Credit Risk
measurement

Founded in 1807, John Wiley & Sons is the oldest independent publishing company in the United States. With offices in North America, Europe, Australia, and Asia, Wiley is globally committed to developing and marketing print and electronic products and services for our customers' professional and personal knowledge and understanding.

The Wiley Finance series contains books written specifically for finance and investment professionals as well as sophisticated individual investors and their financial advisors. Book topics range from portfolio management to e-commerce, risk management, financial engineering, valuation and financial instrument analysis, as well as much more.

For a list of available titles, visit our Web site at www.WileyFinance.com.

Credit Risk
measurement

*New Approaches to Value at Risk
and Other Paradigms*

Second Edition

ANTHONY SAUNDERS
LINDA ALLEN

John Wiley & Sons, Inc.

Published by John Wiley & Sons, Inc., New York.
Published simultaneously in Canada.

This publication is designed to provide accurate and authoritative information in regard to the subject matter covered. It is sold with the understanding that the publisher is not engaged in rendering professional services. If professional advice or other expert assistance is required, the services of a competent professional person should be sought.

ISBN 0-471-21910-X

Printed in the United States of America.

10 9 8 7 6 5 4 3 2 1

preface to second edition

It is quite astonishing that the state of the credit risk measurement art has progressed so far in just two years. Many of the models are entering their second generation. A consensus has developed about certain model parameters and approaches. As is perhaps inevitable for a maturing body of knowledge, two schools of thought have emerged. One "school" traces its intellectual roots to Merton's options theoretic approach and explains default in structural terms related to the market value of the firm's assets as compared to its debt obligations. The other "reduced form school" statistically decomposes observed risky debt prices into default risk premiums that price credit risk events without necessarily examining their underlying causalities.

The need for books such as this one has increased as regulatory and market conditions encourage greater proliferation of credit risk models. We have tried to be faithful to the original book's paradigm and present the economic intuition of each of the models accurately, but in terms that are accessible to a reader without a PhD in quantum mechanics. We start with a look back. Chapter 1 describes recent conditions that have made advances in credit risk measurement both desirable and attainable. Chapter 2 describes traditional approaches. Chapter 3 includes comprehensive coverage of the proposed BIS New Capital Accord with commentary. The new models are described in Chapters 4 through 9, with portfolio models described in Chapters 10 and 11. In this edition, we more clearly delineate the options theoretic approach (Chapter 4) from the reduced form approach (Chapter 5). Back-testing models are described in Chapter 12. Applications to internal capital allocation using RAROC models are presented in Chapter 13 and off-balance-sheet credit risk measurement is covered in Chapters 14 and 15.

Finally, we would like to thank Victoria Ivashina, Dina Layish, Indrani de Basak, and Farah Yunus for excellent research assistance and Bill Falloon for being such an accommodating editor at John Wiley & Sons. The standard caveat with regard to responsibility for errors applies here as well.

ANTHONY SAUNDERS
LINDA ALLEN

New York, New York
January 2002

preface to first edition

In recent years, enormous strides have been made in the art and science of credit risk measurement and management. Much of the energy in this area has resulted from dissatisfaction with traditional approaches to credit risk measurement and with the current Bank for International Settlements (BIS) regulatory model. Specifically, under the current regulatory structure, established by the BIS in 1988 in cooperation with the world's major central banks, and implemented in January 1993, virtually all private-sector loans are subject to an 8 percent capital requirement with no account being taken of either: (1) credit quality differences among private-sector borrowers or (2) the potential for credit risk reduction via loan portfolio diversification.

The new models—some publicly available and some partially proprietary—seek to offer alternative "internal model" approaches to measuring the credit risk of a loan or a portfolio of loans. As with market risk in 1993, a debate currently rages as to the extent to which internal models can replace regulatory models—and in which areas of credit risk measurement and management.

Much of the research in this area has been quite technical and not easily accessible to the interested practitioner, student, economist, or regulator. The aim of this book is to bring the debate regarding the "value" of the new internal credit risk models to a wider audience. In doing so, I have tried to simplify the technical details and analytics surrounding these models, while concentrating on their underlying economics and economic intuition.

In many cases, providing a full description of the new models has been hampered because of their semiproprietary nature and because only parts of the modeling approach have been made publicly available through working papers, published papers, and other outlets. Thus, many model details are "translucent" rather than transparent.[*] I have tried to be as accurate as possible in describing the different models. Where the full details of a modeling approach are uncertain or unclear, I have used the description "type," as in a "KMV-type" model. This is an indication (1) of my understanding of the general approach used or (2) that a similar approach has been followed in the publicly available literature by other researchers.

---

[*]I'd like to thank Stuart Turnbull of CIBC for this description.

This literature is very new. At the time of writing, it can be regarded as being at a stage similar to that of market risk modeling when J.P. Morgan's RiskMetrics first appeared in 1994.

The book follows a "building blocks" approach. Chapter 1 provides the motivation for the recent growth of the new credit risk models. Chapter 2 briefly overviews traditional models of credit risk measurement. Chapters 3 through 8 examine the approaches of the new models to evaluating individual borrower (or counterparty) credit risk and to the valuation of individual loans. One of the major features of the newer models is that they consider credit risk in a portfolio context; consequently, Chapters 9 through 12 examine the application of modern portfolio theory concepts to evaluation of the risk of loan portfolios. Finally, many of the new models are equally applicable to assessing credit risk off-balance-sheet as well as on-balance-sheet. Thus, Chapters 13 and 14 look at the application of the new models to assessing the risk of derivative contracts, and the use of such contracts in managing credit risk.

I thank a number of people for their encouragement, insights, and comments. They include, in no particular order: Mark Carey, Lazarus Angbazo, Frank Diebold, Larry Wall, Jim Gilkeson, Kobi Boudoukh, Anthony Morris, Sinan Cebonoyan, Marti Subrahmanyam, Ranga Sundaram, Anil Bangia, Anand Srinivasan, Sreedhar Bharath, Alex Shapiro, and Til Schuermann. Finally, I'd like to thank my colleague, Ed Altman, for encouraging me to look into this area and for keeping the "torchlight" of credit risk analysis burning during the past 30 years. Nevertheless, at the end of the day, I take full responsibility for any errors of omission or commission that may be found here.

ANTHONY SAUNDERS

New York, New York
May 1999

contents

list of abbreviations

ABS	asset backed security
AE	average exposure
AMA	advanced measurement approach
ARS	adjusted relative spread
BIS	Bank for International Settlements
BISTRO	Broad Index Secured Trust Offering
BRW	benchmark risk weight
BSM	Black–Scholes–Merton Model
CAPM	capital asset pricing model
CDO	collateralized debt obligation
CDS	credit default swap
CLN	credit-linked note
CLO	collateralized lending obligation
CMR	cumulative mortality rate
CS	credit spread
CSFP	Crédit Suisse Financial Products
CWI	creditworthiness index
CYC	current yield curve
DD	distance to default
DM	default mode model
EAD	exposure at default
EBITDA	earnings before interest, taxes, depreciation, and amortization
EC	European Community
ECA	Export Credit Agency
EDF	expected default frequency
EDP	estimated default probability
EE	expected exposure
EL	expected losses
EVA	economic value added
EVT	extreme value theory
FA	foundation approach
FIs	financial institutions
FV	future value

FX	foreign exchange
FYC	forward yield curve
GEV	generalized extreme value
GPD	Generalized Pareto Distribution
GSF	granularity scaling factor
IDR	implied debenture rating
IIF	Institute of International Finance
IMF	International Monetary Fund
IRB	internal ratings-based model
ISDA	International Swaps and Derivatives Association
LAS	Loan Analysis System (KPMG)
LDCs	less developed countries
LGD	loss given default
LIBOR	London Inter-Bank Offered Rate
M	maturity
MD	modified duration
MMR	marginal mortality rate
MPT	modern portfolio theory
MRC	marginal risk contribution
MTM	mark-to-market model
NAIC	National Association of Insurance Commissioners
NASD	National Association of Securities Dealers
NGR	net to gross (current exposure) ratio
NPV	net present value
NRSRO	nationally recognized statistical rating organization
OAEM	other assets especially mentioned
OBS	off-balance-sheet
OCC	Office of the Comptroller of the Currency
OECD	Organization for Economic Cooperation and Development
OPM	option-pricing model
OTC	over-the-counter
PD	probability of default
QDF	quasi default frequency
QIS	Quantitative Impact Study
RAROC	risk-adjusted return on capital
RBC	risk-based capital
Repo	repurchase agreement
RN	risk-neutral
ROA	return on assets
ROE	return on equity
RORAC	return on risk-adjusted capital
RW	risk weight

RWA	risk weighted assets
SBC	Swiss Bank Corporation
SM	standardized model
SPV	special-purpose vehicle
UL	unexpected losses
VAR	value at risk
WACC	weighted-average cost of capital
WAL	weighted average life
WARR	weighted-average risk ratio
ZYC	zero yield curve

Credit Risk
measurement

CHAPTER 1

Why New Approaches to Credit Risk Measurement and Management?

In recent years, a revolution has been brewing in risk as it is both measured and managed. Contradicting the relatively dull and routine history of credit risk, new technologies and ideas have emerged among a new generation of financial engineering professionals who are applying their model-building skills and analysis to this area.

The question arises: Why now? There are at least seven reasons for this sudden surge in interest.

1. STRUCTURAL INCREASE IN BANKRUPTCIES

Although the most recent recession hit at different times in different countries, most statistics show a significant increase in bankruptcies, compared to the prior recessions. To the extent that there has been a permanent or structural increase in bankruptcies worldwide—possibly due to the increase in global competition—accurate credit risk analysis becomes even more important today than in the past.

2. DISINTERMEDIATION

As capital markets have expanded and become accessible to small and mid-size firms (e.g., it is estimated that as many as 20,000 U.S. companies have actual or potential access to the U.S. commercial paper market), the firms or borrowers "left behind" to raise funds from banks and other traditional financial institutions (FIs) are increasingly likely to be smaller and to have weaker credit ratings. Capital market growth has produced a "winner's curse" effect on the credit portfolios of traditional FIs.

3. MORE COMPETITIVE MARGINS

Almost paradoxically, despite the decline in the average quality of loans (described above), interest margins or spreads, especially in wholesale loan markets, have become very thin. In short, the risk-return trade-off from lending has gotten worse. A number of reasons can be cited, but an important factor has been the enhanced competition for lower quality borrowers, especially from finance companies, much of whose lending activity has been concentrated at the higher risk/lower quality end of the market.

4. DECLINING AND VOLATILE VALUES OF COLLATERAL

Concurrent with recent Asian and Russian debt crises, banking crises in well-developed countries such as Switzerland and Japan have shown that property values and real asset values are very hard to predict and to realize through liquidation. The weaker (and more uncertain) collateral values are, the riskier lending is likely to be. Indeed, current concerns about "deflation" worldwide have accentuated concerns about the value of real assets such as property and other physical assets.

5. THE GROWTH OF OFF-BALANCE-SHEET DERIVATIVES

Because of the phenomenal expansion of derivative markets, the growth of credit exposure, or counterparty risk, has extended the need for credit analysis beyond the loan book. In many of the very largest U.S. banks, the notional (not market) value of off-balance-sheet exposure to instruments such as over-the-counter (OTC) swaps and forwards is more than 10 times the size of their loan books. Indeed, the growth in credit risk off the balance sheet was one of the main reasons for the introduction, by the Bank for International Settlements (BIS), of risk-based capital (RBC) requirements in 1993. Under the BIS system, banks have to hold a capital requirement based on the mark-to-market current value of each OTC derivatives contract (so-called current exposure) plus an add-on for potential future exposure (see Chapter 14).

6. TECHNOLOGY

Advances in computer systems and related advances in information technology—for example, the development of historic loan databases by the Loan Pricing Corporation and other companies—have given banks and FIs the opportunity to test high-powered modeling techniques. A survey conducted by the International Swaps and Derivatives Association (ISDA) and the Institute of International Finance (IIF) in 2000 found that survey participants (consisting of 25 commercial banks from 10 countries, with varying sizes and specialties) used commercial and internal databases to assess the credit risk on rated and unrated commercial, retail, and mortgage loans.[1] For example, besides being able to analyze loan loss and value distribution functions—and (especially) the tails of such distributions—FIs can move toward actively managing loan portfolios based on modern portfolio theory (MPT) models and techniques.[2]

7. THE BIS RISK-BASED CAPITAL REQUIREMENTS

Despite the importance of these six reasons, probably the greatest incentive for banks to develop new credit risk models has been dissatisfaction with the BIS and central banks' post-1992 imposition of capital requirements on loans, so-called BIS I. The current BIS approach has been described as a "one-size-fits-all" policy; virtually all loans to private-sector counterparties are subjected to the same 8 percent capital ratio (or capital reserve requirement), irrespective of the size of the loan, its maturity, and, most importantly, the credit quality of the borrowing counterparty. Thus, loans to a firm near bankruptcy are treated (in capital requirement terms) in the same fashion as loans to an AAA borrower. Further, the current capital requirement is additive across all loans; there is no allowance for lower capital requirements because of a greater degree of diversification in the loan portfolio.

At the beginning of 1998, in the United States (1997, in the European Community), regulators allowed certain large banks the discretion to calculate capital requirements for their trading books—or market risk exposures—using "internal models" rather than the alternative regulatory ("standardized") model. Internal models have had certain constraints imposed on them by regulators and are subjected to back-testing verification; nevertheless, they potentially allow for (1) the Value at Risk (VAR) of each tradable instrument to be more accurately measured (e.g., based on its price volatility, maturity, and so on) and (2) correlations among assets to be taken into account. In the context of market risk, VAR measures the market value exposure of a financial instrument in case tomorrow is a statistically defined "bad day." For example, under the BIS market risk regulations, when banks calculate their VAR-based capital requirements using their internal models, they are required to measure the bad day as the one bad day that happens every 100 business days. (See Appendix 1.1, in this chapter, for a summary of basic VAR concepts.)

Much of the current interest in fine-tuning credit risk measurement models has been fueled by the proposed BIS New Capital Accord (or so-called BIS II), which would more closely link capital charges to the credit risk exposures for individual retail, commercial, sovereign, and interbank credits. Controversy regarding this proposal (discussed at length in Chapter 3) is evident from the one-year delay in finalization and implementation of BIS II (now proposed to be implemented in 2005). This delay occurred because of difficulties in: agreeing on how credit risk should be modeled, technical problems arising from the nontradability of loans compared to marketable instruments, and the lack of deep historic databases on loan defaults. For this reason, BIS II offers three alternative approaches to the calculation of capital requirements for regulatory purposes: a standardized approach (which utilizes external credit ratings to assess risk weights for capital charges) and two separate internal ratings-based approaches (which utilize the bank's internal database to assess a loan's default probability and loss given default). The internal ratings-based approaches are patterned after the market risk capital regulations using internal models, such that the capital required is calibrated to cover a "bad credit period," defined to be the worst year out of 1,000 years.[3]

Regardless of whether internal models are used to set bank capital requirements, the new models have contributed to the lending process. Specifically, internal models potentially offer better ways to value outstanding loans and credit-risk-exposed instruments such as bonds (corporate and emerging market), as well as better methods for predicting default risk exposures to borrowers and derivative counterparties. Moreover, internal models (1) allow (in many cases) the credit risk of portfolios of loans and credit-risk-sensitive instruments to be better evaluated and (2) can be used to improve the pricing of new loans, in the context of an FI's risk-adjusted return on capital (RAROC), as well as the pricing of relatively new instruments in the credit-derivatives markets, such as credit options, credit swaps, and credit forwards. Finally, the models provide an opportunity to measure the privately optimal or economic amount of capital a bank (or FI) should hold as part of its capital structure.

Before we look at some of these new approaches to credit risk measurement, a brief analysis of the more traditional approaches will heighten the contrast between the new and traditional approaches to credit risk measurement.

APPENDIX 1.1:
A BRIEF OVERVIEW OF KEY *VAR* CONCEPTS

The Role of Capital

Banks hold capital (mostly equity and long-term subordinated debt obligations) as a cushion against losses stemming from adverse credit, market, and operational circumstances. By absorbing these losses, capital protects the bank from insolvency. Bank regulators set minimum capital requirements so as to reduce the likelihood of bank insolvencies that are costly to the economy. To determine how much capital should be required, two questions must be answered. First, what is the acceptable probability of bank insolvency? It is neither practical nor desirable to completely indemnify the banking system against all insolvencies; instead, an "acceptable" level of risk is necessary to prevent moral hazard considerations that would encourage banks to take on excessive risk exposures. The proposed BIS II Internal Ratings-Based model sets this risk threshold at the 99.9 percentile; that is, the capital charge is sufficient to cover losses in all but the worst 0.1 percent of adverse credit risk events. Stated directly: There is a 0.1 percent chance that adverse credit conditions will cause bank insolvency.

Measuring Expected and Unexpected Losses

The second input into capital regulations is a methodology for measuring losses in the event of adverse market conditions called *credit events*. Losses are defined as the change in the security's (loan's) value over a fixed period of time ("the credit horizon period"). Typically, the credit horizon period is chosen to be one year. Thus, losses are calculated as the impact of a credit event on the security's market value,[4] less any cash flows received during the one-year credit horizon period. Losses may be negative (that is, there are gains) if the security's value increases over the year and if a credit event does not occur.

Figure 1.1 illustrates a loss distribution that relates all possible values of securities' losses/gains to the probability of occurrence for each value (determined by the likelihood that a credit event will occur). The area under the probability distribution of security losses must sum to one. The probability distribution in Figure 1.1 is a normal distribution, which suggests that losses or gains are symmetrically distributed around the mean value. Two important loss concepts are illustrated in Figure 1.1. Expected losses (EL) are estimated by the mean of the distribution, and unexpected losses (UL) are measured by the chosen percentile cutoff of extreme losses. If the loss percentile cutoff is set at 0.1 percent (as in BIS II proposals), then UL is the value that just marks off the shaded area in Figure 1.1, which comprises

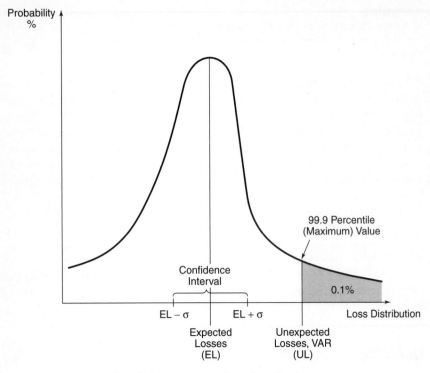

FIGURE 1.1   Normal loss distribution.

0.1 percent of the area under the entire loss distribution. That is, there is only a 0.1 percent likelihood that losses will exceed UL. The UL is considered the measure of Value at Risk (*VAR*).

The standard deviation, denoted σ, is a commonly used measure of risk because it measures the loss dispersion around EL weighted by the likelihood of occurrence. For the normal distribution, there is approximately a 67 percent probability that losses will fall within the region from $EL-\sigma$ to $EL+\sigma$, which is called the *confidence interval*.

The loss distribution shown in Figure 1.1 is normal, although most financial loss distributions are skewed with fat tails; that is, there is a greater likelihood of extreme outcomes than is shown by the normal distribution. Figure 1.2 shows a skewed loss distribution with the loss measures EL and UL. We can solve for the σ of the loss distribution in Figure 1.2, but because it is not normal, we cannot specify the likelihood that losses will fall within the $EL-\sigma$ to $EL+\sigma$ confidence interval unless we have information about the particular shape of the distribution, for example, its skewness (lack of symmetry) and its kurtosis (the probability of extreme loss outcomes).

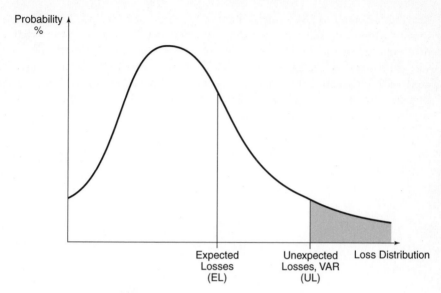

FIGURE 1.2 Skewed loss distribution.

Figures 1.1 and 1.2 are loss distributions for individual security (loan) investments. However, diversification across different securities causes the risk of a portfolio to be lower than the risk of individual security investments. The lower the correlation between pairs of securities, the greater the benefits of diversification in reducing the risk of the portfolio. The correlation coefficient, denoted ρ, measures the comovement between pairs of securities on a scale of −1 to +1: −1 for perfectly negatively correlated (the securities' values move in exactly opposite directions), 0 for uncorrelated, and +1 for perfectly positively correlated (the securities' values move together in lock step). Most securities are positively correlated (thereby preventing the elimination of risk through simple portfolio creation), but not *perfectly* positively correlated (thereby providing substantial benefits to diversification).

As we will see in later chapters (for example, Chapter 6), estimating UL (or *VAR*) for credit risk is challenging. Not only do volatilities and correlations have to be estimated for both probability of default (*PD*) and the loss given default (*LGD*), but the definition of a credit event must also be determined. A credit event may be defined only as default, as in default mode (DM) models. However, mark-to-market (MTM) models define a credit event to be any migration in credit quality, including, but not limited to, default. Thus, if a particular loan or bond is downgraded from an A to a B rating, the adverse change in the bond's price would be included in the loss distribution of an MTM model, whereas it would not be included for a DM model. Moreover, since credit events (particularly default) are somewhat rare events, historical loss rates may not provide accurate estimates of future exposures such as EL and UL. Finally, data availability problems plague credit risk measurement models, in contrast to the market risk *VAR* models that can use series of daily price databases. The challenge, for the modern models of credit risk measurement, is to compensate for these problems.

CHAPTER 2

Traditional Approaches to Credit Risk Measurement

It is hard to draw the line between traditional and new approaches, especially because many of the better ideas of traditional models are used in the new models. We view four classes of models as comprising the traditional approach: (1) expert systems; (2) neural networks; (3) rating systems, including bank internal rating systems; and (4) credit scoring systems. For a more complete discussion of these models, see Caouette, Altman, and Narayanan (1998), listed in the Bibliography.

EXPERT SYSTEMS

In an expert system, the credit decision is left to the local or branch lending officer or relationship manager. Implicitly, this person's expertise, subjective judgment, and weighting of certain key factors are the most important determinants in the decision to grant credit. The potential factors and expert systems a lending officer could look at are infinite; however, one of the most common expert systems—the five "Cs" of credit—will yield sufficient understanding. The expert analyzes these five key factors, subjectively weights them, and reaches a credit decision:

1. *Character.* A measure of the reputation of the firm, its willingness to repay, and its repayment history. In particular, it has been established empirically that the age of a firm is a good proxy for its repayment reputation.
2. *Capital.* The equity contribution of owners and its ratio to debt (leverage). These are viewed as good predictors of bankruptcy probability. High leverage suggests a greater probability of bankruptcy.
3. *Capacity.* The ability to repay, which reflects the volatility of the borrower's earnings. If repayments on debt contracts follow a constant

stream over time, but earnings are volatile (or have a high standard deviation), there may be periods when the firm's capacity to repay debt claims is constrained.

4. *Collateral.* In the event of default, a banker has claims on the collateral pledged by the borrower. The greater the priority of this claim and the greater the market value of the underlying collateral, the lower the exposure risk of the loan.

5. *Cycle (or Economic) Conditions.* The state of the business cycle; an important element in determining credit risk exposure, especially for cycle-dependent industries. For example, durable goods sectors tend to be more cycle-dependent than nondurable goods sectors. Similarly, industries that have exposure to international competitive conditions tend to be cycle-sensitive. Taylor (1998), in an analysis of Dun and Bradstreet bankruptcy data by industry (both mean and standard deviation), finds some quite dramatic differences in U.S. industry failure rates during the business cycle.

In addition to these five "Cs," an expert might take into account the level of interest rates. As is well known from economic theory, the relationship between the level of interest rates and the expected return on a loan is highly nonlinear [see Stiglitz and Weiss (1981)]. When interest rates are at "low" levels, the expected return could increase if rates are raised. However, when interest rates are at "high" levels, an increase in rates may lower the return on a loan. This negative relationship between high loan rates and expected loan returns occurs because of (1) adverse selection and (2) risk shifting. When loan rates rise beyond some point, good borrowers drop out of the loan market; they prefer to self-finance their investment projects (adverse selection). The remaining borrowers, who have limited liability and limited equity at stake, have the incentive to shift into riskier projects (risk shifting). In good times, they will be able to repay the bank. If times turn bad and they default, they will have limited downside loss.

Although many banks still use expert systems as part of their credit decision process, these systems face two main problems:

1. *Consistency.* What are the important common factors to analyze across different types of borrowers?

2. *Subjectivity.* What are the optimal weights to apply to the factors chosen?

Potentially, the subjective weights applied to the five Cs by an expert can vary from borrower to borrower if the expert so chooses. This makes comparability of rankings and decisions very difficult for an individual monitoring an expert's decision and for other experts in general. As a result, quite different standards can be applied by credit officers, within any given bank or FI, to similar types of borrowers.[1] It can be argued that loan committees or multilayered signature authorities are key mechanisms in avoiding such consistency problems, but it is unclear how effectively they impose common standards in practice.[2] This disparity in ability across experts has led to the development of computerized expert systems, such as artificial neural networks, that attempt to incorporate the knowledge of the best human experts.

ARTIFICIAL NEURAL NETWORKS

Development of a computerized expert system requires acquisition of the human expert's knowledge. Because this is often a time-consuming and error-prone task, many systems use induction to infer the human experts' decision processes by studying their decisions. Elmer and Borowski (1988) compare the bankruptcy predictions of an expert system to several credit scoring models and find that the expert system correctly anticipated over 60 percent of the failures 7 to 18 months before bankruptcy, whereas the credit scoring models had prediction rates of only 48 percent and 33 percent. Similarly, Messier and Hansen (1988) show that their expert system outperformed credit scoring models and the human experts themselves in forecasting business failures.

The disadvantages of induction-based expert systems include:

1. The time and effort required to translate the human experts' decision processes into a system of rules.
2. The difficulty and costs associated with programming the decision algorithm and maintaining the system.
3. The inability or inflexibility of the expert system to adapt to changing conditions.

Artificial neural networks have been proposed as solutions to these problems. An artificial neural system simulates the human learning process. The system learns the nature of the relationship between inputs and outputs by repeatedly sampling input/output information sets. Neural networks have a particular advantage over expert systems when data are noisy or incomplete: neural networks can make an "educated guess," much as would a human expert. Hawley, Johnson, and Raina (1990) describe how neural networks can incorporate subjective, nonquantifiable information into credit approval decisions. Kim and Scott (1991) use a supervised artificial neural network to predict bankruptcy in a sample of 190 Compustat firms. The system performs well (87 percent prediction rate) during the year of bankruptcy, but its accuracy declines markedly over time, showing only a 75 percent, 59 percent, and 47 percent prediction accuracy one year, two years, and three years prior to bankruptcy, respectively. Altman, Marco, and Varetto (1994) examine 1,000 Italian industrial firms from 1982 to 1992 and find that neural networks have about the same level of accuracy as do credit scoring models. Podding (1994), using data on 300 French firms collected over three years, claims that neural networks outperform credit scoring models in bankruptcy prediction. However, he finds that not all artificial neural systems are equal, noting that the multilayer perception (or back propagation) network is best suited for bankruptcy prediction. Yang, Platt, and Platt (1999) use a sample of an oil and gas company's debt to show that the back propagation neural network obtained the highest classification accuracy overall, when compared to the probabilistic neural network and discriminant analysis. However, discriminant analysis outperforms all models of neural networks in minimizing type 2 classification errors.[3]

Neural networks are characterized by three architectural features: inputs, weights, and hidden units. Figure 2.1 shows a two-layer system with two hidden units and n inputs. The n inputs, $x_1, x_2, \ldots, x_n$ represent the

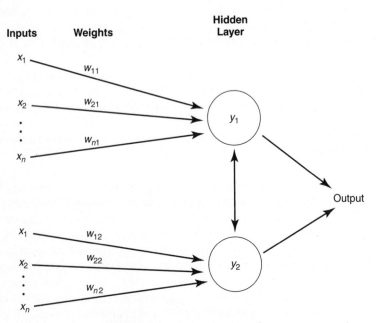

FIGURE 2.1   A neural network.

data received by the system (for example, company financial ratios for the bankruptcy prediction neural networks). Each piece of information is assigned a weight $(w_{11}, w_{21}, \ldots, w_{n1})$ that designates its relative importance to each hidden unit (y_i). These weights are "learned" by the network over the course of "training." For example, by observing the financial characteristics of many bankrupt firms (the training process), the network "learns" the weights. Each hidden unit computes the weighted sum of all inputs and transmits the result to other hidden units. In parallel, the other hidden units are weighting their inputs so as to transmit their signal to all other connected hidden units. Receipt of the signal from other hidden units further transforms the output from each node, and the system continues to iterate until all the information is incorporated. This model incorporates complex correlations among the hidden units to improve model fit and reduce type 1 and type 2 errors. But, care should be taken not to overfit the model. Overfitting results in a model that explains well in-sample but may perform quite poorly in predicting out-of-sample.

Because of the large number of possible connections, the neural network can grow prohibitively large rather quickly. For a set of networks with 10 inputs and 12 hidden units, the maximum possible number of network configurations[4] is 4.46×10^{43}. Thus, various pruning methods exist to economize on the number of connections in the system. Weights and hidden units are pruned during the training stage so as to incorporate only those inputs that are relevant in obtaining the desired output.

A major disadvantage of neural networks is their lack of transparency. The internal structure of the network is hidden and may not be easy to duplicate, even using the same data inputs. This leads to a lack of accountability because the system's intermediate steps cannot be checked. Moreover, although the neural network is useful as a tool of classification or prediction, it does nothing to illuminate the process or the relative importance of the variables; that is, the neural net does not reveal anything about the intermediate steps that lead to the final output.

Because independent rating agencies, such as Moody's and Standard & Poor's, use human expert systems to incorporate subjective factors and nonquantifiable influences (such as changes in management or business cycle effects), neural networks can be used to forecast the corporate bond ratings issued by independent rating agencies. Moody and Utans (1994) find that neural networks outperform linear regressions in accurately classifying corporate bond ratings. Singleton and Surkan (1994) show a 73 percent accuracy rate in predicting bond rating changes, as compared to a 57 percent accuracy rate using a credit scoring discriminant model. These results suggest that there is more to bond credit ratings than simply a weighted average of financial ratios.

RATING SYSTEMS

One of the oldest rating systems for loans was developed by the U.S. Office of the Comptroller of the Currency (OCC).[5] The system has been used in the United States (and abroad) by regulators and bankers to assess the adequacy of their loan loss reserves. The OCC rating system places an existing loan portfolio into five categories: four low-quality ratings and one high-quality rating.[6] In Table 2.1, the minimum required loss reserve appears next to each category.

In the United States, the National Association of Insurance Commissioners (NAIC) utilizes the six-grade regulatory classification scheme, as shown in Table 2.2. NAIC regulatory ratings have been used to assess capital requirements for U.S. insurance companies since the mid-1990s.[7] Insurance companies' internal ratings, as examined by Carey (2001a) for private placements, are highly consistent with the external regulatory ratings. They agree in 76.1 percent of the cases and vary by one grade or less in 96.7 percent of the cases. Moreover, internal ratings of debt (bonds) are highly consistent across insurance companies. There is complete agreement in 64.2 percent of the cases and variation by one grade or less in 90.5 percent of the cases. However, Carey (2001a) finds less consistency across insurance company internal ratings for below-investment-grade debt; that is, when one insurance company rates an obligation as BB or lower, other insurance companies holding the loan assign the same rating in only 37 percent of the cases. This inconsistency is potentially damaging to the case for internal

TABLE 2.1   Loss Reserves

	Percent
Low-quality ratings:	
Other assets especially mentioned (OAEM)	0
Substandard assets	20
Doubtful assets	50
Loss assets	100
High-quality rating:	
Pass/performing	0

Note: Technically speaking, the 0 percent loss reserves for OAEM and pass loans are lower bounds. In practice, the reserve rates on these categories are determined by the bank in consultation with examiners, depending on some type of "historical analysis" of charge-off rates for the bank.

TABLE 2.2 NAIC Ratings

NAIC Ratings	Rating Agency Equivalent	Insurance Company Internal Ratings	Required Capital for Life Insurance Companies
1	AAA, AA, A	1, 2, 3	0.3%
2	BBB	4	1.0
3	BB	5	4.0
4	B	6	9.0
5	Less than B	7	20.0
6	Default	7	30.0
Cash and U.S. government bonds		1	0.0
Residential mortgages			0.5
Commercial mortgages			3.0
Common stock			30.0
Preferred stock	NAIC Rating Capital Factor Plus 2.0		

Source: Carey (2001a), Kupiec et al. (2001). The factors are multiplied by the book value of the life insurance company's year end principal balances in each NAIC rating category in order to calculate the preliminary dollar capital requirement.

ratings models at banks because, whereas only 13 percent of the private placements at insurance companies were below investment grade, typically more than 50 percent of large bank portfolios were below investment grade as of year end 1997 [see Treacy and Carey (2000)].

Internal Ratings at Banks

Over the years, bankers have extended the OCC rating system by developing internal rating systems that more finely subdivide the pass/performing rating category. For example, at any given moment, there is always a chance that some pass or performing loans will go into default, and that some reserves, even if very low, should be held against these loans (e.g., see the 0.003 capital factor levied against top-rated private placements in Table 2.2). Currently, it is estimated that about 60 percent of U.S. bank holding companies have developed internal rating systems for loans on a 1 to 9 or 1 to 10 scale [see Fadil (1997)], including the top 50 FIs in the United States.[8] The BIS (2000) survey of 30 FIs found that internal ratings were used for 96 percent of all large and middle market loans, but for only 71 percent of small corporate loans, and 54 percent of retail customers' obligations.[9] An example of a 1 to 10 loan rating system and its mapping into equivalent bond ratings is shown in Table 2.3.

TABLE 2.3 An Example of a Loan Rating System and Bond Rating Mapping

Bond Rating	Score	Risk Level	Description
AAA	1	Minimal	Excellent business credit, superior asset quality, excellent debt capacity and coverage; excellent management with depth. Company is a market leader and has access to capital markets.
AA	2	Modest	Good business credit, very good asset quality and liquidity, strong debt capacity and coverage, very good management in all positions. Company is highly regarded in industry and has a very strong market share.
A	3	Average	Average business credit, within normal credit standards: satisfactory asset quality and liquidity, good debt capacity and coverage; good management in all critical positions. Company is of average size and position within the industry.
BBB	4	Acceptable	Acceptable business credit, but with more than average risk: acceptable asset quality, little excess liquidity, modest debt capacity. May be highly or fully leveraged. Requires above-average levels of supervision and attention from lender. Company is not strong enough to sustain major setbacks. Loans are highly leveraged transactions due to regulatory constraints.
BB	5	Acceptable with care	Acceptable business credit, but with considerable risk: acceptable asset quality, smaller and/or less diverse asset base, very little liquidity, limited debt capacity.

TABLE 2.3 (*Continued*)

Bond Rating	Score	Risk Level	Description
BB (continued)			Covenants structured to ensure adequate protection. May be highly or fully leveraged. May be of below-average size or a lower-tier competitor. Requires significant supervision and attention from lender. Company is not strong enough to sustain major setbacks. Loans are highly leveraged transactions due to the obligor's financial status.
B	6	Management attention	Watch list credit: generally acceptable asset quality, somewhat strained liquidity, fully leveraged. Some management weakness. Requires continual supervision and attention from lender.
CCC	7	Special mention (OAEM)	Marginally acceptable business credit; some weakness. Generally undesirable business constituting an undue and unwarranted credit risk but not to the point of justifying a substandard classification. Although the asset is currently protected, it is potentially weak. No loss of principal or interest is envisioned. Potential weaknesses might include a weakening financial condition; an unrealistic repayment program; inadequate sources of funds, or lack of adequate collateral, credit information, or documentation. Company is undistinguished and mediocre.
CC	8	Substandard	Unacceptable business credit; normal repayment in jeopardy. Although no loss of principal or interest is envisioned, a positive

(continued)

TABLE 2.3   (*Continued*)

Bond Rating	Score	Risk Level	Description
CC (continued)			and well-defined weakness jeopardizes collection of debt. The asset is inadequately protected by the current sound net worth and paying capacity of the obligor or pledged collateral. There may already have been a partial loss of interest.
C	9	Doubtful	Full repayment questionable. Serious problems exist to the point where a partial loss of principal is likely. Weaknesses are so pronounced that, on the basis of current information, conditions, and values, collection in full is highly improbable.
D	10	Loss	Expected total loss. An uncollectible asset or one of such little value that it does not warrant classification as an active asset. Such an asset may, however, have recovery or salvage value, but not to the point where a write-off should be deferred, even though a partial recovery may occur in the future.

In Table 2.3, the OCC pass grade is divided into six different categories (ratings 1 to 6). Ratings 7 to 10 correspond to the OCC's four low-quality loan ratings. These loan-rating systems do not exactly map into bond-rating systems, especially at the lower-quality end. One reason is that bond-rating systems are supposed to rate an individual loan (including its covenants and collateral backing), whereas loan-rating systems are more oriented to rating the overall borrower. This lack of one-to-one mapping between bond ratings and loan ratings raises a flag as to (1) the merits of newer models that rely on bond data to value loans and (2) the proposed new standardized model of the BIS capital requirements (see Chapter 3) that ties capital requirements to external ratings.

Treacy and Carey (2000), in their survey of the 50 largest U.S. bank holding companies and the BIS (2000) survey of 30 FIs across the G-10 countries, find considerable diversity in internal ratings models. Although all the FIs used similar financial risk factors, there were differences across FIs with regard to the relative importance of each of the factors, as well as the weight assigned to statistically based processes according to expert judgment. Treacy and Carey (2000) find that qualitative factors played a greater role in determining the ratings of loans to small and medium-size firms when the loan officer was chiefly responsible for the ratings. This finding does not apply to loans to large firms in which the credit staff primarily sets the ratings, using quantitative methods such as credit scoring models. Typically, ratings were set with a one-year time horizon, although data were often available for three to five years.[10]

The architecture of the internal rating system can be one-dimensional (an overall rating is assigned to each loan) or two-dimensional; in the latter, each borrower's overall creditworthiness (the probability of default, *PD*) is assessed separately from the loss severity of the individual loan (the loss given default, *LGD*, taking into account any collateral or guarantees). Treacy and Carey (2000), who recommend a two-dimensional rating system, estimate that 60 percent of the FIs in their survey had one-dimensional systems. Moreover, BIS (2000) find that banks are better able to assess the *PD* of their borrowers relative to estimating *LGD*.[11]

Figure 2.2 shows the uses of internal rating systems at the 30 FIs surveyed by BIS (2000). The dominant applications of such systems are the construction of risk reports for senior management and the pricing of loans. However, there are other uses of internal ratings: the allocation of capital using a RAROC-type approach, the setting of economic capital requirements,

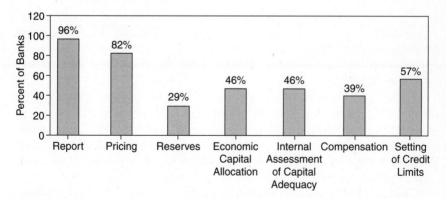

FIGURE 2.2 Use of internal ratings. *Source:* "Range of Practice in Banks' Internal Ratings Systems," Bank for International Settlements, Basel Committee on Banking Supervision, Document No. 66 (January 2000).

the assignment of credit limits, the calculation of incentive-based compensation, and the determination of loss reserves.

More banks can be expected to adopt internal rating systems in response to the incentives built in to the proposed new Basel Capital Accord.[12] Therefore, some words of caution are in order. Adoption of internal ratings for the purpose of assessing regulatory capital requirements has the potential to distort the integrity of the rating system, especially if banks view capital as costly and wish to minimize that cost. Supervisors will have to validate the accuracy of a wide variety of internal rating systems. This may prove impossible without access to large amounts of data, as well as in the presence of nonquantifiable subjective factors that make the rating system into an unverifiable black box. Moreover, reliance on internal ratings raises concerns about: (1) the ongoing integrity of each system; (2) the consistency and comparability of the ratings, particularly across national boundaries; and (3) the evolution and disclosure of best-practices methods that become international standards. [See Griep and De Stefano (2001).]

CREDIT SCORING SYSTEMS

Credit scoring systems can be found in virtually all types of credit analysis, from consumer credit to commercial loans. The idea is essentially the same: Pre-identify certain key factors that determine the probability of default (as opposed to repayment), and combine or weight them into a quantitative score. In some cases, the score can be literally interpreted as a probability of default; in others, the score can be used as a classification system: it places a potential borrower into either a good or a bad group, based on a score and a cut-off point. Full reviews of the traditional approach to credit scoring, and the various methodologies, can be found in Caouette, Altman, and Narayanan (1998) and Saunders (1997). A good review of the worldwide application of credit-scoring models can be found in Altman and Narayanan (1997).

There are four methodological forms of multivariate credit-scoring models: (1) the linear probability model, (2) the logit model, (3) the probit model, and (4) the discriminant analysis model. Mester (1997) documents the widespread use of credit-scoring models: 97 percent of banks use credit scoring to approve credit card applications, whereas 70 percent of the banks use credit scoring in their small business lending.[13]

Because this book is concerned with newer models of credit risk measurement, one simple example of this type of model will suffice to exhibit some of the issues supposedly addressed by many of the newer models.[14] Consider the Altman (1968) Z-score model, which is a classificatory model for corporate borrowers (but can also be used to get a default probability prediction). Based on a matched sample (by year, size, and industry) of failed and solvent firms, and using linear discriminant analysis, the best-fitting scoring model for commercial loans took this form:

$$Z = 1.2X_1 + 1.4X_2 + 3.3X_3 + 0.6X_4 + 1.0X_5$$

where X_1 = working capital/total assets ratio;
X_2 = retained earnings/total assets ratio;
X_3 = earnings before interest and taxes/total assets ratio;
X_4 = market value of equity/book value of total liabilities ratio;
X_5 = sales/total assets ratio.

As used by the credit officer, if a corporate borrower's accounting ratios (the X_i's), when weighted by the estimated coefficients in the Z function, result in a Z score below a critical value (in Altman's initial study, 1.81), they would be classified as "bad" and the loan would be refused. The choice of the optimal cut-off credit score can incorporate changes in economic conditions. That is, if the economy is expected to decline, the cut-off point could be raised in order to decrease the probability of granting bad loans. This reduces the model's type 1 error (lending to bad customers), but increases the model's type 2 error (the likelihood that good customers will be denied credit).[15]

A number of issues need to be raised here. First, the model is linear whereas the path to bankruptcy may be highly nonlinear (the relationship between the X_i's is likely to be nonlinear as well). Second, with the exception of the market value of equity term in the leverage ratio, the model is essentially based on accounting ratios. In most countries, accounting data appear only at discrete intervals (e.g., quarterly) and are generally based on historic or book-value accounting principles. It is also questionable whether such models can pick up a firm that is rapidly deteriorating (such as during the Asian crisis). Indeed, as the world becomes more complex and competitive, the predictability of simple Z-score models may worsen. A good example is Brazil. When fitted in the mid-1970s, the Z-score model did quite a good job of predicting default even two or three years prior to bankruptcy [Altman, Baidya, and Dias (1979)]. More recently, even with low inflation and greater economic stability, this type of model has performed less well as the Brazilian economy has become more open [Sanvicente and Bader (1998)]. Moreover, Mester (1998) reports that 56 percent of the 33 banks that used credit scoring as a way of approving credit card applications failed to predict loan quality problems. If credit-scoring models are inaccurate for relatively homogeneous credit card applications, how are they to evaluate complex large business loans?[16]

Finally, the issue of economic meaning is probably what troubles financial economists the most. For example, what is the economic meaning of an exponentially transformed sum of the leverage ratio and the sales-to-total-assets ratio? The ad hoc economic nature of these models and their tenuous links to existing financial theory separate them from some of the newer models that will be discussed in Chapters 3 through 8.

CHAPTER 3

The BIS Basel International Bank Capital Accord

January 2002

The 1988 Basel[1] Capital Accord (BIS I) was revolutionary in that it sought to develop a single capital requirement for credit risk across the major banking countries of the world.[2] A major focus of BIS I was to distinguish the credit risk of sovereign, bank, and mortgage obligations (accorded lower risk weights) from nonbank private sector or commercial loan obligations (accorded the highest risk weight). There was little or no attempt to differentiate the credit risk exposure within the commercial loan classification. All commercial loans implicitly required an 8 percent total capital requirement (Tier 1 plus Tier 2),[3] regardless of the inherent creditworthiness of the borrower, its external credit rating, the collateral offered, or the covenants extended.[4] Because the capital requirement was set too low for high-risk/low-quality business loans and too high for low-risk/high-quality loans, the mispricing of commercial lending risk created an incentive for banks to shift portfolios toward loans that were more underpriced from a regulatory risk capital perspective; for example, banks tended to retain the most credit risky tranches of securitized loan portfolios. [See Jones (2000) for a discussion of these regulatory capital arbitrage activities.] Thus, the BIS I had the unintended consequence of encouraging a long-term deterioration in the overall credit quality of bank portfolios.[5] The proposed goal of the new Basel Capital Accord of 2002 (BIS II)—to be fully introduced, if approved as proposed, in 2005—is to correct the mispricing inherent in BIS I and incorporate more risk-sensitive credit exposure measures into bank capital requirements.[6]

The BIS proposals presented in this chapter are updated until December 2001. For updates after this date, please see the Web site http://www.stern.nyu.edu/~asaunder/.

Hammes and Shapiro (2001) delineate several key drivers motivating BIS II, including:

1. *Structural changes in the credit markets.* Regulatory capital requirements must reflect the increased competitiveness of credit markets, particularly in the high default risk categories; the trading of credit risk through credit derivatives or collateralized loan obligations; modern credit risk measurement technology; and increased liquidity in the new credit risk markets.
2. *Opportunities to remove inefficiencies in the lending market.* In contrast to the insurance industry which uses derivatives markets and reinsurance companies to transfer risk, the banking industry is dominated by the "originate and hold" approach in which the bank fully absorbs credit risk.
3. *Ballooning debt levels during the economic upturn, with a potential debt servicing crisis in an economic downturn.* For example, in 1999, debt-to-equity ratios at S&P 500 companies rose to 115.8 percent (as compared to 84.4 percent in 1990) and household debt to personal disposable income rose to 95 percent (as compared to 72 percent in 1985) [Hammes and Shapiro (2001), p. 102].[7]

BIS II follows a three-step (potentially evolutionary) paradigm. Banks can choose from among: (1) the basic standardized model, (2) the internal ratings-based (IRB) model foundation approach, and (3) the advanced internal ratings-based model. The standardized model is based on external credit ratings assigned by independent ratings agencies (such as Moody's, Standard & Poor's and Fitch IBCA). Both internal ratings approaches require the bank to formulate and use its own internal ratings system (see Chapter 2). The risk weight assigned to each commercial obligation is based on the ratings assignment (either external or internal), so that higher (lower) rated, high (low) credit quality obligations have lower (higher) risk weights and therefore lower (higher) capital requirements, thereby eliminating the incentives to engage in risk shifting and regulatory arbitrage.

Whichever of the three models is chosen, the BIS II proposal states that overall capital adequacy after 2005 will be measured as follows:[8]

$$
\begin{aligned}
\text{Regulatory total capital } = &\text{ Credit risk capital requirement} \\
&+ \text{ Market risk capital requirement} \\
&+ \text{ Operational risk capital requirement}
\end{aligned}
$$

where

1. The credit risk capital requirement depends on the bank's choice of either the standardized approach or an internal ratings-based (foundation or advanced) models.
2. The market risk capital requirement depends on the bank's choice of either the standardized approach or internal model (e.g., RiskMetrics, historical simulation, or Monte Carlo simulation). This capital requirement was introduced in 1996 in the European Union and in 1998 in the United States.
3. The operational risk capital requirement (as proposed in 2001) depends on the bank's choice among a basic indicator approach, a standardized approach, and an advanced measurement approach (AMA).[9] While part of the 8 percent ratio under BIS I was viewed as capital allocated to absorb operational risk, the proposed new operational risk requirement (to be introduced in 2005) aims to separate out operational risk from credit risk and, at least for the basic indicator approach, has attempted to calibrate operational risk capital to equal 12 percent of a bank's total regulatory capital requirement.[10] Specifically, on November 5, 2001, the BIS released potential modifications to the BIS II proposals that reduced the proposed target of operational risk capital as a percent of minimum regulatory capital requirements from 20 percent to 12 percent.

BIS II incorporates both expected and unexpected losses into capital requirements, in contrast to the market risk amendment of BIS I which is only concerned with unexpected losses. Thus, loan loss reserves are considered the portion of capital that cushions expected credit losses, whereas economic capital covers unexpected losses. The BIS (2000) sound practices for loan accounting state that allowances for loan losses (loan loss reserves) should be sufficient to "absorb estimated credit losses" (p. 4). However, loan loss reserves may be distorted by the stipulation that they are considered eligible for Tier 2 capital up to a maximum 1.25 percent of risk-weighted assets.[11] That is, if expected credit losses exceed 1.25 percent of risk-weighted assets, then some portion of loan loss reserves would not be eligible to meet the bank's capital requirement, thereby requiring excess capital to meet some portion of expected losses and leading to redundant capital charges. In November 2001, the BIS proposed modifications that would relax these constraints and permit the use of "excess" provisions to offset expected losses. Capital requirements for credit and operational risk can be satisfied only with Tier 1 and Tier 2 capital, but part of the market risk capital requirement can be satisfied with Tier 3 capital, which includes subordinated debt of more than two years maturity.[12]

The new capital requirements in BIS II are applied, on both a consolidated and an unconsolidated basis, to holding companies of banking firms.[13] When BIS II is completely adopted, overall regulatory capital levels, on average, are targeted (by the BIS) to remain unchanged for the system as a whole.[14] However, recent tests conducted by 138 banks in 25 countries have led to a downward calibration of the capital levels required to cover credit risk (under the internal ratings-based foundation approach) and operational risk (under the standardized model, basic indicator model, and advanced measurement approach). See BIS (September 2001) and BIS (November 5, 2001a).

THE STANDARDIZED MODEL FOR CREDIT RISK

The standardized model follows the same methodology as BIS I, but makes it more risk sensitive by dividing the commercial obligor designation into finer gradations of risk classifications (risk buckets), with risk weights that are a function of external credit ratings. Under the current system (BIS I), all commercial loans are viewed as having the same credit risk (and thus the same risk weight). Essentially, the book value of each loan is multiplied by a risk weight of 100 percent, and then by 8 percent, to generate the Tier 1 plus Tier 2 minimum capital requirement of 8 percent of risk-adjusted assets, the so-called 8 percent rule. Table 3.1 compares the risk weights for corporate obligations under the proposed new standardized model to the old BIS I risk weights. Under BIS II, the bank's assets are classified into each of the five risk buckets shown in Table 3.1, according to the credit rating assigned to the obligor by independent rating agencies, such as Standard & Poor's, Moody's, and Fitch. Appendix 3.1 shows how credit ratings provided by the three major rating agencies are mapped on a comparable basis. To obtain the minimum capital requirement for credit risk purposes, all

TABLE 3.1   Total Capital Requirements on Corporate Obligations under the Standardized Model of BIS II

External Credit Rating	AAA to AA–	A+ to A–	BBB+ to BB–	Below BB–	Unrated
Risk weight under BIS II	20%	50%	100%	150%	100%
Capital requirement under BIS II	1.6%	4%	8%	12%	8%
Risk weight under BIS I	100%	100%	100%	100%	100%
Capital requirement under BIS I	8%	8%	8%	8%	8%

credit exposures—each is known as the exposure at default, EAD[15]—in each risk weight bucket are summed up, weighted by the appropriate risk weight from Table 3.1, and then multiplied by the overall total capital requirement of 8 percent.

The standardized approach takes credit risk mitigation into account by adjusting the transaction's EAD to reflect collateral, credit derivatives, guarantees, and offsetting on-balance-sheet netting. However, any collateral value is reduced by a haircut to adjust for the volatility of the instrument's market value. Moreover, a floor capital level ensures that the credit quality of the borrower will always impact capital requirements.

The risk weights for claims on sovereigns and their central banks are shown in Table 3.2. The new weights allow for differentiation of credit risk within the classification of Organization for Economic Cooperation and Development (OECD) nations. Under BIS I, all OECD nations carried preferential risk weights of 0 percent on their government obligations. BIS II levies a risk weight that depends on the sovereign's external rating, not on its political affiliation.[16] However, claims on the BIS, the International Monetary Fund (IMF), the European Central Bank (ECB), and the European Community (EC) all carry a 0 percent risk weight.

There are two options for standardized risk weighting of claims on banks and securities firms. Under option 1, all banks incorporated in a

TABLE 3.2 Total Capital Requirements on Sovereigns under the Standardized Model of BIS II

External Credit Rating	AAA to AA– or ECA Rating 1	A+ to A– or ECA Rating 2	BBB+ to BBB– or ECA Rating 3	BB+ to B– or ECA Rating 4 to 6	Below B– or ECA Rating 7
Risk weight under BIS II	0%	20%	50%	100%	150%
Capital requirement under BIS II	0%	1.6%	4%	8%	12%

Notes: ECA denotes Export Credit Agencies. To qualify, the ECA must publish its risk scores and use the OECD methodology. If there are two different assessments by ECAs, then the higher risk weight is used. Sovereigns also have an unrated category with a 100 percent risk weight (not shown). Under BIS I, the risk weight for OECD government obligations is 0 percent. OECD interbank deposits and guaranteed claims, as well as some non-OECD bank and government deposits and securities carry a 20 percent risk weight under BIS I. All other claims on non-OECD governments and banks carry a 100 percent risk weight under BIS I. [See Saunders (1997), Chapter 20.]

TABLE 3.3 Total Capital Requirements on Banks under the Standardized Model of BIS II

External Credit Rating	AAA to AA−	A+ to A−	BBB+ to BBB−	BB+ to B−	Below B−	Unrated
Risk Weight under BIS II Option 1	20%	50%	100%	100%	150%	100%
Capital requirement under BIS II Option 1	1.6%	4%	8%	8%	12%	8%
Risk Weight under BIS II, Option 2	20%	50%	50%	100%	150%	50%
Risk weight for short-term claims under BIS II Option 2	20%	20%	20%	50%	150%	20%

Notes: The capital requirements for option 2 can be calculated by multiplying the risk weight by the 8 percent capital requirement.

given country are assigned a risk weight that is one category less favorable than the sovereign country's risk weight (with the exception of sovereigns rated BB+ or below). Thus, the risk ratings for option 1 shown in the heading in Table 3.3 pertain to the *sovereign's* risk rating. For example, a bank that is incorporated in a country with an AAA rating will have a 20 percent risk weight under option 1, which will result in a 1.6 percent capital requirement.[17] Option 2 uses the external credit rating of the bank itself to set the risk weight. Thus, the risk ratings for option 2, shown in the heading in Table 3.3, pertain to the *bank's* credit rating. For example, a bank with an AAA rating would receive a 20 percent risk weight (and a 1.6 percent capital requirement) regardless of the sovereign's credit rating. The choice of which option applies is left to national bank regulators and must be uniformly adopted for all banks in the country. Table 3.3 also shows that BIS II reduced the risk weights for all bank claims with original maturity of three months or less.[18]

Assessment

BIS II is a step in the right direction in that it adds risk sensitivity to the regulatory treatment of capital requirements to absorb credit losses. However, Altman and Saunders (2001a, b) and the Institute of International Finance (2000) find insufficient risk sensitivity in the proposed risk buckets of the standardized model, especially in the lowest rated bucket for corporates (rated below BB−) which would require a risk weight three times greater than was proposed under BIS II to cover unexpected losses based on empirical evidence on corporate bond loss data.[19] By contrast, the risk weight in the first two corporate loan buckets may be too high. Table 3.4 shows the one-year unexpected losses on a bond portfolio using a normal loss distribution (default mode) at the 99.97 percent confidence level [such that credit losses will exceed the capital amounts as a percent of assets (loans) shown in Table 3.4 in just 3 out of 10,000 years; see Appendix 1.1].[20] The 1.6 percent capital charge for the first risk bucket (AAA to AA− ratings) is too high, given the 0 percent historical loss experience. However, the 35.032 percent historical one-year loss experience for the lowest risk bucket (ratings below BB−) over the period 1981 to 2000 is significantly larger than the 12 percent capital requirement. Thus, capital regulation arbitrage incentives will not be completely eliminated by the BIS II credit risk weights.[21]

The unrated risk bucket (of 100 percent) has also been criticized [see Altman and Saunders (2001a, b)]. Table 3.5 shows that more than 70 percent of corporate exposures were unrated in the 138 banks that participated in a BIS survey (the Quantitative Impact Study, QIS2). Because the majority of obligations held by the world's banks are not rated [see Ferri, Liu, and Majnoni (2001)]—for example, it is estimated that fewer than 1,000 European companies are rated[22]—the retention of an unrated risk bucket is a major lapse that threatens to undermine the risk sensitivity of BIS II.[23] Specifically, actual default data on nonrated loans put them closer to the 150 percent bucket risk weight than the specified 100 percent risk weight. In addition, low-quality borrowers that anticipate receiving an external credit rating below BB− have an incentive to eschew independent rating

TABLE 3.4 Comparison of BIS II Proposed Risk Buckets to Actual Loss Values, Altman and Saunders (2001b)

	AAA to AA−	A+ to A−	BBB+ to BB−	Below BB−
BIS II risk weight	20%	50%	100%	150%
BIS II capital requirement	1.6%	4%	8%	12%
Unexpected losses on all bonds 1981–1999	0%	2.142%	7.369%	35.434%
Unexpected losses on senior bonds 1981–1999	0%	0.659%	10.200%	42.143%
Unexpected losses on all bonds 1981–2000	0%	2.042%	11.753%	35.032%
Unexpected losses for year 2000	0%	5.761%	27.429%	71.159%

TABLE 3.5 Quality Distribution of Corporate Exposures, 138 Banks from 25 Countries Participating in the QIS2 Survey

	AAA–AA	A	BBB–BB	Below B	Higher Risk Loans	Unrated
Large banks in G10 countries	6%	9%	11%	1%	1%	72%
Small banks in G10 countries	11%	9%	6%	2%	2%	70%
Large banks in the EU	6%	8%	8%	1%	1%	75%
Small banks in the EU	8%	10%	5%	2%	2%	73%
Developing countries	7%	3%	4%	2%	3%	81%

Source: BIS, "Results of the Second Quantitative Impact Study," November 5, 2001a.

agencies altogether and may choose to reduce their costs of borrowing by remaining unrated, thereby reducing the availability of credit information available to the market.[24]

On a more fundamental basis, concern has been expressed about tying capital requirements to external ratings produced by rating agencies. Ratings are issue-specific audits; they are not opinions about the overall credit quality of an obligor. There is a certain amount of heterogeneity within each rating class, because a single-letter grade represents a multidimensional concept that includes default probability, loss severity, and transition risk.[25] Moreover, because rating agencies try to avoid discrete jumps in ratings classifications, the rating may be a lagging, not a leading, indicator of credit quality. [See Reisen and von Maltzan (1999) and Reinhart (2001) for discussions of lags in sovereign credit ratings; Kealhofer (2000) and Altman and Saunders (2001a) for lags in publicly traded corporate ratings; and Bongini, Laeven, and Majnoni (2001) for lags in credit ratings of banks.] Ratings change over time, so the transaction may be shifted from one risk bucket to another, thereby injecting excessive volatility into capital requirements [see Linnell (2001)], and may lead to an increase in systemic risk because, with increased downgrades in a recession, banks may find their capital requirements peaking at the worst time (i.e., in the middle of a recession when earnings are relatively weak). Indeed, there is evidence [see Ferri et al. (2001) and Monfort and Mulder (2000), Altman and Saunders (2001a)] that rating agencies behave procyclically because ratings are downgraded in a financial crisis, thereby increasing capital requirements at just the point in the business cycle when stimulation is required [see Reisen (2000)]. Thus, pegging capital requirements to external ratings may exacerbate systemic risk concerns and concern about systemic risk may lead to regulatory attempts to influence rating agencies, thereby undermining their independence and credibility.[26]

Although an important advantage of external ratings is their validation by the market, the credit-rating industry is not very competitive. There are only a handful of well-regarded rating agencies. This leads to the risk of *rating shopping*.[27] The obligors are free to choose a rating agency, so moral hazard may lead rating agencies to shade their ratings upward in a bid to obtain business. Moreover, because there is no single, universally accepted standard for credit ratings, they may not be comparable across rating agencies and across countries. [See discussions in White (2001), Cantor (2001), Griep and De Stefano (2001).] This is likely to distort capital requirements more in less developed countries (LDCs), because of greater volatility in LDC sovereign ratings, less transparent financial reporting in those countries, and the greater impact of the sovereign rating as a de facto ceiling for the private sector in LDCs.[28]

Finally, banks are also considered "delegated monitors" [see Diamond (1984)] that have a comparative advantage in assessing and monitoring the credit risks of their borrowers. Indeed, this function is viewed as making banks "special." This appears to be inconsistent with the concept underlying the standardized model, which essentially attributes this bank-monitoring function to external rating agencies for the purposes of setting capital requirements. Adoption of this model may well reduce banks' incentives to invest time and effort in monitoring, thereby reducing the availability of information and further undermining the value of the banking franchise.

THE INTERNAL RATINGS-BASED MODELS FOR CREDIT RISK

Under the internal ratings-based (IRB) model[29] each bank is required to establish an internal ratings model to classify the credit risk exposure of each activity (e.g., commercial lending, consumer lending) whether on or off the balance sheet. For the foundation IRB approach, the required outputs obtained from the internal ratings model are estimates of one-year[30] probability of default (PD) and exposure at default (EAD) for each transaction. In addition to these estimates, independent estimates of both the loss given default (LGD) and maturity (M)[31] are required to implement the advanced IRB approach. The bank computes risk weights for each individual exposure (e.g., corporate loan) by incorporating its estimates of PD, EAD, LGD, and M obtained from its internal ratings model and its own internal data systems. The model also assumes that the average default correlation among individual borrowers is between 10 percent and 20 percent with the correlation a decreasing function of PD; see BIS (November 5, 2001b).[32]

Expected losses upon default can be calculated as follows:

$$\text{Expected losses} = PD \times LGD$$

where *PD* is the probability of default and *LGD* is the loss given default.[33] However, this considers only one possible credit event—default—and ignores the possibility of losses resulting from credit-rating downgrades. That is, deterioration in credit quality caused by increases in *PD* or *LGD* will cause the value of the loan to be written down—in a mark-to-market sense—even prior to default, thereby resulting in portfolio losses (if the loan's value is marked to market). Thus, credit risk measurement models can be differentiated on the basis of whether the definition of a "credit event" includes only default (the default mode or DM models) or whether it also includes nondefault credit quality deterioration (the mark-to-market or MTM models). The mark-to-market approach considers the impact of credit downgrades and upgrades on market value, whereas the default mode is only concerned about the economic value of an obligation in the event of default. There are five elements to any IRB approach:

1. A classification of the obligation by credit risk exposure—the internal ratings model.
2. Risk components—*PD* and *EAD* for the foundation model and *PD*, *EAD*, *LGD*, and *M* for the advanced model.
3. A risk weight function that uses the risk components to calculate the risk weights.
4. A set of minimum requirements of eligibility to apply the IRB approach (i.e., demonstration that the bank maintains the necessary information systems to accurately implement the IRB approach).
5. Supervisory review of compliance with the minimum requirements.

The Foundation IRB Approach

The bank is allowed to use its own estimate of probability of default (*PD*) over a one-year time horizon, as well as each loan's exposure at default (*EAD*). However, there is a lower bound on *PD* that is equal to three basis points, so as to create a nonzero floor on the credit risk weights (and hence capital required to be held against any individual loan). The average *PD* for each internal grade is used to calculate the risk weight for each internal rating. The *PD* may be based on historical experience or even potentially on a credit scoring model. (See Chapter 2 for traditional credit scoring models and Chapters 4 through 8 for newer models.) The *EAD* for on-balance-sheet transactions is equal to the nominal (book value) amount of the exposure outstanding. Credit mitigation factors (e.g., collateral, credit derivatives or guarantees, on-balance-sheet netting) are incorporated following the rules of the standard IRB approach by adjusting the *EAD* for the collateral amount, less a haircut determined by supervisory advice under Pillar II. The *EAD* for off-balance-sheet activities is computed using the BIS I approach of translating off-balance-sheet items into on-balance-sheet equivalents mostly using the BIS I conversion factors [see Saunders (1997), Chapter 20].[34] The foundation IRB approach sets a benchmark for *M*, maturity [or weighted average life (WAL) of the loan] at three years. Moreover, the foundation approach assumes that loss given default for each unsecured loan is set at *LGD* = 50 percent for senior claims and *LGD* = 75 percent for subordinated claims on corporate obligations.[35] However, in November 2001, the Basel Committee on Banking Supervision presented potential modifications that would reduce the *LGD* on secured loans to 45 percent if fully secured by physical, nonreal estate collateral and 40 percent if fully secured by receivables.

Under the January 2001 proposal, the foundation approach formula for the risk weight (*RW*) on corporate obligations (loans) is:[36]

$$RW = \left(\frac{LGD}{50}\right) \times BRW \tag{3.1}$$

or

$$12.50 \times LGD$$

whichever is smaller; where the benchmark risk weight (*BRW*) is calculated for each risk classification using the following formula:

$$BRW = 976.5 \times N(1.118 \times G(PD) + 1.288) \times \left(1 + .0470 \times \frac{(1-PD)}{PD^{0.44}}\right) \tag{3.2}$$

The term $N(y)$ denotes the cumulative distribution function for a standard normal random variable (i.e., the probability that a normal random variable with mean zero and variance of one is less than or equal to y) and the term $G(z)$ denotes the inverse cumulative distribution function for a standard normal random variable (i.e., the value y such that $N(y) = z$). The *BRW* formula is calibrated so that a three year corporate loan with a *PD* equal to 0.7 percent and a *LGD* equal to 50 percent will have a capital requirement of 8 percent, calibrated to an assumed loss coverage target of 99.5 percent (i.e., losses can exceed the capital allocation that occur only 0.5 percent of the time, or five years in 1,000).[37] Appendix 3.2 shows the calibration of equation (3.2) for retail loans, demonstrating that the *BRW* for retail loans is set lower than the *BRW* for corporate loans for all levels of *PD*. Figure 3.1 shows the continuous relationship between the *BRW* and the *PD*. Note that this continuous function allows the bank to choose the number of risk categories in the internal risk rating system, as long as there is a minimum of six to nine grades for performing borrowers and two grades for nonperforming borrowers.[38]

Consultation between the Basel Committee on Banking Supervision and the public fueled concerns about the calibration of the foundation approach as presented in equations (3.1) and (3.2). This concern was galvanized by the results of a Quantitative Impact Study (QIS2) that examined the impact of the BIS II proposals on the capital requirements of 138 large and small banks from 25 countries. Banks that would have adopted the IRB foundation approach would have seen an unintended 14 percent increase in their capital requirements. Potential modifications were released on November 5, 2001 to lower the risk weights and make the risk weighting function less steep for the IRB foundation approach only. Moreover, the potential modifications (if incorporated into the BIS II proposals) would make the correlation coefficient a function of the *PD,* such that the correlation coefficient between assets decreases as the *PD* increases. Finally, the confidence level built into the risk weighting function would be increased from 99.5 percent to 99.9 percent.

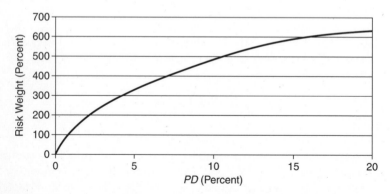

FIGURE 3.1 Proposed IRB risk weights for hypothetical corporate exposure having *LGD* equal to 50 percent. *Source:* "The Internal Ratings-Based Approach," The New Basel Capital Accord, Bank for International Settlements (2001).

The potential modifications to equations (3.1) and (3.2) corporate loan risk weight curves are as follows:

$$BRW = 12.5 \times LGD \times M$$

$$\times N \left[(1-R)^{-0.5} \times G(PD) + \left(\frac{R}{(1-R)} \right)^{.05} \times G(0.999) \right] \qquad (3.3)$$

where

$$M = 1 + 0.047 \times \left(\frac{(1-PD)}{PD^{0.44}} \right) \qquad (3.4)$$

$$R = 0.10 \times \left[\frac{\left(1 - exp^{-50\,PD}\right)}{\left(1 - exp^{-50}\right)} \right] + 0.20 \times \left[1 - \frac{\left(1 - exp^{-50\,PD}\right)}{1 - exp^{-50}} \right] \qquad (3.5)$$

and

$$RW = \left(\frac{X}{50} \right) \times BRW \qquad (3.6)$$

where $X = 75$ for a subordinated loan,
  $X = 50$ for an unsecured loan,
  $X = 45$ for a loan fully secured by physical, nonreal estate collateral, and
  $X = 40$ for a loan fully secured by receivables.

In equations (3.3) through (3.6), *exp* stands for the natural exponential function, $N(.)$ stands for the standard normal cumulative distribution function, and $G(.)$ stands for the inverse standard normal cumulative distribution function.

Equation (3.4) denotes the maturity factor *M*. This is reportedly unchanged from the BIS II proposals shown in equation (3.2) in that it is still benchmarked to a fixed three year weighted average life of the loan.[39] The correlation coefficient *R* is computed in equation (3.5). The correlation ranges from 0.20 for the lowest *PD* value to 0.10 for the highest *PD* value.

This inverse relationship appears to be somewhat counterintuitive in that empirically asset correlations increase during systemic crises when *PD*s also tend to increase, thereby implying a direct positive (rather than inverse) relationship between correlation and *PD*; see Carey (1998) and Erlenmaier and Gersbach (2001).

Using the potential modifications of November 2001, the benchmark risk weight (*BRW*) is calculated from equations (3.3) through (3.5). The actual risk weight (*RW*) is then calculated in equation (3.6) where $RW = (X/50) \times BRW$ and X = the stipulated fixed *LGD* for each type of loan. For example, under the potential modifications of November 2001, the *LGD* takes on a value of either 40 percent (if the loan is fully secured by receivables), 45 percent (if fully secured by physical, non-real estate collateral), 50 percent (if unsecured but senior), or 75 percent (if subordinated). Risk-weighted assets (*RWA*) are then computed by multiplying the risk weight (*RW*) times the exposure at default *EAD*. Finally, the minimum capital requirement is computed by multiplying the risk-weighted assets times 8 percent; that is, the minimum capital requirement on the individual loan = $RW \times EAD \times 8$ percent.

Table 3.6 shows the impact of the November 2001 modified risk weighting function on the capital requirements under the IRB foundation approach. For

TABLE 3.6 Comparison of BIS II Proposals and Potential Modifications: Capital Requirements under the IRB Foundation Approach

Probability of Default (Basis Points)	January 2001 BIS II Proposal Capital Requirements (%)	November 2001 BIS Modified Capital Requirements (%)
3	1.1	1.4
10	2.3	2.7
25	4.2	4.3
50	6.4	5.9
75	8.3	7.1
100	10.0	8.0
125	11.5	8.7
150	12.9	9.3
200	15.4	10.3
250	17.6	11.1
300	19.7	11.9
400	23.3	13.4
500	26.5	14.8
1,000	38.6	21.0
2,000	50.0	30.0

Notes: The minimum capital requirements shown are a percent of *EAD* (exposure at default) assuming *LGD* = 50 percent. *Source:* BIS (November 5, 2001b).

example, an unsecured $100 million corporate loan with a *PD* of 10 percent would have a 2.62 percent benchmark risk weight under the November 2001 modifications, computed using equations (3.3) through (3.5). Because the loan in our example is unsecured, using equation (3.1) the $RW = (50/50) \times BRW = 2.62$. Thus, the loan's minimum capital requirement would be $100m \times .08 \times 2.62 = 21 million shown in Table 3.6 column (3). In contrast, Table 3.6 shows that the same loan's minimum capital requirement under the January 2001 proposals would have been $38.6 million shown in column (2). Moreover, under BIS I the capital requirement would have been $100 million $\times$ 8 percent = $8 million. Table 3.6 also shows that the capital requirement for the highest quality (lowest *PD*) exposures increases slightly in the modified proposals, whereas the capital requirement for the lowest quality (highest *PD*) exposures decreases significantly as compared to the January 2001 BIS II proposals.

This example is for a single loan. In practice, the BIS makes an additional adjustment for loan portfolio concentration. In the foundation model, the *RW* in equation (3.1) is multiplied by the *EAD* for each internal rating classification (on a transaction by transaction basis) in order to obtain a measure of risk-weighted assets for each loan; that is, $RWA = RW \times EAD$. The risk-weighted assets are summed across all ratings classes to obtain the baseline level of credit risk-weighted assets. Then an adjustment for granularity (i.e., the degree of single-borrower risk concentration) is applied.[40] The adjustment may be positive or negative and reflects the undiversified idiosyncratic risk of the portfolio. Although the granularity adjustment incorporates correlations (such that the adjustment increases as asset correlations increase), it differs from the *R* factor in equation (3.5) because it measures overall portfolio concentration rather than pairwise asset correlation. Thus, the effect of the granularity adjustment is to increase (decrease) the total risk-weighted assets of portfolios with relatively large (small) borrower risk concentration.

The *BRW* in equation (3.2) is calibrated using CreditMetrics (see Chapter 6) to an assumed $PD = 0.7025$ percent, $LGD = 50$ percent, maturity of three years, and a granularity scaling factor of 4 percent. That is, about 4 percent of baseline capital is allocated to cover the expected and unexpected losses associated with undiversified idiosyncratic risk resulting from the fact that the portfolio does not contain an infinite number of equal-sized loans. Thus, the portion of risk-weighted assets that is levied as a granularity charge is $.04 \times RWA$. To determine the effect of actual portfolio granulation, the portfolio's granularity must be compared to this baseline level, such that if the actual portfolio's granularity is higher (lower), the portfolio's minimum capital requirement is higher (lower).

Calculation of the portfolio's granularity capital charge is based on the property that the *VAR* of a granular portfolio consisting of *n* homogenous loans is equal to the *VAR* for an infinitely fine-grained portfolio (assumed in calculating the baseline risk weights) plus an adjustment factor that is inversely proportional to n. The constant of proportionality is a function of PD, LGD, and F (the systematic risk sensitivity of the exposures in the portfolio). Thus, the additional capital charge (as a fraction of portfolio size) that is required to cover the undiversified idiosyncratic risk of a granular portfolio is GSF/n, where GSF is the constant factor of proportionality (shown in equation (3.8) to be a function of PD, LGD, and F) and n is the number of exposures in the portfolio. This granularity capital charge must be compared to the baseline 4 percent granularity charge. The form of the granularity adjustment is then as follows:[41]

$$\left(Portfolio\ TEAD \times \frac{GSF}{n^*} \right) - \left(.04 \times RWA \right) \tag{3.7}$$

where $Portfolio\ TEAD$ = the portfolio's total non-retail exposure,[42]
GSF = the granularity scaling factor; see equation (3.8),
n^* = effective number of loans, taking into account their size distribution,[43]
RWA = risk-weighted assets under the baseline assumptions of equation (3.1).

Credit Risk Plus (see Chapter 8) is used to calibrate the granularity scaling factor (GSF); see also Gordy (2000). The form is:

$$GSF = \left(0.6 + 1.8 \times LGD \right) \times \left(9.5 + 13.57 \times \frac{PD}{F} \right) \tag{3.8}$$

where LGD = the weighted average of the portfolio's loss given default,
PD = the weighted average of the portfolio's default probability,
F = the measure of systematic risk sensitivity, is defined as follows:

$$F = N\left(\alpha_1 \times G(PD) + \alpha_0 \right) - PD \tag{3.9}$$

where as in equation (3.2), $N(y)$ denotes the cumulative distribution function for a standard normal random variable (i.e., the probability that a normal random variable with mean zero and variance of one is less than or equal to y) and the term $G(z)$ denotes the inverse cumulative distribution function for a standard normal random variable (i.e., the value y such that $N(y)=z$). α_0 and α_1 are the same terms as in equation (3.2) (e.g., $\alpha_0 = 1.288$ and $\alpha_1 = 1.118$ for corporate loans). The granularity adjustment is applied to the entire portfolio as a whole (excluding the retail portfolio, which is generally assumed to be infinitely granular) after the sum of all baseline risk-weighted assets for all portfolio exposures is computed.

The Advanced IRB Approach

Sophisticated banks are encouraged to move from the foundation approach to the advanced approach. A primary source for this incentive results from the use of the bank's *actual LGD* experience in place of the fixed assumption of a 40, 45, 50, or 75 percent *LGD*. Evidence suggests that historical *LGD* for bank loans is significantly lower than 50 percent[44] and, therefore, the shift to the advanced approach is expected to reduce bank capital requirements by 2 to 3 percent. However, the quid pro quo for permission to use actual *LGD* is compliance with an additional set of minimum requirements attesting to the efficacy of the bank's information systems in maintaining data on *LGD*.

Another adjustment to the foundation approach's benchmark risk weight (*BRW*) is the incorporation of a maturity adjustment that reflects the transaction's effective maturity, defined as the greater of either one year or nominal maturity, which is the weighted average life (= $\Sigma_t tP_t / \Sigma_t P_t$ where P_t is the minimum amount of principal contractually payable at time t) for all instruments with a predetermined minimum amortization schedule. The maturity is capped at seven years to avoid overstating the impact of maturity on credit risk exposure.

The advanced IRB approach allows the bank to use its own credit risk mitigation estimates to adjust *PD*, *LGD*, and *EAD* for collateral, credit derivatives, guarantees, and on-balance-sheet netting. The risk weights for the mark-to-market Advanced IRB approach are calculated as follows:

$$RW = \left(\frac{LGD}{50}\right) \times BRW \times \left[1 + b(PD) \times (M - 3)\right] \tag{3.10}$$

where

$$b(PD) = \frac{\left[.0235 \times (1 - PD)\right]}{\left[PD^{0.44} + .0470 \times (1 - PD)\right]} \tag{3.11}$$

and *BRW* is as defined in the foundation IRB approach. The effect of the [1 + $b(PD) \times M(-3)$] term in equation (3.10) is to adjust the risk of loans for its maturity.[45] For longer maturity instruments, the maturity adjustments increase for low *PD*-rated borrowers (i.e., higher rated borrowers). The intuition is that maturity matters most for low *PD* borrowers since they can move only in one direction (downward) and the longer the maturity of the loan, the more this is likely to occur. For high *PD* (low-quality) borrowers who are near default, the maturity adjustment will not matter as much because they may be close to default regardless of the length of the maturity of the loan.[46]

The advanced IRB approach entails the estimation of parameters requiring long histories of data that are unavailable to most banks [see the Basel Committee on Banking Supervision (April 1999) for a survey of current credit risk modeling practices at 20 large international banks located in 10 countries]. Given the costs of developing these models and databases, there is the possibility of dichotomizing the banking industry into "haves and have-nots." For example, some anecdotal estimates suggest that no more than 15 U.S. banks will choose to use either IRB approach. Moreover, capital requirements are highly sensitive to the accuracy of certain parameter values; in particular, estimates of *LGD* and the granularity in *PD* are important [see Gordy (2000) and Carey (2000)]. Because credit losses are affected by economic conditions, the model parameters should also be adjusted to reflect expected levels of economic activity. Thus, the data requirements are so substantial that full implementation of the advanced IRB approach lies far in the future, even for the most sophisticated banks. When that date comes, regulators will have commensurate challenges in obtaining the necessary data to validate the banks' models.

ASSESSMENT

In its sophistication in measuring credit risk, BIS II is a potential improvement over BIS I. Moreover, it moves regulatory capital in the direction of economic capital. However, it is far from an integrated portfolio management approach to credit risk measurement. Focus on individual ratings classifications (whether external or internal) prevents an aggregated view of credit risk across all transactions, and regulatory concerns about systemic risk prevent full consideration of cross-asset correlations that might reduce capital requirements further.[47] Thus, capital requirements are likely to be higher than is economically necessary when considering actual portfolio correlations.[48] Moreover, incompatible approaches to assessing the capital adequacy of insurance companies and other nonbanking firms may obscure their impact on financial system instability. In the United States, the insurance industry and government-sponsored enterprises (such as Fannie Mae and Freddie Mac) and, in the United Kingdom, the Financial Services Authority all use a variety of models ranging from minimum ratios and stress-test survivorship requirements to a dynamic risk-of-ruin scenario analysis that includes the asset and the liability sides of the balance sheet to measure capital requirements.

The advanced IRB approach also contains some properties that may distort bank incentives to manage their credit risk exposure. For example, Allen (2002) finds that the maturity adjustment in the advanced IRB approach [see equation (3.10)] creates perverse incentives when dealing with loans with maturities greater than three years such that the loan adjustment factor *decreases* the loan's risk weight as the loan quality (credit rating) declines. Moreover, the advanced IRB approach penalizes increases in *LGD* more than increases in *PD*. Table 3.7 uses data from Altman and Saunders (2001b) to determine the impact of increases in *LGD* on the advanced IRB risk weights for loans with maturity of three years keeping expected losses (i.e., $LGD \times PD$) constant. For all risk buckets (for illustrative purposes only, the standardized approach's risk classifications are used), the advanced IRB risk weights increase as the *LGD* increases, although the *PD* decreases offset the *LGD* increases so as to keep expected losses constant.

BIS II is based on a prespecified threshold insolvency level; that is, capital levels are set so that the estimated probability of insolvency of each bank is lower than a threshold level such as 99.9 percent (or 0.1 percent probability of failure per year, or 1 bank insolvency every 1,000 years).[49]

TABLE 3.7 The Impact of Increases in *LGD* on Advanced Internal Ratings-Based Risk Weights under BIS II Holding Expected Losses Constant

BIS II Risk Buckets (1)	Actual LGD (2)	PD (%) (3)	Increased LGD (4)	Decreased PD (%) (5)	Advanced IRB Risk Weight Using Cols. (2) and (3)	Advanced IRB Risk Weight Using Cols. (4) and (5)
AAA to AA−	0	0	0	0	0	0
A+ to A−	20.714	0.058	25	0.048	3.585	4.327
BBB+ to BB−	18.964	0.857	20	0.813	16.315	17.206
Below BB−	28.321	9.787	35	7.919	153.063	189.160

Notes: The *LGD* and *PD* values in columns (2) and (3) are taken from Altman and Saunders (2001b). The *LGD* and *PD* values in columns (4) and (5) are adjusted to increase *LGD* while keeping expected losses ($LGD \times PD$) constant.

However, from the regulator's point of view, there are two potential short-comings to this approach. First, without considering the relationship between individual banks' insolvency probabilities, BIS II cannot specify an aggregate, systemwide insolvency risk threshold [see Acharya (2001)]. Second, there is no information about the magnitude of loss given bank insolvency. The deposit insurer, for example, may be concerned about the cost to the deposit insurance fund in the event that the bank's capital is exhausted. [See Gordy (2000) and Appendix 6.2 for a discussion of the estimation of the "expected tail loss."] BIS II does not address either of these concerns. However, there is evidence [see Jackson et al. (2001)] that banks hold capital in excess of the regulatory minimum in response to market pressures; for example, in order to participate in the swap market, the bank's credit quality must be higher than would be induced by complying with either BIS I or II.[50] Thus, regulatory capital requirements may be considered lower bounds that do not obviate the need for more precise credit risk measurement.

SUMMARY

The new Basel Accord on bank capital (BIS II) makes capital requirements more sensitive to credit risk exposure. Regulations governing minimum capital requirements allow the bank to evolve through three steps: (1) the standardized model, (2) the internal ratings-based (IRB) foundation approach, and (3) the advanced IRB approach. In the standardized model, credit risk weights are determined using external ratings assigned by independent credit-rating agencies. For commercial loans, there are four risk buckets (plus an unrated classification) corresponding to prespecified corporate credit ratings.

The IRB approaches require banks to formulate their own internal ratings models in order to classify the credit risk of their activities. The foundation approach requires that banks estimate only the probability of default (PD) and the exposure at default (EAD). There are two additional parameter estimates required to implement the advanced approach: the loss given default (LGD) and the maturity (M). BIS II requires supervisors to validate the internal models developed by the banks, in conjunction with enhanced disclosure requirements that reveal more detailed credit risk information to the market.

APPENDIX 3.1

Tables 3.1 through 3.5 use Standard & Poor's credit ratings in order to derive the risk weights under the standardized approach. Table 3.8 shows how

TABLE 3.8 Mapping of Standard & Poor's, Moody's, and Fitch IBCA Credit Ratings

Standard & Poor's Credit Rating	Moody's Credit Rating	Fitch IBCA Credit Rating
AAA	Aaa	AAA
AA+	Aa1	AA+
AA	Aa2	AA
AA–	Aa3	AA–
A+	A1	A+
A	A2	A
A–	A3	A–
BBB+	Baa1	BBB+
BBB	Baa2	BBB
BBB–	Baa3	BBB–
BB+	Ba1	BB+
BB	Ba2	BB
BB–	Ba3	BB–
B+	B1	B+
B	B2	B
B–	B3	B–
CCC+	Caa1	CCC+
CCC	Caa2	CCC
CCC–	Caa3	CCC–
CC	Ca	CC
C	C	C
D		D

Source: BIS (April 30, 2001).

Standard & Poor's ratings can be mapped onto comparable Moody's and Fitch IBCA ratings.

APPENDIX 3.2
BIS II TREATMENT OF RETAIL EXPOSURES UNDER THE INTERNAL RATINGS-BASED APPROACH

The retail portfolio is defined as a "large number of small, low-value loans with either a consumer or a business focus, in which the incremental risk of any particular exposure is small" [BIS (2001), "The Internal Ratings-Based

Approach," p. 59]. This includes credit cards, installment loans (e.g., personal finance, education loans, auto loans, leasing), revolving credits (e.g., overdrafts, home equity lines of credit), residential mortgages, and small business facilities. To be considered "retail," the loans must be managed by the bank as a large pool of fairly homogenous loans. The retail loan portfolio is typically divided into segments based on each segment's *PD, LGD,* and *EAD*. For each loan, the bank determines the *EAD* and multiplies that by the risk weight,[51] which in turn is dependent on a benchmark risk weight following the methodology shown in equation (3.2), but calibrated to different constants as follows:

$$BRW = 976.5 \times N\left(1.043 \times G(PD) + 0.766\right) \times \left(1 + .0470 \times \frac{(1-PD)}{PD^{0.44}}\right) \quad (3.12)$$

The term $N(y)$, where y reflects the variables in equation (3.4), denotes the cumulative distribution function for a standard normal random variable (i.e., the probability that a normal random variable with mean zero and variance of one is less than or equal to y) and the term $G(z)$, where z reflects the term in brackets in equation (3.12), denotes the inverse cumulative distribution function for a standard normal random variable (i.e., the value

TABLE 3.9 Comparison of Benchmark Risk Weights under BIS Internal Ratings-Based Foundation Approach for Corporate versus Retail Loans: January 2001

Probability of Default PD (%)	Corporate Loan Benchmark Risk Weight (%)	Retail Loan Benchmark Risk Weight (%)
0.03	14	6
0.05	19	9
0.1	29	14
0.2	45	21
0.4	70	34
0.5	81	40
0.7	100	50
1.0	125	64
2.0	192	104
3.0	246	137
5.0	331	195
10.0	482	310
15.0	588	401
20.0	625	479

Notes: Both the corporate and retail loans are calibrated to a three-year maturity and a *LGD* = 50 percent. *Source:* BIS (January 2001).

y such that $N(y) = z$). The risk weight formula is calibrated to a three-year retail loan maturity with an $LGD = 50$ percent. As for corporate loans, the BRW is substituted into equation (3.1) to determine the retail loan's risk weight. In Table 3.9, the benchmark risk weights for retail loans are compared to the BRW for corporate loans; both sets of loans assume a three-year maturity and an $LGD = 50$ percent. As shown in Table 3.9, retail loans have lower benchmark risk weights for every value of PD reflecting lower minimum capital requirements for the retail sector.[52]

In November 2001, the Basel Committee on Banking Supervision published potential modifications to the BIS II proposals for retail obligations. Under the modifications, residential mortgages would have a higher risk weight curve than other retail exposures, but both retail risk weight curves would be lower than the one specified in equation (3.12) under the BIS II proposals.

The residential mortgage risk weight curve under the IRB foundation approach November (2001) proposal is:

$$BRW = 12.50 \times LGD$$
$$\times N\left[(1-R)^{-0.5} \times G(PD) + \left(\frac{R}{(1-R)} \right)^{0.5} \times G(0.999) \right] \quad (3.13)$$

where the correlation R is calibrated to equal 0.15. The LGD is set at 50 percent for the IRB foundation approach; there may be a scaling factor (up or down) to reflect actual LGD.

The other retail exposures risk weight curve is:

$$BRW = 12.50$$
$$\times \left| LGD \times N\left[(1-R)^{-0.5} \times G(PD) + \left(\frac{R}{(1-R)} \right)^{0.5} \times G(0.999) \right] - LGD \times PD \right| \quad (3.14)$$

where

$$R = 0.04 \times \frac{\left(1 - exp^{-25\,PD}\right)}{\left(1 - exp^{-25}\right)} + 0.15 \times \left[1 - \frac{\left(1 - exp^{-25\,PD}\right)}{\left(1 - exp\right)^{-25}} \right] \quad (3.15)$$

The correlation R ranges from a minimum value of 0.04 (for the highest PD) to a maximum value of 0.15 (for the lowest PD). All expected losses on retail exposures are covered by margin income. LGD is set equal to 50 percent unless scaled to actual LGD.

CHAPTER 4

Loans as Options

The KMV and Moody's Models

The idea of applying option pricing theory to the valuation of risky loans and bonds has been in the literature at least as far back as Merton (1974). In recent years, Merton's ideas have been extended in many directions. One example is the generation of default prediction models (by KMV and Moody's) that produce (and update) default predictions for all major companies and banks that have their equity publicly traded.[1] In this chapter, we first look at the link between loans and options and then investigate how this link can be used to derive a default prediction model.

THE LINK BETWEEN LOANS AND OPTIONALITY

Figure 4.1 shows the payoff function to a bank lender of a simple loan. Assume that this is a one-year loan and the amount *(OB)* is borrowed on a discount basis. Technically, option formulas (discussed later) model loans as zero-coupon "bonds" with fixed maturities. Over the year, a borrowing firm will invest the funds in various projects or assets. Assume that, at the end of the year, the market value of the borrowing firm's assets is OA_2. The owners of the firm have an incentive to repay the loan (*OB*) and keep the residual as "profit" or return on investment ($OA_2 - OB$). Indeed, for any value of the firm's assets exceeding *OB*, the owners of the firm will have an incentive to repay the loan. However, if the market value of the firm's assets is less than *OB* (e.g., OA_1 in Figure 4.1), the owners have an incentive (or option) to default and to turn over the remaining assets of the firm to the lender (the bank).

For market values of assets exceeding *OB*, the bank will earn a fixed upside return on the loan; essentially, interest and principal will be repaid in full. For asset values less than *OB*, the bank suffers increasingly larger losses.

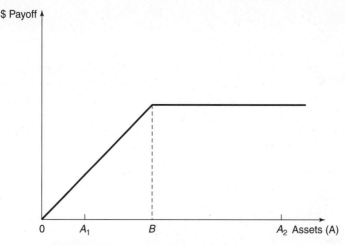

FIGURE 4.1   The payoff to a bank lender.

In the extreme case, the bank's payoff is zero: principal and interest are totally lost.[2]

The loan payoff function shown in Figure 4.1—a fixed payoff on the upside, and long-tailed downside risk—might be immediately familiar to an option theorist. Compare it with the payoff to a writer of a put option on a stock (shown in Figure 4.2). If the price of the stock (S) exceeds the exercise price (X), the writer of the option will keep the put premium. If the price of the stock falls below X, the writer will lose successively larger amounts.

Merton (1974) noted this formal payoff equivalence; that is, when a bank makes a loan, its payoff is isomorphic to writing a put option on the assets of the borrowing firm. Moreover, just as five variables enter the classic Black-Scholes-Merton (BSM) model of put option valuation for stocks, the value of the default option (or, more generally, the value of a risky loan) will also depend on the value of five similar variables.

In general form:

$$\text{Value of a put option on a stock} = f\left(\bar{S}, \bar{X}, \bar{r}, \bar{\sigma}, \bar{\tau}\right) \qquad (4.1)$$

$$\text{Value of a default option on a risky loan} = f\left(A, \bar{B}, \bar{r}, \sigma_A, \bar{\tau}\right) \quad (4.2)$$

where S, X, A, and B are as defined above (a bar above a variable denotes that it is directly observable); r is the short-term interest rate; σ and σ_A are,

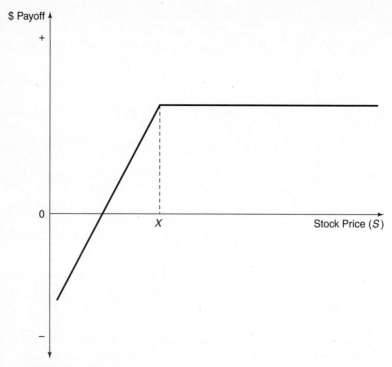

FIGURE 4.2   The payoff to the writer of a put option on a stock.

respectively, the volatilities of the firm's equity value and the market value of its assets; and τ is the maturity of the put option or, in the case of loans, the time horizon (default horizon) for the loan.

In general, for options on stocks, all five variables on the right side of equation (4.1) are directly observable; however, this is true for only three variables on the right side of equation (4.2). The market value of a firm's assets (A) and the volatility of the market value of a firm's assets (σ_A) are *not* directly observable. If A and σ_A could be directly measured, the value of a risky loan, the value of the default option, and the equilibrium spread on a risky loan over the risk-free rate could all be calculated directly. [See Merton (1974) and Saunders (1997) for examples; see also Appendix 4.1.]

Some analysts have substituted the observed market value of risky debt on the left-hand-side of equation (4.2) (or, where appropriate, the observed interest spread between a firm's risky bonds and a matched risk-free Treasury rate) and have assumed that the book value of assets equals the market value of assets. This allows the implied volatility of assets (σ_A) to be "backed out" from equation (4.2). [See, for example, Gorton and Santomero (1990) and Flannery and Sorescu (1996).] However, without additional assumptions, it is impossible to impute two unobservable values (A and σ_A), based solely on one equation (4.2). Moreover, the market values and trading dynamics of risky corporate debt are hard to get for all but a few firms [see Schultz (2001) and Saunders et al. (2002)]. Corporate bond price information is generally not easily available to the public, and quoted bond prices are often artificial "matrix" prices.[3,4]

THE KMV CREDIT MONITOR MODEL[5]

The innovation of the KMV Credit Monitor Model is that it turns the bank's lending problem around and considers the loan repayment incentive problem from the viewpoint of the borrowing firm's equity holders. To solve the two unknowns, A and σ_A, the model uses (1) the "structural" relationship between the market value of a firm's equity and the market value of its assets, and (2) the relationship between the volatility of a firm's assets and the volatility of a firm's equity. After values of these variables are derived, an expected default frequency (*EDF*) or probability of default measure for the borrower can be calculated.

Figure 4.3 shows the loan repayment problem from the side of the borrower (the equity owner of the firm). Suppose the firm borrows *OB* and the end-of-period market value of the firm's assets is OA_2 (where $OA_2 > OB$). The firm will then repay the loan, and the equity owners will keep the residual value of the firm's assets ($OA_2 - OB$). The larger the market value of the firm's assets at the end of the loan period, the greater the residual value of the firm's assets to the equity holders. However, if the firm's assets fall below *OB* (e.g., are equal to OA_1), the equity owners of the firm will not be able to repay the loan.[6] They will be economically insolvent and will turn the firm's assets over to the bank.[7] Note that the downside risk of the equity owners is truncated no matter how low asset values are, compared to the amount borrowed. Specifically, "limited liability" protects the equity owners against losing more than *OL* (the owners' original stake in the firm). As shown in Figure 4.3, the payoff to the equity holder of a leveraged firm has a limited downside and a long-tailed upside. Those familiar with options will immediately recognize the similarity between the payoff function of an equity owner in a leveraged firm and buying a call option on a stock. Thus, we can view the market-value position of equity holders in a borrowing firm (*E*) as isomorphic to holding a call option on the assets of the firm (*A*).

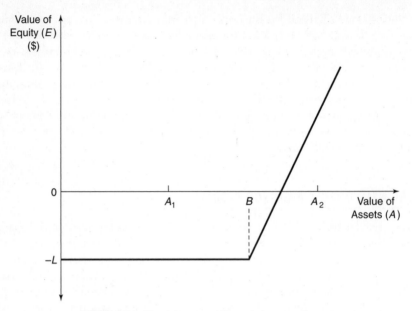

FIGURE 4.3 Equity as a call option on a firm.

In general terms, equity can be valued as:

$$\overline{E} = h\!\left(A, \sigma_A, \overline{B}, \overline{r}, \overline{\tau}\right) \tag{4.3}$$

In equation (4.3), the observed market value of a borrowing firm's equity (price of shares times the number of shares) depends on the same five variables as in equation (4.2), as per the BSM model for valuing a call option (on the assets of a firm). However, a problem still remains: How to solve two unknowns (A and σ_A) from one equation (where $\overline{E}$, $\overline{r}$, $\overline{B}$, and $\overline{\tau}$ are all observable, as denoted by the bar above each of them)?

KMV and others in the literature have resolved this problem by noting that a second relationship can be exploited: the theoretical relationship between the observable volatility of a firm's equity value (σ) and the "unobservable" volatility of a firm's asset value (σ_A).[8] In general terms:

$$\overline{\sigma} = g\!\left(\sigma_A\right) \tag{4.4}$$

With two equations and two unknowns, equations (4.3) and (4.4) can be used to solve for A and σ_A by successive iteration. Explicit functional forms for the option-pricing model (*OPM*) in equation (4.3) and for the stock price-asset volatility linkage in equation (4.4) have to be specified. [A good discussion of these issues can be found in Jarrow and Turnbull (2000) and Delianedis and Geske (1998).] KMV uses an option-pricing BSM-type model that allows for dividends. B, the default exercise point, is taken as the value of all short-term liabilities (one year and under) plus half the book value of long-term debt outstanding.[9] (The precise strike price or "default point" has varied under different generations of the model, and there is a question as to whether net short-term liabilities should be used instead of total short-term liabilities.[10]) The maturity variable (τ) also can be altered according to the default horizon of the analyst; most commonly, it is set equal to one year. A slightly different *OPM* was used by Ronn and Verma (1986, p. 878) to solve a very similar problem in estimating the default risk of U.S. banks.[11]

After they have been calculated, the A and σ_A values can be employed, along with assumptions about the values of B, r, and τ, to generate a theoretically based expected default frequency (*EDF*) score for any given borrower.

The idea is shown in Figure 4.4. Suppose that the values backed out of equations (4.3) and (4.4) for any given borrower are, respectively: $A = \$100$

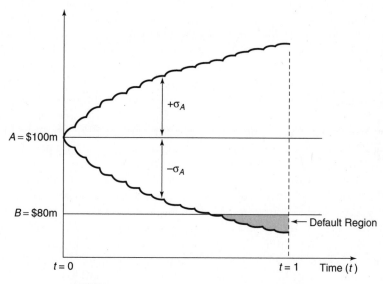

FIGURE 4.4 Calculating the theoretical *EDF*.

million and $\sigma_A = \$10$ million.[12] The value of $B = \$80$ million. In practice, the user can set the default point or "exercise price" (B) equal to any proportion of total debt outstanding that is of interest. Suppose we want to calculate the EDF for a one-year horizon. Given the values of A, σ_A, B, and r, and with τ = one year, what is the (theoretical) probability of a borrowing firm's failure at the one-year horizon? As can be seen in Figure 4.4, the EDF is the shaded area of the distribution of asset values below B. This area represents the probability that the current value of the firm's assets, $100 million, will drop below $80 million at the one-year time horizon. The size of the shaded area, and therefore the EDF, increases as (1) the asset volatility, σ_A, increases, (2) the value of debt, B, increases, and (3) the initial market value of assets, A, decreases.

If it is assumed that future asset values are normally distributed around the firm's current asset value, we can measure the $t = 0$ (or today's) distance to default (DD) at the one-year horizon as:

$$\text{Distance to default } (DD) = \frac{A - B}{\sigma_A} = \frac{\$100m - \$80m}{\$10m} \qquad (4.5)$$

For the firm to enter the default region (the shaded area), asset values would have to drop by $20 million, or two standard deviations, during the next year. If asset values are normally distributed, we know that there is a 95 percent probability that asset values will vary between plus and minus 2σ from their mean value. Thus, there is a $2\frac{1}{2}$ percent probability that asset values will increase by more than 2σ over the next year, and a $2\frac{1}{2}$ percent probability that they will fall by more than 2σ. In other words, there is an (EDF) of $2\frac{1}{2}$ percent. In Figure 4.4, we have shown no growth in expected or mean asset values over the one-year period, but this can easily be incorporated. For example, if we project that the value of the firm's assets will grow 10 percent over the next year, then the relevant EDF would be lower because, for the firm to default at year-end, asset values would have to drop by 3σ, below the firm's expected asset growth path.[13]

The idea of asset values normally distributed around some mean level plays a crucial role in calculating joint default transition probabilities in CreditMetrics (see Chapter 6), yet there is an important issue as to whether it is (theoretically or empirically) reasonable to make this assumption.[14] With this in mind, rather than producing theoretical EDFs, the KMV approach generates an empirical EDF along the following lines.[15] Suppose that we have a large historic database of firm defaults and loan repayments, and we calculate that the firm we are analyzing has a theoretical distance to default of 2σ. We then ask the empirical question: What percentage of firms in the database actually defaulted within the one-year time horizon when their asset values placed them a distance of 2σ away from default at the beginning of the year, and how does that compare to the total population of firms that were 2σ away from default at the beginning of the year? As shown in Figure 4.5, this produces a (nonparametric) empirical *EDF*:

$$\text{Empirical } EDF = \frac{\substack{\text{Number of firms that defaulted within a year with} \\ \text{asset values of } 2\sigma \text{ from } B \text{ at the beginning of the year}}}{\substack{\text{Total population of firms with asset} \\ \text{values of } 2\sigma \text{ from } B \text{ at the beginning of the year}}}$$

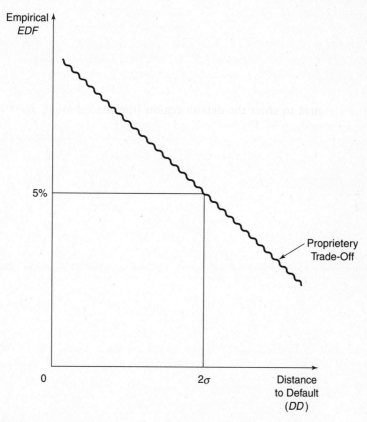

FIGURE 4.5 Empirical *EDF* and the distance to default (*DD*): A hypothetical example.

Suppose, based on a worldwide database, it was estimated that 50 of 1,000 possible firms defaulted. The equation would be:

$$\text{Empirical } EDF = \frac{50 \text{ Defaults}}{\text{Firm population of 1,000}} = 5 \text{ percent}$$

As a result, this empirically-based *EDF* can differ quite significantly from the theoretically-based *EDF*. From a proprietary perspective, KMV's advantage comes from building up a large worldwide database of firms (and firm defaults: over 40,000 private firms and over 3,400 public companies defaulted) that can produce such empirically-based *EDF* scores. KMV's empirical *EDF* is an overall statistic that can be calculated for every possible distance to default (*DD*) using data either aggregated or segmented by industry or region. To find the *EDF* for any particular firm at any point in time, one must simply look up the firm's *EDF* as implied by its calculated *DD*.[16] Firm-specific empirical *EDF*s, as shown in Figures 4.6, 4.7, and 4.8 fluctuate over time as the firm's *DD* fluctuates (caused by changes in *A*, *B*, and σ_A) and as the overall empirical *EDF* value changes for each *DD* measure (caused by changes in the historical distribution of defaults across all firms in the database).[17] For actively traded firms, it would be possible, in

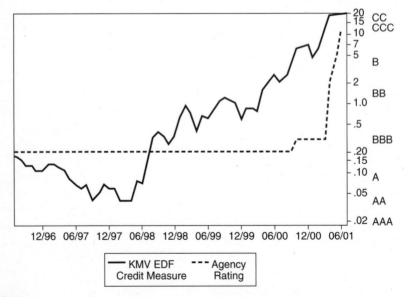

FIGURE 4.6   KMV Expected Default Frequency™ and agency rating for Comdisco Inc. *Source:* KMV LLC, http://www.kmv.com/ (2001).

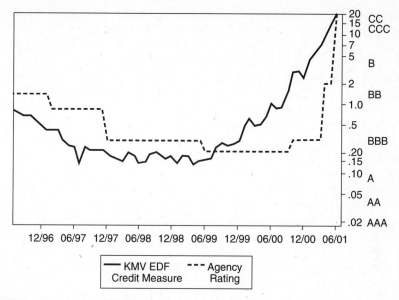

FIGURE 4.7 KMV Expected Default Frequency™ and agency rating for USG Corp. *Source:* KMV LLC, http://www.kmv.com/ (2001).

theory, to update an *EDF* every few minutes. In actuality, KMV can update *EDF* scores frequently (in many cases, monthly) for some 29,000 firms worldwide.[18]

A question arises as to how *EDF* scores perform relative to the rating systems described in Chapter 2. Figure 4.6 shows how the KMV-produced *EDF* scores for Comdisco Inc., over a five-year period (using a log-scale), compared to S&P ratings. The significant increase in Comdisco's *EDF* in June 1998, followed by further deteriorations during 1999–2000, provided early warning signs of credit problems. Comdisco filed for Chapter 11 bankruptcy protection on July 16, 2001. The company's S&P rating was unchanged at BBB until it was first slightly downgraded in July 2000; it was not changed again until March 2001. If rating agencies are reluctant to precipitously downgrade their customers, it may not be surprising that credit ratings lag *EDF* scores when credit quality is deteriorating. However, Figure 4.7 shows that agency ratings lag *EDF* scores in forecasting credit quality *improvements* as well as deteriorations. USG Corporation's credit rating was upgraded three times during the period from September 1996 to June 1999. During that entire period of credit quality improvement, KMV *EDF* scores were below the implied agency ratings, suggesting that S&P ratings lagged *EDF* scores even for credit upgrades. Moreover, when USG Corporation's credit began to deteriorate, in June 1999, S&P ratings lagged behind EDF scores in forecasting the turnaround in USG's credit quality (not reflected in ratings until October 2000) as well as its ultimate descent into bankruptcy. USG Corporation filed for Chapter 11 on June 25, 2001.

On December 2, 2001, Enron Corporation filed for Chapter 11 bankruptcy protection. At an asset value of $49.53 billion, this was the largest bankruptcy filing in U.S. history. For months prior to the bankruptcy filing, a steadily declining stock price reflected negative information about the firm's financial condition, potential undisclosed conflicts of interest, and dwindling prospects for a merger with Dynegy Inc. However, as Figure 4.8 shows, the S&P rating stayed constant throughout the period from the end of 1996 until November 28, 2001, when Enron's debt was downgraded to "junk" status just days before the bankruptcy filing. In contrast, KMV *EDF* scores provided early warning of the start of a deterioration in credit quality as early as January 2000, with a marked increase in *EDF* after January 2001, 11 months prior to the bankruptcy filing.[19]

Another way to compare KMV *EDFs* to ratings is shown in the power curve in Figure 4.9, which analyzes all publicly rated defaults from 1990 to 1999—a total of 83 defaults and 1,202 nondefaults.[20] KMV *EDFs* are compared to both Moody's and S&P implied ratings using publicly available bond issue ratings. *Implied ratings* are constructed to be a nonissue-specific

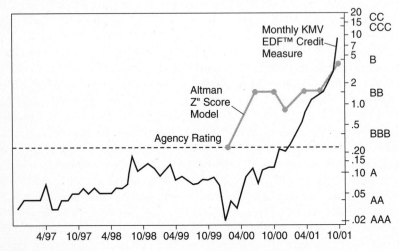

FIGURE 4.8 KMV Expected Default Frequency™ and agency rating for Enron Corp. *Source:* KMV LLC, http://www.kmv.com/ (2001).

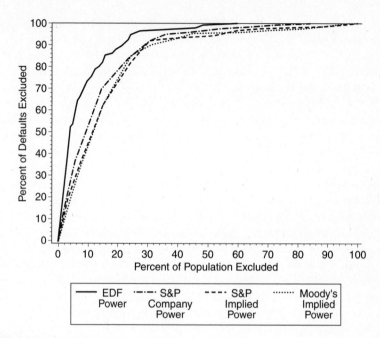

FIGURE 4.9 KMV *EDF* Credit Measure versus agency ratings (1990–1999) for rated U.S. companies. *Source:* Kealhofer (2000); http://www.kmv.com/ (2001).

measure of default probability by adjusting the published ratings as follows: subordinated debt rated BB or worse was lowered two notches (e.g., from B– to B+); subordinated debt rated B or better was lowered one notch; and secured debt was raised one notch. In addition, the S&P obligor-level rating was compared to the performance of the KMV *EDFs*. Thus, Figure 4.9 compares the KMV *EDFs* to the Moody's and S&P implied ratings, as well as to S&P obligor-level ratings. Each methodology is used to rank all observations by default probability. Figure 4.9 shows that if the bottom 20 percent of the rankings using each of the four methods are denied credit [i.e., Type 2 errors (classifying good loans as bad) are held to a maximum of 20 percent], then the KMV *EDFs* eliminate 84 percent of the defaults, whereas the S&P obligor-level ratings exclude only 78 percent of the defaults, and the S&P/Moody's issue-specific ratings exclude only 65 percent of the defaults. Thus, the Type 1 error (i.e., classifying bad loans as good) for the KMV *EDF* score is 16 percent (i.e., the KMV *EDF* cannot exclude 16 percent of the defaults), whereas the obligor-level ratings method's Type 1 error is 22 percent and the issue-specific ratings' Type 1 error is 35 percent for both S&P and Moody's.

This greater sensitivity of *EDF* scores, compared to rating-based systems, comes from the direct link between *EDF* scores and stock market prices. As new information about a borrower is generated, its stock price and stock price volatility will react, as will its implied asset value (A) and standard deviation of asset value (σ_A).[21]

KMV *EDF* scores have been criticized on the basis that they are not true probabilities of default. This is reflected in the poor results obtained when using KMV empirical *EDF*s in order to replicate risky bond prices [see Kao (2000) and Eom et al. (2001)]. These results may obtain because the Merton model solves for risk-neutral probabilities of default (*EDF*s) that represent the probability that the asset value will fall below the value of debt, assuming that the underlying asset return (change in asset value) process has a mean return equal to the risk-free rate. In contrast, the KMV empirical *EDF* uses the assets' expected return in place of the risk-free rate. Thus, if the assets' expected return exceeds the risk-free rate (as would be the case in the presence of systematic risk exposure), then the risk-neutral *EDF* exceeds the KMV empirical *EDF*, and the KMV measure underestimates the true probability of default.[22] The KMV measure can be adjusted to overcome this problem by estimating the systematic risk premium over the risk-free rate. Intuitively, the empirical *EDF* is adjusted upward to reflect the additional return necessary to compensate risk-averse investors for the sensitivity of asset values to unexpected market fluctuations. Thus, there is an additional term in the equity valuation equation (4.3) as follows:

$$\overline{E} = h\left(A, \sigma_A, \overline{B}, \overline{r}, \overline{\tau}, \pi\right) \tag{4.6}$$

where π is the (instantaneous) expected excess return on risky assets. This adds an other unknown, thereby requiring an additional equation for estimation. Kealhofer (2000) estimates π using the continuous time capital asset pricing model (CAPM), which estimates the required return as a function of the risk-free rate and the assets' correlation (ρ_{AM}) with the return on a market index such as the S&P 500. The KMV empirical *EDF* can be transformed into the risk-neutral *EDF* by applying the asset correlation (ρ_{AM}) and a scaling parameter equal to the Sharpe ratio (i.e., the risk premium on systematic risk, divided by the standard deviation of the market index). Using 24,465 bond prices from 1992 to 1999, Bohn (2000a) is able to fit bond spreads using KMV empirical *EDF*s adjusted by market Sharpe ratios.[23] Credit risk management requires both risk-neutral and empirical *EDF*s. The risk-neutral *EDF* (denoted as *QDF*) is used to value the instruments in the portfolio. The empirical *EDF* is used to calculate Value at Risk (*VAR*); see Chapter 6.

A further potential problem with KMV-type models, and the BSM structural model approach, is the implication for the probability of default and credit spreads as the time to default, or the maturity of debt, shrinks. Under normal BSM continuous time diffusion processes for asset values, the probability that a firm's asset value (A) will fall below its debt boundary (B; see Figure 4.4) declines dramatically as the default horizon (τ) goes to zero. Indeed, the implication of structural models is that the credit spread at the very short end of the risky debt market should be zero [see Leland (1994), for example].

In general, however, observable short-term credit spreads over the risk-free rate (say, in the short-term commercial paper and Fed funds markets) are nonzero. It could be argued that this is due to liquidity and transaction cost effects, but there is a conflicting opinion that the structural models of the BSM (and KMV) type—and especially the underlying assumptions of these models, regarding the diffusion of asset values over time—underestimate the probability of default over short horizons.[24] Not surprisingly, considerable recent research has focused on resolving this issue by modifying the basic assumptions of the BSM model. The work by Zhou (1997, 2001) attempts to address underestimation of short-horizon risk by allowing for jumps in the asset value (A) of the firm. Duffie and Lando (2001) propose that asset values, in the context of the structural model, are noisy in that they cannot be perfectly observed by outsiders. In this context, accounting information releases may partially resolve this information gap and lead to jumps in asset values as investors revise their expectations. Thus, imperfect information and fuzziness in observed asset values may potentially be integrated into the *OPM* (structural) framework and resolve the underestimation of default risk at the short horizon. Work by Leland (1994), Anderson, Sundaresan, and Tychon (1996), and Mella-Barral and Perraudin (1997), which extends the BSM model by allowing for debt renegotiations (i.e., renegotiations of the debt boundary value, or B), can be thought of as work in a similar spirit,[25] as can that of Leland (1998), who built in agency costs as a friction to the traditional BSM model.

Because an *EDF* score reflects information signals transmitted from equity markets, it might be argued that the model is likely to work best in highly efficient equity market conditions and might not work well in many emerging markets. This argument ignores the fact that many thinly traded stocks are those of relatively closely held companies. Thus, major trades by "insiders," such as sales of large blocks of shares (and thus, major movements in a firm's stock price), may carry powerful informational signals about the future prospects of a borrowing firm.[26]

In sum, the option pricing approach to bankruptcy prediction has a number of strengths. First, it can be applied to any public company. Second, by being based on stock market data rather than "historic" book value accounting data, it is forward looking. Third, it has strong theoretical underpinnings because it is a "structural model" based on the modern theory of corporate finance, where equity is viewed as a call option on the assets of a firm, and loans are viewed as put options written on the value of a firm's assets.

Against these strengths are four weaknesses: (1) it is difficult to construct theoretical *EDFs* without the assumption of normality of asset returns; (2) private firms' *EDFs* can be calculated only by using some comparability analysis based on accounting data and other observable characteristics of the borrower;[27] (3) it does not distinguish among different types of debt according to their seniority, collateral, covenants, or convertibility;[28] and (4) it is "static" in that the Merton model assumes that once management puts a debt structure in place, it leaves it unchanged—even if the value of a firm's assets has doubled. As a result, the Merton model cannot capture the behavior of those firms that seek to maintain a constant or target leverage ratio across time [see Jarrow and van Deventer (1999) and Collin-Dufresne and Goldstein (2001)]. In contrast, Mueller (2000) models leverage as a function of sensitivity to macroeconomic factors (e.g., GDP growth and risk-free interest rates). Thus, the long-run leverage ratio changes stochastically over time, thereby fitting the model to observed term structures of default.[29]

MOODY'S PUBLIC FIRM MODEL[30]

Although the KMV Credit Monitor is considered a structural model of default, it deviates from the purely theoretical Merton model in its incorporation of a statistical approach to calculating empirical *EDF* scores. Moody's carries this one step further by combining the distance to default obtained from a Merton model with ratings and financial statement variables in order to obtain its own "empirical *EDF*" measure.

In explaining the firm's *EDF*, Moody's uses a nonlinear artificial neural network (see the discussion in Chapter 2) to weight the relative importance of the nine key variables shown in Table 4.1. The neural network solves a system of nested logistic regressions in order to obtain the influence of each of the variables on the *EDF* score at any point in time. The neural system is "trained" using a hold-out sample that is representative of the entire population. In Figure 4.10, the case of Applied Magnetics Corporation illustrates how each variable's relative influence changes over time.[31] In January 1998, shown in Panel (A), when the company's *EDF* was slightly below the population's average, the most influential variable was the equity growth rate. In contrast, Panel (B) shows that in January 1999, one year prior to the company's filing for Chapter 11 protection on January 7, 2000, the influence of

TABLE 4.1 Key Variables of the Moody's Default Prediction Model

Model Variable	Definition	Frequency
Credit quality	Moody's Rating when available. Proprietary rating model for unrated firms.	Credit history when available.
Return on assets	Net income/assets	Annual
Firm size	Log (assets)	Annual
Operating liquidity	Working capital/assets	Annual
Leverage	Liabilities/assets	Annual
Market sensitivity	Stock price volatility	Monthly
Equity growth	Equity growth rate	Monthly
Return on equity	Net income/equity	Monthly
Distance to default	Merton model DD (equation 4.5)	Monthly

Source: Sobehart, Stein, Mikityanskaya, and Li (2000), p. 10.

equity growth, distance to default, return on assets (ROA), and leverage all signaled significantly higher *EDF*s.

The data used to estimate and validate the Moody's empirical *EDF* scores consist of 14,447 public, nonfinancial firms during the period from 1980 to 1999; more than 100,000 firm-year observations; and 1,406 default events.[32] The Moody's model has been criticized as being overfit to a particular sample, and therefore unlikely to perform well out-of-sample; see Kealhofer (2000).[33] However, Sobehart, Keenan, and Stein (2000) showed an out-of-sample, out-of-time Type 1 error of only 26 percent and a Type 2 error of 17 percent. In addition, Sobehart, Keenan, and Stein (2000) conducted a performance test of Moody's empirical *EDF* versus the theoretical *EDF* (not the KMV empirical *EDF*) and versus several statistical models, including: two variants of the Z-score discriminant model (see the discussion of credit scoring models in Chapter 2), a hazard model based on financial data, and a univariate model based on return on assets (ROA) only. The power curve, shown in Figure 4.11, suggests that the Moody's empirical *EDF* outperforms all other methods; for example, if the bottom 20 percent of the rankings using each of the methods are denied credit (i.e., Type 2 errors are held to 20 percent), then the Moody's empirical *EDF*s eliminate 80 percent of the defaults. This may be compared to the results for the KMV empirical *EDF* shown in Figure 4.9, which shows a power of 84 percent for the 20 percent cutoff point.[34] However, this is not proof of superiority for either model because statistical significance tests are subject to sample

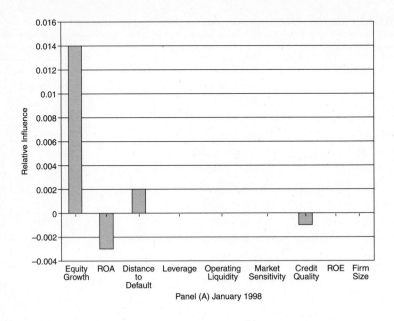

Panel (A) January 1998

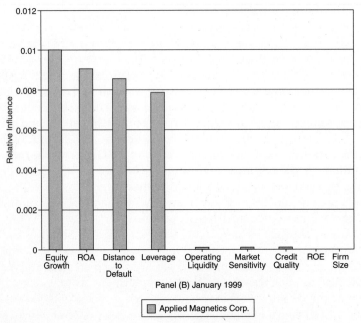

Panel (B) January 1999

Applied Magnetics Corp.

FIGURE 4.10 An example of influence analysis of model factors. *Source:* Sobehart, Keenan, and Stein (2000).

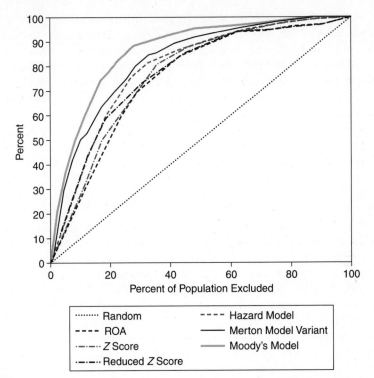

FIGURE 4.11 Power curves for the tested models. *Notes:* All models were tested on the same validation data set. The 45° line represents the naive case which is equivalent to a random assignment of scores. All models perform considerably better than the random case. The Merton model variant performs almost as well as the Moody's model in the case of extremely poor quality firms. However, the Moody's model clearly performs better beyond about the bottom 10% of the population and is much better at discriminating defaults in the middle ranges of credit. *Source:* Sobehart, Keenan, and Stein (2000).

variations, and it is unclear whether 84 percent is statistically significantly higher than 80 percent.[35]

SUMMARY

The economic cause of default (or insolvency), as modeled by structural models of default probability, is the decline in the market value of the firm's assets below the value of the firm's debt obligations at a given horizon. Only if the assets' value exceeds the debt value will it be rational for shareholders to exercise their "call option" on the firm's assets and repay the firm's debt. Thus, debt can be viewed as a short put option on the firm's assets; the shareholders will "sell" the firm's assets to the lenders (i.e., exercise the put option and default on the debt) if the market value of assets is less than the put's exercise price, which is the repayment value of the debt. The probability of default (the risk-neutral expected default frequency, *EDF*) is the area under the asset value probability distribution below the default point. The distance to default (*DD*) is the number of standard deviations of the asset probability distribution between current asset value and the default point.

The KMV Corporation applies structural models of default to its substantial credit history database in order to determine an empirical *EDF* by examining the historical likelihood of default for any given *DD* level. Moody's incorporates ratings and financial statement variables together with the theoretical risk-neutral *EDF* in an artificial neural network that measures another empirical *EDF* score. Both empirical *EDFs* outperform ratings and statistical models in terms of their accuracy at predicting defaults. The primary advantage of structural models is that they utilize stock price data that are predictive and highly responsive to changes in the firm's financial condition. The primary disadvantage of structural models is their reliance on distributional assumptions (i.e., normality) that imply default probabilities that are not reflected in observed bond spreads.

APPENDIX 4.1
MERTON'S VALUATION MODEL

The equation for the market value of risky debt, $F(\tau)$, takes the form:

$$F(\tau) = Be^{-r\tau}\left[\left(\frac{1}{d}\right)N(h_1) + N(h_2)\right] \qquad (4.7)$$

where τ = the length of time remaining to loan maturity; that is, $\tau = T - t$, where T is the maturity date, and t is current time (today);

d = the firm's (the borrower's) leverage ratio measured as $\dfrac{Be^{-r\tau}}{A}$, where the market value of debt is valued at the rate r, the risk-free rate of interest;

$N(h)$ = a value computed from the standardized normal distribution statistical tables. This value reflects the probability that a deviation exceeding the calculated value of h will occur:

$$h_1 = -\frac{\left[\frac{1}{2}\sigma^2\tau - ln(d)\right]}{\sigma\sqrt{\tau}}$$

$$h_2 = -\frac{\left[\frac{1}{2}\sigma^2\tau + ln(d)\right]}{\sigma\sqrt{\tau}}$$

where σ^2 measures the asset risk of the borrower—technically, the variance of the rate of change in the value of the underlying assets of the borrower.

This equation also can be written in terms of a yield spread that reflects an equilibrium default risk premium that the borrower should be charged:

$$k(\tau) - r = \left(\frac{-1}{\tau}\right)ln\left[N(h_2) + \left(\frac{1}{d}\right)N(h_1)\right]$$

where $k(\tau)$ = the required yield on risky debt,
ln = natural logarithm,
r = the risk-free rate on debt of equivalent maturity (here, one period).

An example:[36]

$$B = \$100,000,$$
$$\tau = 1 \text{ year,}$$
$$r = 5 \text{ percent,}$$
$$d = 90 \text{ percent or .9,}$$
$$\sigma = 12 \text{ percent.}$$

Substituting these values into the equations for h_1 and h_2, and solving for the areas under the standardized normal distribution, we find:

$$N(h_1) = .174120$$
$$N(h_2) = .793323$$

where

$$h_1 = \frac{-\left[\frac{1}{2}(.12)^2 - ln(.9)\right]}{.12} = -0.938$$

and

$$h_2 = \frac{-\left[\frac{1}{2}(.12)^2 + ln(.9)\right]}{.12} = +0.818$$

Thus, the current market value of the risky $100,000 loan (L) is:

$$L(t) = Be^{-r\tau}\left[N(h_2) + \left(\frac{1}{d}\right)N(h_1)\right]$$

$$= \frac{\$100,000}{1.05127}\left[.793323 + (1.1111)(.17412)\right]$$

$$= \frac{\$100,000}{1.05127}\left[.986788\right]$$

$$= \$93,866.18$$

and the required risk spread or premium is:

$$k(\tau) - r = \left(\frac{-1}{\tau}\right)ln\left[N(h_2) + \left(\frac{1}{d}\right)N(h_1)\right]$$

$$= (-1)ln\left[.986788\right]$$

$$= 1.33 \text{ percent}$$

CHAPTER 5

Reduced Form Models

KPMG's Loan Analysis System and Kamakura's Risk Manager

The structural models described in Chapter 4 use the information embedded in equity prices to solve for default probabilities. Reduced form models use debt prices to accomplish the same goal. However, whereas structural models posit an economic process driving default (i.e., the point at which asset values fall below the repayment value of debt), reduced form models offer no economic model of default causality. Although in reduced form models the default process itself is exogenous, the default risk premium is observable in debt prices and yields. In a world free of arbitrage opportunities, expected returns on a risky asset must equal the return on a risk-free asset (the risk-free rate). More specifically, the observed yield on risky debt can be decomposed into a risk-free rate plus a risk premium. Reduced form models utilize this decomposition to solve for default probabilities, recovery rates, and risky debt prices.

The use of risk neutral probabilities to value risky assets has been in the finance literature at least as far back as Arrow (1953) and has been subsequently developed by Harrison and Kreps (1979), Harrison and Pliska (1981), and Kreps (1982). In finance, it has been traditional to value risky assets by discounting cash flows on an asset by a risk-adjusted discount rate. To do this, you need to know a probability distribution for cash flows and the risk-return preferences of investors. The latter are especially difficult to obtain. Suppose, however, it is assumed that assets trade in a market where *all* investors are willing to accept, from any risky asset, the same *expected* return as that promised by the risk-free asset. Such a market can be described as behaving in a "risk-neutral" fashion. In a financial market where investors behave in a risk-neutral fashion, the prices of all assets can be determined by simply discounting the expected future cash flows on the asset by the risk-free rate.[1]

The equilibrium relationship—where the expected return on a risky asset equals the risk-free rate—can be utilized to back out an implied risk-neutral probability of default (also called the equivalent martingale measure). In this chapter, we derive the risk-neutral default probability from observed bond spreads. Two proprietary reduced form models are then examined: KPMG's Loan Analysis System and Kamakura's Risk Manager. The major shortcoming of all reduced form models is their reliance on noisy bond price data. That is, the difference between risky bond yields (prices) and the equivalent maturity risk-free rate (price) may be the result of credit risk, but it can also be due to a liquidity premium, carrying costs, taxes, or simply pricing errors. Therefore, in this chapter, we also discuss the determinants of bond spreads.

DERIVING RISK-NEUTRAL PROBABILITIES OF DEFAULT

We first consider a discrete version of reduced form models in order to demonstrate the intuition behind the continuous time versions often used in practice. We proceed from very simple assumptions and gradually add complexity.

Consider a B rated $100 face value, zero-coupon debt security with one year until maturity and a fixed recovery rate (which is the same as one minus the loss given default, LGD). For simplicity, assume that the $LGD = 100$ percent, or that the recovery rate is zero (i.e., the entire loan is lost in the event of default). The current price of this debt instrument can be evaluated in two equivalent ways: First, the expected cash flows may be discounted at the risk-free rate, assumed to be 8 percent per annum (p.a.) in our example. Since the security is worthless upon default, the expected cash flows are $100 (1 - PD)$, where PD is the probability of default. If the security's price is observed to be $87.96, then we can solve for PD as follows:

$$\frac{100(1-PD)}{1+.08} = 87.96 \qquad (5.1)$$

thereby obtaining a PD of 5 percent p.a. that satisfies the equality in equation (5.1). Equivalently,[2] the security could be discounted at a risk-adjusted rate of return, denoted y such that:

$$\frac{100}{1+y} = 87.96 \qquad (5.2)$$

thereby obtaining a value of $y = 13.69$ percent p.a. that satisfies equation (5.2). The present value of this security is \$87.96.

Under our simplifying assumptions, the relationship between the risk-adjusted return, y, and the risk-free rate, denoted r, is:

$$1 + r = (1 - PD)(1 + y) \tag{5.3}$$

or

$$1.08 = (1 - .05)(1.1369)$$

Since r and y are observable for traded debt securities (see for example, the yield curves shown in Figure 5.1), equation (5.3) could be used to solve directly for the probability of default (PD) for B rated corporate bonds.

In general, the PD is not constant, but instead varies over time; therefore, we can express the probability of default as $PD(t)$. If we convert equation (5.3) to its time varying equivalent, still assuming a zero recovery rate, we have:

$$y = r + PD(t) \tag{5.4}$$

That is, the yield on risky debt is composed of a riskless rate plus a credit spread equal to the probability of default at any point in time t where $PD(t)$ is the stochastic default rate intensity.

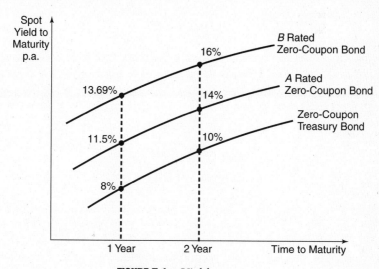

FIGURE 5.1 Yield curves.

Considering two other points on the B rated yield curve shown in Figure 5.1, let us decompose the credit spread included in the two-year zero-coupon B rated corporate bond, shown as earning a yield to maturity of 16 percent p.a. To divide this rate into its component parts, we must first solve for the one-year forward rate; that is, the rate on a B rated one-year zero-coupon corporate bond to be received one year from now, denoted[3] $_1y_1$. Assuming that the expectations hypothesis holds, we can solve for the one-year forward rate on the corporate bond as:

$$(1 + {_0}y_2)^2 = (1 + {_0}y_1)(1 + {_1}y_1)$$

or substituting the values from Figure 5.1:

$$(1 + .16)^2 = (1 + .1369)(1 + {_1}y_1)$$

Solving for $_1y_1$ yields a one-year forward rate on the one-year maturity B rated corporate bond of 18.36 percent p.a. A similar exercise can be performed to determine the one-year forward rate on the one-year Treasury (risk-free) bond as follows:

$$(1 + {_0}r_2)^2 = (1 + {_0}r_1)(1 + {_1}r_1) \tag{5.5}$$

or substituting the values from Figure 5.1:

$$(1 + .10)^2 = (1 + .08)(1 + {_1}r_1)$$

Solving for $_1r_1$ yields a one-year forward Treasury rate of 12.04 percent p.a. We can now use these one-year forward rates to decompose the risky yield into its risk-free and credit risk spread components. Replicating the analysis in equation (5.3) for one-year maturities, but using one-year forward rates instead, we have:

$$1 + {_1}r_1 = (1 - PD)(1 + {_1}y_1) \tag{5.6}$$

$$1 + .1204 = (1 - PD)(1 + .1836)$$

obtaining the probability of default during the second year (conditional on no default occurring in the first year) of $PD = 5.34$ percent p.a. That is, the probability of default for the B rated corporate bond is 5 percent in the first year and 5.34 percent in the second year, and (assuming independence across time) the two-year cumulative PD is:

$$\text{Cumulative } PD = 1 - [(1 - PD_1)(1 - PD_2)]$$
$$= 1 - [(1 - .05)(1 - .0534)] = 10.07\%$$

That is, the B rated corporate bond has a 10.07 percent chance of defaulting sometime over the next two years.

THE LOSS INTENSITY PROCESS

Let us return to the simplified static model and remove the simplifying assumption that the recovery rate is zero. Then the expected loss on default (*EL*) equals probability of default (*PD*) times severity or loss given default (*LGD*). That is, $EL = PD \times LGD$; we can rewrite equation (5.3) as:

$$1 + r = (1 - EL)(1 + y) = (1 - PD \times LGD)(1 + y) \qquad (5.3')$$

or in time varying form, we can rewrite equation (5.4) as:[4]

$$y = r(t) + [PD(t) \times LGD(t)] \qquad (5.4')$$

Equation (5.4') expresses the yield on risky debt as the sum of the riskless rate and the credit spread, comprised of $PD \times LGD$. Using the rates from the yield curve in Figure 5.1, $r = 8\%$ and $y = 13.69\%$, we can solve for $PD \times LGD = 5\%$, but there is an identification problem which requires additional equations in order to untangle PD from LGD.[5]

Reduced form models resolve the identification problem by specifying a functional form for the statistical distribution of $PD(t)$, called the intensity process; hence their pseudonym of "intensity-based" models. In contrast to structural models, in which default is always triggered by an understood and expected economic event (e.g., asset value falling below debt payments), default occurs at random intervals in reduced form models.[6] Jarrow and Turnbull (1995) introduced one of the first reduced form models, assuming a constant *LGD* and an exponentially distributed exogenous default process. Default follows a Poisson distribution and arises contingent on the arrival of some "hazard," meant in the insurance context as an unexpected loss event.[7] The intensity of the hazard arrival process is estimated empirically from bond price data, thereby eliminating the need to model the economic explanation for default. Because these types of models do not posit a causal relationship between firm value and default, they are more dependent on the quality of the bond pricing data than are structural models. Moreover, the parameters of the default intensity function may shift over time. The results, therefore, are very specific to the particular database used and the time period over which the parameters are estimated. For an explanation of the Poisson intensity process and a simulation of credit spreads using different parameter estimates, see Appendix 5.1.

Many of the earlier reduced form models focused on modeling the default intensity, PD, in order to disentangle the two components of the credit spread, $PD \times LGD$. Their simplifying assumptions that the LGD was either constant or proportional to bond values were counterfactual; observed recovery rates are volatile and show a cyclical component. Moreover, the default intensity also fluctuates with the business cycle and systemic risk conditions. Das and Tufano (1996) allow a proportional LGD to vary over time, but maintain the assumption of independence between LGD and PD. Duffie and Singleton (1999) allow for (economic) state-dependence of both LGD and PD, as well as interdependence between LGD and PD; however, they assume independence between firm asset value and the LGD and PD processes, an assumption that does not hold if, for example, the debt obligation is a large part of the issuer's capital structure.

The pure recovery model of Unal et al. (2001) decomposes the difference between the prices of senior versus junior debt to obtain a measure of recovery rates on senior debt relative to junior debt (LGD) that is independent of default probabilities (PD). The adjusted relative spread, ARS, is defined as:

$$ARS = p_s \left(\frac{v_s v_j}{G - v_j} \right) = \phi\left(\lambda, \theta, \mu, \sigma, p_s\right) + \varepsilon_t$$

where p_s = the fraction of senior debt to total debt,
       v_s = the price of senior debt,
       v_j = the price of junior debt, and
       G = the price of risk-free U.S. Treasury debt.

An intensity process specifies the parameters λ and θ allowing for the possibility of deviations from absolute priority in which junior debtholders receive payment before senior debtholders are fully paid off; μ is the mean recovery rate, estimated using a two-factor model where the time dependent factors are the business cycle, proxied by the risk-free interest rate, and firm-specific tangible assets; and the deviation of mean recovery rates is σ. Table 5.1 shows that the estimated mean recovery rates ($1 - LGD$) for the 11 companies in the sample[8] are extremely volatile both across time and cross-sectionally, thereby casting doubt on the assumption of a constant LGD rate (such as in the BIS II IRB foundation approach to capital regulations—see Chapter 3).

In this chapter, we describe two examples of reduced form models: (1) KPMG's loan analysis system (LAS), which uses risky bond prices to

TABLE 5.1 Estimating Recovery Rates (1–*LGD*) using a Reduced Form Model

Company	Estimated Mean Recovery Rate	Volatility of Recovery Rate σ	Industry Average	Root Mean Squared Error
AMC	52.2	2.969	37.1	0.042
American Medical	12.5	0.500	26.5	0.037
Coastal Corporation	63.3	0.010	70.5	0.100
Envirotest Systems	34.3	0.118	46.2	0.075
Flagstar	12.7	0.713	33.2	0.045
Revlon	40.5	0.447	62.7	0.083
Sequa Corporation	59.2	0.081	38.4	0.073
Stone Container	9.6	0.113	29.8	0.082
Sweetheart Cup	56.7	0.124	62.7	0.064
Valassis Insterts	19.1	0.010	46.2	0.086
Del Webb Corporation	39.3	1.163	35.3	0.026

Source: Unal et al. (2001). Industry averages are obtained from Altman and Kishore (1996).

decompose credit spreads by incorporating default probabilities and credit migration probability data into the intensity process and (2) Kamakura Corporation's Risk Manager (KRM), which uses bond prices, equity prices, and accounting data in order to solve a reduced form model with stochastic default-free interest rates, a liquidity premium, and endogenously determined *LGD*.

Both of these models decompose observed yields on risky debt into a riskless rate and a credit spread. Most often, they use corporate bond yields in order to solve for the credit spread.[9] However, estimates of *PD* and *LGD* will be biased if corporate bond yields are affected by factors other than just the risk-free rate and the credit spread. Huang and Huang (2000) suggest that only a very small portion (only 24 percent for a 10-year Baa-Treasury yield spread) of the yields on investment grade corporate bonds are determined by credit risk exposure.[10] Thus, before we proceed to the reduced form models themselves, it is useful to consider what factors, other than credit risk, determine actual bond spreads and prices.

DETERMINANTS OF BOND SPREADS

The U.S. corporate bond market had a market value close to $3 trillion in 1998.[11] Although this makes it several times the size of U.S. equity markets, it is not nearly as transparent.[12] One reason is that less than 2 percent of the volume of corporate bond trading occurs on the NYSE or AMEX. The rest of the trades are conducted over the counter by bond dealers. Saunders, Srinivasan, and Walter (2002) show that this interdealer market is not very competitive. It is characterized by large spreads and infrequent trades. Pricing data are often inaccurate, consisting of matrix prices that use simplistic algorithms to price infrequently traded bonds. Even the commercially available pricing services are often unreliable. Hancock and Kwast (2001) find significant discrepancies between commercial bond pricing services, Bloomberg and Interactive Data Corporation, in all but the most liquid bond issues. Bohn (1999) finds that there is more noise in senior issues than in subordinated debt prices. Corporate bond price performance is particularly erratic for maturities of less than one year. The sparsity of trading makes it difficult to obtain anything more frequent than monthly pricing data, see Warga (1999). A study by Schwartz (1998) indicated that even for monthly bond data, the number of outliers (measured relative to similar debt issues) is significant. We can attribute these outliers to the illiquidity in the market.

The considerable noise in bond prices, as well as investors' preferences for liquidity, suggest that there is a liquidity premium built into bond spreads. Thus, if risky bond yields are decomposed into the riskless rate plus the credit spread only, the estimate of credit risk exposure will be biased upward.

Risky corporate bonds also contain embedded options, such as call and conversion features, as well as covenants and sinking funds. These features have value that must be incorporated into the analysis of bond spreads. A common practice is to avoid this complex valuation process and only consider option-free corporate bonds in empirical studies. However, this biases the sample since the subset of option-free bonds tends to have lower credit risk exposure than the general population. Thus, observed bond yields must be adjusted to reflect the value of increasingly complicated embedded options.

Even the specification of the risk-free rate can be troublesome. Duffee (1998) finds that changes in credit spreads are negatively related to changes in risk-free interest rates for lower credit quality bonds.[13] Although Treasury yields are typically used to measure the risk-free rate, it may be more appropriate to use the highest quality corporate bond yield as the benchmark default-free rate. Part of this stems from the asymmetric tax treatments of corporate and Treasury bonds. Bohn (2000b) claims that use of a default-free rate is more appropriate unless all other sources of risk are explicitly modeled.

There are also administrative costs of holding a portfolio of risky debt. This cost of carry was measured by Aguais et al. (1998) at about 15 to 16 basis points for high credit quality (rated A and AA) short-term loans.

Incorporating all of these considerations into our representa[tion] risky bond yields requires the following restatement of equation (5[...] follows:

$$y = r(t) + (PD(t) \times LGD(t) + L(t) + O(t) + C + \varepsilon(t) \qquad (5.4'')$$

where $r(t)$ is the stochastic risk-free rate, $PD \times LGD$ is the credit spread, $L(t)$ is the liquidity risk factor, $O(t)$ is the value of embedded options, C is the carrying costs, including tax considerations, and $\varepsilon(t)$ is the bond pricing error term. Reduced form models focus on the problem of identifying the credit spread portion of observed bond yields and separating it into its two component parts: PD and LGD.

KPMG'S LOAN ANALYSIS SYSTEM (LAS)

Using current market debt prices, KPMG uses a net present value (NPV) approach to credit risk pricing that evaluates the loan's structure. That is, the impact of revaluations, embedded options, exercise strategies, covenants, and penalties on credit risk pricing is evaluated using a lattice or "tree" analysis. The loan's value is computed for all possible transitions through various states, ranging from credit upgrades and prepayments, to restructurings, to default.

Figure 5.2 from KPMG shows, in a simplified fashion,[14] the potential transitions of the credit rating of a B rated borrower over a four-year loan period using a tree diagram. Given transition probabilities, the original grade B borrower can migrate up or down over the loan's life to different

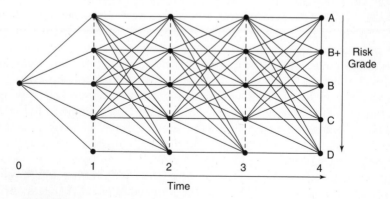

FIGURE 5.2 The multiperiod loan migrates over many periods.

nodes (ratings), and may even migrate to D or default (an absorbing state). Along with these migrations, you can build in a pricing grid that reflects the bank's current policy on spread repricing for borrowers of different quality (or, alternatively, a grid that reflects the spreads that the "market" charges on loans of different quality). Potentially, at least, this methodology can tell the bank whether it has a "good" or "bad" repricing grid in an expected net present value (NPV) sense (basically, whether the expected return on the loan equals the risk-free rate). When valuing a loan in this framework, valuation takes place recursively (from right to left in Figure 5.2), as it does when valuing bonds under binomial or multinomial models. For example, if the expected NPV of the loan in its final year is too "high," and given some prepayment fee, the model can allow prepayment of the loan to take place at the end of period 3. Working backward through the tree from right to left, the total expected NPV of the four-year loan can be determined. Moreover, the analyst can make different assumptions about spreads (the pricing grid) at different ratings and prepayment fees to determine the loan's value. In addition, other aspects of a loan's structure, such as caps, amortization schedules, and so on can be built in and a Value at Risk (VAR, see Appendix 1.1) can also be calculated.[15]

Inputs to the LAS include the credit spreads for one-year option-free zero-coupon primary bonds for each of the 18 S&P or Moody's ratings classifications. Each node (reflecting annual revaluations) incorporates the risk-neutral probability of transition from one risk rating to another. The LAS uses an average of Moody's and S&P transition probabilities.[16] The loan value at each node is then revalued using the market-based credit spread for each rating classification.

Using the market data on bond yields from Figure 5.1 we can illustrate the LAS approach to price a $100 two-year zero-coupon loan. Using an internal rating system, the loan is given a B rating upon its origination. Assuming $LGD = 100$ percent (for a zero recovery rate), we have shown earlier in this chapter that the PD for B rated corporate debt in the first year is 5 percent and, assuming there was no default in the first year, the PD is 5.34 percent in the second year. However, default is not the only possibility that will affect the loan's value. For simplicity, we consider only two other possibilities: the loan's rating will remain at its current B rating or it will be upgraded one full letter grade to an A rating.[17] In our example, a hypothetical ratings transition matrix shows that the probability of an upgrade from B to A (in any period) is 1 percent and the PD is 5 percent (assuming that the beginning period rating was B). Moreover, the probability of a downgrade from A to B is 5.66 percent and the probability of migrating from A to default is 0.34 percent.[18] Finally, the probability of no change in credit rating is assumed to be 94 percent for all ratings classifications.

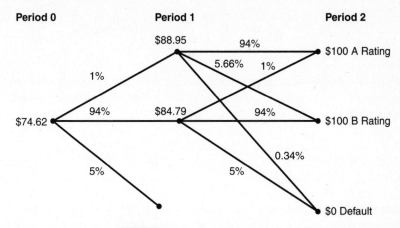

FIGURE 5.3 Risky debt pricing.

Figure 5.3 shows the backward recursion process used by the LAS in order to price the loan. Starting from period 2, the value of the loan is $100 as long as there is no default and $0 recovery in the event of default. Moving back one year to period 1, let us first examine the B rated node. If the loan is B rated in period 1, then there is a 94 percent chance that it will retain that rating until period 2, a 1 percent chance that it will be upgraded to an A rating, and a 5 percent chance that it will default at the beginning of period 2. The D rated node (default) is an absorbing state with a value of zero. Using equation (5.2) and the risk-free forward rates obtained from the yield curve in Figure 5.1,[19] risk-neutral evaluation of the B rated node in period 1 is as follows:

$$0.94\left(\frac{100}{1.1204}\right) + 0.01\left(\frac{100}{1.1204}\right) + 0.05(0) = \$84.79$$

Similarly, the A rated node in period 1 is valued at:

$$0.94\left(\frac{100}{1.1204}\right) + 0.0566\left(\frac{100}{1.1204}\right) + .0034(0) = \$88.95$$

Moving back one more year to period 0, using the one-year risk-free spot rate of 8 percent p.a., the loan can be valued as:

$$0.94\left(\frac{84.79}{1.08}\right) + 0.01\left(\frac{88.95}{1.08}\right) + 0.05(0) = \$74.62$$

Using a two period version of equation (5.2), we can also solve for the loan's credit spread, denoted CS, defined to be a constant risk premium added to the risk-free rate to reflect the loan's risk exposure:[20]

$$74.62 = \frac{100}{(1 + .08 + CS)(1 + .1204 + CS)}$$

Using the one-year risk-free rate of 8 percent p.a. and the one year forward risk-free rate of 12.04 percent p.a., we obtain a credit spread of $CS = 5.8$ percent p.a.[21] This credit spread evaluates unexpected losses/gains from rating migration over the life of the loan as well as the probability of default. The credit spread can be further decomposed into expected and unexpected losses. Expected losses are derived using actual or historical default rates observed in ratings transition matrices. Unexpected losses are derived as the remaining portion of the total credit spread that compensates the lender for the (higher) risk-neutral default probability.[22]

This simplified example, while providing the flavor of the LAS, abstracts from many of its features. For example, in our example, we assumed that the transition matrix was fixed over the two-year life of the loan. In reality, transition matrices are themselves volatile and may be related to economic conditions.[23] In particular, during economic upturns, default rates tend to be low and ratings upgrades tend to be high relative to downgrades, whereas the opposite holds true during economic downturns. KPMG defines a Z-risk index of migrations that measures how good or bad credit conditions are after controlling for ratings. That is, if $Z < 0$ ($Z > 0$) then default rates are higher (lower) than average and there are more downgrades (upgrades) than upgrades (downgrades). Thus, the LAS credit spreads fluctuate with economic conditions, since credit rating migrations are driven by the systematic Z-risk component as well as the company-specific component.

Following Ginzberg et al. (1994), it can be argued that this extended risk-neutral valuation framework is valid as long as a replicating (no-arbitrage) portfolio of underlying assets is available. However, it is unclear how such a replicating portfolio could be established in reality when most loans are not traded in active markets. Moreover, if bond spreads include a liquidity premium, carrying costs, and factors other than credit spreads, then the LAS will overestimate credit risk exposure. Kamakura's Risk Manager models some of these "noise" factors explicitly.

KAMAKURA'S RISK MANAGER (KRM)

Jarrow and Turnbull (1995) decompose credit spreads into a constant *LGD* and an independent default intensity process with a Poisson distribution that determines the time of default. In their model, the risk neutral *PD* is the probability that the unpredictable default event precedes the maturity of the debt, given the assumption of a Poisson hazard process. However, this makes the counterfactual assumption that default intensities are constant across firm types (e.g., as measured by firm credit rating) and over time (e.g., across business cycles).[24] Jarrow, Lando, and Turnbull (1997) incorporate historical transition probability matrices to estimate default as a Markov process contingent on firm credit rating and assume a constant fractional *LGD*. Duffie and Singleton (1998) improve the model fit by assuming a stochastic risk-free interest rate process and an empirically derived *LGD*. Longstaff and Schwartz (1995) utilize a two-factor model that specifies a negative relationship between the stochastic processes determining credit spreads and default-free interest rates. Madan and Unal (2000) and Unal et al. (2001) compare senior and subordinated bond spreads (for firms with both securities outstanding) in order to isolate the *LGD*. Zhou (2001) examines default correlations across firms.

Kamakura's Risk Manager (KRM) is based on Jarrow (2001). Credit spreads are decomposed into *PD* and *LGD* by the use of both debt and equity prices in order to better separate the default intensity process from the loss recovery process.[25] The default hazard rate is modeled as a function of stochastic default-free interest rates, liquidity factors, and lognormal risk factors, such as a stochastic process for the market index. KRM is benchmarked using credit spreads or bond prices, equity prices, and accounting data over the period from 1962 to 1990, with out-of-sample forecasting from 1991 to 1999. The five explanatory variables, denoted *X(t)*, used to parameterize the system are: (1) return on assets = (net income)/(total assets); (2) leverage = (total liabilities)/(total assets); (3) relative size = (firm equity value)/(total market value of the NYSE and AMEX); (4) excess return (monthly) over the CRSP NYSE/AMEX index return; and (5) monthly equity volatility. Kamakura claims that the public (private) firm model correctly ranks 81.38 percent (65.33 percent) of bankrupt firms in the top decile of risk, thereby producing a Type 1 error rate of 18.62 percent for public firms and 34.67 percent for private firms.

The liquidity factor is modeled as a convenience yield, such that when the supply of a particular issue is tight (i.e., when one cannot buy the issue because asking prices are high and special rates on repurchase agreements are low), then there is a positive convenience yield incorporated into bond spreads.[26] Alternatively, when there is a glut of a particular issue (i.e., in times of credit crises and high market volatilities, when some bonds can only be sold at discount prices), then there is a negative convenience yield incorporated into bond spreads. The Jarrow model measures liquidity risk by estimating these convenience yields implicit in bond prices.

Recovery rates are modeled as a fixed percentage of debt prices just prior to default, with equity prices used to determine that percentage.[27] That is, since the equity price is not a function of either the liquidity premium or the *LGD* and the bond price is a function of both variables (as well as others), then the use of both price series can be used to separate out the *LGD* from the *PD*. Prices can be expressed as:

Bond prices: $B = B[t, T, i, \lambda(t, X(t)), \delta(t, X(t)), \gamma(t, T, X(t)), \mu, S(t, X(t))]$

Equity price: $\xi = \xi[t, T, i, \lambda(t, X(t)), \mu, S(t, X(t))]$

where t = the current period;
T = the bond's maturity date;
i = the stochastic default-free interest rate process;
$\lambda(t, X(t))$ = the default intensity process (i.e., the risk neutral *PD*);
$\delta(t, X(t))$ = the recovery rate $(1 - LGD)$;
$\gamma(t, T, X(t))$ = the liquidity premium;
μ = a stock market bubble factor; and
$S(t, X(t))$ = the liquidating dividend on equity in the event of bond default.

Since reduced form models are purely empirical, they cannot be evaluated by interpreting their economic assumptions and implications; they are data-driven and should therefore provide results that conform to the data better than structural models. KRM results suggest that this is the case for comparisons with the pure Merton model (although the KMV and Moody's versions are not tested). The average pricing error using the Merton model is six times the error using the reduced form model forecast two years into the future and 40 times forecast 10 years into the future. Estimates of credit spreads using the Jarrow model are better fit to observed values at all maturities. Merton *PD*s are five times more volatile over time than Jarrow loss intensities. Moreover, since an important test of a credit risk measurement model is its ability to construct a dynamic hedge for the market value of a bond, the Jarrow hedging errors average about 50 percent of the errors for the Merton model. Despite these encouraging results, the noise inherent in bond pricing data makes it an open question as to how valuable is a model that is tailored to a somewhat fickle standard [see Anderson and Sundaresan (1998)].

SUMMARY

Reduced form models decompose risky bond yields into the risk-free rate plus a credit risk premium. The credit spread consists of the risk neutral probability of default (*PD*) multiplied by the loss given default (*LGD*). KPMG's Loan Analysis System uses this information to price untraded risky debt securities (loans). Kamakura's Risk Manager extends the analysis by estimating the liquidity premium and carrying costs included in bond spreads to back out estimates of credit spreads. The primary advantages of reduced form models over structural models like KMV and Moody's are: (1) their relative ease of computation, and (2) their better fit to observed credit spread data.

APPENDIX 5.1
UNDERSTANDING A BASIC INTENSITY PROCESS[28]

Default probabilities can be modeled as a Poisson process with intensity *h* such that the probability of default over the next short time period, Δ, is approximately Δh and the expected time to default is $1/h$; therefore, in continuous time, the probability of survival without default for *t* years is:

$$1 - PD(t) = e^{-ht} \tag{5.7}$$

Thus, if an A rated firm has an $h = .001$, it is expected to default once in 1,000 years; using equation (5.7) to compute the probability of survival over the next year we obtain .999. Thus, the firm's *PD* over a one-year horizon is .001. Alternatively, if a B rated firm has an $h = .05$, it is expected to default once in 20 years and substituting into equation (5.7), we find that the probability of survival over the next year is .95 and the *PD* is .05.[29] If a portfolio consists of 1,000 loans to A rated firms and 100 loans to B rated firms, then there are six defaults expected per year.[30] A hazard rate can be defined as the arrival time of default (i.e., $-p'(t)/p(t)$ where $p(t)$ is the probability of survival and $p'(t)$ is the first derivative of the survival probability function, assumed to be differentiable with respect to t. Since the probability of survival depends on the intensity h, the terms hazard rate and intensity are often used interchangeably.[31]

Default intensities may be affected by external macroeconomic events. Thus, default intensities may change over time. The probability of survival for t years can be expressed in discrete terms as $E[e^{-(h0 + h1 + h2 + \ldots + ht-1)}]$, where $h_0 \ldots h_{t-1}$ are the time-varying default intensities in years $0, \ldots, t - 1$.[32] If there is a joint macroeconomic or systemic factor J that impacts the default intensity of each firm i, then the total default intensity of firm i at time t can be expressed as:

$$h_{it} = p_{it}J_t + H_{it} \qquad (5.8)$$

where J_t is the intensity of arrival of systemic events, p_{it} is the probability that firm i defaults given a systemic event, and H_{it} is the firm-specific

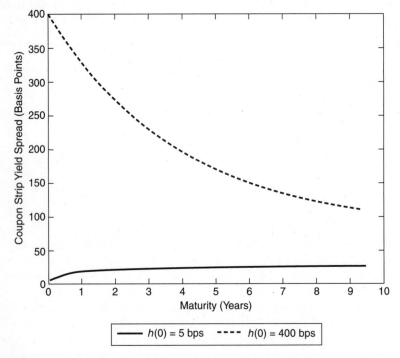

FIGURE 5.4   Term structure of coupon-strip (zero-recovery) yield spreads.
Source: Duffie and Singleton (1998), p. 20.

intensity of default arrival. Thus, the intensity of arrival of any kind of event is: $H_t = J_t + H_{lt} + \ldots + H_{nt}$. Substituting the parameters of our earlier example into equation (5.7), if the A rated firm defaults with probability 0.02 in the event of a systemic breakdown that occurs with a 1 percent probability, then the firm's default intensity increases to 0.0012 and it is expected to default once within the next 833 (as opposed to 1,000) years. Moreover, if the B rated firm defaults with probability 50 percent if the systemic event occurs, then the firm's default intensity increases to 0.055 for one expected default within the next 18 (rather than 20) years. The introduction of time-varying default intensities causes the portfolio to have an expected 6.7 (rather than 6) defaults per year.

Duffie and Singleton (1998) formulate the firm-specific intensity process h in equation (5.8) as a mean-reverting process with independently distributed jumps that arrive at some constant intensity λ; otherwise h reverts at rate κ to a constant θ. Figure 5.4 plots the credit spreads for two obligations with the same parameters[33] ($\tau = 10$ basis points, $\lambda = 10$ basis points, $\kappa = .5$, and $J = 5$), but with different initial default intensities. The credit obligation with high credit risk has an initial default intensity of 400 basis points whereas the low risk obligation has an initial default intensity of 5 basis points.[34] Figure 5.4 shows that credit spreads are clearly sensitive to parameter estimates.

CHAPTER 6

The *VAR* Approach

CreditMetrics and Other Models

Since 1993, when the Bank for International Settlements (BIS) announced its intention to introduce a capital requirement for market risk, great strides have been made in developing and testing Value at Risk (*VAR*) methodologies. The incentive to develop internal *VAR* models was given a further boost in 1996, when the BIS amended its market risk proposal and agreed to allow certain banks to use their own internal models, rather than the standardized model proposed by regulators, to calculate their market risk exposures. Since the end of 1996 in the European Union and 1998 in the United States, the largest banks (subject to regulatory approval) have been able to use their internal models to calculate *VAR* exposures for the trading book and, thus, capital requirements for market risk.[1]

In this chapter, we first review the basic *VAR* concept and then look at its potential extension to nontradable loans and its use in calculating the capital requirement for loans in the banking book. Considerable attention will be paid to CreditMetrics, originally developed by J.P. Morgan in conjunction with several other sponsors (including KMV). CreditMetrics provides a useful benchmark for analyzing the issues and problems of *VAR* modeling for loans. The *VAR* approach will be revisited again in Chapter 11 in the context of loan portfolio risk.

THE CONCEPT OF VALUE AT RISK *(VAR)*

Essentially, *VAR* models seek to measure the minimum loss (of value) on a given asset or liability over a given time period at a given confidence level (e.g., 95 percent, 97½ percent, 99 percent). A simple example of a tradable instrument such as equity will suffice to describe the basic concept of *VAR* methodology (see Figure 6.1). Suppose the market price (*P*) of equity today is

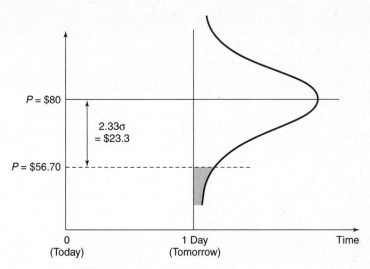

FIGURE 6.1 The *VAR* of traded equity.

$80, and the estimated daily standard deviation of its value (σ) is $10. Because the trading book is managed over a relatively short horizon, a trader or risk manager may ask: "If tomorrow is a 'bad day,' what is my *VAR* [size of loss in value, at some confidence level]?" Assume that the trader is concerned with the value loss on a bad day that occurs, on average, once in every 100 days, and that daily asset values (returns) are "normally" distributed around the current equity value of $80. Statistically speaking, the one bad day has a 1 percent probability of occurring tomorrow. The area under a normal distribution carries information about probabilities. We know that roughly 68 percent of return observations must lie between +1 and −1 standard deviation from the mean; 95 percent of observations lie between +1.96 and −1.96 standard deviations from the mean; and 98 percent of observations lie between +2.33 and −2.33 standard deviations from the mean. With respect to the latter, and in terms of dollars, there is a 1 percent chance that the value of the equity will increase to a value of $80 + 2.33σ (or above) tomorrow, and a 1 percent chance it will fall to a value of $80 − 2.33σ (or below). Because σ is assumed to be $10, there is a 1 percent chance that the value of the equity will fall to $56.70 or below; alternatively, there is a 99 percent probability that the equity holder will lose less than $80 − $56.70 = $23.30 in value; that is, $23.30 can be viewed as the *VAR* on the equity at the 99 percent confidence level. Note that, by implication, there is a 1 percent chance of losing $23.30 *or more* tomorrow. Because, by assumption, asset values are normally distributed, the one bad day in every 100 can lead to the loss being placed anywhere in the shaded region below $56.70, in Figure 6.1. (In reality, losses on nonleveraged financial instruments are truncated at −100 percent of value, and the normal curve is at best an approximation to the log-normal.)

Thus, the key inputs in calculating the *VAR* of a marketable instrument are its current market value (P) and the volatility or standard deviation of that market value (σ). Given an assumed "risk" horizon and a required confidence level (e.g., 99 percent), the *VAR* can be directly calculated.

Application of this methodology to nontradable loans has some immediate problems. First, P, or the current market value of a loan, is not directly observable because most loans are not traded. Second, because P is not observable, we have no time series to calculate σ, the volatility of P. At best, the assumption of a normal distribution for returns on some tradable assets is a rough approximation, and the approximation becomes even rougher when applied to the possible distribution of values for loans. Specifically, as discussed in Chapter 4 in the context of option-theoretic structural models, loans have both severely truncated upside returns and long downside risks. As a result, even if we can and do measure P and σ, we still need to take into account the asymmetry of returns on making a loan.

CREDITMETRICS

CreditMetrics was first introduced in 1997 by J.P. Morgan and its co-sponsors (Bank of America, KMV, Union Bank of Switzerland, and others) as a *VAR* framework to apply to the valuation and risk of nontradable assets such as loans and privately placed bonds.[2] RiskMetrics seeks to answer the question: "If tomorrow is a bad day, how much will I lose on tradable assets such as stocks, bonds, and equities?" CreditMetrics asks: "If next year is a bad year, how much will I lose on my loans and loan portfolio?[3]

As noted, because loans are not publicly traded, we observe neither P (the loan's market value) nor σ (the volatility of the loan value over the horizon of interest). However, using (1) available data on a borrower's credit rating, (2) the probability that the rating will change over the next year (the rating transition matrix), (3) recovery rates on defaulted loans, and (4) credit spreads and yields in the bond (or loan) market, it is possible to calculate a hypothetical P and σ for any nontraded loan or bond, and, thus, a *VAR* figure for individual loans and the loan portfolio.[4]

We examine, first, a simple example of calculating the *VAR* on a loan and, second, technical issues surrounding this calculation. Consider, as the example, a five-year fixed-rate loan of $100 million made at 6 percent annual interest.[5] The borrower is rated BBB.

Rating Migration

Based on historical data on publicly traded bonds (or loans) collected by
Standard and Poor's (S&P), Moody's, KMV, or other bond or loan analysts,[6] the probability that a BBB borrower will stay at BBB over the next
year is estimated at 86.93 percent. There is also some probability that the
borrower will be upgraded (e.g., to A) or will be downgraded (e.g., to CCC
or even to default, D). Indeed, eight transitions are possible for the borrower during the next year. Seven involve upgrades, downgrades, and no
rating change, and one involves default.[7] The estimated probabilities of
these transitions are shown in Table 6.1.[8]

Valuation

The effect of rating upgrades and downgrades is to impact the required
credit risk spreads or premiums on the loan's remaining cash flows, and,
thus, the implied market (or present) value of the loan. If a loan is downgraded, the required credit spread premium should rise (remember that the
contractual loan rate in our example is assumed fixed at 6 percent) so that
the present value of the loan to the FI should fall. A credit rating upgrade
has the opposite effect. Technically, because we are revaluing the five-year,
$100 million, 6 percent loan at the end of the first year (the credit horizon),
after a "credit-event" has occurred during that year, then (measured in millions of dollars):[9]

$$P = 6 + \frac{6}{\left(1 + {}_1r_1 + s_1\right)} + \frac{6}{\left(1 + {}_1r_2 + s_2\right)^2} + \frac{6}{\left(1 + {}_1r_3 + s_3\right)^3} + \frac{106}{\left(1 + {}_1r_4 + s_4\right)^4} \quad (6.1)$$

TABLE 6.1   One-Year Transition Problabilites for BBB-Rated Borrower

AAA	0.02%
AA	0.33
A	5.95
BBB	86.93 ⟵——— Most likely to stay in the same class
BB	5.30
B	1.17
CCC	0.12
Default	0.18

Source: Gupton et al., *Technical Document*, J.P. Morgan, April 2, 1997, p. 11.

where [10] $_1r_i$ are the risk-free rates (so called forward zero rates) on zero-coupon U.S. Treasury bonds *expected* to exist one year into the future; the one-year forward zero rates are calculated from the current Treasury yield curve (see Appendix 6.1). Further, s_i is the annual credit spread on (zero coupon) loans of a particular rating class of one-year, two-year, three-year, and four-year maturities (the latter are derived from observed spreads in the corporate bond market over Treasuries). In this example, the first year's coupon or interest payment of $6 million (to be received on the valuation date at the end of the first year) is undiscounted and can be regarded as equivalent to accrued interest earned on a bond or a loan.

In CreditMetrics, interest rates are assumed to be deterministic.[11] Thus, the risk-free rates, $_1r_i$, are obtained by decomposing the current spot yield curve to obtain the one-year forward zero curve following the procedure outlined in Appendix 6.1 in which fixed credit spreads are added to the forward zero-coupon Treasury yield curve. An example is shown in Table 6.2. That is, the risk-free zero-coupon yield curve is first derived using U.S. Treasury securities to obtain the pure discount equivalent of the risk-free rates. Then the zero-coupon yield curve is used to derive the forward risk-free rates for U.S. Treasury securities of varying maturities expected to prevail one year into the future (e.g., $_1r_1, {}_1r_2, \ldots {}_1r_T$ [$T = 4$ in the example shown in equation (6.1)]. Finally, a fixed credit spread, s_i, for each maturity i is added to the one-year forward risk-free discount rate (see, for example, Table 6.5). We obtain one forward yield curve for each of the seven ratings, as shown in Table 6.2. Each coupon and principal payment on the defaultable loan is discounted at the rate chosen from Table 6.2 that matches the coupon's maturity and the loan's rating. Suppose that, during the first year, the

TABLE 6.2 One Year Forward Zero Curves Plus Credit Spreads by Credit Rating Category (%)

Category	Year 1	Year 2	Year 3	Year 4
AAA	3.60	4.17	4.73	5.12
AA	3.65	4.22	4.78	5.17
A	3.72	4.32	4.93	5.32
BBB	4.10	4.67	5.25	5.63
BB	5.55	6.02	6.78	7.27
B	6.05	7.02	8.03	8.52
CCC	15.05	15.02	14.03	13.52

Source: Gupton et al., *Technical Document,* J.P. Morgan, April 2, 1997, p. 27.

borrower gets upgraded from BBB to A. That is, a credit event occurs during the first year of the loan's life (see Figure 6.2). The present value, or market value, of the loan to the FI at the end of the one-year risk horizon (in millions) including the first year's $6 million of "accrued interest" is then:[12]

$$P = 6 + \frac{6}{(1.0372)} + \frac{6}{(1.0432)^2} + \frac{6}{(1.0493)^3} + \frac{106}{(1.0532)^4} = \$108.66 \quad (6.2)$$

At the end of the first year, if the loan borrower is upgraded from BBB to A, the $100 million (book value) loan has a market value to the FI of $108.66 million. (This is the value the FI would theoretically be able to obtain at the year-1 horizon if it "sold" the loan in the loan sales market to another FI, at the fair market price or value, inclusive of the first year's coupon payment of $6 million.[13]) Table 6.3 shows the value of the loan if other credit events occur. Note that the loan has a maximum market value of $109.37 million (if the borrower is upgraded from BBB to AAA) and a minimum value of $51.13 million if the borrower defaults. The latter is the estimated recovery value of the loan [or one minus the loss given default (LGD)] if the borrower defaults.[14]

The probability-distribution of loan values is shown in Figure 6.3. The value of the loan has a relatively fixed upside and a long downside (i.e., a negative skew). The value of the loan is not symmetrically (or normally) distributed. Thus, CreditMetrics produces two *VAR* measures:

1. Based on the normal distribution of loan values.
2. Based on the actual distribution of loan values.

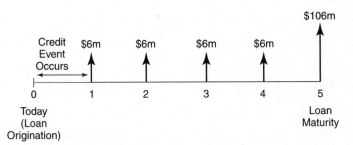

FIGURE 6.2 Cash flows on the five-year BBB loan. Credit events are: upgrades, downgrades, or defaults.

TABLE 6.3 Value of the Loan at the End of Year 1, under Different Ratings (Including First-Year Coupon)

Year-End Rating	Value (Millions)
AAA	$109.37
AA	109.19
A	108.66
BBB	107.55
BB	102.02
B	98.10
CCC	83.64
Default	51.13

Source: Gupton et al., *Technical Document,* J.P. Morgan, April 2, 1997, p. 10.

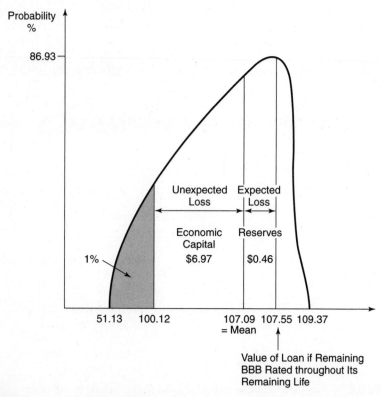

FIGURE 6.3 Actual distribution of loan values on five-year BBB loan at the end of year one (including first-year coupon payment).

Calculation of *VAR*

Table 6.4 shows the calculation of the *VAR*, based on each approach, for both the 5 percent and 1 percent worst-case scenarios around the mean (rather than original) loan value. The first step in determining *VAR* is to calculate the mean of the loan's value, or its expected value, at year 1. This is the sum of each possible loan value at the end of year 1, times its transition probability over the year. The mean value of the loan is $107.09 (see Figure 6.3). However, the FI is concerned about unexpected losses or volatility in value. In particular, if next year is a bad year, how much can it expect to lose with a certain probability? We could define a "bad year" as occurring once every 20 years (the 5 percent *VAR*) or once every 100 years (the 1 percent *VAR*). This definition is similar to market risk *VAR* except that, for credit risk the risk horizon is longer (i.e., 1 year rather than 1 day).

TABLE 6.4   VAR Calculations for the BBB Loan (Benchmark Is Mean Value of Loan)

Year-End Rating	Probability of State (%)	New Loan Value Plus Coupon (millions)	Probability Weighted Value ($)	Difference of Value from Mean ($)	Probability Weighted Difference Squared
AAA	0.02	$109.37	0.02	2.28	0.0010
AA	0.33	109.19	0.36	2.10	0.0146
A	5.95	108.66	6.47	1.57	0.1474
BBB	86.93	107.55	93.49	0.46	0.1853
BB	5.30	102.02	5.41	(5.06)	1.3592
B	1.17	98.10	1.15	(8.99)	0.9446
CCC	0.12	83.64	1.10	(23.45)	0.6598
Default	0.18	51.13	0.09	(55.96)	5.6358
			$107.09 = Mean Value		8.9477 = Variance of Value

σ = Standard deviation = $2.99

Assuming normal distribution
$$\text{5 percent } VAR = 1.65 \times \sigma = \$4.93.$$
$$\text{1 percent } VAR = 2.33 \times \sigma = \$6.97.$$

Assuming actual distribution*
$$6.77 \text{ percent } VAR = \frac{93.23 \text{ percent of}}{\text{actual distribution}} = \$107.09 - \$102.02 = \$5.07.$$
$$1.47 \text{ percent } VAR = \frac{98.53 \text{ percent of}}{\text{actual distribution}} = \$107.09 - \$98.10 = \$8.99.$$
$$1 \text{ percent } VAR = \frac{99 \text{ percent of}}{\text{actual distribution}} = \$107.09 - \$92.29 = \$14.80.$$

Note: 5% VAR approximated by 6.77% VAR (i.e., 5.3%+1.17%+0.12%+0.18%) and 1% *VAR* approximated by 1.47% VAR (i.e., 1.17%+0.12%+0.18%). *Source:* Gupton et al., *Technical Document,* April 2, 1997, p. 28.

Assuming that loan values are normally distributed, the variance of loan value (in millions) around its mean is $8.9477 (squared), and its standard deviation, or volatility, is the square root of the variance, equal to $2.99 million. Thus, the 5 percent VAR for the loan is $1.65 \times \$2.99 = \$4.93$ million. The 1 percent VAR is $2.33 \times \$2.99 = \$6.97$ million. However, this likely underestimates the actual or true VAR of the loan because, as shown in Figure 6.3, the distribution of the loan's value is clearly non-normal. In particular, it demonstrates a negative skew or a long-tailed downside risk.

Using the actual distribution of loan values and probabilities in Table 6.4, we can see that there is a 6.77 percent probability that the loan value will fall below $102.02, implying an "approximate" 5 percent actual VAR of $5.07 million ($107.09 – $102.02 = $5.07 million), and there is a 1.47 percent probability that the loan value will fall below $98.10, implying an "approximate" 1 percent actual VAR of $8.99 million ($107.09 – $98.10 = $8.99). These actual VARs could be made less approximate by using linear interpolation to get at the 5 percent and 1 percent VAR measures. For example, because the 1.47 percentile equals $98.10 and the 0.3 percentile equals $83.64, using linear interpolation, the 1.00 percentile equals approximately $92.29. This suggests an actual 1 percent VAR of $107.09 – $92.29 = $14.80 million.[15]

CAPITAL REQUIREMENTS

It is interesting to compare these VAR figures with the standardized approach to capital requirements under the January 2001 proposals for BIS II (the new Capital Accord, see Chapter 3). For a $100 million face (book) value BBB loan to a private-sector borrower, the capital requirement under the standardized approach (100 percent risk bucket) would be $8 million. Note the contrast to the two VAR measures developed previously. Using the 1 percent VAR based on the normal distribution, the capital requirement against unexpected losses on the loan (i.e., economic capital) would be $6.97 million (i.e., less than the BIS requirement).[16] Capital requirements under the January 2001 BIS II proposals also include loan loss reserves since under the VAR approach, loan loss reserves are held to meet expected loan losses, which in the case of the BBB loan are $0.46 million, or $107.55 million (the value of the BBB loan if no rating changes or default occurs) minus $107.09 million (the expected value of the BBB loan taking into account transition and default probabilities). Adding the expected losses of $0.46 million to $6.97 million produces a total capital requirement of $7.43 million (see Figure 6.3 for a breakdown of the capital requirement). In contrast, however, using the 1 percent VAR based on the interpolated value from the actual distribution shown in Table 6.4, the economic capital requirement would be $14.80 million for unexpected losses plus the loan loss reserve for expected losses of $0.46 million (an amount much greater than the BIS II capital requirement).

Using the CreditMetrics approach, every loan is likely to have a different *VAR* and thus a different implied or economic capital requirement. If regulatory capital requirements were based on an internal model using CreditMetrics, regulators would most likely require that the *VAR* estimate be increased using a stress-test multiplier. In particular, the 99 percent loss-of-value estimate can be expected to have a distribution. In extremely bad (catastrophic) years, a loan's loss will exceed, by a significant margin, the 99 percent measure calculated in the previous example. Under the BIS approach to market risk, this extreme loss or stress-test issue is addressed by requiring banks to multiply their *VAR* number by a factor ranging between 3 and 4. Research by Boudoukh, Richardson, and Whitelaw (1995) shows (in simulation exercises) that, for some financial assets with normally distributed returns, the 3-to-4 multiplication factor may well pick up extreme losses such as the mean in the tail beyond the 99th percentile.[17] Applying such a multiplication factor to low-quality loans would raise capital requirements considerably. The introduction of an internal ratings-based (IRB) approach to capital requirements makes the estimation of the appropriate size of such a multiplication factor particularly important, given the problems of stress-testing credit risk models (see Chapter 12).

Using CreditMetrics to set capital requirements tells us nothing about the potential size of losses that exceed the *VAR* measure. That is, the *VAR* measure is the *minimum* loss that will occur with a certain probability. Extreme Value Theory (EVT) examines the tail of the loss distribution conditional on the expectation that the size of the loss exceeds *VAR*.[18] Tail events are those loss events that occur rarely, but when they do, they have dramatic consequences.[19] Figure 6.4 depicts the size of unexpected losses when catastrophic events occur.[20] Using the estimates from Table 6.4 assuming a normal distribution, the 5 percent *VAR* for unexpected losses is $4.93 million. We set this to be the threshold level; that is, EVT considers only the distribution of unexpected losses that exceed $4.93 million. However, Figure 6.4 assumes that unexpected losses beyond the 95 percent threshold level follow the Generalized Pareto Distribution (GPD) with "fat tails;" see Appendix 6.2 for derivation of the values shown in Figure 6.4. Thus, the estimated 1 percent *VAR*, distributed according to the GPD is larger than the normally distributed 1 percent *VAR* of $6.97 million (from Table 6.4). Under the parameter assumptions described in Appendix 6.2, the 1 percent *VAR* for the GPD, denoted $\overline{VAR}_{.99}$, is $22.23 million. The Expected Shortfall, denoted $\overline{ES}_{.99}$, is calculated as the mean of the excess distribution of unexpected losses beyond the threshold $\overline{VAR}_{.99}$, which is shown as $53.53

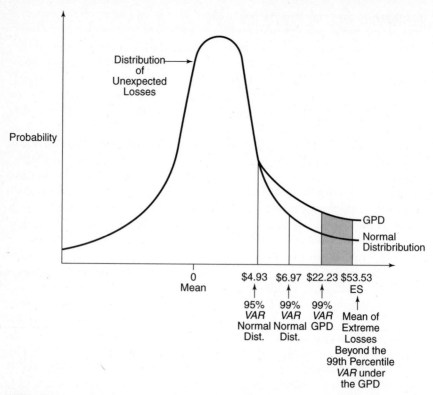

FIGURE 6.4 Estimating unexpected losses using extreme value theory. *Note:* ES = the expected shortfall assuming a Generalized Pareto Distribution (GPD) with fat tails.

million in Figure 6.4. This would be the capital charge for the mean of the most extreme events (i.e., those in the 1 percent tail of the distribution). As such, the $ES_{.99}$ amount can be viewed as the capital charge that would incorporate risks posed by extreme or catastrophic events, or alternatively, a capital charge that internally incorporates an extreme, catastrophic stress-test multiplier. Since the GPD is fat tailed, the increase in losses is quite large at high confidence levels; that is, the extreme values of ES_q (i.e., for high values of q, where q is a risk percentile) correspond to extremely rare catastrophic events that result in enormous losses. Some have argued that the use of EVT may result in unrealistically large capital requirements [see Cruz et al. (1998)].

TECHNICAL ISSUES AND PROBLEMS

In this section, we address some of the main technical issues surrounding CreditMetrics. Some of these issues (and assumptions) can be incorporated quite smoothly into the basic model; others are less easy to deal with.

Rating Migration

A number of issues arise when we use the bond-rating transitions assumed in Table 6.1 to calculate the probabilities of moving to different rating categories (or to default) over the one-year horizon. First, underlying the calculation of the transition numbers, which involves averaging one-year transitions over a past data period (e.g., 20 years), is an important assumption about the way defaults and transitions occur.[21] Specifically, we assume that the transition probabilities follow a stable Markov process [see Altman and Kao (1992)], which means that the probability that a bond or loan will move to any particular state during this period is independent of (not correlated with) any outcome in the past period. However, there is evidence that rating transitions are autocorrelated over time. For example, a bond or loan that was downgraded in the previous period has a higher probability (compared to a loan that was not downgraded) of being downgraded in the current period [see, for example, the results in Nickell et al. (2001a)]. This suggests that a second or higher Markov process may better describe rating transitions over time.[22]

The second issue involves transition matrix stability. The use of a single transition matrix assumes that transitions do not differ across borrower types (e.g., industrial firms versus banks, or the United States versus Japan) or across time (e.g., peaks versus troughs in the business cycle). Indeed, there is considerable evidence to suggest that important industry factors, country factors, and business cycle factors impact rating transitions [see Nickell et al. (2001a) and Bangia et al. (2000)]. For example, when we examine a loan to a Japanese industrial company, we may need to use a rating transition matrix built around data for that country and industry. Indeed, CreditPortfolioView, discussed in Chapter 7, can be viewed as a direct attempt to deal with the issues of cyclical and sectoral impacts on the bond/loan transition matrix.

In 1999, CreditMetrics introduced modifications to allow for cyclicality to be incorporated into the transition matrix.[23] Kim (1999) and Finger (1999) considered a market factor (the credit cycle index),[24] denoted as Z, such that all debt instruments are independent and conditional on the market factor. Figure 6.5 shows the conditional default probability, $p(Z)$, such that the entire distribution shifts down when Z is negative (i.e., the

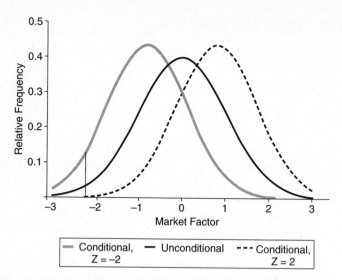

FIGURE 6.5 Unconditional asset distribution and conditional distributions with positive and negative Z. *Source:* Finger (1999), p. 16.

"market" declines during a bad year), thereby increasing the probability of default; when Z is positive (in a good year), the entire $p(Z)$ distribution shifts upward, thereby decreasing the default probability. The impact of market forces on the conditional default probability depends on the index weight w, such that when w is close to one (zero), values are highly correlated (uncorrelated) with the market factor, and the conditional default probability is highly dependent on (independent of) market forces.

The third issue relates to the portfolio of bonds used in calculating the transition matrix. Altman and Kishore (1997) found noticeable impact of bond "aging" on the probabilities calculated in the transition matrix. Indeed, a material difference is noted, depending on whether the bond sample used to calculate transitions is based on new bonds or on all bonds outstanding in a rating class at a particular moment in time. This undermines the assumption of credit risk homogeneity for all obligations in the same ratings classification. Kealhofer, Kwok, and Weng (1998) showed that default rates are skewed within each ratings class so that the mean may be twice as large as median default rates. Simulating Moody's bond ratings transition matrices 50,000 times using Monte Carlo simulation techniques, they find that approximately 75 percent of borrowers within a rating grade may have default rates below the mean, leading to adverse selection among borrowers; that is, only the riskiest 25 percent of all borrowers within each rating classification obtain loans if they are priced at the mean default spread. Moreover, there was such an overlap in the range of default probabilities for each class that a bond rated BBB may have a default probability in the AAA rating class range.

The fourth issue relates to the general problem of using bond transition matrices to value loans. As noted earlier, to the extent that collateral, covenants, and other features make loans behave differently from bonds, using bond transition matrices may result in an inherent valuation bias. Moreover, bond ratings lag market-based measures of default risk, such as KMV's *EDF* in forecasting default probabilities (see Chapter 4). This suggests that the internal development of loan rating transitions by banks (discussed in Chapter 2) based on *EDF*s and historic loan databases, might be viewed as crucial in improving the accuracy of *VAR* measures of loan risk.[25]

Valuation

In the *VAR* calculation shown earlier in this chapter, the amount recoverable on default (assumed to be $51.13 per $100), the forward zero interest rates $(_1r_i)$, and the credit spreads (s_i) are all nonstochastic (or at least hedged). Making any or all of them stochastic generally will increase any *VAR* calculation and capital requirement. In particular, loan recovery rates have quite substantial variability [see Carty and Lieberman (1996)], and the credit spread on, say, an AA loan might be expected to vary over some rating class at any moment in time (e.g., AA+ and AA− bonds or loans are likely to have different credit spreads). More generally, credit spreads and interest rates are likely to vary over time, with the credit-cycle, and shifts in the term structure, rather than being deterministic. One reason for assuming that interest rates are nonstochastic or deterministic is to separate market risk from credit risk,[26] but this remains highly controversial, especially to those who feel that their measurement should be integrated rather than separated and that credit risk is positively correlated with the interest rate cycle [see Crouhy et al. (2000)]. Kiesel et al. (2001) incorporate spread risk into CreditMetrics, arguing that stochastically varying spreads are strongly correlated across different exposures and thus are not diversified away, and find spread risks of about 7 percent of asset values for a portfolio of five-year maturity bonds. However, Kim (2000) contends, in the limited context of market *VAR*, that time horizon mismatches (up to 10 days for market risk and up to one year for credit risk) create problems in integrating spread risk and credit migration risk that may lead to overestimation of economic capital requirements.

Regarding recovery rates, if the standard deviation of recovery rates is $25.45 around a mean value of $51.13 per $100 of loans, it can be shown that the 99 percent *VAR* for the BBB loan in our example under the normal distribution will increase to $2.33 \times \$3.18$ million = $7.41 million, or a *VAR*-based capital requirement of 7.41 percent of the face value of the BBB loan (as compared to $6.97 million under the fixed *LGD* assumption) for unexpected losses only.[27] A related question is whether the volatility of *LGD*s of bonds is the same as for loans given the greater contract flexibility of the latter.[28]

Mark-to-Market Model versus Default Model

By allowing for the effects of credit rating changes (and hence, spread changes) on loan values, as well as default, CreditMetrics can be viewed as a mark-to-market (MTM) model. Other models—for example, CreditRisk Plus (see Chapter 8)—view spread risk as part of market risk and concentrate on expected and unexpected loss calculations rather than on expected and unexpected changes in value (or *VAR*) as in CreditMetrics. This alternative approach is often called the default model or default mode (DM).

It is useful to compare the effects of the MTM model versus the DM model by calculating the expected and, more importantly, the unexpected losses for the same example (the BBB loan) considered earlier. Table 6.1 shows that, in a two-state, default/no-default world, the probability of default is $p = 0.18$ percent and the probability of no default $(1 - p)$ is 99.82 percent. After default, the recovery rate is $51.13 per $100 (see Table 6.3), and the loss given default (*LGD*) is 1 minus the recovery rate, or $48.87 per $100. The book value exposure amount of the BBB loan is $100 million.

Given these figures, the expected loss on the loan is:

$$\text{Expected loss} = p \times LGD \times \text{Exposure}$$

$$= .0018 \times .4887 \times \$100,000,000 \quad (6.3)$$

$$= \$87,966$$

To calculate the unexpected loss, we have to make some assumptions regarding the distribution of default probabilities and recoveries. The simplest assumption is that recoveries are fixed and are independent of the distribution of default probabilities. Moreover, because the borrower either defaults or does not default, the probability of default can (most simply) be assumed to be binomially distributed with a standard deviation of:

$$\sigma = \sqrt{p(1 - p)} \quad (6.4)$$

Given a fixed recovery rate and exposure amount, the unexpected loss on the loan is:

$$\text{Unexpected loss} = \sqrt{p(1-p)} \times LGD \times \text{Exposure}$$
$$= \sqrt{(.0018)(.9982)} \times .4887 \times \$100,000,000 \quad (6.5)$$
$$= \$2,071,512$$

To make this number comparable with the *VAR* number calculated under CreditMetrics for the normal distribution, we can see that the one standard deviation loss of value (*VAR*) on the loan is $2.99 million versus $2.07 million under the DM approach.[29] This difference occurs partly because the MTM approach allows an upside as well as a downside to the loan's value, and the DM approach fixes the maximum upside value of the loan to its book or face value of $100 million. Thus, economic capital under the DM approach is more closely related to book value accounting concepts than to the market value accounting concepts used in the MTM approach.

SUMMARY

In this chapter, we outlined the *VAR* approach to calculating the capital requirement on a loan or a bond. We used one application of the *VAR* methodology—CreditMetrics—to illustrate the approach and raise the technical issues involved. Its key characteristics are: (1) it involves a full valuation or MTM approach in which both an upside and a downside to loan values are considered, and (2) the analyst can consider the actual distribution of estimated future loan values in calculating a capital requirement on a loan. We will revisit *VAR* methodology and CreditMetrics again in Chapter 11, when we consider calculating the *VAR* and capital requirements for a loan portfolio.

APPENDIX 6.1
CALCULATING THE FORWARD ZERO CURVE
FOR LOAN VALUATION

Yields on U.S. Treasury securities can be used as the foundation for the valuation of risky debt because U.S. Treasury note and bond markets are more liquid than corporate debt markets. To derive the credit risk-adjusted discount factor, CreditMetrics uses the following procedure: (1) Obtain the current yield curve, denoted CYC_{RF}, on risk-free (U.S. Treasury) coupon-bearing instruments, (2) Decompose CYC_{RF} into a zero yield curve, denoted ZYC_{RF}, using a no arbitrage condition, (3) Solve for a one-year forward zero risk-free yield curve, FYC_{RF}, and finally (4) Add fixed credit spreads obtained from historical loss experience in order to obtain the one-year forward zero risky debt yield curve, FYC_R.[30] Figure 6.6 illustrates data input into the CreditMetrics approach.

The Current Yield Curve on Risk-Free (U.S. Treasury) Coupon-Bearing Instruments

From the current yield curve (CYC_{RF}) for risk-free coupon bonds, shown in Figure 6.6, a zero-coupon yield curve for risk-free bonds (ZYC_{RF}) can be derived using "no arbitrage" pricing relationships between coupon bonds and zero-coupon bonds, and solving by successive substitution.

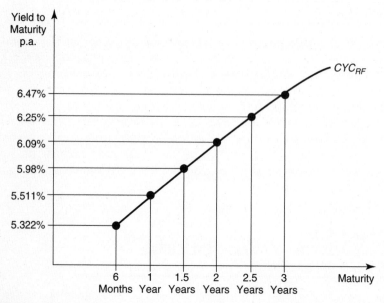

FIGURE 6.6 The current yield curve on risk-free U.S. Treasury coupon-bearing instruments.

Calculation of the Current Zero Risk-Free Curve Using No Arbitrage

U.S. Treasury notes and bonds carry semiannual coupon payments; therefore all yields are halved to reflect semiannual rates.[31] We utilize the double subscript notation introduced in Chapter 5, with the exception that the semiannual, rather than annual periods are numbered consecutively [i.e., $_0r_1$ is the spot (current) rate on the risk-free U.S. Treasury security maturing in 6 months, $_0r_2$ is the spot (current) rate on the risk-free U.S. Treasury security maturing in one year, $_2r_1$ is the one-year forward rate on a six-month U.S. Treasury security, and so on]. Thus:

$$\text{Six-month zero: } 100 = \frac{C+F}{1+_0r_1} = \frac{C+F}{1+_0z_1} = \frac{100+\left(\dfrac{5.322}{2}\right)}{1+\left(\dfrac{.05322}{2}\right)}$$

Therefore, the six-month zero risk-free rate is: $_0z_1 = 5.322$ percent per annum:

$$\text{One-year zero: } 100 = \frac{C}{1+_0r_2} + \frac{C+F}{\left(1+_0r_2\right)^2} = \frac{C}{1+_0z_1} + \frac{C+F}{\left(1+_0z_2\right)^2}$$

$$100 = \frac{\left(\dfrac{5.511}{2}\right)}{1+\left(\dfrac{.05511}{2}\right)} + \frac{100+\left(\dfrac{5.511}{2}\right)}{\left(1+\dfrac{.05511}{2}\right)^2}$$

$$= \frac{\left(\dfrac{5.11}{2}\right)}{1+\left(\dfrac{.05322}{2}\right)} + \frac{100+\left(\dfrac{5.511}{2}\right)}{\left(1+\dfrac{0.55136}{2}\right)^2}$$

Therefore, the one-year zero risk-free rate is: $_0z_2 = 5.5136$ percent per annum. And so on to trace out the zero-coupon yield curve for risk-free U.S. Treasury securities—shown as ZYC_{RF} in Figure 6.7. The next step is to trace out the risk-free forward yield curve, denoted FYC_{RF}, using ZYC_{RF}.

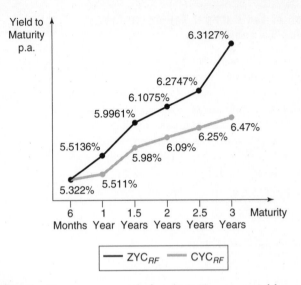

FIGURE 6.7   Zero coupon risk-free U.S. Treasury yield curve.

Derivation of the One-Year Forward Government Yield Curve Using the Current Risk-Free Zero Yield Curve

We can use the expectations hypothesis to derive the risk-free ZYC expected next year, or the risk-free one year forward zero yield curve, FYC_{RF} shown in Figure 6.8. But first we derive a series of six-month forward rates using the rates on the ZYC_{RF} curve.[32]

$$\left(1 + {}_0z_2\right)^2 = \left(1 + {}_0z_1\right)\left(1 + {}_1z_1\right)$$

$$\left(1 + \frac{.055136}{2}\right)^2 = \left(1 + \frac{.05322}{2}\right)\left(1 + {}_1z_1\right)$$

Therefore, the rate for six-months forward delivery of six-month maturity U.S. Treasury securities is expected to be: ${}_1z_1 = 5.7054$ percent p.a.

$$\left(1 + {}_0z_3\right)^3 = \left(1 + {}_0z_2\right)^2\left(1 + {}_2z_1\right)$$

$$\left(1 + \frac{.059961}{2}\right)^3 = \left(1 + \frac{.055136}{2}\right)^2\left(1 + {}_2z_1\right)$$

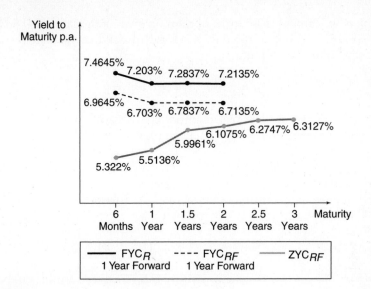

FIGURE 6.8 Derivation of the one-year forward risky debt yield curve.

Therefore, the rate for one-year forward delivery of six-month maturity U.S. Treasury securities is expected to be: $_2z_1 = 6.9645$ percent p.a.

$$\left(1+_0z_4\right)^4 = \left(1+_0z_3\right)^3\left(1+_3z_1\right)$$

$$\left(1+\frac{.061075}{2}\right)^4 = \left(1+\frac{.059961}{2}\right)^3\left(1+_3z_1\right)$$

Therefore, the rate for six-month maturity U.S. Treasury securities to be delivered in 1.5 years is: $_3z_1 = 6.4421$ percent p.a.

$$\left(1+_0z_5\right)^5 = \left(1+_0z_4\right)^4\left(1+_4z_1\right)$$

$$\left(1+\frac{.062747}{2}\right)^5 = \left(1+\frac{.061075}{2}\right)^4\left(1+_4z_1\right)$$

Therefore, the rate for six-month rate maturity U.S. Treasury securities to be delivered in two-years is $_4z_1 = 6.9452$ percent p.a.

Now we can use these forward rates on six-month maturity U.S. Treasury securities to obtain the one-year forward risk-free yield curve FYC_{RF} shown in Figure 6.8 as follows:

$$(1 + {_2}z_2)^2 = (1 + {_2}z_1)(1 + {_3}z_1)$$

Therefore, the rate for one-year maturity U.S. Treasury securities to be delivered in one-year is: ${_2}z_2 = 6.703$ percent p.a.

$$(1 + {_2}z_3)^3 = (1 + {_2}z_1)(1 + {_3}z_1)(1 + {_4}z_1)$$

Therefore, the rate for 18-month maturity U.S. Treasury securities to be delivered in one-year is ${_2}z_3 = 6.7837$ percent p.a.

$$(1 + {_2}z_4)^4 = (1 + {_2}z_1)(1 + {_3}z_1)(1 + {_4}z_1)(1 + {_5}z_1)$$

Therefore, the rate for two-year maturity U.S. Treasury securities to be delivered in one-year is: ${_2}z_4 = 6.7135$ percent p.a.

Derivation of One-Year Forward Risky Yield Curve—FYC_R

CreditMetrics adds a fixed credit spread (s_i) to the risk-free forward zero yield curve in order to obtain the risky debt forward yield curve, FYC_R, shown in Figure 6.8. Table 6.5 shows credit spreads provided by commercial firms such as Bridge Information Systems for different maturities.

TABLE 6.5 Credit Spreads for AAA Bonds

Maturity (in Years, Compounded Annually)	Credit Spread, s_i
2	0.007071
3	0.008660
5	0.011180
10	0.015811
15	0.019365
20	0.022361

Source: Gupton et al., *Technical Document,* J.P. Morgan, April 2, 1997, p. 164, from Bridge Information Systems, February 15, 1997.

Typically, commercially-provided credit spreads are calculated using historical averages. The one-year forward yield curve for risky debt in Figure 6.8 is illustrated assuming a fixed 50 basis point credit spread.

A Last Methodological Word

The methodology presented in this Appendix has been criticized for, among other reasons, its assumptions of deterministic interest rates (fixed yield curves) and constant credit spreads, s_i. The second criticism could be addressed by decomposing risky debt yield curves directly rather than decomposing the risk-free U.S. Treasury yield curve and then adding on a fixed credit spread. However, this approach injects noise into valuations if risky debt markets are illiquid and prices subject to error (see discussion in Chapter 5).

APPENDIX 6.2
ESTIMATING UNEXPECTED LOSSES USING
EXTREME VALUE THEORY

The Generalized Pareto Distribution (GPD) is a two-parameter distribution with the following functional form:

$$G_{\xi\beta}(x) = 1 - \left(1 + \frac{\xi x}{\beta}\right)^{-\frac{1}{\xi}} \text{ if } \xi \neq 0,$$

$$= 1 - exp\left(\frac{-x}{\beta}\right) \text{ if } \xi = 0$$

The two parameters that describe the GPD are ξ (the shape parameter) and β (the scaling parameter). If $\xi > 0$, then the GPD is characterized by fat tails.[33]

Suppose that the GPD describes the portion of the distribution of unexpected losses that exceeds the 5 percent *VAR* and assume that a normal distribution best describes the distribution of values for the BBB rated loan described in Table 6.4 up to the 95th percentile, denoted as the "threshold value" $u = \$4.93$ million. If we had 10,000 observations of unexpected losses on this loan, denoted $n = 10,000$, the 95 percent threshold is set by the 500 observations with the largest unexpected losses; that is

$$\frac{(10,000 - 500)}{10,000} = 95\%$$

denoted as $N_u = 500$. Suppose that fitting the GPD parameters to the data yields $\xi = 0.5$ and $\beta = 7.$[34] McNeil (1999) shows that the estimate of a *VAR* beyond the 95th percentile, taking into account the heaviness of the tails in the GPD (denoted $\overline{VAR}_{99}$) can be calculated as follows:

$$\overline{VAR}_q = u + \left(\frac{\beta}{\xi}\right)\left[\left(\frac{n(1-q)}{N_u}\right)^{-\xi} - 1\right]$$

Substituting in the parameters of this example for the 99th percentile *VAR*, or $\overline{VAR}_{99}$, yields:

$$\$22.23 = \$4.93 + \left(\frac{7}{.5}\right)\left[\left(\frac{10,000(1-.99)}{500}\right)^{-.5} - 1\right]$$

McNeil (1999) also shows that the expected shortfall (i.e., the mean of the credit losses exceeding $\overline{VAR}_{99}$) can be estimated as follows:

$$\overline{ES}_q = \left(\frac{\overline{VAR}_q}{(1-\xi)}\right) + \frac{(\beta - \xi u)}{(1-\xi)}$$

where q is set equal to the 99th percentile. Thus,

$$\overline{ES}_q = \frac{(\$22.23)}{.5} + \frac{(7 - .5(4.93))}{.5} = \$53.53$$

to obtain the values shown in Figure 6.4. As can be seen, the ratio of the extreme (shortfall) loss to the 99th percentile loss is quite high:

$$\frac{\overline{ES}_{.99}}{\overline{VAR}_{.99}} = \frac{\$53.53}{\$22.23} = 2.4$$

This means that nearly 2½ times more capital would be needed to secure the bank against catastrophic credit losses compared to unexpected losses occurring up to the 99th percentile level, even when allowing for "fat tails" in the $VAR_{.99}$ measure. It also suggests that a catastrophic credit "stress-test" multiplier of between 2 and 3 would be appropriate in this case.

CHAPTER 7

The Macro Simulation Approach

The CreditPortfolio View Model and Other Models

As discussed in Chapter 6, the basic methodology underlying CreditMetrics *VAR* calculations assumes that transition probabilities are stable across borrower types and across the business cycle.[1] The assumption of stability is problematic. A recent survey of the internal rating systems of 26 major bank holding companies suggested that as much as 50 percent of their collective loan portfolios may be below the equivalent of investment grade [see Treacy and Carey (2000)].[2] The default rates on low-quality credits (including junk bonds) are highly sensitive to the state of the business cycle. Moreover, there is empirical evidence that rating transitions in general may depend on the state of the economy [see Wilson (1997a, b) and Nickell, Perraudin, and Varotto (2001a)]. This evidence suggests that the probability of downgrades and defaults may be significantly greater in a cyclical downturn than in an upturn.[3]

DEALING WITH CYCLICAL FACTORS

There are at least two ways to deal with cyclical factors and effects:

1. Divide the past sample period into recession years and nonrecession years, and calculate two separate historic transition matrices (a recession matrix and a nonrecession matrix) to yield two separate *VAR* calculations.
2. Directly model the relationship between transition probabilities and macroeconomic factors, and, when a model is fitted, simulate the evolution of transition probabilities over time by generating macroeconomic "shocks" to the model.

A version of the first approach is taken by CreditPortfolio View[4] in its newer product, CPV-Direct, as well as in the advanced versions of Credit-Metrics and other *VAR* models discussed in Chapter 6.[5] The second approach is taken by CPV-Macro. In this chapter, we first illustrate the basic dynamics of the CPV-Macro model and then briefly describe CPV-Direct.

THE MACRO SIMULATION APPROACH: CPV-MACRO

The essential idea is represented in the transition matrix for a given country, shown in Figure 7.1. Note especially the cell of the matrix in the bottom right-hand corner (p_{CD}). Each cell in the transition matrix shows the probability that a particular counterparty, rated at a given grade at the beginning of the period, will move to another rating by the end of the period. In Figure 7.1, p_{CD} shows the estimated probability that a C-rated borrower (a speculative-grade borrower) will default over the next year, that is, it will move from a C rating to a D (default) rating. The unconditional one-year transition matrix shown in Figure 7.1 is derived as follows: the historic frequency of transitions from each initial rating to each other rating divided by the total number of issuers that began the year in the initial rating classification; that is, p_{CD} is the observed number of issues, averaged over the entire sample period, that started out the year with a C rating and ended up with a D rating one year later divided by the total number of C ratings at the

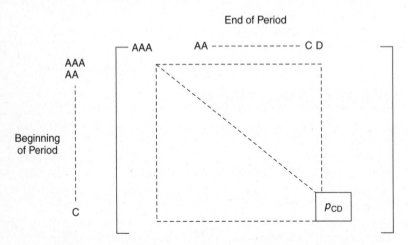

FIGURE 7.1 Historical (unconditional) transition matrix.

start of each year. This approach assumes that each rating transition (e.g., p_{CD}) is a constant parameter.

In general, we would expect this probability to move significantly during the business cycle and to be higher in recessions than in expansions.[6] Because the probabilities in each row of the transition matrix must sum to 1, an increase in p_{CD} must be compensated for by a decrease in other probabilities, for example, those involving upgrades of initially C-rated debt, where p_{CB} and p_{CA} represent the probabilities of the C-rated borrower's moving to, respectively, a B grade and an A grade during the next year. The density, or mass, of the probabilities in the transition matrix moves increasingly in a southeast direction as a recession proceeds.[7]

With this in mind, let p_{CD} vary at time t along with a set of macro factors indexed by variable y. For convenience, the subscripts (C and D) will be dropped. However, we are implicitly modeling the probability that a C-rated borrower will default over the next period (say, one year). In general terms:[8]

$$p_t = f(y_t) \qquad (7.1)$$

where $f' < 0$; that is, there is an inverse link between the state of the economy and the probability of default. The macro indicator variable y_t can be viewed as being driven by a set of i (systematic) macroeconomic variables at time t (X_{it}) as well as (unsystematic) random shocks or innovations to the economic system (V_t). In general:[9]

$$y_t = g(X_{it}, V_t) \qquad (7.2)$$

where $i = 1, \ldots, n$ and $V_t \sim N(0, \sigma^2)$.

In turn, macroeconomic variables (X_{it}) such as gross domestic product (GDP) growth, unemployment, and so on, can themselves be viewed as being determined by their past histories (e.g., lagged GDP growth) as well as being sensitive to shocks themselves (ε_{it}).[10] Thus:

$$X_{it} = h(X_{it-1}, X_{it-2}, \ldots, \varepsilon_{it}) \qquad (7.3)$$

where $i = 1, \ldots, n$ and $\varepsilon_{it} \sim N(0, \sigma_\varepsilon^2)$.

Different macro model specifications can be used in the context of equations (7.2) and (7.3) to improve model fit, and different models can be used to explain transitions for different countries and industries. This is discussed in greater detail in Appendix 7.1.

Substituting equation (7.3) into equation (7.2), and equation (7.2) into equation (7.1), the probability of a speculative (grade C) loan moving to grade D during the next year will be determined by:

$$p_t = f(X_{it-j}; V_t, \varepsilon_{it}) \qquad (7.4)$$

Essentially, equation (7.4) models the determinants of this transition probability as a function of lagged macro variables, a general economic shock factor or "innovation" (V_t), and shock factors or innovations for each of the i macro variables (ε_{it}). Because the X_{it-j} are predetermined, the key variables driving p_t will be the innovations or shocks V_t and ε_{it}. Using a structured Monte Carlo simulation approach, values for V_t and ε_{it} can be generated for periods in the future that occur with the same probability as that observed from history.[11] We can use the simulated V's and ε's, along with the fitted macro model, to simulate scenario values for p_{CD} in periods t, $t + 1$, $t + 2$, . . . , $t + n$, and on into the future.

Suppose that, based on current macroeconomic conditions, the simulated value for p_{CD}, labeled p_t^*, is 0.174, and the number in the historic (unconditional) transition matrix is 0.15 (where * indicates the simulated value of the transition probability). Because the (unconditional) transition value, of 0.15 is less than the value estimated conditional on the macro economic state (0.174), we are likely to underestimate the VAR of loans and a loan portfolio—especially at the low-quality end.

Define the migration adjustment ratio (R_t):[12]

$$R_t = \frac{p_t^*}{p_t} = \frac{.174}{.15} = 1.16 \qquad (7.5)$$

Based on the simulated macro model, the probability of a C-rated borrower's defaulting over the next year is 16 percent higher than the average (unconditional) historical transition relationship implies. We can also calculate this ratio for periods $t + 1$, $t + 2$, and so on. For example, suppose, based on simulated innovations and macro-factor relationships, the simulation predicts p^*_{t+1} to be 0.21. The migration adjustment ratio relevant for the next year (R_{t+1}) is then:

$$R_{t+1} = \frac{p^*_{t+1}}{p_{t+1}} = \frac{.21}{.15} = 1.4 \qquad (7.6)$$

Again, the unconditional transition matrix will underestimate the risk of default on low-grade loans in this period. These calculated ratios can be used to adjust the elements in the projected $t, t + 1, \ldots, t + n$ transition matrices. In CPV–Macro, the unconditional value of p_{CD} is adjusted by the ratio of the conditional value of p_{CD} to its unconditional value. Consider the transition matrix for period t; then $R \times 0.15 = 0.174$ (which is the same as p_t^*). Thus, we replace 0.15 with 0.174 in the transition matrix (M_t), as shown in Figure 7.2. This also means that we need to adjust all the other elements in the transition matrix (e.g., p_{CA}, p_{CB}, and so on). A number of procedures can be used to do this, including linear and nonlinear regressions of each element or cell in the transition matrix on the ratio R_t and the use of a diffusion parameter, λ [see Wilson (1997a, b) and Appendix 7.1; remember that the rows of the transition matrix must sum to one[13]]. For the next period $(t + 1)$, the transition matrix would have to be similarly adjusted by multiplying the unconditional value of p by R_{t+1}, or $.15 \times 1.4 = .21$.

Thus, there would be different transition matrices for each year into the future $(t, t + 1, \ldots, t + n)$, reflecting the simulated effect of the macroeconomic shocks on transition probabilities. We could use this type of approach, along with CreditMetrics, to calculate a cyclically sensitive *VAR* for one year, two years, $\ldots n$ years.[14] Specifically, the simulated transition matrix M_t, would replace the historically based unconditional (stable Markov) transition matrix, and, given any current rating for the loan (say, C), the distribution of loan values based on the macro-adjusted transition probabilities in the C row of the matrix M_t could be used to calculate *VAR* at the

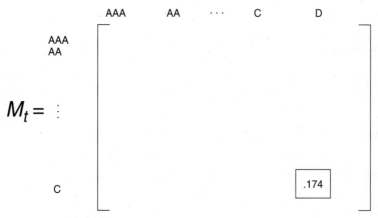

FIGURE 7.2 Conditional transition matrix (M_t).

one-year horizon, in a fashion similar to that used under CreditMetrics in Chapter 6.

We could also calculate VAR estimates using longer horizons. Suppose we are interested in transitions over the next two years (t and $t + 1$). Multiplying the two matrixes,

$$M_{t, t+1} = M_t \times M_{t+1} \qquad (7.7)$$

produces a new matrix, $M_{t,t+1}$. The final column of this new matrix will give the simulated (cumulative) probabilities of default on loans of all ratings over the next two years.

We have considered just one simulation of values for $p_t{}^*$ from one set of shocks (V_t, ε_{it}). Repeating the exercise over and over again (e.g., taking 10,000 random draws) would produce 10,000 values of $p_t{}^*$ and 10,000 possible transition matrices.

Consider the current year (t). We can plot hypothetical simulated values for $p_t{}^*$, as shown in Figure 7.3. The mean simulated value of $p_t{}^*$ is .174, but the extreme value (99th percentile, or worst-case value) is .45. When

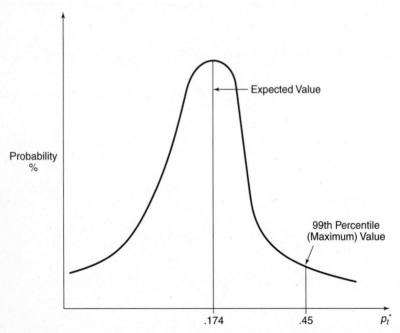

FIGURE 7.3   Probability distribution of simulated values of $p_t{}^*$ in year t.

calculating capital requirements—that is, when considering unexpected declines in loan values—the latter figure for p_t^*, and the transition matrix associated with this value, might be considered most relevant.

CPV DIRECT

The derivation of implicit risk factors as reflected in credit migration matrices in CPV-Macro, discussed previously, can be summarized as follows:

1. Obtain a time series of macroeconomic variables and default histories.
2. Regress default rates on macroeconomic variables to identify systemic factor coefficients.[15]
3. Extrapolate forecasts of macroeconomic variables using a two-period distributed lag, multiple regression analysis.[16]
4. Calculate default rates by regressing default on the forecast of macroeconomic conditions.[17]
5. Simulate default rates over many different possible macroeconomic states of the world to trace out the distribution of conditional default probabilities for each rating. The distribution of simulated default rates is used to define the shift parameter (the ratio R) and the diffusion parameter (λ) defined in Appendix 7.1 for the conditional migration matrix, such that the higher the volatility of the default risk factor, the larger the shift of the migration matrix.

CPV-Macro simulates default probabilities using forecast values of macroeconomic variables, y, following equation (7.1), and therefore makes no explicit assumptions about the distribution of default probabilities; that is, the default probability distribution is implicitly determined by the simulated values of macroeconomic conditions. An alternative version of Credit-Portfolio View, called CPV-Direct, instead directly specifies the default distribution (and correlations across industry risk segments). That is, historic default probabilities can be used to directly estimate the distributional form (e.g., gamma), as well as the correlations of default probabilities across industry segments. Then the shift parameters, R and λ, are determined depending on the value of the risk factor for each risk segment. The model is simulated by taking correlated draws of the risk factors depending on the assumed default probability distributions. The shift parameters for the migration matrix are therefore directly dependent on the assumed distribution of default probabilities.

Macroeconomic conditions can be introduced into CPV-Direct by varying the distributional assumptions so that the form and the variability of default probabilities are affected by the business cycle. Figure 7.4 shows two possible distributional assumptions. The stress scenario illustrates how the default probability distribution is affected by the expectation of a deep recession. The tail probability weight in the high default region increases (relative to the "normal scenario" shown in Figure 7.4) to reflect the assumption that high risk borrowers are more likely to default when economic conditions deteriorate. Since the volatility of the stress scenario distribution is higher than the volatility of the normal scenario default distribution, the shift parameter R is higher under the stress scenario than under the normal scenario.

An important drawback of models like CPV-Direct is that estimating distributions of default probabilities directly from observed credit histories requires large amounts of data. Bond databases for U.S. industrial corporations have been maintained by the rating agencies for more than 30 years. However, coverage of loans, non-U.S. industrials, or sovereign nations began only in the last decade. Hu et al. (2001) use the ordered probit model to estimate transition matrices for sovereigns by creating "fitted" rating histories and then using this simulated credit history to estimate transition matrices along the lines outlined by Nickell et al. (2001a). They find that they

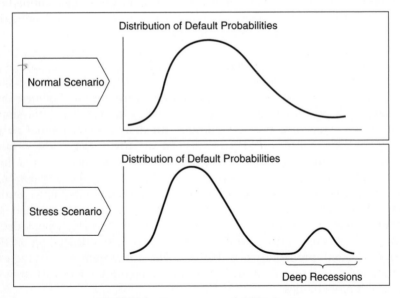

FIGURE 7.4   Stress tests of CPV-direct.

could compensate for gaps in the data and obtained useful estimates of conditional default probability distributions.

SUMMARY

One way to build in business cycle effects and to take a forward-looking view of *VAR* is to model macroeconomic effects, both systematic and unsystematic, on the probability of default and associated rating transitions. The macro simulation approach should be viewed as being complementary to CreditMetrics, overcoming some of the biases resulting from assuming static or stationary transition probabilities period to period.

APPENDIX 7.1
CALCULATING CONDITIONAL MIGRATION MATRICES IN CREDITPORTFOLIO VIEW–MACRO[18]

There are three components necessary to obtain the conditional migration matrix:

1. *Explanatory processes.* Macroeconomic variables must be identified to simulate future values of macroeconomic states (i.e., systematic risk factors).
2. *Speculative default rate processes.* The stochastic relationship between the macroeconomic explanatory variables and default rates for speculative rating grades must be estimated. Different relationships are estimated for each industry segment.
3. *Shift factors to transform unconditional into conditional migration matrices.* Assesses the impact of changes in each segment's conditional speculative default rate on the one-year unconditional rating migration matrix.

Explanatory Processes

CPV-Macro uses fundamental macroeconomic variables to describe the evolution of the macroeconomy. Although varying from country to country, some examples of explanatory variables are: unemployment rates, GDP growth, long-term interest rates, foreign exchange rates, public disbursements, and aggregate savings rates. Wilson (1997b) suggests that at least three different macroeconomic factors are required to capture the systematic variation in speculative default rates for each country.[19] Since different industry segments have different sensitivities to these macroeconomic factors, CPV-Macro estimates the model for each industry segment in each country individually. Throughout this appendix, it is assumed (and therefore subscript notation is suppressed for ease of exposition) that we are focused on a particular industry segment, j; in a particular country, c; for a particular initial rating class, Z; at time period, t. The analysis is then replicated for each industry segment, for all possible rating classes, at different time periods across different countries.

The estimation of the explanatory process captures the momentum (cyclical dynamics) of each macroeconomic variable. The momentum is measured by the coefficients on the lagged macroecomic variables and the error terms, $k_{i,p}$ and $k_{i,q}$ from a set of univariate, auto-regressive, moving average processes, ARMA(p,q), for each macroeconomic variable, i, as follows: [20]

$$X_{i,t} = k_{i,0} + \Sigma_{p=1\ldots P}(k_{i,p}X_{i,t-p}) + \Sigma_{q=1\ldots Q}(k_{i,q}\varepsilon_{i,t-q}) \qquad (7.8)$$

where $k_{i,p}$ and $k_{i,q}$ are the moving average constants to be estimated for each macroeconomic variable i, and $\varepsilon_{i,t-q}$ are the moving average error terms, assumed to be independent and identically distributed as $N(0, \sigma_i^2)$. This estimation is performed separately for each macroeconomic variable (e.g., GDP innovations, unemployment rates, interest rates), thereby yielding i sets of cyclical momentum estimates, $k_{i,p}$ and $k_{i,q}$.[21]

Speculative Default Rate Processes

Macroeconomic conditions have the most impact on the default probabilities of bonds rated in the speculative grades. Thus, CPV-Macro estimates a speculative grade default probability, denoted PD, conditional on the cyclical macroeconomic risk factors estimated in the previous section. Suppressing all subscripts for simplicity, the following estimation is performed for each industry segment j at time period t:

$$PD = \frac{1}{\left[1 + e^{-y}\right]} \qquad (7.9)$$

where PD is the default probability for a speculative grade issue from industry segment j at time t,[22] and y is an explanatory index variable that is estimated using the N different macroeconomic factors X_i estimated in equation (7.8), constructed for each segment j at time t (subscripts suppressed) as follows:

$$y = \beta_0 + \Sigma_{i=1\ldots N}\, \beta_i X_i + V \qquad (7.10)$$

where the β_i coefficients are estimated specifically for each industry segment j at each point in time t. Thus, the β_i coefficients reflect the impact of the cyclical dynamics estimated in equation (7.8) on the probability of default for speculative grades of debt. The error term V represents the unsystematic risk component remaining after the systematic risk component is captured by the (sector-weighted) influence of the macroeconomic variables from equation (7.8). The error term V can be interpreted as a segment-specific surprise that is similar in function to the jump process assumed in intensity-based models; that is, V reflects sudden shifts in default probabilities that are not a function of domestic macroeconomic conditions. (However, V could include the effect of an external macroeconomic shock; e.g., an Asian crisis on Germany.)

The functional form of equation (7.9) was chosen because it offered, on average, a better fit to the historical data, as measured by R-squared, and because for any value of the index y, equation (7.9) yields a *PD* between 0 and 1.

Once the relationships in equations (7.8 through 7.10) are estimated, the implementation of the model proceeds as follows:

- *Step 1.* Simulate the future value of each macroeconomic explanatory variables, X_i, using equation (7.8). These will largely reflect the shocks in the X_i since the lagged variables of X_i are predetermined. Indeed, the ε_{it} and V will drive y.
- *Step 2.* Use the simulated values of all of the macroeconomic variables X_i along with V to construct the index y [equation (7.10)] for each industry sector.
- *Step 3.* Estimate the conditional default probabilities for speculative grade debt in each industry segment using equation (7.9). The simulated *PD* is normalized so that the mean of the first year's *PD* across all simulation runs is equal to its historical average. This assures that the mean of the first-year conditional migration matrix is equal to its unconditional expected value; that is, the migration adjustment ratio R (defined in the text of this chapter) is centered around 1.
- *Step 4.* Define the ratio of the simulated value of *PD* for each industry sector from equation (7.9) divided by the long run average default probability (calculated over the historical data series), denoted $\overline{PD}$; $\overline{PD}$ is used in the next section to construct a left- and right-shift operator. Intuitively, if $\overline{PD} > 1$, then the simulated speculative default probability for the segment is greater than the long-run average and the right shift operator increases the probability of being downgraded; alternatively,

if $\overline{PD} < 1$, then the simulated speculative default probability for the segment is less than the long-run average and downgrades are less likely.

Shift Factors to Transform Unconditional into Conditional Migration Matrices

To transform the unconditional migration matrix (obtained from historical migration probabilities) into a migration matrix that is conditional on macroeconomic conditions, the model estimates both a systematic risk sensitivity parameter, denoted λ, and an unsystematic risk sensitivity parameter θ.

The Systematic Risk Sensitivity Parameter, λ   To understand how systematic risk is diffused through the conditional migration matrix, let us elaborate on the example in the text. We consider an unconditional default probability for C rated debt, p_{CD}, equal to 0.15. Let us fill in the last line of the unconditional transition matrix as shown in Table 7.1.[23] Beginning with p_{CD}, we derive the migration adjustment ratio, R, as a function of simulated default probabilities for speculative grade debt. In Step 4 above we defined $\overline{PD}$ to be the ratio of the simulated default probability PD, estimated from equation (7.9), to the historic average speculative default probability. CPV-Macro posits a relationship between downgrade/upgrade probabilities and $\overline{PD}$ such that if $\overline{PD} > 1$, the probability of downgrades increases and if $\overline{PD} < 1$ then more of the mass of the transition matrix is shifted into upgrades. This can be estimated as:

$$\frac{D_t}{\overline{D}} = (1+\alpha) + \alpha\overline{PD}$$

$$\frac{U_t}{\overline{U}} = (1+\beta) + \beta\overline{PD}$$

(7.11)

where D_t (U_t) is the actual, historical single rating downgrade (upgrade) percentages at time period t and, $\overline{D}$ $(\overline{U})$ are the average downgrade (upgrade) rates over the entire period. Using historic data to consecutively re-estimate the empirical relationships in equation (7.11), we can obtain measures for one rating classification downgrade (upgrade) α_1 (β_1), and two rating classifications downgrade (upgrade) α_2 (β_2), and so on. However, because historic data includes downgrades to the absorbing state of default, the historic relationship introduces an upward drift in expected defaults for all rating classes. Therefore, CPV-Macro constrains each rating downgrade factor to be equal to the upgrade factor for the equivalent number of ratings

TABLE 7.1 Unconditional Transition Matrix

	A	B	C	D
A	. . .	. . .	. . .	. . .
B	. . .	. . .	. . .	. . .
C	0.01	0.04	0.80	0.15

classifications, such that $\alpha_i = \beta_i$ and sets them equal to λ_i, which is defined as the systematic risk sensitivity parameter for i shifts in ratings classifications.

To illustrate the transformation of the unconditional matrix into a conditional transition matrix, we use the example shown in Table 7.1. Suppose that estimation of equation (7.11) yields the following estimates of the systematic risk sensitivity parameter $\lambda_0 = 1.18$, $\lambda_1 = 0.4$, $\lambda_2 = 4$.[24] Beginning with the bottom right entry in the unconditional transition matrix, $p_{CD} = 0.15$, we define the (discrete) transition ratio for a one rating shift from C to D to be:

$$R = 1 + \lambda_1 \tau \qquad (7.12)$$

where λ_1 is the risk sensitivity parameter estimated from equation (7.11) for a one-rating classification shift and τ is defined to be $\overline{PD} - 1$ for $\overline{PD} > 1$ and $-(\overline{PD} - 1)$ for $\overline{PD} < 1$; therefore, $\tau \geq 0$. Suppose that the estimation of equation (7.9) yields $\overline{PD} = 1.4$, then $\tau = 0.4$. Suppose further that we estimated the systematic risk sensitivity parameter for one rating transition from equation (7.11) to be $\lambda_1 = 0.4$. Therefore, solving equation (7.12), $R = 1.16$. Thus, the conditional value of $p^*_{CD} = rp_{CD} = 1.16(.15) = 0.174$. This is shown in the bottom right hand entry of the conditional transition matrix shown in Table 7.2.

Note that the $\Delta p_{CD} = 0.174 - 0.15 = .024$. To see how the diffusion term (the shift operator) is obtained, note that the shift in transition probabilities must be diffused throughout the row so that the sum of all probabilities still equals one. We use the systematic risk sensitivity parameter λ in

TABLE 7.2 Conditional Transition Matrix

	A	B	C	D
A				
B				
C	0.0124	0.034	0.7796	0.174

order to define the diffusion term for the last row of the conditional transition matrix shown in Table 7.2 as follows:

$$\Delta p_{CC} = \lambda_1 \Delta p_{CB} - \lambda_1 \Delta p_{CD}$$
$$\Delta p_{CB} = \lambda_2 \Delta p_{CA} - \lambda_0 \Delta p_{CC} \qquad (7.13)$$
$$\Delta p_{CA} = \lambda_1 \Delta p_{CB}$$

That is, the shift operator is defined to be the risk sensitivity parameter times the difference between the change in the transition probability in the next higher class minus the change in the transition probability in the next lower class. Equation (7.13) is a system of three equations with three unknowns which, in our example, can be solved for: $\Delta p_{CC} = -0.0204$, $\Delta p_{CB} = -0.006$, and $\Delta p_{CA} = 0.0024$ to obtain the last row in the conditional transition matrix shown in Table 7.2.[25] This is repeated for each row of the unconditional transition matrix.

The Unsystematic Risk Sensitivity Parameter, θ   Transition probabilities for low grade and speculative grade debt closely follow the cyclical dynamics estimated in the previous section. However, high credit quality debt tends to be less sensitive to cyclical movements. Thus, reliance on the systematic risk sensitivity parameter alone will underestimate the default probabilities for highly rated debt classifications.[26] CPV-Macro allows users to input a "spontaneous combustion" unsystematic risk parameter for highly rated obligors. Rather than a gradual shift in the probability mass across the entire row, the unsystematic risk sensitivity parameter, θ, is applied directly to the probability of default entry. Thus, the probability of default for investment grade ratings would be increased by a discrete value. This would be netted out in the diffusion of the conditional transition matrix following the procedure outlined in the previous section.

The conditional transition matrix in our example shown in Table 7.2 is obtained for one simulated value of PD which corresponds to one set of macroeconomic conditions, X_i. To obtain the loss distribution, this process must be simulated using Monte Carlo simulation techniques for many different possible future states of the world. CPV-Macro recommends the use of between 250 and 5,000 macroeconomic scenarios in order to ensure that the results are robust.

CHAPTER 8

The Insurance Approach

Mortality Models and the CSFP
Credit Risk Plus Model

Only quite recently have ideas from insurance found their way into the new tools for credit risk measurement and management. In this chapter, we look at two applications of insurance ideas—one from life insurance and one from property insurance. Altman (1989) and others have developed mortality tables for loans and bonds using ideas (and models) similar to those that insurance actuaries apply when they set premiums for life insurance policies. Credit Suisse Financial Products (CSFP) has developed a model similar to the one a property insurer selling household fire insurance might use when assessing the risk of policy losses in setting premiums. We look first at the mortality model and then at the CSFP Credit Risk Plus model.

MORTALITY ANALYSIS

The idea is very simple. Based on a portfolio of loans or bonds and their historic default experience, develop a table that can be used in a predictive sense for one-year, or marginal, mortality rates (*MMR*) and for multiyear, or cumulative, mortality rates (*CMR*). Combining such calculations with *LGD*s can produce estimates of expected losses.[1]

To calculate say, the *MMR*s of grade B bonds (loans) defaulting in each year of their "life," the analyst will pick a sample of years—say, 1971 through 2000—and, for *each year*, will look at:

$$MMR_1 = \frac{\text{Total value of grade B bonds defaulting in year 1 of issue}}{\text{Total value of grade B bonds outstanding in year 1 of issue}} \qquad (8.1)$$

$$MMR_2 = \frac{\text{Total value of grade B bonds defaulting in year 2 of issue}}{\text{Total value of grade B bonds outstanding in year 2 of issue (adjusted for defaults, calls, sinking fund redemptions, and maturities in the prior year)}} \qquad (8.2)$$

and so on for $MMR_3, \ldots, MMR_n$.

When an individual year MMR_i has been calculated, the analyst calculates a weighted average over the entire sample period, which becomes the figure entered into the mortality table. The weights (w_i) used should reflect the relative issue sizes in different years, thus biasing the results toward the larger-issue years. The average MMR in year 1 after issue for a particular grade would be calculated as:

$$MMR_1 = \sum_{i=1971}^{2000} MMR_{1i} \times w_i \qquad (8.3)$$

To calculate a cumulative mortality rate (CMR)—the probability that a loan or bond will default over a period longer than a year (say, 2 years)—it is first necessary to specify the relationship between $MMRs$ and survival rates (SRs):

$$MMR_i = 1 - SR_i$$

or $\qquad (8.4)$

$$SR_i = 1 - MMR_i$$

Consequently,

$$CMR_T = 1 - \prod_{i=1}^{T} SR_i \qquad (8.5)$$

where Π is the geometric sum or product, $SR_1 \times SR_2 \times \ldots SR_T$, and T denotes the number of years over which the cumulative mortality rate is calculated.

Mortality Tables

Table 8.1 shows marginal and cumulative mortality rates for syndicated loans and bonds over a ten-year horizon, as computed by Altman and Karlin (2001a). The table has an interesting feature: Marginal mortality rates fluctuate nonmonotonically over the life of the corporate bond. In particular, although not shown, each of the MMR estimates has an implied standard-error and confidence interval. Moreover, it can be shown that as the number of loans or bonds in the sample increases (i.e., as N gets bigger), the standard error on a mortality rate will fall (i.e., the degree of confidence we have in using the MMR estimate to predict expected losses out-of-sample increases). Because, in any period a loan or bond either dies or survives,[2] the standard error (σ) of an MMR is:

$$\sigma = \sqrt{\frac{MMR_i(1 - MMR_i)}{N}} \tag{8.6}$$

and rearranging:

$$N = \frac{MMR_i(1 - MMR_i)}{\sigma^2} \tag{8.7}$$

As can be seen from equations (8.6) and (8.7), there is an inverse relationship between N (sample size) and the σ (standard error) of a mortality rate estimate.

Suppose that $MMR_1 = 0.01$ is a mortality rate estimate, and we want to apply extreme actuarial principles of confidence in the stability of the estimate for pricing and prediction out of sample. Extreme actuarial principles might require σ to be one-tenth the size of the mortality rate estimate (or $\sigma = .001$). Plugging the values into equation (8.7), we have:

$$N = \frac{(.01)(.99)}{(.001)^2} = 9,900$$

This suggests that we would need almost 10,000 loan observations per rating class to get this type of confidence in the estimate. With 10 rating classes (as under most bank rating systems), we would need to analyze a portfolio of some 100,000 loans. With respect to commercial loans, very few banks have built information systems of this type. To get to the requisite large size, a cooperative effort among the banks themselves may be

TABLE 8.1 Mortality Rates by Original Rating—All Rated Corporated Bonds* (1971–2000)

		Years after Issuance									
		1	2	3	4	5	6	7	8	9	10
AAA	Marginal	0.00%	0.00%	0.00%	0.00%	0.03%	0.00%	0.00%	0.00%	0.00%	0.00%
	Cumulative	0.00%	0.00%	0.00%	0.00%	0.03%	0.03%	0.03%	0.03%	0.03%	0.03%
AA	Marginal	0.00%	0.00%	0.35%	0.19%	0.00%	0.00%	0.00%	0.00%	0.03%	0.02%
	Cumulative	0.00%	0.00%	0.35%	0.54%	0.54%	0.54%	0.54%	0.54%	0.57%	0.59%
A	Marginal	0.00%	0.00%	0.02%	0.07%	0.03%	0.08%	0.05%	0.09%	0.06%	0.00%
	Cumulative	0.00%	0.00%	0.02%	0.09%	0.12%	0.20%	0.25%	0.34%	0.40%	0.40%
BBB	Marginal	0.12%	0.48%	0.55%	0.59%	0.56%	0.58%	0.72%	0.15%	0.05%	0.26%
	Cumulative	0.12%	0.60%	1.14%	1.73%	2.28%	2.85%	3.55%	3.70%	3.75%	3.98%
BB	Marginal	0.96%	1.65%	3.15%	1.54%	2.15%	0.95%	1.65%	0.45%	1.75%	3.75%
	Cumulative	0.96%	2.59%	6.50%	7.12%	9.12%	9.98%	11.47%	11.87%	13.41%	16.66%
B	Marginal	1.60%	4.94%	5.95%	6.72%	5.94%	4.15%	3.12%	2.10%	1.65%	0.85%
	Cumulative	1.60%	6.46%	12.03%	17.85%	22.73%	25.94%	28.25%	29.76%	30.92%	31.51%
CCC	Marginal	4.35%	13.26%	14.84%	8.15%	3.02%	9.15%	4.56%	3.26%	0.00%	4.15%
	Cumulative	4.35%	17.03%	31.00%	36.62%	38.53%	44.15%	46.70%	48.44%	48.44%	50.58%

*Rated by S&P at Issuance, based on 933 issues.

Source: Standard & Poor's (New York) and Altman and Karlin (2001a).

required. The end result of such a cooperative effort might be a National Loan Mortality table that could be as useful in establishing banks' loan loss reserves (based on expected losses) as the National Life Mortality tables are in pricing life insurance.[3]

CSFP CREDIT RISK PLUS

The model developed by CSFP stands in direct contrast to CreditMetrics in its objectives and its theoretical foundations. CreditMetrics seeks to estimate the full *VAR* of a loan or loan portfolio by viewing rating upgrades and downgrades and the associated effects of spread changes in the discount rate as part of the *VAR* exposure of a loan. Credit Risk Plus views spread risk as part of market risk rather than credit risk. As a result, in any period, only two states of the world are considered—default and nondefault—and the focus is on measuring expected and unexpected losses rather than expected value and unexpected changes in value (or *VAR*) as under CreditMetrics. Thus, CreditMetrics is a mark-to-market (MTM) model; whereas Credit Risk Plus is a default mode (DM) model.

The second major difference is that, in CreditMetrics, the default probability in any year is discrete (as are the upgrade/downgrade probabilities). In Credit Risk Plus, default is modeled as a continuous variable with a probability distribution. An analogy from property fire insurance is relevant. When a whole portfolio of homes is insured, there is a small probability that each house will burn down, and (in general) the probability that each house will burn down can be viewed as an independent event.[4] Similarly, many types of loans, such as mortgages and small business loans, can be thought of in the same way, with respect to their default risk. Thus, under Credit Risk Plus, each individual loan is regarded as having a small probability of default, and each loan's probability of default is independent of the default on other loans.[5] This assumption makes the distribution of the default probabilities of a loan portfolio resemble a Poisson distribution.[6] The difference in assumptions regarding default probabilities, between Credit Risk Plus and CreditMetrics, is shown in Figure 8.1.

Default rate uncertainty is only one type of uncertainty modeled in Credit Risk Plus. A second type of uncertainty surrounds the size or severity of the losses themselves. Borrowing again from the fire insurance analogy, when a house "catches fire," the degree of loss severity can vary from the loss of a roof to the complete destruction of the house. In Credit Risk Plus, the fact that severity rates are uncertain is acknowledged, but because of the difficulty of measuring severity on an individual loan-by-loan basis, loss severities or loan exposures are rounded and banded (for example, into

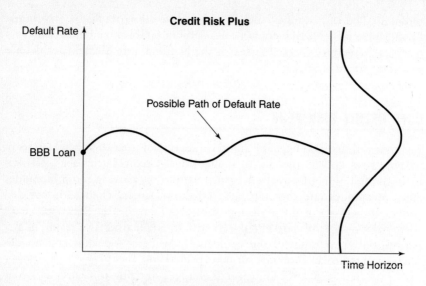

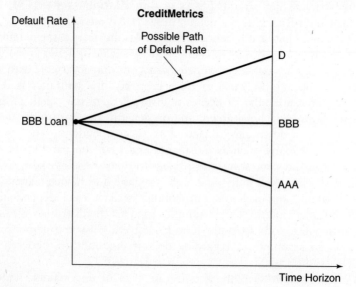

FIGURE 8.1 Comparison of Credit Risk Plus and CreditMetrics.

discrete $20,000 severity or loss bands). The smaller the bands, the less the degree of inaccuracy that is built into the model as a result of banding.

The two degrees of uncertainty—the frequency of defaults and the severity of losses—produce a distribution of losses for each exposure band. Summing (or accumulating) these losses across exposure bands produces a distribution of losses for the portfolio of loans. Figure 8.2 shows the link between the two types of uncertainty and the distribution of default losses. Although not labeled by CSFP as such, we call the model in Figure 8.2 *Model 1*. The computed loss function, assuming the Poisson distribution for individual default rates and the banding of losses, is shown in Figure 8.3. The loss function is quite "symmetric" and is close to the normal distribution, which it increasingly approximates as the number of loans in the portfolio increases. However, as discussed by CSFB (1997), default rates and loss rates tend to exhibit "fatter tails" than are implied by Figure 8.3. Specifically, the Poisson distribution implies that the mean default rate of a portfolio of loans should equal its variance, that is,

$$\sigma^2 = \text{mean} \tag{8.8}$$

or

$$\sigma = \sqrt{\text{mean}} \tag{8.9}$$

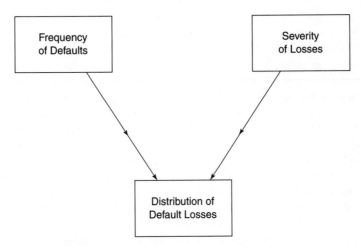

FIGURE 8.2 The CSFP Credit Risk Plus model.

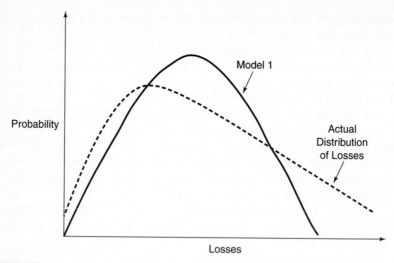

FIGURE 8.3 Distribution of losses with default rate uncertainty and severity uncertainty.

Using figures from Carty and Lieberman (1996) on default rates, CSFP shows that, in general, equation (8.9) does not hold, especially for lower quality credits. For B-rated bonds, Carty and Lieberman find the mean default rate is 7.62 percent and the square root of the mean is 2.76 percent, but the observed σ is 5.1 percent, or almost twice as large as the square root of the mean (see Figure 8.3). Thus, the Poisson distribution appears to underestimate the actual probability of default.

The question is: What extra degree of uncertainty might explain the higher variance (fatter tails) in observed loss distributions? The additional uncertainty modeled by CSFP is that the mean default rate itself can vary over time (or over the business cycle). For example, in economic expansions, the mean default rate will be low; whereas in economic contractions, it may rise significantly.[7] In the extended model (which we shall call Model 2), there are three types of uncertainty: (1) the uncertainty of the default rate around any given mean default rate, (2) the uncertainty about the severity of loss, and (3) the uncertainty about the mean default rate itself [modeled as a gamma distribution by CSFB (1997)]. Credit Risk Plus derives a closed-form solution for the loss distribution by assuming that these types of uncertainty are all independent.[8]

Appropriately modeled, a loss distribution can be generated along with expected losses and unexpected losses that exhibit observable fatter tails. The latter can then be used to calculate a capital requirement, as shown in

Figure 8.4. Note that this economic capital measure is not the same as the *VAR* measured in Chapter 6 under CreditMetrics because CreditMetrics allows for upgrades and downgrades that affect a loan's value. By contrast, there are no nondefault migrations in the CSFP model. Thus, the CSFP capital measure is closer to a loss-of-earnings or book-value capital measure than a full market value of economic capital measure. Nevertheless, its great advantage is in its parsimonious data requirements. The key data inputs are mean loss rates and loss severities, for various bands in the loan portfolio, both of which are potentially amenable to collection, either internally or externally. A simple "discrete" example of the CSFP Model 1 will illustrate the minimal data input that is required.

An Example

Suppose a bank divides its loan portfolio into exposure bands (denoted as v by CSFP); that is, it has many different sizes of loans, and each potentially has a different loss exposure. At the lowest end of the exposure levels, it identifies 100 loans, each of which has $20,000 of exposure.[9] We can think of this band ($v = 1$) as containing all loans for which the exposures, when rounded up to "the nearest $20,000," are $20,000. The next two exposure bands

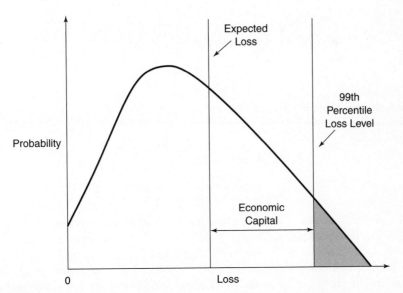

FIGURE 8.4 Capital requirement under the CSFP Credit Risk Plus model.

would represent all loans with a "rounded" exposure of \$40,000 ($v = 2$) and \$60,000 ($v = 3$), respectively.

As a first step, we want to compute the distribution of losses for the first band. In CSFP Credit Risk Plus, each band can be viewed as a separate portfolio, and the total loss distribution is then an aggregation of the (independent) individual loss distributions.

Suppose that, based on historic data, an average of 3 percent of loans with this level of loss exposure (\$20,000) default. There are currently 100 loans in the portfolio of this type, so the expected mean default rate (m) is 3. However, the actual default rate is uncertain and is assumed to follow a Poisson distribution (see Figure 8.1). Given this assumption, we can compute the probability of 0 defaults . . . n defaults, and so on, by using the formula, for the Poisson distribution:

$$\text{Prob. } (n \text{ defaults}) = \frac{e^{-m} m^n}{n!} \tag{8.10}$$

where e = exponential = 2.71828, m = mean number of defaults, $!$ = factorial, n = number of defaults of interest, $n = 1 \ldots N$.

Thus, the probability of 3 defaults is:[10]

$$\text{Prob. } (3 \text{ defaults}) = \frac{(2.71828)^{-3} \times 3^3}{3!}$$
$$= .224 = 22.4\%$$

and, the probability of 8 defaults is:

$$\text{Prob. } (8 \text{ defaults}) = \frac{(2.71828)^{-3} \times 3^8}{8!}$$
$$= .008 = 0.8\%$$

The probability that a different number of defaults will occur and the cumulative probabilities are listed in Table 8.2. The distribution of defaults for band 1 is shown in Figure 8.5. Calculation of the distribution of losses in band 1 is straightforward because, by assumption (and rounding), the loss severity is constant in the $v = 1$ band at \$20,000 per loan. Figure 8.6

TABLE 8.2 Calculation of the Probability of Default Using the Poisson Distribution

N	Probability	Cumulative Probability
0	0.049787	0.049789
1	0.149361	0.199148
2	0.224042	0.423190
3	0.224042	0.647232
⋮		
8	0.008102	0.996197

shows the distribution of losses where the mean number of defaults is 3. The expected loss is then \$60,000 (= 3 × \$20,000) in band 1 of the loan portfolio. The 99th percentile (unexpected) loss rate shows slightly less than 8 loans out of 100 defaulting, which puts the probability of 8 loans defaulting equal to 0.8 percent. Using 8 loans as an approximation,[11] the 99 percent unexpected loss rate is \$160,000 (= 8 × \$20,000) on portfolio $v = 1$. Viewed in isolation from the rest of the loan portfolio, the capital requirement would

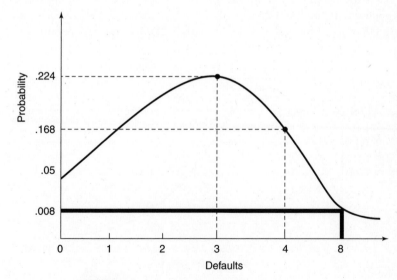

FIGURE 8.5 Distribution of defaults: Band 1.

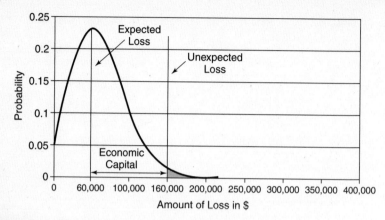

FIGURE 8.6 Loss Distribution for single loan portfolio. Severity rate = $20,000 per $100,000 loan.

be $100,000 (the unexpected loss minus the expected loss, or, $160,000 − $60,000).[12] This type of analysis would be repeated for each loss severity band—$40,000, $60,000, and so on—taking into account the mean default rates for these higher exposure bands and then aggregating the band exposures into a total loan loss distribution.

Continuing the discrete example of a CSFP-type model, suppose, for simplicity, that the band 2 portfolio ($v = 2$), with average loss exposure of $40,000, also contained 100 loans with a historic average default rate of

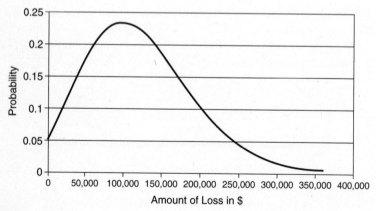

FIGURE 8.7 Single loan portfolio. Severity rate = $40,000 per $100,000 loan.

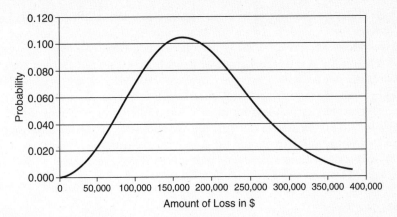

FIGURE 8.8 Loss distribution for two loan portfolios with severity rates of $20,000 and $40,000.

3 percent ($m = 3$). Figure 8.7 shows the loss distribution for the $40,000 band ($v = 2$) portfolio alone. Figure 8.8 shows the aggregation of losses across the two portfolio bands, $v = 1$ and $v = 2$. If these were the only types of loans made, this would be the loss distribution for the entire loan portfolio. Notice that, in adding the loan distributions for the two bands, the total loss distribution in Figure 8.8 looks more "normal" than the individual loss distributions for $v = 1$ and $v = 2$.[13]

Finally, this calculation is likely to underestimate the true capital requirement because we assumed that the mean default rate was constant in each band. To the extent that mean default rates themselves are variable (e.g., they increase systematically in each band as the "national" default rate increases), the loss distribution will have fatter tails than are implied in this example (and shown in Figure 8.8). Moreover, when the mean default rate in the economy varies and the default rates in each band are linked to economywide default rates, then the default rates in each band can no longer be viewed as independent. (There is a systematic default correlation element among loans; see Chapter 11.)[14] Indeed, exposure amounts themselves may even be affected by systemic risk factors; something not incorporated into even advanced versions of Credit Risk Plus.

SUMMARY

We have reviewed two insurance-based approaches to credit risk analysis. Mortality analysis offers an actuarial approach to predicting default rates, which might be thought of as an alternative to some of the traditional accounting-based models for calculating expected losses and loan loss reserves. However, the predictive usefulness of mortality rates very much depends on the size of the sample of loans/bonds from which they are calculated. Credit Risk Plus, an alternative to CreditMetrics, calculates capital requirements based on actuarial approaches found in the property insurance literature. Its major advantage is the rather minimal data input required (e.g., no data on credit spreads are required). Its major limitation is that it is not a full *VAR* model because it concentrates on loss rates rather than loan value changes. It is a default model (DM) rather than a mark-to-market (MTM) model.

CHAPTER 9

A Summary and Comparison of New Internal Model Approaches

In Chapters 4 through 8, we described key features of some of the more prominent new models of credit risk measurement. At first sight, these approaches appear to be very different and likely to produce considerably different loan loss exposures and *VAR* figures. This chapter summarizes these new models and discusses key differences and similarities among them. Empirical evidence on predictive differences among these models is also discussed.

MODEL COMPARISON

There are many dimensions along which to compare the new models. We focus on 10 key dimensions of five types of models:

1. Options pricing models such as KMV and Moody's (Chapter 4);
2. Reduced form models such as KPMG and Kamakura Corporation (Chapter 5);
3. *VAR* models such as CreditMetrics (Chapter 6);
4. Time varying models such as CreditPortfolio View (Chapter 7); and
5. Mortality models such as Credit Risk Plus (Chapter 8).

Analytically and empirically, these models are not as different as they may first appear. Indeed, similar arguments stressing the structural similarities have been made by Gordy (2000), Koyluoglu and Hickman (1999), and Crouhy et al. (2000), using different model anatomies. Table 9.1 lists the 10 dimensions for comparing the models. Each row of the table is discussed in turn.

TABLE 9.1 Comparison of Different Credit Risk Measurement Models

	CreditMetrics	CreditPortfolio View	Credit Risk Plus	Merton OPM KMV/Moody's	Reduced Form KPMG/Kamakura
Definition of risk	MTM	MTM or DM	DM	MTM or DM	MTM
Risk drivers	Asset values	Macroeconomic factors	Expected default rates	Asset values	Debt and equity prices
Data requirements	Historical transition matrix, credit spreads and yield curves, *LGD*, correlations, exposures	Historical transition matrix, macroeconomic variables, credit spreads, *LGD*, exposures	Default rates and volatility, macro factors, *LGD*, exposures	Equity prices, credit spreads, correlations, exposures	Debt and equity prices, historical transition matrix, correlations, exposures
Characterization of credit events	Credit migration	Migration conditional on macroeconomic factors	Actuarial random default rate	Distance to default: structural and empirical	Default intensity
Volatility of credit events	Constant or variable	Variable	Variable	Variable	Variable
Correlation of credit events	Multivariate normal asset returns	Macroeconomic factor loadings	Independence assumption or correlation with expected default rate	Multivariate normal asset returns	Poisson intensity processes with joint systemic factors
Recovery rates	Random (beta distribution)	Random	Constant within band	Constant or random	Constant or random
Numerical approach	Simulation or analytic	Simulation	Analytic	Analytic and econometric	Econometric
Interest rates	Constant	Constant	Constant	Constant	Stochastic
Risk classification	Ratings	Ratings	Exposure bands	Empirical EDF	Ratings or credit spreads

Definition of Risk

As described in Chapters 4 through 8, we need to distinguish between models that calculate *VAR* based on the change in the market value of loans [mark-to-market (MTM) models], and models that concentrate on predicting default losses [default mode (DM) models]. The MTM models allow for credit upgrades and downgrades as well as defaults in calculating loan value losses and gains and hence capital reserves. The DM models consider only two states of the world: default and no-default.

As discussed earlier, the key difference between the MTM and DM approaches is the inclusion of credit migration risk in MTM models. This is often referred to as *spread risk*. However, spread risk also includes the risk of changes in credit spreads for any given rating classification. Therefore, changes in valuation may result from (1) default, (2) changes in credit quality (e.g., ratings migration), and (3) changes in credit spreads that are not caused by credit quality changes. MTM models measure the first two of these components of valuation changes; the third is considered market risk and the 1996 market risk amendment of BIS I levies capital requirements to cover this component of spread risk.[1] In contrast, DM models measure changes in valuation resulting from default only. Not surprisingly, if models measure different things, they are likely to produce different results. CreditMetrics is an MTM model. Credit Risk Plus and KMV are essentially DM models. (Although, as discussed in Chapter 11, KMV also offers an MTM version.)[2] CreditPortfolio View can be used as either an MTM or a DM model. Reduced form models such as KPMG's LAS is an MTM model.

Risk Drivers

At first sight, the key risk drivers of these models appear to be quite different. CreditMetrics, KMV, and Moody's have their analytic foundations in a Merton-type options pricing model (OPM); a firm's asset values and the volatility of asset values are the key drivers of default risk. In CreditPortfolio View, the risk drivers are macroeconomic factors (such as the unemployment rate); in Credit Risk Plus, it is the mean level of default risk and its volatility; in reduced form models, it is the credit spreads obtained from risky debt yields. Yet, if couched in terms of multifactor models, all five models can be viewed as having similar roots.[3] Specifically, the variability of a firm's asset returns in CreditMetrics (as in KMV and Moody's) is modeled as being directly linked to the variability in a firm's stock returns. To the extent that multifactor asset pricing models drive all risky security prices, the credit spreads of reduced form models are driven by the same risk factors. In turn, in calculating correlations among firms' asset returns (see Chapter 11), the equities of individual firms are viewed as being driven by a set of systematic risk factors (industry factors, country factors, and so on) and unsystematic risk factors. The systematic risk factors, along with correlations among systematic risk factors (and their weighted importance), drive the asset returns of individual firms and the default correlations among firms.[4]

The risk drivers in CreditPortfolio View have origins similar to those of CreditMetrics. In particular, systematic countrywide macroeconomic factors and unsystematic macroeconomic shocks drive default risk and the correlations of default risks among borrowers. The key risk driver in Credit Risk Plus is the variable mean default rate in the economy. This mean default rate can be viewed as being linked systematically to the "state of the macroeconomy"; when the macro economy deteriorates, the mean default rate is likely to rise, as are default losses. An improvement in economic conditions has the opposite effect.

Thus, the risk drivers and correlations in all five models can be viewed as being linked, to some degree, to a set of macroeconomic and systematic risk factors that describe the evolution of economywide conditions.

Data Requirements

Where the five models differ considerably is in the format of the data required to estimate credit risk exposure. Indeed, participants in the IIF/ISDA study of credit risk modeling (to be discussed later in this chapter) noted the critical role of data management and standardization in obtaining usable estimates from any model. Historical transition matrices represent the fundamental data input for CreditMetrics, CreditPortfolio View, and KPMG's LAS. In contrast, Credit Risk Plus is built around mortality tables used to estimate the default rate distribution for each exposure band. Because of Credit Risk Plus' light data requirements, it can be most readily applied to retail portfolios. In contrast, KMV, Moody's, and Kamakura require a series of security prices consisting of risky debt, risk-free debt, and equity prices. All models input credit exposures from the portfolio's composition. As Table 9.1 shows, most models input asset correlations, with the exception of CreditPortfolio View, which estimates asset correlations with common macroeconomic risk factors and Credit Risk Plus, in which correlations are obtained from default distributions conditional on macroeconomic factors.

Characterization of Credit Events

A credit event is said to occur when there is a material change in the creditworthiness of a particular obligation. In CreditMetrics and CreditPortfolio View, a credit event occurs whenever there is a rating migration. KMV and Moody's characterize a credit event as a change in the distance to default, resulting in a change in the empirical *EDF*. In Chapter 4, we demonstrated that rating changes lag behind empirical *EDF* changes in forecasting changes in credit quality. Therefore, credit events are realized with greater speed and frequency in KMV and Moody's than in CreditMetrics and CreditPortfolio View.

Similar in focus to KMV and Moody's is the reduced form KPMG LAS and Kamakura models. Because they also rely on market prices (of debt and equity), reduced form models show greater sensitivity to credit events, defined as changes in the default intensity, than a model such as Credit Risk Plus, which limits characterization of credit events to default since it is a pure DM. However, changes in the actuarial default rate could be considered a deterioration in credit quality. Because the distribution of the mean actuarial default rate is estimated from mortality rates, Credit Risk Plus definitions of credit events are related to ratings transitions, at least for the entry that measures the probability of default.

Volatility of Credit Events

A key difference among the models is in the modeling of the one-year default probability or the probability of default distribution function. In CreditMetrics, the probability of default (as well as upgrades and downgrades) is modeled as a fixed or discrete value based on historic data. In KMV and Moody's, expected default frequencies (*EDF*s) vary as new information is impounded in stock prices. Changes in stock prices and the volatility of stock prices underlie empirical *EDF* scores. Similarly, changes in debt and equity prices drive changes in default intensities estimated by Kamakura's reduced form model. In CreditPortfolio View, the probability of default is a logistic function of a set of macroeconomic factors and shocks that are normally distributed; thus, as the macroeconomy evolves, so will the probability of default and the cells, or probabilities, in the rest of the transition matrix. In Credit Risk Plus, the probability of each loan's defaulting is viewed as variable, conforming to a Poisson distribution around some mean default rate. In turn, the mean default rate is modeled as a variable with a gamma distribution. This produces a distribution of losses that may have fatter tails than those produced by either CreditMetrics or CreditPortfolio View.

Correlation of Credit Events

The similarity of the determinants of credit risk correlations has already been discussed in the context of risk drivers. Specifically, the correlation structure in all five models can be linked to systematic linkages of loans to key factors. The correlations among borrowers will be discussed in greater length in Chapters 10 through 12, where the application of the new models, and modern portfolio theory, to the credit portfolio decision is analyzed.

Recovery Rates

The distribution of losses and *VAR* calculations depend not only on the probability of defaults but also on the severity of losses or loss given default. Empirical evidence suggests that default severities and recoveries are quite volatile over time. Further, building in a volatile recovery rate is likely to increase the *VAR* or unexpected loss rate. (See, for example, the discussion on CreditMetrics in Chapter 6.)

CreditMetrics, in the context of its *VAR* calculations, allows for recoveries to be variable. In the normal distribution version of the model, the estimated standard deviation of recoveries is built in to the *VAR* calculation. In the "actual" distribution version which recognizes a skew in the tail of the loan value loss distribution function, recoveries are assumed to follow a beta distribution, and the *VAR* of loans is calculated via a Monte Carlo simulation. In KMV's simplest model, recoveries are viewed as a constant. In extended versions of the model, recoveries are allowed to follow a beta distribution as well. In CreditPortfolio View, recoveries are also estimated via a Monte Carlo simulation approach and severities are drawn from a beta distribution. By contrast, under Credit Risk Plus, loss severities are rounded and banded into subportfolios, and the loss severity in any subportfolio is viewed as a constant. In reduced form models, the recovery rate is estimated from debt and equity prices, and either follows a stochastic process (Kamakura) or else is assumed to be constant (KPMG).

Numerical Approach

The numerical approach to estimation of *VAR*s, or unexpected losses, also differs across models. A *VAR*, at both the individual loan level and the portfolio-of-loans level, can be calculated analytically under CreditMetrics, but this approach becomes increasingly intractable as the number of loans in the portfolio increases. (This is discussed in more detail in Chapter 11.) As a result, for large loan portfolios, Monte Carlo simulation techniques are used to generate an "approximate" aggregate distribution of portfolio loan values and hence a *VAR*. Similarly, CreditPortfolio View uses repeated Monte Carlo simulations to generate macro shocks and the distribution of losses (or loan values) on a loan portfolio. By comparison, Credit Risk Plus, based on its convenient distributional assumptions (the Poisson distribution for individual loans and the gamma distribution for the mean default rate, along with the fixed recovery assumption for loan losses in each subportfolio of loans), allows an analytic or closed-form solution to be generated for the probability density function of losses. KMV also allows an analytic solution to the loss function as well as a Monte Carlo simulation solution. Moody's combines the analytic and econometric approaches. Finally, the reduced form models utilize a closed form, econometric approach to solve for the form of the intensity process.

Interest Rates

Although several academic (structural) models have incorporated stochastic interest rates into the credit risk measurement models, most of the basic commercial models assume constant interest rates (i.e., assuming a stable yield curve). Indeed, CreditMetrics even assumes a fixed credit spread. Only reduced form models (e.g., Kamakura) explicitly model the stochastic processes governing interest rate fluctuations.

Risk Classification

A critical step in implementing credit risk models is the risk classification of each obligation. This is particularly difficult for loan portfolios, since most of the obligations are untraded. That is, there is no external risk classification of loans for the most part, whereas rating systems and credit spreads are available for risky debt securities. In Chapter 2, we discussed the internal ratings systems and credit scoring models that have been developed by financial institutions to remedy this problem. CreditMetrics, CreditPortfolio View, and KPMG's LAS utilize ratings (either external or internal) to classify risk. Credit Risk Plus uses exposure bands to classify the default risk of any obligation. Reduced form models use default intensity levels. Finally, KMV and Moody's estimate empirical *EDF*s. The differences in these methodologies imply that the same loan may be classified differently by each of the different models. The question is whether these classification differences significantly impact the measure of credit risk. To answer this question, we examine comparative studies that measure the credit risk of a standardized portfolio using each of the different credit risk models.

COMPARATIVE STUDIES

Overview of the IIF/ISDA (2000) Study

In February 2000, the International Swaps and Derivatives Association (ISDA) and the Institute of International Finance (IIF) published the results of an ambitious joint project to test credit risk measurement models in 25 commercial banks from 10 countries with varying sizes and specialties. In the report, hereinafter referred to as IIF/ISDA, four models (CreditMetrics,

CreditPortfolio View, Credit Risk Plus, and KMV's Portfolio Manager) were compared to internal models for standardized portfolios (without option components) created to replicate four markets: corporate bonds and loans, middle markets, mortgages,[5] and retail credits. The most important conclusions of the study are:[6]

- Models yield directionally consistent outputs when given similar inputs. For some model types, the outputs are almost identical.
- Where there are discrepancies, they reflect differences in: model inputs, preprocessing (i.e., packaging transactions into a readable format), valuation, errors in model usage during testing, and misunderstandings by participants regarding application of standardized parameters.
- Substantive differences in results across models can be attributed to different approaches to valuations and correlation calculation methods. Model outputs are significantly affected by: valuation methods, changes in spreads, discount rates, and the treatment of cash flows.
- The most significant drivers of portfolio risk are credit quality (tested by subjecting portfolios to specified downgrade scenarios), asset correlation, and loss given default.
- Internal models focus on scoring methodologies and aggregate measures of default, not default probabilities and credit migrations.

IIF/ISDA Results on the Portfolio of Corporate Bonds and Loans   Two hypothetical portfolios were created for testing purposes: a small portfolio valued at US\$12,543.3 million consisting of 588 obligors, and a large portfolio valued at US\$50,173.3 million consisting of four times as many (2,352) obligors. In both portfolios, 39 percent of the exposures were rated below investment grade. The recovery rate was set at 60 percent for loans and 40 percent for bonds (implying $LGD = 40$ percent for loans and $LGD = 60$ percent for bonds). The standard deviation of the recovery rate was set at 25 percent for loans and 20 percent for bonds. The median 1 percent *VAR* risk value on the small (large) corporate bond portfolio was calculated as 4.4 (4.1) percent.

Table 9.2 shows that the models are quite consistent when it came to measuring expected losses, *EL*. KMV's lower estimates for *EL* can be attributed to the risk-neutral pricing technique. That is, risk-neutral expected cash flows are computed by multiplying risky cash flows by a forward *QDF*. Then each of these risk-free cash flows are discounted at the forward risk-free rate (see Appendix 11.1). Alternatively, the KMV model also utilizes a matrix pricing approach that discounts the risky cash flows at a risk adjusted rate (i.e., the risk adjusted discount rate consists of a fixed credit

TABLE 9.2 Summary of IIF/ISDA Results for the Portfolio of Corporate Bonds and Loans

Model	Exposure ($)	Expected Loss (%)	Unexpected Loss (%)	1% VAR
Small Portfolio				
Median values	12,439	1.7	1.9	4.4
Credit Risk Plus	12,484	1.7	1.9	6.9
CreditMetrics	12,439	1.7	1.5	4.4
KMV	11,654	1.0	2.0	3.6
Internal models	12,412	1.7	1.3	4.7
Large Portfolio				
Median values	49,730	1.7	1.5	4.1
Credit risk plus	49,786	1.7	1.8	6.4
CreditMetrics	49,726	1.7	1.4	4.0
KMV	48,834	1.1	1.6	3.3
Internal models	49,845	1.9	1.7	4.9
Scenario Analysis				
Reduced asset correlations CR+	12,543	1.7	0.8	2.2
2-notch downgrade KMV (book values)	50,173	5.6	2.7	7.9
All investment grade (book values) CreditMetrics	30,712	0.4	0.1	0.5
All noninvestment grade (book values) CreditMetrics	19,466	4.5	2.7	8.5

Source: IIF/ISDA Study, Chapter I, pp. 13–14. The results assume that all assets in the portfolio are carried at market value except if noted otherwise. Reprinted with permission from the Institute of International Finance. The complete study is available for purchase from http://www.iif.org.

spread plus the risk-free rate). This matrix pricing approach follows the valuation methodology used by CreditMetrics (see Appendix 6.1). Therefore, it is not surprising that KMV estimates of *EL* using the matrix pricing approach are consistent with those obtained from CreditMetrics.

Sensitivity tests were performed on the base case scenario for selected models and selected portfolios. Decreases in correlations caused the risk estimates to drop considerably for all models. For example, Table 9.2 shows that the Credit Risk Plus estimates of the 1 percent *VAR* for the small portfolio dropped from 6.9 to 2.2 upon assumption of a uniform 0 percent asset correlation. Credit quality also was found to be a key credit risk driver. For example, Table 9.2 shows that a two-notch downgrade in credit quality caused the large portfolio's 1 percent *VAR*, computed using KMV's Portfolio Manager, to increase from 3.3 percent to 7.9 percent. In other sensitivity tests shown in Table 9.2, if the entire large portfolio consisted of investment grade debt only, then the 1 percent *VAR* estimated using CreditMetrics, decreased from 4.0 percent to 0.5 percent. Finally, in the last row of Table 9.2, if all debt were non-investment grade, then the 1 percent *VAR* for the large portfolio measured by CreditMetrics increased to 8.5 percent.

IIF/ISDA Results on the Middle Market Portfolio   The results for the middle markets, mortgages, and retail credit showed a greater range of credit risk estimates than was obtained for the corporate portfolio. Moreover, proprietary internal models were used most often by the banks participating in the survey for the middle markets portfolio as compared to any other portfolio. These internal models typically focused on default only. The standardized test portfolio for middle markets was a composite of 2,500 real-world exposures, averaging £894,000 per obligor. Five percent of the total exposures came from one obligor and the next five obligors represented an additional 6 percent of the exposures. To replicate portfolio concentration, all exposures were assumed to be in the United Kingdom.

As shown in Table 9.3, there were significant differences in the risk measures estimated by the different models for the middle market portfolio.

TABLE 9.3   Summary of IIF/ISDA Results for the Middle Market Portfolio

Model	Exposure GBP Millions	Expected Loss (%)	Unexpected Loss (%)	1% VAR
Median values	2,276	0.6	N/A	2.4
CreditMetrics	2,276	0.6	0.4	1.6
KMV	2,276	0.6	0.7	3.0
Internal models	2,276	0.4–0.7	0.3–1.1	2.3–6.6
Migration Risk				
CreditMetrics	2,283	0.6	0.5	1.8
KMV	2,213	0.6	1.6	4.2
Internal models	2,276	0.1	0.7	1.5

Source: IIF/ISDA Study, Chapter I, pp. 21–23. The results assume that all assets in the portfolio are carried at market value. Reprinted with permission from the Institute of International Finance. The complete study is available for purchase from http://www.iif.org.

KMV generated 1 percent *VAR* estimates of 3.0 percent in contrast to the CreditMetrics estimates of 1.6 percent. Part of this discrepancy may be the result of differences in maturity assumptions; the KMV users rounded maturities of less than one year to one year, whereas CreditMetrics users left all maturities as specified in the portfolio. Moreover, the corporate bond and loan portfolio was standardized for an entire range of model parameters (see discussion in previous section). In contrast, the middle market portfolio left more flexibility for individual interpretation.[7] This may account for the greater variability in outputs shown in Table 9.3 as compared to Table 9.2. Examining the source of this variability, IIF/ISDA found that migration risk increases estimates of unexpected losses (*UL*) and *VAR* estimates for all models in Table 9.3. The one exception is for the internal models. However, the low amount of credit risk estimates for the internal model shown in Table 9.3 stems from the model's assumption that it takes a certain amount of time for a loan to migrate to default.

IIF/ISDA Results on the Retail Portfolio   Only KMV's Portfolio Manager was tested against internal models for the retail portfolio,[8] using two alternative (small and large) standardized portfolios. The median 99.97 percentile *VAR* estimate for the small (large) portfolio using KMV was 3.6 (2.3) percent, whereas for internal models the 99.97 percentile *VAR* was 3.2 (2.7) percent. The lower risk estimates for the large portfolio reflect the benefit of diversification.[9] Scenario analysis was performed on the retail portfolio to measure the sensitivity of credit risk measures to correlations, domestic macroeconomic factors, *LGD,* and credit quality. As expected, credit risk estimates increase with increases in correlations, domestic risk factors, *LGD,* and default probability. For example, *VAR* estimates obtained using KMV increased from 0.9 when *LGD* was set equal to 25 percent to 2.7 when *LGD* was set equal to 90 percent. In another scenario, default probabilities across the board were doubled, resulting in an increase in the KMV estimate of *VAR* from 2.9 percent to 4.8 percent for the small retail portfolio. Doubling both default probabilities and asset correlations together magnified the impact on *VAR*, causing a further increase in the KMV estimate of *VAR* to 8.1 percent.

Other Comparative Studies

The usual approach to comparisons of credit risk measurement models has been to make the definition of risk and the assumption about recoveries common, and to concentrate on modeling the effects of other assumptions on the loss distributions. In particular, Crouhy et al. (2000) compare

CreditMetrics (DM version) and Credit Risk Plus with KMV and CIBC's (Canadian Imperial Bank of Commerce) own internal model (Credit *VAR* 1). Examining a diversified portfolio of more than 1,800 bonds across 13 currencies and a whole spectrum of qualities and maturities, they find that unexpected losses fall in quite a narrow range.

Gordy (2000) shows the structural similarities between Credit Risk Plus and CreditMetrics. In CreditMetrics, the default probabilities are assumed to be conditional on cutoff values corresponding to historic transition matrices, presumably driven by macroeconomic factors.[10] Similarly, Credit Risk Plus directly models the probability of default conditional on historical macroeconomic risk factors. The differences between these models are limited to distributional assumptions and functional forms, not substance. However, it would be wrong to ignore the importance of distributional assumptions and parameter calibration on model results. CreditMetrics assumes that the macroeconomic factors are normally distributed, whereas Credit Risk Plus assumes that the mean default probability follows a gamma distribution. These distributional differences can have significant impacts on model estimates.[11] For instance, Gordy (2000) finds that the constrained form of CreditMetrics produced unexpected loss values similar to those of Credit Risk Plus, as long as the volatility (σ) of the mean default rate (systematic risk factor) followed its historically estimated value. However, for extremely large values of the volatility of the mean default rate, the unexpected loss figures of the two models began to diverge. This occurred because of (1) the greater kurtotic nature of the loss tails under the Credit Risk Plus model and (2) the fact that the kurtosis and fat tailedness of Credit Risk Plus directly depend on the value of σ.

The importance of model parameters in driving credit risk estimates was underscored by Koyluoglu and Hickman (1999), who conduct a study on the default mode (DM) versions of three models with fixed recovery rates. Using a statistic that measured the degree of agreement in the tails ($\bar{p} + 2\sigma$ to infinity) of default rate distributions, they find that the degree of similarity depended crucially on the extent to which they harmonized key parameter values across the three models (CreditMetrics, CreditPortfolio View, and Credit Risk Plus). In particular, "unsurprisingly, when the parameters do not imply consistent mean and standard deviation of default rate distributions, the result is that the models are significantly different" (p. 15).

Koyluoglu et al. (1999) suggest that comparative studies should focus more on differential parameter assumptions as opposed to the similar structural nature across models. Using a simulated corporate loan portfolio to compare the DM versions of CreditMetrics, KMV's Portfolio Manager, Credit Risk Plus, a simplified Merton OPM, and a Markowitz portfolio approach (see Chapter 10), they find significant discrepancies in estimates of

EL, UL, and *VAR* resulting from parameter inconsistency and model mis-specification. Simply reestimating each model using the same portfolio did not eliminate these discrepancies. In particular, potential sources of inconsistencies include differences across empirical *EDF* calibrations, recovery rates, exposure amounts, and asset correlations. For example, using the same database, CreditMetrics and KMV assigned higher asset correlations than the other models, thereby resulting in higher 1 percent *VAR* levels (3.2 and 2.7 percent for CreditMetrics and KMV, respectively, as compared to 2.0 percent for Credit Risk Plus). This difference may result from the tendency of Credit Risk Plus' historically-based default volatility to understate true volatility.[12]

Koyluoglu et al. (1999) recommend segmenting the portfolio and re-estimating credit risk for each subportfolio separately. They show smaller discrepancies in estimates across models for portfolio segments as compared to the entire portfolio. For example, Figure 9.1 shows the discrepancies in unexpected losses (*UL*), as estimated by KMV's Portfolio Manager versus CreditMetrics. In contrast, Figures 9.2 and 9.3 show the model discrepancies in *UL* estimates when the portfolios are subdivided into high and low credit quality. The differences in asset correlations assigned by KMV versus CreditMetrics are smaller for high-quality loans than for a low-quality portfolio; that is, the greater discrepancies in model parameters for the low-quality portfolio distorts the estimates of *UL* when combined with a high-quality portfolio.

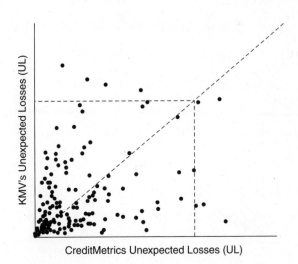

FIGURE 9.1   CreditMetrics versus KMV's Portfolio Manager: Entire portfolio. *Source:* Koyluoglu, Bangia, and Garside (1999).

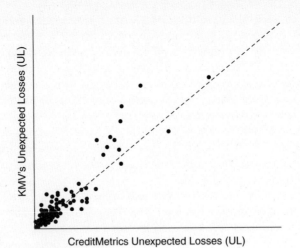

FIGURE 9.2 Unexpected losses for high credit quality portfolio. *Source:* Koyluoglu, Bangia, and Garside (1999).

Similarly, the discrepancy across models is less for high-credit quality port-folios than for low-credit quality portfolios when comparing Credit Risk Plus to KMV and CreditMetrics.

Another possible source of model discrepancy is the parameterization of *EDF.* Koyluoglu et al. (1999) estimate both KMV and Moody's empirical

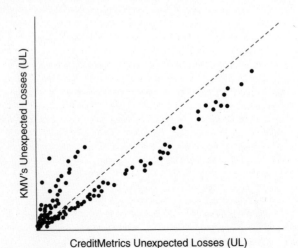

FIGURE 9.3 Unexpected losses for low credit quality portfolio. *Source:* Koyluoglu, Bangia, and Garside (1999).

*EDF*s (see Chapter 4) and find that the Moody's empirical *EDF* exceeded the KMV *EDF* for their sample of firms at a single point in time.[13] Table 9.4 shows the relative importance of parameter inconsistencies on estimates of *UL*—comparing differences in asset correlations (as discussed in the previous paragraph) to differences in empirical *EDF* calculations. For high-credit quality loans, the *EDF* effect dominates, whereas for low-credit quality loans, the correlation effect dominates.

Reduced form models can take on the structure of Merton-based options pricing models (OPM) with a few assumptions about the observability of asset values (see Chapter 5). Thus, it is perhaps not surprising that these models yield similar credit risk estimates. Keswami (1999) uses a portfolio of Brady bonds for Mexico, Argentina, and Venezuela in order to estimate credit risk using the Longstaff and Schwartz (1995) OPM and the intensity-based model of Duffee (1999) over the period 1993 to 1996. He finds that the credit risk estimates are comparable across models, with goodness of fit estimates ranging from 84.1 percent to 94.2 percent *R*-squared. Similarly, Finger (2000b) finds that the estimates of two-year default probabilities using advanced versions of CreditMetrics are quite close to those obtained using the Duffie and Singleton (1998) reduced form model for a portfolio consisting of investment grade debt with low asset correlations. However, the model estimates diverged widely for speculative grade portfolios as well as for portfolios comprised of investment grade debt with high correlations. Moreover, these discrepancies are compounded over a multiple year horizon. Finger (2000b) finds that the capital required to achieve a given target investment grade rating may vary by as much as a factor of two across models.

TABLE 9.4 Contribution of Parameter Discrepancies to Differences in Model Estimates of Unexpected Losses (*UL*)

Paramater Discrepancies	High Credit Quality Portfolio	Low Credit Quality Portfolio
Correlation effect	0.3 %	0.3 %
EDF effect	1.1 %	0.1 %
Combined effect	1.3 %	0.3 %

Note: The table shows the standard deviation of differences in marginal *UL* estimates normalized by the average *UL* for the portfolio using the following models: Credit Risk Plus, CreditMetrics, KMV Portfolio Manager, a simplified Merton OPM, and a Markowitz portfolio model. The correlation effect refers to discrepancies in estimates of asset correlations for the equal exposure case. The *EDF* effect compares the use of KMV versus Moody's empirical *EDF*s. Both the high- and low-credit quality portfolios each contain 180 obligors. *Source:* Koyluoglu et al. (1999), p. 25.

The comparative studies described in this chapter can be criticized on the grounds that they focus on the discrepancies among various credit risk measurement models, rather than on how accurate these models are at measuring the risks they purport to evaluate. This issue of back-testing (more fully discussed in Chapter 12) is a particular challenge for credit risk models since their conventional one-year time horizon limits the length of the times series of data available for testing. Lopez and Saidenberg (2000) suggest, but do not test a statistical test of model accuracy. Keswani (1999) finds that although an intensity-based model marginally outperforms a Merton OPM, the fitting errors rise by approximately 25 percent in out-of-sample tests using Brady bonds. Nickell et al. (2001b) compare credit risk estimates for a large portfolio of dollar-denominated Eurobonds using Creditmetrics and KMV's Portfolio Manager. They find that both models significantly underestimate the credit risks of the Eurobond portfolio. Thus, achieving consistency across models is of limited benefit if all of those consistent estimates are wrong.

SUMMARY

Comparison of credit risk measurement models reveals a large degree of consistency in underlying structure. However, differing parameter assumptions and functional forms can produce dramatically different credit risk estimates across different models. Thus, before a consensus model of credit risk measurement can emerge, there must be a consensus regarding data inputs and fundamental model assumptions. This process may be rather prolonged because of the data limitations inherent in measuring the credit risk of portfolios consisting of thinly traded debt instruments. In contrast, market risk models did not have to overcome these hurdles and therefore proceeded more rapidly in their theoretical and model development.

CHAPTER 10

Overview of Modern Portfolio Theory and Its Application to Loan Portfolios

So far, we have considered default-risk and credit risk exposure on a single-borrower basis. This is not unreasonable; much of the banking theory literature views the personnel at banks and similar financial institutions (FIs) as credit specialists who, through monitoring and the development of long-term relationships with customers, gain a comparative advantage in lending to a specific borrower or group of borrowers.[1]

This advantage, developed by making (and holding to maturity) loans to a select subset of long-term borrowers, may nevertheless be inefficient from a risk-return perspective. Suppose, instead, loans were publicly traded (or could be swapped with other FIs) and could be viewed as being similar to "commodity" type assets such as equities, which are freely traded at low transaction costs and with high liquidity in public securities markets. By separating the credit-granting decision from the credit portfolio management decision, a bank may be able to generate a better risk-return trade-off and offset what KMV and others have called the "paradox of credit."

In Figure 10.1, which illustrates the paradox of credit, portfolio A is a relatively concentrated loan portfolio for a traditional bank that makes and monitors loans, and holds those loans to maturity. Portfolios B and C are on the "efficient frontier" of loan portfolios. They achieve either the maximum return for any level of risk (B) or the minimum risk for a given expected return (C). To move from A to either B or C, the bank must actively manage its loan portfolio in a manner similar to the tenets of modern portfolio theory (MPT), where the key focus for improving the risk-return trade-off is on (1) the (default) correlations among the assets held in the portfolio and (2) a willingness, as market conditions change, to flexibly adjust the amount of different assets held, rather than to make and hold loans to maturity, as is the practice under traditional relationship banking.

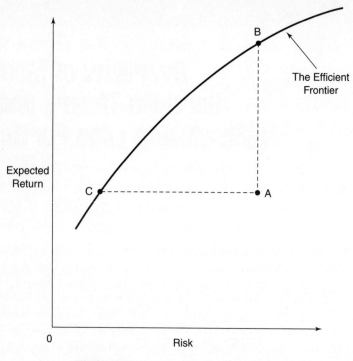

FIGURE 10.1   The paradox of credit.

In this chapter, we first describe the main features of MPT and then raise important issues regarding applications of MPT to nontraded loans and bonds.

MODERN PORTFOLIO THEORY: AN OVERVIEW

The (mean) return and risk of a portfolio of assets, under the assumption that returns on individual assets are normally distributed (or that asset managers have a quadratic utility function), are given in equations (10.1), (10.2), and (10.3). An assumption either that individual asset returns are normally distributed or that managers of an FI exhibit a particular set of preferences (quadratic utility) toward returns implies that only two moments of the distribution of asset returns are necessary to analyze portfolio decisions: (1) the mean return of a portfolio and (2) its variance (or the standard deviation of the returns on that portfolio). MPT itself, being

based on expected returns and risks, is forward-looking; these, by definition, are unobservable. As a result, portfolio returns and risks are usually
estimated from historic time series of the returns and risks on individual
assets.

Given these assumptions, the mean return on a portfolio of assets ($\bar{R}_p$)
and the variance of returns (σ_p^2) on a portfolio of assets can be computed
as:

$$\bar{R}_p = \sum_{i=1}^{n} X_i \bar{R}_i \tag{10.1}$$

$$\sigma_p^2 = \sum_{i=1}^{n} X_i^2 \sigma_i^2 + \sum_{i=1}^{n} \sum_{\substack{j=1 \\ i \neq j}}^{n} X_i X_j \sigma_{ij} \tag{10.2}$$

or

$$\sigma_p^2 = \sum_{i=1}^{n} X_i^2 \sigma_i^2 + \sum_{i=1}^{n} \sum_{\substack{j=1 \\ i \neq j}}^{n} X_i X_j \rho_{ij} \sigma_i \sigma_j \tag{10.3}$$

where $\bar{R}_p$ = the mean return on the asset portfolio,
Σ = summation,
$\bar{R}_i$ = the mean return on the ith asset in the portfolio,
X_i = the proportion of the asset portfolio invested in the ith
asset; and $i = 1, \ldots, n$,
σ_i^2 = the variance of returns on the ith asset,
σ_{ij} = the covariance of returns between the ith and jth assets,
ρ_{ij} = the correlation between the returns on the ith and jth
assets, and $-1 \leq \rho_{ij} \leq +1$

From equation (10.1), the mean return on a portfolio of assets ($\bar{R}_p$) is
simply a weighted (X_i) sum of the mean returns on the individual assets in
that portfolio ($\bar{R}_i$). By comparison, the variance of returns on a portfolio of
assets (σ_p^2) is decomposable into two terms. The first term reflects the
weighted (X_i^2) sum of the variances of returns on the individual assets (σ_i^2),

and the second term reflects the weighted sums of the covariances among the assets (σ_{ij}). Because a covariance is unbounded, it is common in MPT-type models to substitute the correlation among asset returns for the covariance term, using the statistical definition:

$$\sigma_{ij} = \rho_{ij}\sigma_i\sigma_j \qquad (10.4)$$

Because a correlation is constrained to lie between plus and minus unity, we can evaluate the effect of ρ_{ij} varying on asset portfolio risk. For example, in the two-asset case, if ρ_{ij} is negative, the second term in equation (10.3) will also be negative and will offset the first term, which will always be positive.[2] By appropriately exploiting correlation relationships among assets, a portfolio manager can significantly reduce risk and improve a portfolio's risk-return trade-off (which, in the context of Figure 10.1, is to move the portfolio from A to B or C).[3] Computationally, the efficient frontier, or the portfolio of assets with the lowest risk for any given level of return, can be calculated by solving for the asset proportions (X_j) that minimize σ_p for each given level of returns ($\overline{R}_p$). Both B and C are efficient asset portfolios in this sense.

The best of all the risky asset portfolios on the efficient frontier is the one that exhibits the highest excess return over the risk-free rate (r_f) relative to the level of portfolio risk, or the highest risk-adjusted excess return:

$$\frac{\overline{R}_p - r_f}{\sigma_p} \qquad (10.5)$$

This risk-return ratio is usually called the *Sharpe ratio*. Diagrammatically, the optimal risky asset portfolio is the one in which a line drawn from the return axis, with an origin at r_f is just tangential to the efficient frontier (this is shown as portfolio D in Figure 10.2). Because the slope of this line reflects the $(\overline{R}_p - r_f)/\sigma_p$ ratio for that portfolio, it is also the portfolio with the highest Sharpe ratio.[4]

APPLYING MPT TO NONTRADED BONDS AND LOANS

For over 40 years, MPT has been a portfolio management tool commonly used by most mutual fund and pension fund managers. It has also been applied with some success to publicly traded junk bonds when their returns

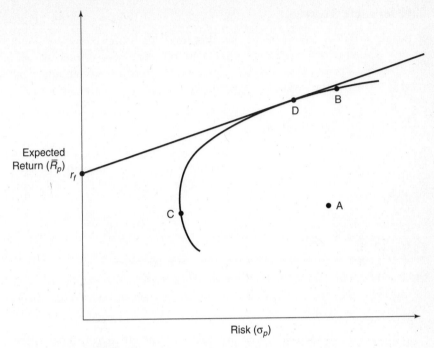

FIGURE 10.2 The optimum risky loan portfolio.

have tended to be more equity-like than bond-like and when historical returns are available [see Altman and Saunders (1997)]. With respect to most loans and bonds, however, there are problems with non-normal returns, unobservable returns, and unobservable correlations.

Non-Normal Returns

As discussed in Chapters 4 through 9, loans and bonds tend to have relatively fixed upside returns and long-tailed downside risks. Thus, returns on these assets tend to exhibit a strong negative skew and kurtosis (fat-tailedness) as well. MPT is built around a model in which only two moments—the mean and variance—are required to describe the whole distribution of returns. To the extent that the third (skewness) and fourth (kurtosis) moments of returns are important in fully describing the distribution of asset returns, the use of simple, two-moment, MPT models becomes difficult to justify.[5]

Unobservable Returns

A further problem relates to the fact that most loans and corporate bonds are not traded or are traded over-the-counter at very uneven intervals with little historical price or volume data. This makes it difficult to compute mean returns ($\overline{R_i}$) and the variance of returns (σ_i^2) using historic time series.

Unobservable Correlations

Relatedly, if price and return data are unavailable, calculating the covariance (σ_{ij}) or correlation (ρ_{ij}) among asset returns also becomes difficult. Yet, as discussed above, these correlations are a key building block in MPT-type analysis.

SUMMARY

MPT provides an extremely useful framework for a loan portfolio manager considering risk-return trade-offs. The lower the correlation among loans in a portfolio, the greater the potential for a manager to reduce a bank's risk exposure through diversification. Further, to the extent that a VAR-based capital requirement reflects the concentration risk and default correlations of the loan portfolio, such a portfolio may have lower credit risk than when loan exposures are considered independently additive (as under the standardized approach to BIS II capital requirements).

Unfortunately, there are a number of problems in applying MPT to loans (and many bonds)—in particular, the non-normality of loan returns and the unobservability of market-based loan returns (and, thus, correlations) as a result of the fact that most loans are "nontraded."[6] In the next chapter, we examine portfolio models suggested by KMV, CreditMetrics, and others in an attempt to overcome these problems. Specific attention will be given to how these models calculate returns, risk, and correlations of loans and loan portfolios.

CHAPTER 11

Loan Portfolio Selection and Risk Measurement

In this chapter, we look at a number of applications of MPT-type techniques to the loan portfolio. We distinguish between models that seek to calculate the full risk-return trade-off for a portfolio of loans (such as KMV's Portfolio Manager) and models that can be viewed as concentrating mostly on the risk dimension of a portfolio (such as intensity-based models and Credit Risk Plus).

KMV's PORTFOLIO MANAGER

KMV's Portfolio Manager can be viewed as a full-fledged MPT optimization approach because all three key variables—returns, risks, and correlations—are calculated. However, it can also be used to analyze risk effects alone, as will be discussed next. This section explains how the three key

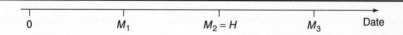

0	M_1	$M_2 = H$	M_3	Date

- If the loan's maturity is M_1, then the loan matures before the credit horizon, H.
- If the loan's maturity is M_2, then the loan matures at the credit risk horizon (simple case).
- If the loan's maturity is M_3, then the loan matures after the credit horizon.

Only when the loan's maturity exceeds the credit horizon (e.g., at maturity M_3) does the effect of credit migration on the loan portfolio value become important. See Appendix 11.1.

FIGURE 11.1   Loan maturity (M) versus loan horizon (H).

variables that enter into any MPT model can be calculated. In this model (as well as in Chapter 4) we assume that loans mature at or before the credit horizon (e.g., one year; maturity M_1 or M_2 in Figure 11.1). If loans mature beyond the credit horizon, credit migrations need to be accounted for between the horizon date and loan maturity. In this case (apart from using a different risk-neutral approach to valuing loan changes), KMV becomes quite similar to the CreditMetrics approach (discussed below) to portfolio risk calculations.

Returns

In the absence of historic returns on traded loans, the (expected) excess return over the risk-free rate on the ith loan (R_{it}) over any given horizon (t) can be set equal to:

$$R_{it} = \left[\text{Spread}_i + \text{Fees}_i\right] - \left[\text{Expected loss}_i\right] - r_f \qquad (11.1)$$

or:

$$R_{it} = \left[\text{Spread}_i + \text{Fees}_i\right] - \left[EDF_i \times LGD_i\right] - r_f \qquad (11.2)$$

The first component of returns is the spread of the loan rate over a benchmark rate such as the London Inter-Bank Offered Rate (LIBOR), plus any fees directly earned from the loan and expected over a given period (say, a year). Expected losses on the loan are then deducted because they can be viewed as part of the normal cost of doing banking business. In the context of a KMV-type model, where the expected default frequency (EDF) is calculated from stock returns (the Credit Monitor model), for any given borrower, expected losses will equal $EDF_i \times LGD_i$, where LGD_i is the loss given default for the ith borrower (usually estimated from the bank's internal database). KMV then deducts the risk-free rate, r_f, to present loan returns in an "excess return" format. If the bank desires, it can calculate the portfolio model using gross returns instead (i.e., not deducting r_f).[1]

Loan Risks

Assume that the loan matures on or before the chosen credit risk horizon date. In the absence of return data on loans, a loan's risk (σ_i) can be approximated by the unexpected loss rate on the loan (UL_i)—essentially, the variability of the loss rate around its expected loss value ($EDF_i \times LGD_i$). There are a number of ways in which UL_i might be calculated, depending on the assumptions made about the maturity of the loan relative to the credit horizon, the variability of *LGD*, and the correlation of loan *LGD*s with *EDF*s. For example, in the simplest form, when a loan matures before the horizon a DM model can be employed where the borrower either defaults or doesn't default (i.e., there are no credit migrations), so that defaults are binomially distributed with *LGD* assumed to be fixed across all borrowers. Then:

$$\sigma_i = UL_i = LGD \times \sqrt{(EDF_i)(1 - EDF_i)} \tag{11.3}$$

where $\sqrt{(EDF_i)(1 - EDF_i)}$ reflects the variability of a default rate frequency that is binomially distributed.[2] A slightly more sophisticated DM version would allow *LGD* to be variable, but factors affecting *EDF*s are assumed to be different from those affecting *LGD*s, which are assumed to be independent across borrowers.[3] In this case [see Kealhofer (1995)]:

$$\sigma_i = \sqrt{EDF_i(1 - EDF_i)\overline{LGD}_i^2 + EDF_i VOL_i^2} \tag{11.4}$$

where $\overline{LGD}_i$ is the expected value of *LGD*, and VOL_i is the standard deviation of borrower *i*'s *LGD*. Equation (11.4) can be generalized to solve for σ_i under a full MTM model with credit upgrades and downgrades as well as default. That is, for the case where the maturity of the loan exceeds the loan's credit horizon, the loan's risk is measured as:

$$\sigma_i = \sqrt{EDF_i(1 - EDF_i)\overline{LGD}_i^2 + EDF_i(VVOL_i)^2 + (1 - EDF_i)VVOL_i^2} \tag{11.4'}$$

where $VVOL_i$ (or valuation volatility) is the standard deviation of borrower *i*'s MTM loan value in the nondefault state. $VVOL_i$ can be viewed as the standard deviation of asset values and can be calculated using the methodology outlined in Chapter 4. However, in Chapter 4 we focused on the area under the valuation distribution that fell below the default point (i.e., the region in which the value of assets fell below the debt repayment). Here we examine only the distribution of asset values above the default point in order to estimate the *VVOL*.[4] Appendix 11.1 examines the calculation of *VVOL* in more detail.

Another difference between KMV's Portfolio Manager (PM) and the discussion of KMV in Chapter 4 is that PM does not assume normally distributed asset portfolios. Both an analytical approximation and the Monte Carlo method are used in the MTM version of PM so as to allow for the possibility of fat tails in the distribution of portfolio returns. The analytical approximation adjusts tail probabilities based on returns, the weighted average of individual loan ULs, and minimum and maximum possible portfolio values. The analytical approximation is most accurate for the 10-basis point level of tail risk (i.e., the worst one-thousandth possible outcomes). Monte Carlo simulation draws states of the world to estimate whether each borrower in the portfolio defaults and, if so, what the LGD would be, conditional on the random draw of overall business factors.[5] This process is repeated 50,000 to 200,000 to determine a frequency distribution that approximates the distribution of the portfolio's value.[6] Appendix 11.1 demonstrates this procedure.

Correlations

One important intuition from a KMV-type approach is that default correlations are "generally" likely to be low. To see why, consider the context of the two-state DM version of a KMV-type model. A default correlation would reflect the joint probability of two firms G and F—say, for example, General Electric and Ford—having their asset values fall below their debt values over the same horizon (say, one year). In the context of Figure 11.2, the General Electric asset value would have to fall below its debt value (B_G) in Figure 11.2, and the Ford asset value would have to fall below its debt value (B_F). The joint area of default is shaded, and the joint probability distribution of asset values are represented by the isocircles. The isocircles are similar to those used in geography charts to describe the topographical characteristics (e.g., height) of hills. The inner circle is the top of the hill (high probability), and the outer circles are the bottom of the hill (low probability). The joint probability that asset values will fall in the shaded region is low (as shown) and will depend, in part, on the asset correlations between the two borrowers.[7] The two graphs below and to the left of the graph of the isocircles represent the payoff on each firm's debt as a function of the market value of the firm's assets. In the context of the simple binomial DM model [for Ford (F) and General Electric (G)] the correlation between F and G (ρ_{GF}) is:

$$\rho_{GF} = \frac{COV_{GF}}{SD_F \times SD_G} \qquad (11.5)$$

or:

$$\rho_{GF} = \frac{JDF_{GF} - (EDF_G \times EDF_F)}{\sqrt{(EDF_G)(1 - EDF_G)}\sqrt{(EDF_F)(1 - EDF_F)}} \qquad (11.6)$$

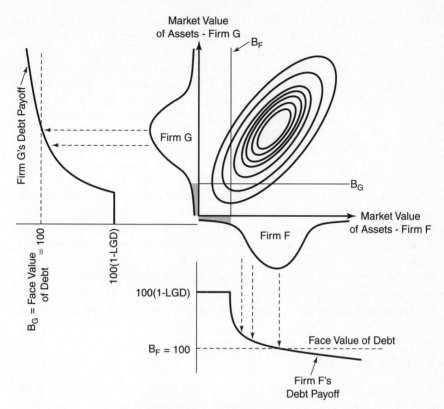

FIGURE 11.2 Value correlation.

The numerator of equation (11.6) is the covariance (COV_{GF}) between the asset values of the two firms, G and F. It reflects the difference between when the two asset values are jointly distributed (JDF_{GF}) and when they are independent $(EDF_G \times EDF_F)$.[8] The denominator reflects the standard deviation (SD) of default rates under the binomial distribution for each firm.

Although correlations may generally be "low," Figure 11.2 can be used to understand the dynamics of how correlations may rise over time. For example, KMV correlations among U.S. firms have recently been rising. To see why, note that the leverage ratios of U.S. corporations have more than doubled over the past decade (i.e., in the context of Figure 11.2, B_F and B_G have both shifted up along their respective axes) and thus the shaded area of joint default has expanded.[9]

Rather than seeking to directly estimate correlations using equation (11.6), KMV uses a multifactor stock-return model from which correlations are derived.[10] The model reflects the correlation among the systematic risk factors affecting each firm and their appropriate weights. KMV's multifactor approach to calculating correlations is somewhat similar to the CreditMetrics stock-return factor approach to correlation calculation discussed more fully later in this chapter, except that KMV uses asset correlations rather than equity correlations.[11] KMV typically finds that correlations lie in the range 0.002 to 0.15. Credit Risk Plus finds default correlations on the order of 0.01 to 0.05. Gupton (1997) employs Moody's data over the period 1970 through 1995 to obtain implied default correlations between 0.0013 and 0.033 using CreditMetrics.[12] The low correlations obtained using all of these models are consistent with evidence showing a significant reduction in credit risk for diversified debt portfolios. KMV shows that 54 percent of the risk can be diversified away by simply choosing a portfolio comprised of the debt issued by five different BBB rated firms.[13] Barnhill and Maxwell (2001) show that diversification can reduce a bond portfolio's standard deviation from $23,433 to $8,102 ($9,518) if the portfolio consists of 100 bonds from 24 industry sectors (a single sector). Carey (1998) also find significant diversification benefits across size, obligor concentration, and rating classification for a portfolio consisting of private placements.[14]

Calculating Correlations Using KMV's Portfolio Manager

To estimate correlations, KMV's Portfolio Manager decomposes asset returns into systematic and unsystematic risk using a three-level structural model. Asset returns are extracted from equity returns using the KMV Credit Manager approach outlined in Chapter 4 for imputing firm asset values. Using a time series of such asset values, asset returns can be calculated. Once asset returns are estimated, the first-level decomposition into risk factors is a single index model that regresses asset returns on a composite market factor that is constructed individually for each firm. The composite market factor used in the first-level analysis is comprised of a weighted sum of country and industry factors. These factors are estimated at the second level of analysis and may be correlated with each other.[15] The second level separates out the systematic component of industry and country risk, each of which is further decomposed into three sets of independent factors at the third level. These third-level factors are: (1) two global economic factors—a market-weighted index of returns for all firms and the return index weighted by the log of market values; (2) five regional factors—Europe, North America, Japan, Southeast Asia, and Australia/New Zealand; (3) seven sector factors—interest sensitive (banks, real estate, and utilities), extraction (oil and gas, mining), consumer nondurables, consumer durables, technology, medical services, and other (materials processing, chemicals, paper, steel production).[16]

For any firm k, the multifactor model is:

$$r_k = \sum_{G=1,2} \beta_{kG} r_G + \sum_{R=1,\ldots,5} \beta_{kR} r_R + \sum_{S=1,\ldots,7} \beta_{kS} r_S + \sum_I \beta_{kI} \varepsilon_I + \sum_C \beta_{kC} \varepsilon_C + \varepsilon_k \quad (11.7)$$

Third Level Factors   Second Level   First Level

where $\beta_{kG}, \beta_{kR}, \beta_{kS}$ = firm k's beta coefficients on global, regional, and sector factors (from the third regression level),

r_G = the return on the two independent global economic factors,

r_R = the return on the five independent regional economic factors,

r_S = the return on the seven independent industrial sector effects,

β_{kI}, β_{kC} = firm k's beta coefficients on the country and industry-specific systematic risk components (from the second level),

ε_I = the industry-specific effect for industry I,

ε_C = the country-specific effect for country C,

ε_k = firm k's company-specific risk (from the first level).

We can express the asset variance for firm k as follows:

$$\sigma_k^2 = \sum_{G=1,2} \beta_{kG}^2 \sigma_G^2 + \sum_{R=1,\ldots,5} \beta_{kR}^2 \sigma_R^2 + \sum_{S=1,\ldots,7} \beta_{kS}^2 \sigma_S^2 + \sum_I \beta_{kI}^2 \sigma_I^2 + \sum_C \beta_{kC}^2 \sigma_C + \varepsilon_k^2 \quad (11.8)$$

Equation (11.8) can be used to calculate correlations between firms j and k as follows:

$$\sigma_{jk} = \sum_{G=1,2} \beta_{jG} \beta_{kG} \sigma_G^2 + \sum_{R=1,\ldots,5} \beta_{jR} \beta_{kR} \sigma_R^2 + \sum_{S=1,\ldots,7} \beta_{jS} \beta_{kS} \sigma_S^2 + \sum_I \beta_{jI} \beta_{kI} \sigma_I^2 + \sum_C \beta_{jC} \beta_{kC} \sigma_C \quad (11.9)$$

Thus, the correlation coefficient between firms j and k is: $\rho_{jk} = \sigma_{jk}/\sigma_j\sigma_k$.

After they are calculated, the three inputs (returns, risks, and correlations) can be employed in a number of directions. One potential use would be to calculate a risk-return efficient frontier for the loan portfolio, as discussed in Chapter 10. Reportedly, one large Canadian bank manages its U.S. loan portfolio using a KMV-type model.[17]

A second use would be to measure the risk contribution of expanding lending to any given borrower. As discussed in Chapter 10, the risk (in a portfolio sense) of any one loan will not only depend on the risk of the individual loan on a stand-alone basis, but also on its correlation with the risks of other loans. For example, a loan, when viewed individually, might be thought to be risky, but because its returns are negatively correlated with other loans, it may be quite valuable in a "portfolio" context in constraining or lowering portfolio risk.

The effects of making additional loans to a particular borrower also depend crucially on assumptions made about the balance sheet constraint. For example, if investable or loanable funds are viewed as fixed, then expanding the proportion of assets lent to any borrower i (i.e., increasing X_i) means reducing the proportion invested in all other loans (assets). However, if the funds constraint is viewed as being nonbinding, then the amount lent to borrower i can be expanded without affecting the amount lent to other borrowers. In the KMV-type marginal risk contribution calculation, a funding constraint is assumed to be binding:

$$X_i + X_j + \ldots + X_n = 1$$

By comparison, under CreditMetrics (see the next section), marginal risk contributions are calculated assuming no such funding constraint; for example, a bank can make a loan to a twentieth borrower without reducing the loans outstanding to the nineteen other borrowers.

Assuming a binding funding constraint, the marginal risk contribution for the ith loan (MRC_i) can be calculated as:[18]

$$MRC_i = X_i \frac{d\,UL_p}{dX_i} \tag{11.10}$$

where UL_p is the risk (standard deviation) of the total loan portfolio p and X_i is the proportion of the loan portfolio made to the ith borrower:[19]

$$UL_p = \sqrt{\sum_{i=1}^{N} X_i^2 UL_i^2 + \sum_{i=1}^{N} \sum_{\substack{j=1 \\ i \neq j}}^{N} X_i X_j UL_i UL_j \rho_{ij}} \tag{11.11}$$

and

$$\sum_{i=1}^{N} X_i = 1$$

The marginal risk contribution can be viewed as a measure of the economic capital needed by the bank in order to make a new loan to the ith borrower because it reflects the sensitivity of portfolio risk (specifically, portfolio standard deviation) to a small percentage change in the weight of the asset (dX_i). Note that the sum of *MRCs* are equal to UL_p; consequently, the required capital for each loan is just its *MRC* scaled by the capital multiple (the ratio of capital to UL_p).[20]

CREDITMETRICS

Until recently, when a return dimension was added,[21] CreditMetrics could be viewed more as a loan portfolio *VAR* model (for economic capital calculations) rather than a full-fledged MPT risk-return optimization model. Here, we will concentrate on the measurement of the *VAR* for a loan portfolio. As with individual loans, two approaches to measuring portfolio *VAR* are considered:[22]

1. Loan portfolios are assumed to have normally distributed asset values.
2. The actual loan portfolio value distribution exhibits a long-tailed downside or negative skew.

We will first consider the normal distribution case, which produces a direct analytic solution to *VAR* calculations using conventional MPT techniques.

CreditMetrics: Portfolio *VAR* under the Normal Distribution

In the normal distribution model, a two-loan case provides a useful benchmark. A two-loan case is readily generalizable to the *N*-loan case; that is, the risk of a portfolio of *N* loans can be shown to depend on the risk of each pair of loans in the portfolio and the risk of each individual loan (see the later discussion and Appendix 11.2).

To calculate the *VAR* of a portfolio of two loans, we need to calculate: (1) the joint migration probabilities for each loan (assumed to be the $100 million face value BBB loan discussed in Chapter 6, and an A rated loan with $100 million face value) and (2) the joint payoffs or values of the loans for each possible one-year joint migration probability.

Joint Migration Probabilities

Table 11.1 shows the one-year individual and joint migration probabilities for the BBB and A loans.[23] Given eight possible credit states for the BBB borrower and eight possible credit states for the A borrower over the next year (the one-year horizon), there are 64 joint migration probabilities. (See the cells of Table 11.1.) Importantly, the joint migration probabilities are not simply the product of the two individual migration probabilities. This can be seen by looking at the independent probabilities that the BBB loan will remain BBB (.8693) and the A loan will remain single A (.9105) over the next year. The joint probability, assuming the correlation between the two migration probabilities is zero, would be:

$$.8693 \times .9105 = .7915 \text{ or } 79.15\%$$

Note that the joint probability in Table 11.1 is slightly higher, at 79.69 percent, because the (assumed) correlation is .3 between the two borrowers.

Adjusting the migration table to reflect correlations is a two-step process. First, an economic model is needed to motivate migration transitions. In CreditMetrics, a Merton-type model is used to link asset value or return volatility to discrete rating migrations for individual borrowers. Second, a model is needed to calculate the correlations among the asset value volatilities

TABLE 11.1 Joint Migration Probabilities with 0.30 Asset Correlation (%)

Obligor 1 (BBB)		Obligor 2 (A)							
		AAA	AA	A	BBB	BB	B	CCC	Default
		0.09	2.27	91.05	5.52	0.74	0.26	0.01	0.06
AAA	0.02	0.00	0.00	0.02	0.00	0.00	0.00	0.00	0.00
AA	0.33	0.00	0.04	0.29	0.00	0.00	0.00	0.00	0.00
A	5.95	0.02	0.39	5.44	0.08	0.01	0.00	0.00	0.00
BBB	86.93	0.07	1.81	<u>79.69</u>	4.55	0.57	0.19	0.01	0.04
BB	5.30	0.00	0.02	4.47	0.64	0.11	0.04	0.00	0.01
B	1.17	0.00	0.00	0.92	0.18	0.04	0.02	0.00	0.00
CCC	0.12	0.00	0.00	0.09	0.02	0.00	0.00	0.00	0.00
Default	0.18	0.00	0.00	0.13	0.04	0.01	0.00	0.00	0.00

Source: Gupton et al., *Technical Document,* April 2, 1997, p. 38.

of individual borrowers. Similar to KMV, asset values of borrowers are unobservable, as are correlations among those asset values. The correlations among the individual borrowers are therefore estimated from multifactor models driving borrowers' stock returns.

Example of the Link between Asset Volatilities and Rating Transitions

To see the link between asset volatilities and rating transitions, consider Figure 11.3, which links standardized normal asset return changes (measured in standard deviations) of a BB rated borrower to rating transitions.[24] If the unobservable (standardized) changes in asset values of the firm are assumed to be normally distributed around the firm's current asset value, we can calculate how many standard deviations asset values would have to change to move the firm from BB into default. For example, the historic one-year default probability of this type of BB borrower is 1.06 percent. Using the standardized normal distribution tables, asset values would have to fall by 2.3σ for the firm to default. Also, there is a 1 percent probability that the BB firm will move to a CCC rating over the year. Asset values would have to fall by at least 2.04σ to change the BB borrower's rating to CCC or below.[25] The full range of possibilities is graphed in Figure 11.3. Similar figures could be constructed for a BBB borrower, an A borrower, and so on. The links between asset volatility and rating changes for an A borrower are shown in Table 11.2.

From Figure 11.3, we can see that a BB rated borrower will remain BB as long as the standardized normal asset returns of the borrowing firm fluctuate between -1.23σ and $+1.37\sigma$. The A borrower's rating (see Table 11.2) will remain unchanged as long as the asset returns of the firm vary within

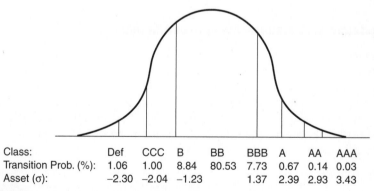

Class:	Def	CCC	B	BB	BBB	A	AA	AAA
Transition Prob. (%):	1.06	1.00	8.84	80.53	7.73	0.67	0.14	0.03
Asset (σ):	-2.30	-2.04	-1.23		1.37	2.39	2.93	3.43

FIGURE 11.3 The link between asset value volatility (σ) and rating transitions for a BB rated borrower.

TABLE 11.2 The Link between Asset Value Volatility (σ) and Rating Transitions for an A Rated Borrower

Class	Default	CCC	B	BB	BBB	A	AA	AAA
Transition probability	0.06	0.01	0.26	0.74	5.52	91.05	2.27	0.09
Asset (σ)	−3.24	−3.19	−2.72	−2.30	−1.51		1.98	3.12

the -1.51σ and $+1.98\sigma$ range. Assume for the sake of this example that the correlation (ρ) between those two firms' asset returns is .2 (to be calculated in more detail in the next section). The joint probability (Pr) that both borrowers will remain in the same rating class during the next year can be found by integrating the bivariate normal density function[26] as follows:

$$Pr\left(-1.23 < BB < 1.37, -1.51 < A < 1.98\right) = \int_{-1.23}^{1.37} \int_{-1.51}^{1.98} f\left(Y_1 Y_2 ; \rho\right) dY_2 dY_1 \quad (11.12)$$
$$= .7365$$

where Y_1 and Y_2 are random, and f is the joint probability distribution of asset values and $\rho = .20$.

In equation (11.12), the ρ (correlation coefficient's value) was assumed to be equal to .2. As described next, these correlations, in general, are calculated in CreditMetrics from multifactor models of stock returns for individual borrowers.[27] This contrasts with KMV, which deleverages equity returns in order to derive implied asset values and thus returns for individual borrowers.

Calculating Correlations Using CreditMetrics

Consider two firms, A and Z. We do not observe their asset values or returns, but we do observe their stock returns if both are publicly traded companies. The returns (R_A) on stocks of company A, a chemical company, are driven by a single industry index factor (R_{CHEM}, the returns on the chemical industry index) and some idiosyncratic risk (U_A) assumed to be diversifiable in a portfolio context. The estimated sensitivity of firm A's returns to the chemical industry's returns is .9. Thus:[28]

$$R_A = .9R_{CHEM} + U_A \quad (11.13)$$

Firm Z can be considered a universal bank. It has return sensitivity to two factors: the German banking industry return index (R_{BANK}) and the

German insurance industry return index (R_{INS}). The estimated independent factor sensitivities are, respectively, .15 and .74. Thus:

$$R_z = .74R_{INS} + .15R_{BANK} + U_Z \tag{11.14}$$

The correlation between the two firms, A and Z, will depend on the correlation between the chemical industry return index and the insurance industry return index and on the correlation between the chemical industry index and the banking industry index:[29]

$$\rho_{AZ} = (.9)(.74)(\rho_{CHEM,INS}) + (.9)(.15)(\rho_{CHEM,BANK}) \tag{11.15}$$

If the correlations $\rho_{CHEM,INS}$ and $\rho_{CHEM,BANK}$ are, respectively, .16 and .08, we have:

$$\rho_{AZ} = (.9)(.74)(.16) + (.9)(.15)(.08) = .1174$$

Firms A and Z have a low but positive default correlation. Correlation values calculated in a similar fashion are inserted into equation (11.12) to solve the bivariate normal density function and, thus, the joint migration probability in tables such as Table 11.1.

Joint Loan Values

In addition to 64 joint migration probabilities, we can calculate 64 joint loan values in the two-loan case. The market value for each loan in each credit state is calculated as in Chapter 6. Individual loan values are then added to get a portfolio loan value, as shown in Table 11.3. Thus, if, over the year, both loans get upgraded to AAA, Table 11.3 shows that the market value of the loan portfolio at the one-year horizon becomes $215.96 million. By comparison, if both loans default, the value of the loan portfolio becomes $102.26 million.

With 64 possible joint probabilities, p_i, and 64 possible loan values, V_i, the mean value of the portfolio and its variance are as computed in equations (11.16) and (11.17):

$$\text{Mean} = p_1 V_1 + p_2 V_2 + \ldots + p_{64} V_{64}$$
$$= \$213.63 \text{ million} \tag{11.16}$$

$$\text{Variance} = p_1 (V_1 - \text{Mean})^2 + p_2 (V_2 - \text{Mean})^2$$
$$+ \ldots + p_{64}(V_{64} - \text{Mean})^2 \tag{11.17}$$
$$= \$11.22 \text{ million}$$

TABLE 11.3   Loan Portfolio Values

	All Possible 64 Year-End Values for a Two-Loan Portfolio ($)							
		Obligor 2 (A)						
Obligor 1		AAA	AA	A	BBB	BB	B	CCC	Default
(BBB)		106.59	106.49	106.30	105.64	103.15	101.39	88.71	51.13
AAA	109.37	215.96	215.86	215.67	215.01	212.52	210.76	198.08	160.50
AA	109.19	215.78	215.68	215.49	214.83	212.34	210.58	197.90	160.32
A	108.66	215.25	215.15	214.96	214.30	211.81	210.05	197.37	159.79
BBB	107.55	214.14	214.04	<u>213.85</u>	213.19	210.70	208.94	196.26	158.68
BB	102.02	208.61	208.51	208.33	207.66	205.17	203.41	190.73	153.15
B	98.10	204.69	204.59	<u>204.40</u>	203.74	210.25	199.49	186.81	149.23
CCC	83.64	190.23	190.13	189.94	189.28	186.79	185.03	172.35	134.77
Default	51.13	157.72	157.62	157.43	156.77	154.28	152.52	139.84	102.26

Source: Gupton et al., *Technical Document,* April 2, 1997, p. 12.

Taking the square root of the solution to equation (11.17), the σ of the loan portfolio value is $3.35 million and the 99 percent *VAR* under the normal distribution is:

$$2.33 \times \$3.35 = \$7.81 \text{ million} \qquad (11.18)$$

Comparing this value of $7.81 million, for a loan portfolio face value of $200 million, with the 99 percent *VAR*-based capital requirement of $6.97 million, for the single BBB loan of $100 million in Chapter 6, we can see that although the loan portfolio has doubled in face value, a *VAR*-based capital requirement (based on the 99th percentile of the loan portfolio's value distribution) has increased by only $7.81 million − $6.97 million = $0.84 million. Perhaps even more illustrative of the diversification effects is that the bank's capital ratio falls from 6.97 percent to $7.81/$200 = 3.91 percent. The reason for this is portfolio diversification. Specifically, built into the joint transition probability matrix in Table 11.1 is an assumed correlation of .3 between the default risks of the two loans.

CreditMetrics: Portfolio *VAR* Using the Actual Distribution

Unfortunately, the capital requirement under the normal distribution is likely to underestimate the true 99 percent *VAR* because of the skewness in the actual distribution of loan values. Using Table 11.1 in conjunction with Table 11.3, the 99 percent (worst) loan value for the portfolio is $204.40 million.[30] Thus, the unexpected change in value of the portfolio from its mean value is:

$$\$213.63 \text{ million} - \$204.40 \text{ million} = \$9.23 \text{ million}$$

This is higher than the capital requirement under the normal distribution discussed earlier ($9.23 million versus $7.81 million), but the benefits of portfolio diversification are clear. In particular, the capital requirement of $9.23 million for the combined $200 million face-value portfolio can be favorably compared to the $14.8 million 99 percent *VAR* using the actual distribution for the single BBB loan of $100 million face value calculated in Chapter 6.[31]

CreditMetrics with Large *N* Loans

The normal distribution model can be extended in either of two directions. The first option is to keep expanding the loan joint transition matrix by directly or analytically computing the mean and standard deviation of the portfolio. This, however, rapidly becomes computationally difficult. For example, in a five-loan portfolio, there are 8^5 possible joint transition probabilities, or over 32,000 joint transitions. The second option is to manipulate the equation for the variance of a loan portfolio. It can be shown that the risk of a portfolio of N loans depends on the risk of each pairwise combination of loans in the portfolio as well as the risk of each loan individually. To estimate the risk of a portfolio of N loans, we only need to calculate the risks of subportfolios containing two assets, as shown in Appendix 11.2.

To compute the distribution of loan values in the large sample case where loan values are not normally distributed, CreditMetrics uses Monte Carlo simulation.[32] Consider the portfolio of 20 loans in Table 11.4 and the correlations among those loans (borrowers) in Table 11.5.

For each loan, 20,000 (or more) different underlying borrower asset values are simulated, based on the original rating of the loan, the joint transition probabilities to other grades, and the historical correlations among the loans.[33] The loan (or borrower) can either stay in its original rating class or migrate to another rating class. (See the earlier discussion and Figure 11.3.) Each loan is then revalued after each simulation (and rating transition). Adding across the simulated values for the 20 loans produces 20,000 different values for the loan portfolio as a whole.[34] A *VAR* for the loan portfolio, based on the 99 percent worst case, can be calculated as the value of the loan portfolio that has the 200th worst value out of 20,000 possible

TABLE 11.4   Example Portfolio

Credit Asset	Principal Rating	Maturity Amount	Market (Years)	Value
1	AAA	$ 7,000,000	3	$ 7,821,049
2	AA	1,000,000	4	1,177,268
3	A	1,000,000	3	1,120,831
4	BBB	1,000,000	4	1,189,432
5	BB	1,000,000	3	1,154,641
6	B	1,000,000	4	1,263,523
7	CCC	1,000,000	2	1,127,628
8	A	10,000,000	8	14,229,071
9	BB	5,000,000	2	5,386,603
10	A	3,000,000	2	3,181,246
11	A	1,000,000	4	1,181,246
12	A	2,000,000	5	2,483,322
13	B	600,000	3	705,409
14	B	1,000,000	2	1,087,841
15	B	3,000,000	2	3,263,523
16	B	2,000,000	4	2,527,046
17	BBB	1,000,000	6	1,315,720
18	BBB	8,000,000	5	10,020,611
19	BBB	1,000,000	3	1,118,178
20	AA	5,000,000	5	6,181,784

Source: Gupton et al., *Technical Document,* April 2, 1997, p. 121.

loan portfolio values. In conjunction with the mean loan portfolio value, a capital requirement (*VAR*) can be calculated.

The CreditMetrics portfolio methodology can also be used for calculating the marginal risk contribution (*MRC*) for individual loans. Unlike the KMV-type approach, funds are viewed as being flexibly adjustable to accommodate an expanded loan supply, and *marginal* means loans are either made or not made to a borrower (rather than having an incremental amount of new loans made to a current borrower). Thus, CreditMetrics defines the risk contribution of an asset to the portfolio as the change in the portfolio's standard deviation due to the addition of the asset into the portfolio. In contrast, KMV and Credit Risk Plus define the asset's risk contribution as the change in the portfolio standard deviation due to a small change in the weight of the asset in the portfolio (see equation (11.10) for KMV's definition of MRC_i).

TABLE 11.5 Asset Correlations for Example Portfolio

	1	2	3	4	5	6	7	8	9	10	11	12	13	14	15	16	17	18	19	20
1	1	0.45	0.45	0.45	0.15	0.15	0.15	0.15	0.15	0.15	0.1	0.1	0.1	0.1	0.1	0.1	0.1	0.1	0.1	0.1
2	0.45	1	0.45	0.45	0.15	0.15	0.15	0.15	0.15	0.15	0.1	0.1	0.1	0.1	0.1	0.1	0.1	0.1	0.1	0.1
3	0.45	0.45	1	0.45	0.15	0.15	0.15	0.15	0.15	0.15	0.1	0.1	0.1	0.1	0.1	0.1	0.1	0.1	0.1	0.1
4	0.45	0.45	0.45	1	0.15	0.15	0.15	0.15	0.15	0.15	0.1	0.1	0.1	0.1	0.1	0.1	0.1	0.1	0.1	0.1
5	0.15	0.15	0.15	0.15	1	0.35	0.35	0.35	0.35	0.35	0.2	0.2	0.2	0.2	0.2	0.15	0.15	0.15	0.1	0.1
6	0.15	0.15	0.15	0.15	0.35	1	0.35	0.35	0.35	0.35	0.2	0.2	0.2	0.2	0.2	0.15	0.15	0.15	0.1	0.1
7	0.15	0.15	0.15	0.15	0.35	0.35	1	0.35	0.35	0.35	0.2	0.2	0.2	0.2	0.2	0.15	0.15	0.15	0.1	0.1
8	0.15	0.15	0.15	0.15	0.35	0.35	0.35	1	0.35	0.35	0.2	0.2	0.2	0.2	0.2	0.15	0.15	0.15	0.1	0.1
9	0.15	0.15	0.15	0.15	0.35	0.35	0.35	0.35	1	0.35	0.2	0.2	0.2	0.2	0.2	0.15	0.15	0.15	0.1	0.1
10	0.15	0.15	0.15	0.15	0.35	0.35	0.35	0.35	0.35	1	0.2	0.2	0.2	0.2	0.2	0.15	0.15	0.15	0.1	0.1
11	0.1	0.1	0.1	0.1	0.2	0.2	0.2	0.2	0.2	0.2	1	0.45	0.45	0.45	0.45	0.2	0.2	0.2	0.1	0.1
12	0.1	0.1	0.1	0.1	0.2	0.2	0.2	0.2	0.2	0.2	0.45	1	0.45	0.45	0.45	0.2	0.2	0.2	0.1	0.1
13	0.1	0.1	0.1	0.1	0.2	0.2	0.2	0.2	0.2	0.2	0.45	0.45	1	0.45	0.45	0.2	0.2	0.2	0.1	0.1
14	0.1	0.1	0.1	0.1	0.2	0.2	0.2	0.2	0.2	0.2	0.45	0.45	0.45	1	0.45	0.2	0.2	0.2	0.1	0.1
15	0.1	0.1	0.1	0.1	0.2	0.2	0.2	0.2	0.2	0.2	0.45	0.45	0.45	0.45	1	0.2	0.2	0.2	0.1	0.1
16	0.1	0.1	0.1	0.1	0.15	0.15	0.15	0.15	0.15	0.15	0.2	0.2	0.2	0.2	0.2	1	0.55	0.55	0.25	0.25
17	0.1	0.1	0.1	0.1	0.15	0.15	0.15	0.15	0.15	0.15	0.2	0.2	0.2	0.2	0.2	0.55	1	0.55	0.25	0.25
18	0.1	0.1	0.1	0.1	0.15	0.15	0.15	0.15	0.15	0.15	0.2	0.2	0.2	0.2	0.2	0.55	0.55	1	0.25	0.25
19	0.1	0.1	0.1	0.1	0.1	0.1	0.1	0.1	0.1	0.1	0.1	0.1	0.1	0.1	0.1	0.25	0.25	0.25	1	0.65
20	0.1	0.1	0.1	0.1	0.1	0.1	0.1	0.1	0.1	0.1	0.1	0.1	0.1	0.1	0.1	0.25	0.25	0.25	0.65	1

Source: Gupton et al., *Technical Document*, April 2, 1997, p. 122.

Table 11.6 shows the stand-alone and marginal risk contributions of 20 loans in a hypothetical loan portfolio based on a standard deviation (σ) measure of risk. The stand-alone columns reflect the dollar and percentage risk of each loan, viewed separately. The stand-alone percentage risk for the CCC rated asset (number 7) is 22.67 percent, and the B rated asset (number 15) is 18.72 percent. The marginal risk contribution columns in Table 11.6 reflect the risk of adding each loan to a portfolio of the remaining 19 loans (the standard deviation risk of a 20-loan portfolio minus the standard deviation risk of a 19-loan portfolio). Interestingly, in Table 11.6, on a stand-alone basis, asset 7 (CCC) is riskier than asset 15 (B), but when risk is measured in a portfolio context (by its marginal risk contribution), asset 15 is riskier. The reason can be seen from the correlation matrix in Table 11.5, where the B rated loan (asset 15) has a "high" correlation level of .45 with

TABLE 11.6 Standard Deviation of Value Change

Asset	Credit Rating	Stand-Alone		Marginal	
		Absolute ($)	Percent	Absolute ($)	Percent
1	AAA	4,905	0.06	239	0.00
2	AA	2,007	0.17	114	0.01
3	A	17,523	1.56	693	0.06
4	BBB	40,043	3.37	2,934	0.25
5	BB	99,607	8.63	16,046	1.39
6	B	162,251	12.84	37,664	2.98
7	CCC	255,680	<u>22.67</u>	73,079	<u>6.48</u>
8	A	197,152	1.39	35,104	0.25
9	BB	380,141	7.06	105,949	1.97
10	A	63,207	1.99	5,068	0.16
11	A	15,360	1.30	1,232	0.10
12	A	43,085	1.73	4,531	0.18
13	B	107,314	15.21	25,684	3.64
14	B	167,511	15.40	44,827	4.12
15	B	610,900	<u>18.72</u>	270,000	<u>8.27</u>
16	B	322,720	12.77	89,190	3.53
17	BBB	28,051	2.13	2,775	0.21
18	BBB	306,892	3.06	69,624	0.69
19	BBB	1,837	0.16	120	0.01
20	AA	9,916	0.16	389	0.01

Source: Gupton et al., *Technical Document*, April 2, 1997, p. 130.

assets 11, 12, 13, and 14. By comparison, the highest correlations of the CCC rated loan (asset 7) are with assets 5, 6, 8, 9, and 10 at the .35 level.

One policy implication is immediate and is shown in Figure 11.4, where the total risk (in a portfolio context) of a loan is broken down into two components: (1) its percentage marginal standard deviation (vertical axis) and (2) the dollar amount of credit exposure (horizontal axis). We then have:

Total risk of a loan ($) = Marginal standard deviation (%)

× Credit exposure ($)

For example, using the credit exposure value for loan 15 (a B rated loan) shown in Table 11.5 and the marginal standard deviation for loan 15 shown in Table 11.6, the total risk of loan 15 can be calculated as follows:

$$\$270,000 = 8.27\% \times \$3,263,523$$

Also plotted in Figure 11.4 is an equal risk *isoquant* of $70,000. Suppose managers wish to impose total credit risk exposure limits of $70,000 on each loan measured in a portfolio context. Then asset 15 (the B rated

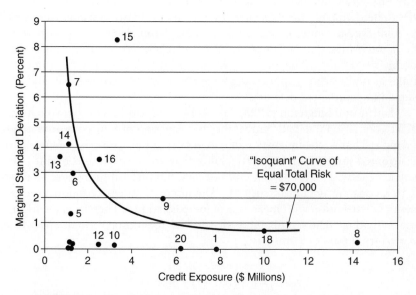

FIGURE 11.4 Credit limits and loan selection in CreditMetrics.

loan) and assets 16 and 9 are clearly *outliers*. One possible solution would be for the bank to sell asset 15 to another bank, or to swap it for another B rated asset that has a lower correlation with the other loans (assets) in the bank's portfolio. In doing so, its expected returns may remain approximately unchanged, but its loan portfolio risk is likely to decrease.[35]

MODELING DEFAULT CORRELATIONS USING REDUCED FORM MODELS

In this section, we discuss default correlations derived from intensity-based models (see Chapter 5). In these models, default correlations reflect the effect of "events" inducing *simultaneous* jumps in the default intensities of obligors. The causes of defaults themselves are not modeled explicitly; however, what is modeled are various approaches to default-arrival intensity that focus on correlated "times to default." This allows the model to answer questions such as: What was the worst week, month, year, and so on, out of the past N years, in terms of loan portfolio risk? That worst period will be when correlated default intensities were highest (defaults arrived at the same time). With joint credit events, some of the default intensity of each obligor is tied to such a marketwide event with some probability. For example, the intensity-based model of Duffie and Singleton (1998) allows default intensities to be correlated through changes in default intensities themselves as well as joint credit events. In the Duffie and Singleton model, obligors have default intensities that mean-revert with correlated Poisson arrivals of randomly sized jumps. They then formulate individual obligor default intensity times as multivariate exponentials which allows them to develop a model for simulating correlated defaults.

Duffie and Singleton (1998)[36] consider a hazard function in which each asset's conditional default probability is a function of four parameters: λ, θ, k, and J. That is, the intensity h of a loan's default process has independently distributed jumps in default probability that arrive at some constant intensity λ; otherwise, if no default event occurs, h returns at mean-reversion rate k to a constant default intensity θ. The jumps in intensity follow an exponential distribution with mean size of jump equal to J. Therefore, the form of the individual firm's probability of survival (conditional upon survival to date t) from time t to time s is:

$$p(t,s) = exp\{\alpha(s-t) + \beta(s-t)h(t)\}$$

where $\beta(t) = \dfrac{-\left(1 - e^{-kt}\right)}{k}$

$$\alpha(t) = -\theta\left[t + \beta(t)\right] - \left[\frac{\lambda}{(J+k)}\right]\left[Jt - ln\left(1 - \beta(t)J\right)\right]$$

As a numerical illustration, suppose that $\lambda = .001$, $k = .5$, $\theta = .001$, $J = 5$, and $h(0) = .001$,[37] then arrival of a jump in default risk reduces the expected remaining life of the loan to less than three months. Thus, as a stand-alone asset, this loan is relatively risky. However, we must consider the credit risk of the loan in a portfolio, allowing for imperfectly correlated default arrival times. That is, the timing of sudden jumps of default arrival intensities may be imperfectly correlated across loans. For simplicity, assume that parameters other than λ (i.e., the sizes of the jumps in default intensities) are equal and independent across loans and across time, thereby fixing the parameter values θ, k, and J.

Correlations across loan default probabilities occur because common factors affect the timing of jumps in default probabilities across assets (loans). Specifically, the intensity jump time, λ, can be separated into a common factor with intensity V_c and an idiosyncratic factor, V. Thus,

$$\lambda = vV_c + V \tag{11.19}$$

where v is the sensitivity of the timing of jumps in default intensities to common factors.[38] These common factors, V_c can be viewed as macroeconomic factors, similar to those used in the multifactor models discussed earlier in this chapter. The correlation coefficient between the time to the next credit event for any pair of loans can be expressed as a simple function of v, V_c, and V.

To illustrate using a numerical example, Figure 11.5 shows a portion of a typical sample path for the total arrival intensity h of defaults for the following parameter values: $\lambda = .002$, $\theta = .001$, $k = .5$, $J = 5$, $v = .02$, and $V_c = .05$. Using equation (11.19), we can compute $V = .002 - (.02)(.05) = .001$. We can also compute the probability that loan i's default intensity jumps at time t, given that loan j's intensity has experienced a jump, as: $vV_c/(V_c + V) = (.02)(.05)/(.05 + .001) = 2$ percent. Figure 11.5 shows a marketwide credit event occurs just prior to year 2.8 on the calendar time axis. This event instigates jumps in default intensity for several firms. These defaults are represented by the symbol "x" in Figure 11.5. Correlations across default intensities cause a rapid increase in default risk in the period immediately

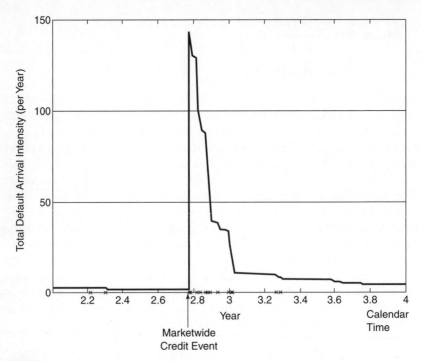

FIGURE 11.5 Correlated Default Intensity. *Note:* The figure shows a portion of a simulated sample path of total default arrival intensity (initially 1,000 firms). An X along the calender time axis denotes a default event. *Source:* Duffie and Singleton (1998), ©2001 by Darrell Duffie and Kenneth Singleton. All rights reserved. You may read and browse this material at this website. However, no further copying, downloading, or linking is permitted. No part of this material may be further reproduced in any form by any electronic or mechanical means (including photocopying, recording, or information storage retrieval) without permission in writing from the publisher. Users are not permitted to mount this file on any network servers.

surrounding the marketwide credit event. However, the mean reversion built into the intensity process (k is assumed to equal .5) causes the total arrival intensity for defaults to drop back almost to pre-event levels within one year.

Taking the scenario illustrated in Figure 11.5 as the base case, Duffie and Singleton (1998) also examine alternative correlation values: zero correlation ($v = V_c = 0$), and high correlations ($v = .02$ and $V_c = .1$). Figure 11.6 plots the probabilities of experiencing four or more defaults in any time window (of m days) for the three different assumptions about correlations: zero (low) correlation, medium correlation (the base case), and high correlation. Figure 11.6 shows the substantial impact that correlation has on the portfolio's credit risk exposure. This implies that the correlations in default

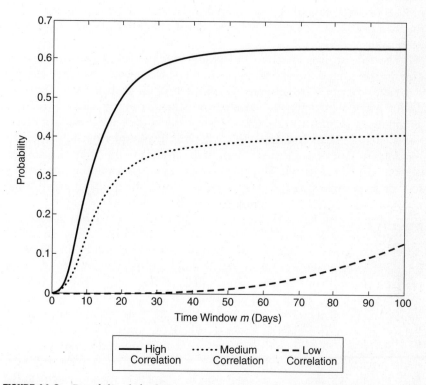

FIGURE 11.6 Portfolio default intensities. *Note:* The figure shows the probability of an m-day interval within 10 years experiencing four or more defaults (base case). *Source:* Duffie and Singleton (1998), ©2001 by Darrell Duffie and Kenneth Singleton. All rights reserved. You may read and browse this material at this website. However, no further copying, downloading, or linking is permitted. No part of this material may be further reproduced in any form by any electronic or mechanical means (including photocopying, recording, or information storage retrieval) without permission in writing from the publisher. Users are not permitted to mount this file on any network servers.

risk shocks (i.e., the correlated jumps in default intensities) may create systemic risk that makes it difficult for banks to recapitalize within one year of experiencing defaults on the loans in their portfolios [see Carey (2001b)].

OTHER PORTFOLIO APPROACHES

CreditPortfolio View and Credit Risk Plus can be viewed as partial MPT models or *VAR* (economic capital models) in that the returns on loans and the loan portfolio are not explicitly modeled, the focus being on loan portfolio risk.

The role of diversification in CreditPortfolio View (CPV) can best be seen in the context of the macroeconomic shock factors (or unsystematic risk factors) ε and V (see Chapter 7), which drive the probability of borrower default over time. As portfolio diversification increases (e.g., across countries and industry segments in the CPV-Macro model), the relative importance of unsystematic risk to systematic risk will shrink, and the exposure of a loan portfolio to shocks will shrink. Thus, in the context of the Monte Carlo simulations of the model, the 99 percent worst-case loss for an internationally well-diversified portfolio is likely to be less (other things being equal) than that for a single country or industry-specialized portfolio of loans.[39]

In Credit Risk Plus, we need to distinguish between two model cases. In what was called Model 1 in Chapter 8, there were two sources of uncertainty in the loan portfolio: (1) the Poisson distribution of the number of defaults (around a constant mean default rate) and (2) the severity of losses (variable across loan exposure bands). Because the Poisson distribution implies that each loan has a small probability of default and that this probability is independent across loans, the correlation of default rates is, by definition, zero. In Model 2, however, where the mean default rate itself is variable (gamma distributed), correlations will be induced among the loans in the portfolio because of their varying systematic linkages to the mean default rate movements. As was discussed in Chapter 8, the movement in the mean default rate can be modeled in terms of factor sensitivities to different independent "sectors" (which could be countries or industries). For example, a company's default probability may be sensitive to both a U.S. factor and a German factor. Given this trait, the default correlations in Credit Risk Plus are shown to be equal to:

$$\rho_{AB} = \left(m_A m_B\right)^{\frac{1}{2}} \sum_{k=1}^{N} \theta_{Ak}\theta_{Bk}\left(\frac{\sigma_k}{m_k}\right)^2 \qquad (11.20)$$

where ρ_{AB} = default correlation between obligor A and B,

m_A = mean default rate for type A obligor,

m_B = mean default rate for type B obligor,

θ_A = allocation of obligor A's default rate volatility across N sectors,

θ_B = allocation of obligor B's default rate volatility across N sectors,

$(\sigma_k/m_k)^2$ = proportional default rate volatility in sector k.

Table 11.7 shows an example of equation (11.20) where each of the two obligors is sensitive to one economywide sector (in this example, the United States) only ($\theta_{Ak} = \theta_{Bk} = 1$) and $\sigma_k/m_k = .7$ is set at an empirically reasonable level, reflecting U.S. national default rate statistics. As can be seen from Table 11.7, as the credit quality of the obligors declines (i.e., m_A and m_B get larger), correlations get larger. Nevertheless, even in the case where individual mean default rates are high ($m_A = 10\%$ and $m_B = 7\%$), the correlation among the borrowers is still quite small (here, 4.1%).

SUMMARY

We reviewed various approaches toward applying MPT-type models to the loan portfolio. Some of the new models are not full-fledged MPT models (returns are often left unmodeled), but their importance is in the link they show between loan portfolio risk (*VAR*) and: (1) default correlations and (2) portfolio diversification. In particular, the consensus of the literature so far appears to be that default correlations on average are generally low and gains through loan portfolio diversification are potentially high. However, that is changing as correlations have increased in recent years. Moreover, an important implication of these models is that any regulatory capital

TABLE 11.7 The Link between Mean Default Rates and Default Correlations

Variables	High Credit Quality	Medium Credit Quality	Low Credit Quality
m_A	0.5%	5%	10%
m_B	1%	2%	7%
θ_{Ak}	1	1	1
θ_{Bk}	1	1	1
σ_k/m_k	70%	70%	70%
ρ_{AB}	0.35%	1.55%	4.1%

Source: Credit Risk Plus, *Technical Document,* Credit Suisse Financial Products, October 1997.

proposal (such as the standardized approach of BIS II), which ignores correlations among loans in setting capital requirements may be flawed. In particular, MPT-based models suggest that loan portfolios in which individual loan default risks are highly correlated should have higher capital requirements than loan portfolios of the same size, in which default risk correlations are relatively low.

APPENDIX 11.1
VALUING A LOAN THAT MATURES AFTER THE CREDIT HORIZON IN THE KMV PORTFOLIO MANAGER MODEL

If the loan matures at the credit horizon, (see Figure 11.1) then the payoffs are binomial—either nondefault (and the loan fully pays off) or default (and the loan pays the *LGD*). Moreover, if the loan matures before the credit horizon, a similar binomial structure prevails—either the loan defaulted or it did not. However, if the loan matures after the credit horizon, then the loan's value must be estimated as of the horizon date taking into account the probability of receiving the loan's remaining promised cash flows as a function of the likelihood that assets may fall below the default point on some date between the horizon date and loan maturity.

As in Chapter 4, the loan's value is determined by the distribution of the firm's asset value as compared to the default point (debt level). Since the future value of the firm's assets is unknown, it must be simulated using a specification of the stochastic process determining asset values. For each possible asset value, the distance to default is converted into an *EDF* score using KMV's empirical database of loan defaults. Four steps are needed to derive the distribution of loan (excess) returns or losses in order to calculate the loan portfolio's risk-return characteristics. They are:

1. Valuation of an individual firm's assets using random sampling of risk-factors.
2. Loan valuation based on the *EDF*s implied by the firm's asset valuation.
3. Aggregation of individual loan values to construct the portfolio's value.
4. Calculation of excess returns and losses for the loan portfolio.

Completion of these four steps yields a single estimate for either the excess returns or expected losses on the loan portfolio. Then the process must be repeated 50,000 to 200,000 times using Monte Carlo iterative techniques in order to trace out an excess return/loss distribution for the loan portfolio. After describing the four steps in more detail, we illustrate the procedure using a numerical example.

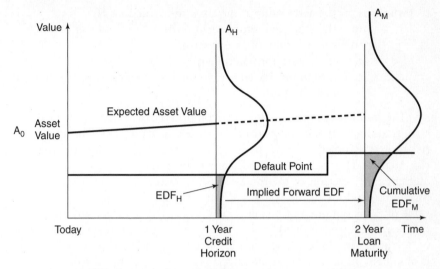

FIGURE 11.7 Valuation of the term structure of EDF.

Step 1: Valuation of an Individual Firm's Assets Using Random Sampling of Risk Factors

KMV's Portfolio Manager specifies a stochastic process to determine future asset values. If the loan matures after the credit horizon date, then the distribution of future expected asset values must be simulated for at least two distinct dates in the future: the credit horizon date (assumed to be one year) and the loan maturity date. Figure 11.7 shows the three asset valuations needed to compute returns for loans that mature after the credit horizon: A_0 (current asset value), A_H (firm asset value at the credit horizon in one year), and A_M (firm asset value at the loan's maturity shown to be two years in Figure 11.7). A_0 is a point value, but A_H and A_M are stochastic. However, the asset value at maturity, A_M, is determined by the realization of the asset value at the horizon date, A_H. Thus, A_H is first simulated using random draws of risk factors and then the value of A_M is calculated for each A_H drawn using the asset drift term.

KMV assumes that the underlying assets' valuation at the credit horizon follow a random walk such that:

$$ln\, A_H = ln\, A_0 + \left(\mu - .5\sigma^2\right)t_H + \sigma\varepsilon_H \sqrt{t_H} \qquad (11.21)$$

where A_H = the asset value at the credit horizon date H,

μ = the expected return (drift term) on the asset valuation,

σ = the volatility of asset returns,

t_H = the credit horizon time period,

ε_H = a random risk term (assumed to follow a standard normal distribution).

The random component, ε_H, is decomposed into a systematic risk portion, f, and a firm-specific portion, u, such that $\varepsilon_H = f + u$. The systematic risk term is assumed to be a function of five country and industry systematic risk factors. The asset R-squared depicts the asset's risk exposure since it measures the fraction of the random risk term that is systematic. For each Monte Carlo draw of the systematic and firm specific risk factors, another value of A_H is obtained using equation (11.21).[40] The possible draws of the risk factors are constrained by the correlations in asset returns for each pair of borrowers in the loan portfolio.[41] Once the simulated value of assets A_H is obtained, an *EDF* score is assigned reflecting the distance to default and therefore the empirical probability that the simulated asset value A_H will fall below the default point.

The maturity asset value A_M is based on the simulated asset value A_H, the asset drift term, and the time between the credit horizon and maturity. The distance to default for each value of A_M implies a cumulative *EDF* value that measures the probability of default at or before loan maturity. Figure 11.7 shows that the distance from each simulated asset value to the firm's debt level (shown to be increasing over time) is used to calculate the *EDF* at each point in time. That is, there is a term structure of *EDF*s consisting of the *EDF* corresponding to the one-year credit horizon, denoted EDF_H, and the *EDF* corresponding to the loan's maturity date, denoted EDF_M. KMV assumes a standard exponential cumulative *EDF* function so that the implied forward *EDF* between time periods H and M can be extrapolated from EDF_H and EDF_M.[42]

Step 2: Loan Valuation Based on the EDFs Implied by the Firm's Asset Valuation

Step 1 has produced a term structure of *EDF* scores that can be used to value the risky loan. However, first the empirical *EDF* must be converted into the risk-neutral quasi-*EDF* (*QDF*) along the lines outlined in Chapter 4. That is, the risk-adjusted expected return (asset drift term) must be replaced by the risk-free rate. Once the *QDF* is derived, the loan value may be split into two components: (1) a risk-free cashflow equal to $1 - LGD$ and (2) a risky cash flow equal to LGD which is paid only if the loan does not default. Thus, the loan's present value at time period $t = 0$ is:

$$V_0 = PV_0\left(1 - LGD\right) + PV_0\left(1 - QDF\right)LGD \qquad (11.22)$$

where V_0 = the loan's present value,
PV_0 = the present value factor using the risk-free rate to discount the loan's cash flows to time $t = 0$,
QDF = the (cumulative) risk-neutral quasi-*EDF*,
LGD = the loss given default.

However, the loan must also be valued as of the credit horizon date, $t = H$. Suppose that the first year's coupon payment is paid on the one year credit horizon date. The expected value of the loan, conditional on nondefault at or before date H is:

$$V_{H|ND} = C_H + PV_H\left(1 - LGD\right) + PV_H\left(1 - QDF\right)LGD \qquad (11.23)$$

where $V_{H|ND}$ = the loan's expected value as of the credit horizon date given that default has not occurred,
C_H = the cash flow on the credit horizon date,
PV_H = the present value factor using the risk-free rate as the discount factor to discount the loan's cash flows to time $t = H$.

However, there is also a possibility that the loan will default on or before the credit horizon date. The expected value of the loan given default is:

$$V_{H|D} = \left(C_H + PV_H\right)LGD \qquad (11.24)$$

Putting together equations (11.23) and (11.24), KMV obtains the expected loan value at the credit horizon date:[43]

$$V_H = \left(EDF\right)V_{H|D} + \left(1 - EDF\right)V_{H|ND} \qquad (11.25)$$

Step 3: Aggregation of Individual Loan Values to Construct the Portfolio's Value

Sum the expected values, V_H, for all loans to calculate the expected value of the portfolio at the credit horizon date for all loans in the portfolio.

$$V_t^P = \sum_i V_t^i \tag{11.26}$$

where V_t^P = the value of the loan portfolio at date $t = 0, H$,
V_t^i = the value of each loan i at date $t = 0, H$.

Step 4: Calculation of Excess Returns and Losses for the Loan Portfolio

The excess return on the portfolio (from time period 0 to the credit horizon date) is:[44]

$$R_H = \frac{V_H^P - V_0^P}{V_0^P} - r_f \tag{11.27}$$

where R_H = the excess return on the loan portfolio from time period 0 to the credit horizon date H,
V_H^P = the expected value of the loan portfolio at the credit horizon date,
V_0^P = the present value of the loan portfolio,
r_f = the risk-free rate.

Equation (11.27) yields a single estimate of excess return on the loan portfolio for each simulated asset valuation.

The expected loss on the loan portfolio for this iteration of asset values is:

$$EL_H = \frac{V_{H|ND}^P - V_H^P}{V_0^P} \tag{11.28}$$

where EL_H = the expected loss on the loan portfolio at the credit horizon date,
$V_{H|ND}^P$ = the portfolio's expected value conditional on nondefault on or before the credit horizon date,
V_H^P = the portfolio's expected value at the credit horizon date,
V_0^P = the portfolio's present value.

KMV's Portfolio Manager then iterates Steps 1 through 4 again 50,000 to 200,000 times in order to generate a distribution of excess returns or expected losses for the entire loan portfolio. We consider the following numerical example to illustrate the entire procedure.

A Numerical Example

Consider the following example of a 5-year maturity, $1 loan paying 10 percent p.a. Table 11.8 values the cash flows on the loan shown in column (2) as of the present, $t = 0$. The risk-free rate is assumed constant at 5 percent p.a. for the entire five years; thus, column (3) of Table 11.8 shows the risk-free discount factor for each period t (i.e., $e^{-.05t}$). Column (4) discounts the loan's cash flows at the risk-free rate, using the continuous risk-free discount factor shown in column (3). Summing up the discounted cash flows in column (4) yields the present value of the risk-free portion of cash flows, denoted PV_0 in the first term of equation (11.22).

For the purposes of this example, suppose that the results of the first iteration of the Step 1 simulation of asset values estimate the annual EDF to be constant at 1 percent. Thus, the cumulative EDF, shown in column (5) of Table 11.8, can be calculated as $1 - (1 - EDF)^t$ for each period t. Each value of the EDF is transformed into an equivalent QDF in column (6) by removing the asset drift factor.[45] Finally, the risk-adjusted present value of each cash flow is obtained by multiplying 1 minus the cumulative QDF in column (6) times the risk-free value in column (4). Summing up the cash flows in column (7) yields the $PV_0(1 - QDF)$ value of the second term in equation (11.22), for the single simulated asset value shown in Table 11.8 to equal $1.0675.

To solve for the loan's present value using equation (11.22) of Step 2, we must consider the LGD. Suppose that the LGD is equal to 50 percent.

TABLE 11.8 Valuing the Loan's Present Value, $t = 0$

Time Period (1)	Cash Flows per Period (2)	Discount Factor $e^{-t r_f}$ (3)	Risk-Free Present Value of Cash Flows $(2) \times (3) = (4)$	EDF_i Cumulative (5)	QDF_i Cumulative (6)	Risky Present Value of Cash Flows (7)
1	.10	.9512	.0951	.0100	.0203	.0932
2	.10	.9048	.0905	.0199	.0471	.0862
3	.10	.8607	.0861	.0297	.0770	.0795
4	.10	.8187	.0819	.0394	.1088	.0730
5	1.10	.7788	.8567	.0490	.1414	.7356
Totals			1.2103			1.0675

Then, we can use the sum of columns (4) and (7) in Table 11.8 to calculate the loan's present value using equation (11.22) as follows:

$$V_0 = PV_0(1 - LGD) + PV_0(1 - QDF)LGD = 1.2103(.50) + (1.0675)(.50) = \$1.1389$$

This procedure must be repeated using equations (11.23) through (11.25) in order to determine the loan value as of the credit horizon date. Table 11.9 shows the remaining cash flows as of the one-year credit horizon date. First consider the nondefault case. Suppose that the first year's coupon payment is paid on the credit horizon date. Thus, the expected value of the loan conditional on the nondefault state is obtained using equation (11.23) as follows:

$$V_{HID} = C_H + PV_H(1 - LGD) + PV_H(1 - QDF)LGD = 0.10 + 1.1723(.50)$$
$$+ (1.0615)(.50) = \$1.2169$$

The expected value of the loan on the credit horizon date conditional on the default state is computed using equation (11.24):

$$V_{HID} = (C_H + PV_H)LGD = (0.10 + 1.1723)(.50) = \$0.63615$$

Using equation (11.25), we obtain the expected loan value at the credit horizon date:

$$V_H = (EDF)V_{HID} + (1 - EDF)V_{HIND} = (.01)(.63615) + (.99)(1.2169) = \$1.2111$$

TABLE 11.9   Valuing the Loan on the Credit Horizon Date, $t = 1$

Time Period (1)	Cash Flows per Period (2)	Discount Factor $e^{-t r_f}$ (3)	Risk-Free Present Value of Cash Flows (2) × (3) = (4)	EDF_i Cumulative (5)	QDF_i Cumulative (6)	Risky Present Value of Cash Flows (7)
1	0	1	0			
2	.10	.9512	.0951	.0100	.0203	.0932
3	.10	.9048	.0905	.0199	.0471	.0862
4	.10	.8607	.0861	.0297	.0770	.0795
5	1.10	.8187	.9006	.0394	.1088	.8026
Totals			1.1723			1.0615

Assuming, for simplicity, that this loan is the only one in the portfolio, equation (11.27) can be used to calculate the loan's excess return as follows:

$$R_H = \frac{V_H^P - V_0^P}{V_0^P} - r_f = \left[\frac{(1.2111 - 1.1389)}{1.1389} \right] - .05 = 1.34\%$$

This would constitute one point on the distribution of loan excess returns. The procedure would then begin again at Step 1, drawing another asset value from the distribution of risk factors, solving for *EDF* and *QDF*, and then valuing the loan at time periods *0* and *H* to fill in another point on the loan's excess return distribution.

If the goal is to draw a loss distribution instead, we use equation (11.28) to obtain the point estimate of expected losses consistent with the first draw of the firm's asset value and iterate using Monte Carlo simulation to obtain the entire loss distribution. For this numerical example, expected losses are:

$$EL_H = \frac{V_{HIND} - V_H}{V_0} = \left[\frac{1.2169 - 1.2111}{1.1389} \right] = 0.0051$$

KMV's PRIVATE FIRM MODEL

Privately held firms do not have a series of equity prices that can be used to estimate asset values using the procedures discussed in Chapter 4. Therefore, KMV's private firm model requires four additional steps that proceed the four steps outlined earlier. They are:

1. Calculate the earnings before interest, taxes, depreciation, and amortization (EBITDA) for the private firm *j* in industry *i*.
2. Calculate the average equity multiple for industry *i* by dividing the industry average market value of equity by the industry average EBITDA.
3. Obtain an estimate of the market value of equity for the private firm *j* by multiplying the industry equity multiple from Step 2 by firm *j*'s EBITDA.
4. Firm *j*'s assets equal the Step 3 estimate of the market value of equity plus the book value of firm *j*'s debt. Once the private firm's asset values can be estimated, then the public firm model can be utilized to estimate the return/loss distribution for the loan portfolio as shown earlier.

APPENDIX 11.2
THE SIMPLIFIED TWO-ASSET SUBPORTFOLIO
SOLUTION TO THE *N* ASSET PORTFOLIO CASE

The standard formula for the risk of a portfolio is:

$$\sigma_P^2 = \sum_{i=1}^{n} \sigma^2\left(V_i\right) + 2\sum_{i=1}^{n-1} \sum_{j \neq i=1}^{n} Cov\left(V_i, V_j\right) \tag{11.29}$$

Alternatively, we may relate the covariance terms to the variances of pairs of assets, where

$$\sigma^2\left(V_i + V_j\right) = \sigma^2\left(V_i\right) + 2\,Cov\left(V_i, V_j\right) + \sigma^2\left(V_j\right) \tag{11.30}$$

and thus

$$2\,Cov\left(V_i, V_j\right) = \sigma^2\left(V_i + V_j\right) - \sigma^2\left(V_i\right) - \sigma^2\left(V_j\right) \tag{11.31}$$

substituting the equation for $2\,Cov(V_i, V_j)$ into equation (11.29), we can express the portfolio standard deviation in terms of the risk of individual assets and the standard deviations of subportfolios containing two assets.

$$\sigma_P^2 = \sum_{i=1}^{n-1} \sum_{j \neq i=1}^{n} \sigma^2\left(V_i + V_j\right) - \left(n - 2\right)\sum_{i=1}^{n} \sigma^2\left(V_i\right) \tag{11.32}$$

CHAPTER 12

Stress Testing Credit Risk Models

Algorithmics Mark-to-Future

A key issue for bankers and regulators is internal model validation and predictive accuracy. In the context of market models, this issue has led to numerous efforts to "back test" models to ascertain their predictive accuracy. The proposed second pillar of BIS II states that "supervisors are expected to evaluate how well banks are assessing their capital needs relative to their risk and to intervene, where appropriate" [BIS (January 2001), p. 104]. Currently, under the BIS market risk-based capital requirements, a bank must back test its internal market model over a minimum of 250 past days if it is used for capital requirement calculations. If the forecast *VAR* errors on those 250 days are too large (i.e., risk is underestimated on too many days), a system of penalties is imposed by regulators to create incentives for bankers to get their models right.[1]

Many observers have argued, however, that back testing over 250 days is not enough, given the high standard errors that are likely to be involved if the period is not representative. To reduce errors of this type, one suggestion has been to increase the number of past daily observations over which a back test of a model is conducted. For example, at least 1,000 past daily observations are commonly felt to be adequate to ensure that the period chosen is "representative" in terms of testing the predictive accuracy of any given model.[2] Unfortunately, even for traded financial assets such as currencies, a period of 1,000 past days requires going back in time over four years and may involve covering a wide and unrepresentative range of regimes. Moreover, Fender et al. (2001) find that although most stress test scenarios emphasize negative shocks (mostly focused on equities and emerging markets), the size of the shocks and cross-market effects vary widely.

BACK TESTING CREDIT RISK MODELS

To appropriately back test or stress test market risk models, 250 observations may be regarded as too few, but it is unlikely that a bank would be able to generate anywhere near that many past time-series observations for back testing its internal credit risk models. For example, with annual observations (which are the most likely to be available) a bank might be able to generate only 40 past observations that cover five or six credit cycles.[3] A banker/regulator is then severely hampered from performing time series back testing similar to that currently available for market risk models.[4]

Even when available for back testing of credit risk models, loan databases are often subject to substantial error in classification. To compute the loss distribution for a loan portfolio, individual loans must be classified according to their default probabilities. Carey and Hrycay (2001) compare three methodologies to accomplish this: (1) the internal ratings method, (2) mapping to external ratings, and (3) credit scoring (see Chapter 2). Each of these methodologies have biases that may undermine the accuracy of the estimated loss distribution. For example, the internal ratings method may be unstable if ratings criteria have changed over time or if there are insufficient data to estimate a time-invariant historical average default rate for each internal rating classification. In contrast, the efficacy of the external ratings mapping method is undermined by possible judgmental biases in assigning each individual loan to a particular external ratings classification. Finally, credit scoring models suffer from biases in model estimates that are exacerbated across different credit cycles. Carey and Hrycay (2001) find that the classification model did well in quantifying rating grades, but correctly identify only one-third of defaulting firms. Moreover, the biases introduced by errors in classification differ for investment grade as opposed to non-investment grade debt instruments. Some, but not all, of these problems can be alleviated if long panels of loan data are collected.[5]

TIME-SERIES VERSUS CROSS-SECTIONAL STRESS TESTING

Granger and Huang (1997), at a theoretical level, and Carey (1998, 2000) and Lopez and Saidenberg (1998), at a simulation/empirical level, show that stress tests similar to those conducted across time for market risk models, can be conducted using cross-sectional or panel data for credit risk models. In particular, suppose that in any given year a bank has a sample of N loans in its portfolio, where N is large. By repeated subsampling of the total loan portfolio, it is possible to build up a cross-sectional distribution of expected losses, unexpected losses, and the full probability density function of losses. By comparing cross-sectional subportfolio loss distributions with the actual full-portfolio loss distribution, it is possible to generate an idea of the predictive accuracy of a credit risk model. For example, if the model is a good predictor or forecaster, the mean average loss rate and the mean 99th percentile loss rate from 10,000 randomly drawn subportfolios of the total loan portfolio should be pretty close to the actual average and 99th percentile loss rates on the full loan portfolio experienced in that year. Indeed, different models may have different prediction errors, and the relative size of the prediction errors can be used to judge the "best" model [see Lopez and Saidenberg (1998) and Carey (2000)].

A number of statistical issues arise with cross-sectional stress testing, but these are generally similar to those that arise with time-series stress testing (or back testing). The first issue is that the number of loans in the portfolio has to be large. For example, Carey's (1998) sample is based on 30,000 privately placed bonds held by a dozen life insurance companies during 1986 to 1992, a period during which over 300 credit-related events (defaults, debt restructurings, and so on) occurred for the issuers of the bonds. The subsamples chosen varied in size; for example, portfolios of $0.5 billion to $15 billion in size containing no more than 3 percent of the bonds of any one issuer. Table 12.1 shows simulated loss rates from 50,000 different subsample portfolios drawn from the 30,000 bond population. Subportfolios were limited to $1 billion in size. Further, using a Moody's database of bond ratings and defaults during 1970 through 1998, Carey (2000) constructs $5 billion subportfolios comprised of around 500 bonds and estimates loss distributions under a DM model.

The loss rates in Table 12.1 vary by year. In 1991, which was the trough of a recession in the United States, 50,000 simulated portfolios containing below-investment-grade (below BBB rated) bonds, produced a (mean) 99 percent loss rate of 8.04 percent, which is quite close to the BIS 8 percent risk-based capital requirement. However, in relatively good years (e.g., 1986 to 1989), the 99 percent loss rate was much lower: 5.11 percent. Carey (2000) also shows that capital ratios in bad years must be about 175 percent of those in the good years if capital is set to cover unexpected losses computed at the 99 percent *VAR* level.[6]

A related issue is the representativeness of any given year or subperiod chosen to evaluate statistical moments such as the mean (expected) loss rate and the 99 percent unexpected loss rate. Suppose we look at 1991, a recession year. A set of systematic and unsystematic risk factors likely determined the intensity of the recession. The more a recession year reflects systematic rather than unsystematic recession risk factors, the more representative the loss experience of that year is, in "a predictive" sense, for

TABLE 12.1　Loss Rate Distribution When Monte Carlo Draws Are from Good versus Bad Years

This table compares Monte Carlo estimates of portfolio loss rates at the mean and at various percentiles of the credit loss rate distribution, when Monte Carlo draws are limited to the "good" years, 1986–1989, the "bad" years, 1990–1992, and the "worst" year, 1991. All drawn portfolios are $1 billion in size. The two panels, each with three rows, report results when all simulated portfolio assets are investment grade and below investment grade (rated below BBB), respectively. An exposure-to-one-borrower limit of 3 percent of the portfolio size was enforced in building simulated portfolios. Results in each row are based on 50,000 simulated portfolios.

Portfolio Characteristics		Simulated Portfolio Loss Rates (%)						
			At Loss Distribution Percentiles					
% Rated Below BBB	Years Used in Monte Carlo	Mean	95	97.5	99	99.5	99.9	99.95
0%	Good: 1986–1989	0.09	0.53	0.74	1.40	1.46	1.98	2.14
0%	Bad: 1990–1992	0.15	0.87	1.26	1.45	1.59	2.22	2.28
0%	Very bad: 1991	0.16	0.91	1.40	1.54	1.67	2.28	2.36
100%	Good: 1986–1989	1.73	4.18	4.63	5.11	5.43	5.91	6.05
100%	Bad: 1990–1992	2.53	5.59	6.31	7.19	7.82	8.95	9.33
100%	Very bad: 1991	3.76	6.68	7.30	8.04	8.55	9.72	10.19

Source: Carey (1998).

future bad recession years. This suggests that some type of screening tests need to be conducted on various recession years before a given year's loss experience is chosen as a benchmark for testing predictive accuracy among credit risk models and for calculating capital requirements.[7]

A second issue is the effect of outliers on simulated loss distributions. A few extreme outliers can seriously affect the mean, variance, skewness, and kurtosis of an estimated distribution, as well as the correlations among the loans implied in the portfolio. In a market risk model context, Stahl (1998) shows how only 5 outliers out of 1,000, in terms of foreign currency exchange rates, can have a major impact on estimated correlations among key currencies. With respect to credit risk, the danger is that a few big defaults in any given year could seriously bias the predictive power of any cross-sectional test of a given model. Carey (2000) demonstrates the importance of portfolio "granularity" (large disparities in loan sizes within the portfolio) on unexpected loss distributions. Table 12.2 shows that expected losses are relatively unaffected, but that unexpected losses, particularly in the extreme 99.9 percent extreme tails of the distribution, are sensitive to both the size disparity across loans (see rows 1 and 2 of Table 12.2) and large loans to single borrowers (rows 3 and 4 of Table 12.2).

A third issue deals with variability in *LGDs* across time and across debt instruments.[8] Table 12.3 shows the wide range of weighted average *LGD* over the period 1978 to 2001. *LGD* also varies across industry sector over time. For example, the telecommunications sector experienced a historically high 88 percent *LGD* during the second quarter of 2001 [see Altman and Karlin (2001b)]. Carey (2000) finds that assumptions about *LGD* significantly affect the loan portfolio's loss distribution. For example, allowing *LGD* to vary causes unexpected losses at the 99 percent tail of the loss distribution to increase from 0.64 percent (assuming a fixed *LGD* of 10 percent for all senior debt and a fixed *LGD* of 5 percent for all senior debt restructurings) to 3.18 percent for variable *LGDs* (assuming a mean *LGD* of 44 percent for senior debt and a mean *LGD* of 22 percent for senior debt restructurings). Moreover, Fraser (2000) uses CreditMetrics to stress test a portfolio of 331 liquid Eurobonds for *LGD* sensitivity, finding a significant 0.048 percent increase in portfolio 99 percent *VAR* for every 1 percent increase in expected *LGD*.

Stress tests of other model parameters show less sensitivity. For example, Fraser (2000) finds that a 1 percent increase in constant correlations assumed for a Eurobond portfolio causes a 0.026 percent increase in Credit-Metrics' estimate of 99 percent *VAR*, but that the impact was nonmonotonic; for certain ranges, as correlations increased, some risk measures actually decreased. Moreover, Carey (2000) finds that the distribution of obligors across industries (with different cross correlations) does not have much of an impact on unexpected loss estimates.

TABLE 12.2 The Impact of Loan Size Distribution on Portfolio Losses
Simulated Loss Rates (in percentage terms) for Different Portfolio Parameters

Simulation Parameters	Mean	95%	99%	99.5%	99.9%
Base case, 500 loans, random sizes	0.67	2.01	2.98	3.39	4.34
Base case, 500 loans, equal sizes	0.65	1.73	2.37	2.58	2.98
Base case, no one-borrower limit	0.66	2.09	3.38	4.16	7.81
Base case, 5% limit on lending to a single borrower	0.66	2.11	3.14	3.55	4.43

Source: Carey (2001), Tables 6 and 7.

TABLE 12.3 Weighted Average Recovery Rates on Defaulted Debt by Seniority per $100 Face Amount (1978–2001 Q2)

Default Year	Senior Secured		Senior Unsecured		Senior Subordinated		Subordinated		Discount and Zero Coupon		All Seniorities	
	No.	%	No.	%	No.	%	No.	%	No.	%	No.	%
2Q 01	5	29.71	85	31.13	25	14.51	0	0.00	20	12.71	135	24.68
2000	13	39.58	47	25.40	61	25.96	26	26.62	17	23.61	164	25.83
1999	14	26.90	60	42.54	40	23.56	2	13.88	11	17.30	127	31.14
1998	6	70.38	21	39.57	6	17.54	0	0	1	17.00	34	37.27
1997	4	74.90	12	70.94	6	31.89	1	60.00	2	19.00	25	53.89
1996	4	59.08	4	50.11	9	48.99	4	44.23	3	11.99	24	51.91
1995	5	44.64	9	50.50	17	39.01	1	20.00	1	17.50	33	41.77
1994	5	48.66	8	51.14	5	19.81	3	37.04	1	5.00	22	39.44
1993	2	55.75	7	33.38	10	51.50	9	28.38	4	31.75	32	38.83
1992	15	59.85	8	35.61	17	58.20	22	49.13	5	19.82	67	50.03
1991	4	44.12	69	55.84	37	31.91	38	24.30	9	27.89	157	40.67
1990	12	32.18	31	29.02	38	25.01	24	18.83	11	15.63	116	24.66
1989	9	82.69	16	53.70	21	19.60	30	23.95			76	35.97
1988	13	67.96	19	41.99	10	30.70	20	35.27			62	43.45
1987	4	90.68	17	72.02	6	56.24	4	35.25			31	66.63
1986	8	48.32	11	37.72	7	35.20	30	33.39			56	36.60
1985	2	74.25	3	34.81	7	36.18	15	41.45			27	41.78
1984	4	53.42	1	50.50	2	65.88	7	44.68			14	50.62
1983	1	71.00	3	67.72			4	41.79			8	55.17
1982			16	39.31			4	32.91			20	38.03
1981	1	72.00									1	72.00
1980			2	26.71			2	16.63			4	21.67
1979							1	31.00			1	31.00
1978			1	60.00							1	60.00
Total/ Average	131	52.81%	450	41.79%	324	29.97%	247	31.03%	85	18.92%	1237	35.81%
Median		57.42%		42.27%		31.90%		31.96%		17.40%		40.05%

Note: No. refers to number of bonds. *Source:* Altman and Karlin (2001b).

ALGORITHMICS MARK-TO-FUTURE

Back testing often takes the form of scenario analysis; that is, how will a credit risk model perform under different market scenarios? Stress testing, in particular, focuses on the extreme crisis scenarios. Algorithmics Mark-to-Future (MtF) is a scenario-based model that focuses on estimating each asset's risk and return characteristics under thousands of different scenarios corresponding to all major risk factors ranging from market risk to operational risk to credit risk. For example, Algorithmics MtF can create 5 to 20 extreme scenarios corresponding to historical "crashes" using 50 to 200 systemic market and credit factors to conduct credit risk stress tests over time horizons between 1 and 10 years. MtF differs from other credit risk measurement models in that it views market risk and credit risk as inseparable.[9] Stress tests show that credit risk measures are quite sensitive to market risk factors.[10] Indeed, it is the systemic risk parameters that drive creditworthiness in MtF.[11]

Dembo et al. (2000) offer an example of credit risk stress testing using MtF for a BB rated swap obligation. The firm's credit risk is estimated using a Merton model of default; that is, a creditworthiness index (CWI) is defined that specifies the distance to default as the distance between the value of the firm's assets and a (nonconstant) default boundary.[12] Figure 12.1 shows the scenario simulation of the CWI, illustrating two possible scenarios of firm

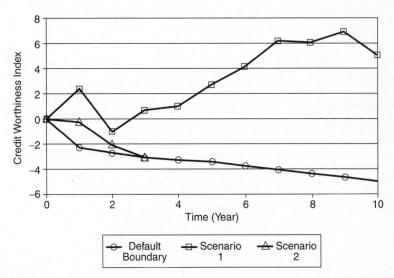

FIGURE 12.1 Merton model of default. *Source:* Dembo et al. (2000), p. 68.

asset values: (Scenario 1) the firm defaults in year 3 and (Scenario 2) the firm remains solvent for the next 10 years. The default date under each scenario is represented by the point at which the firm's asset value first hits the default boundary.[13] MtF assumes that the CWI follows a geometric Brownian motion standardized to have a mean of zero and a variance of one. The basic building block of the CWI is the unconditional cumulative default probabilities for typical BB rated firms, obtained using the Merton model (as discussed in Chapter 4). Using the unconditional default probabilities as a foundation, a conditional cumulative default probability distribution is generated for each scenario. That is, the sensitivity of the default probability to scenario risk factors is estimated for each scenario. For example, suppose that the unconditional likelihood of default within five years for a BB firm is 9.6 percent. Choose a particular scenario of the time path of the S&P 500 and six-month U.S. Treasury rates over the next 10 years. Figure 12.2 plots the hypothesized fluctuations in the S&P 500 (the index return) and U.S. Treasury rates (the interest rate return) for a particular scenario over the next 10 years. This is the credit driver. Suppose that in this particular scenario (call it scenario 9 or S9), the credit driver decreases about 1.2 standard deviations in five years.

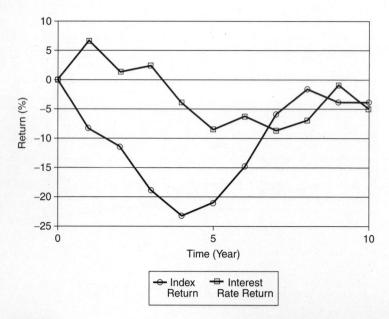

FIGURE 12.2 Scenario S9 returns. *Source:* Dembo et al. (2000), p. 70.

What is the impact of the decline in the credit driver represented in scenario S9 on the default risk of this BB rated firm? MtF estimates all BB rated firms' historical sensitivity to the credit driver using a multifactor model that incorporates both systemic and idiosyncratic credit factors. If the results of the multifactor model suggest that the obligor has a positive correlation to the credit driver, then the swap's credit quality is expected to decrease under scenario S9. The conditional cumulative default probability is calculated based on the results of the multifactor model. In this example, the BB rated firm's five-year probability of default increases from 9.6 percent to 11.4 percent under scenario S9. This process is replicated for several scenarios. Figure 12.3 shows the conditional default probabilities for 10 different credit driver scenarios (including S9). A return distribution can be derived using the full range of possible scenarios.

The results for scenario S9 depend on the assumption that systemic risk explains 5 percent of the total variance of the CWI, with idiosyncratic risk explaining the remaining 95 percent. If on the other hand, systemic risk accounted for 80 percent of the variance, the five-year conditional default probability under scenario S9 would have been 44.4 percent instead of 11.4 percent. Therefore, conditional default probabilities have higher volatility when the systemic risk component is greater.

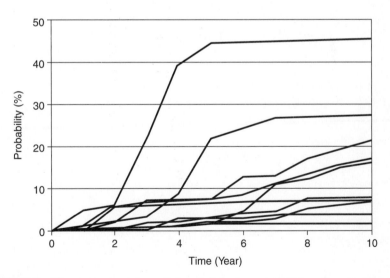

FIGURE 12.3 Ten scenarios of conditional default probabilities. *Source:* Dembo et al. (2000), p. 70.

SUMMARY

A key measure of the usefulness of internal credit risk models is their predictive ability. Tests of predictive ability—such as back testing—are difficult for credit risk models because of the lack of sufficiently long time-series data. Nevertheless, given a large and representative (in a default risk sense) loan portfolio, it is possible to stress test credit risk models by using cross-sectional subportfolio sampling techniques that provide predictive information on average loss rates and unexpected loss rates. Moreover, the predictive accuracy, in a cross-sectional sense, of different models can be used to choose the most appropriate credit risk measurement model. In the future, wider-panel data sets, and even time series of loan loss experience, are likely to be developed by banks and/or consortia of banks.

Another approach to credit risk stress testing, that avoids the problem of scenario-specific data limitations, is the scenario analysis approach, such as adopted by Algorithmics Mark-to-Future. Credit drivers, comprised of market risk factors, are used to estimate conditional default probabilities. Varying the credit driver scenario causes changes in conditional default probabilities which are then used to determine a creditworthiness index. Scenarios can also be chosen to replicate extreme events in order to stress test the portfolio's credit risk exposure.

CHAPTER 13

Risk-Adjusted Return on Capital Models

Today, virtually all major banks and FIs have developed risk-adjusted return on capital (RAROC) models to evaluate the profitability of various
business lines, including their lending. The RAROC concept was first introduced by Bankers Trust in the 1970s. The recent surge among banks and
other FIs to adopt proprietary forms of the RAROC approach can be explained by two major forces: (1) the demand by stockholders for improved
performance, especially the maximization of shareholder value and (2) the
growth of FI conglomerates built around separate business units (or profit
centers). These two developments have been the impetus for banks to develop a measure of performance that is comparable across business units,
especially when the capital of the bank is both costly and limited.

WHAT IS RAROC?

In terms of modern portfolio theory (MPT), RAROC can best be thought of
as a Sharpe ratio for business units, including lending. Its numerator, as explained next, is some measure of adjusted income over either a future period
(the next year) or a past period (last year). The denominator is a measure of
the unexpected loss or economic capital at risk (VAR) as a result of that activity. Thus:

$$\text{RAROC} = \frac{\text{Adjusted income}}{\text{Capital at risk}} \qquad (13.1)$$

In this chapter, we concentrate on the measurement of RAROC in
terms of lending, although, as noted in equation (13.1), it can be applied

across all areas of the bank.[1] Once calculated, the RAROC of a loan is meant to be compared with some hurdle rate reflecting the bank's cost of funds or the opportunity cost of stockholders in holding equity in the bank. Thus, in some RAROC models, the hurdle rate is the bank stockholders' return on equity (ROE); in others, it is some measure of the weighted-average cost of capital (WACC).[2] If:

$$RAROC > \text{Hurdle rate} \qquad (13.2)$$

then the loan is viewed as value adding, and scarce bank capital should be allocated to the activity.[3]

Because RAROC historically has been calculated on a stand-alone basis, with correlations among activities ignored, the number of projects/activities satisfying equation (13.2) often exceeds the available (economic) capital of the bank. It may take time to raise new equity to fund all "valuable" projects (in a RAROC sense), so a second-round allocation of economic capital usually takes place [see Dermine (1998) and Crouhy, Turnbull, and Wakeman (1998)].[4] This is to calculate a weight (w_j) such that:

$$w_j = \frac{EC_B}{\sum_{j=1}^{n} EC_j} \qquad (13.3)$$

where EC_B is the available economic capital of the bank and EC_j is the stand-alone economic capital allocation to the viable (acceptable) projects under equation (13.2).[5] Marginal economic capital allocated for the jth business unit is $w_j EC_j$ and across all business units:

$$\sum_{j=1}^{n} w_j EC_j = EC_B$$

RAROC VERSUS ROA VERSUS RORAC

Before looking at the different forms that RAROC can take, it is worthwhile to briefly compare RAROC with ROA (return on assets) and RORAC (return on risk-adjusted capital). The formulas for these alternative (loan) performance measures are:

$$\text{ROA} = \frac{\text{Adjusted income}}{\text{Assets lent}} \qquad (13.4)$$

$$\text{RORAC} = \frac{\text{Adjusted income}}{\text{BIS risk-based capital requirement}} \qquad (13.5)$$

All three measures—RAROC, ROA, and RORAC—potentially calculate income in a similar fashion, but they differ in the calculation of the denominator. Thus, ROA, a traditional measure of performance, completely ignores the risk of the activity of lending, and uses assets lent as the denominator. RORAC uses the BIS regulatory capital requirement as a measure of the capital at risk from the activity. Under BIS I for private-sector loans, this meant taking the book value of the outstanding loan and multiplying it by 8 percent. Under BIS II the relevant capital amount will depend on the model used (standardized or internal-ratings based) and potentially the *PD*, *LGD*, and maturity of the loan exposure. By comparison, the alternative forms of RAROC discussed next seek to more accurately measure the economic or *VAR* exposure from lending activity. To the extent that the BIS II regulatory proposals are successful at more accurately assessing a capital requirement that covers the credit risk of the loan portfolio, RORAC measures should approach RAROC measures upon adoption of the new capital standards.

ALTERNATIVE FORMS OF RAROC

We next discuss the two components of the ratio: (1) the numerator and (2) the denominator.

The Numerator

As shown in equation (13.1), the numerator reflects the adjusted expected one-year income on a loan. The numerator can reflect all or a subset of the following factors (where τ is the marginal tax rate):

$$\genfrac{}{}{0pt}{}{\text{Adjusted}}{\text{income}} = \left[\text{Spread} + \text{Fees} - \genfrac{}{}{0pt}{}{\text{Expected}}{\text{loss}} - \genfrac{}{}{0pt}{}{\text{Operating}}{\text{costs}} \right] (1 - \tau) \qquad (13.6)$$

The spread term reflects the direct income earned on the loan—essentially, the difference between the loan rate and the bank's cost of funds. To this should be added fees directly attributable to the loan over the next year.

For example, loan origination fees would be added, as would commitment fees. There are, however, a number of "gray" areas. Suppose, in making a loan to a small business, the small business brings its asset management business to the bank (the customer relationship effect) and that business also generates annual fees. A lending officer may view these asset management fees as part of the loan's profitability, and thus the loan's RAROC calculation. The bank's asset manager will also claim some of the fees, as part of his or her RAROC calculation for the asset management unit. The danger is that fees will be double or triple counted. A very careful allocation of fees via some allocation matrix is needed, so as to avoid the "double-counting" problem.[6]

In many RAROC models, two deductions are commonly made, from the spread and fees, to calculate adjusted income. The first recognizes that expected losses are part of normal banking business and deducts these from direct income. One way to do this would be to use a KMV-type model for each loan i, where:

$$\text{Expected loss}_i = EDF_i \times LGD_i \tag{13.7}$$

Alternatively, some annual accounting-based loss reserves can be allocated to the loan. As Dermine (1998) notes, this can bias the calculation if there is a link between the loan's maturity and the size of annual loss reserves. Finally, some RAROC models deduct measures of a loan's operating costs, such as a loan officer's time and resources in originating and monitoring the loan. In practice, precise allocation of such costs across loans has proved to be very difficult.

Finally, equation (13.6) computes the asset's after-tax adjusted income, where τ is often set equal to the statutory tax rate. However, Nakada et al. (1999) use the effective corporate tax rate to measure the tax penalty associated with the double taxation of returns—once at the corporate level and again at the shareholder level.[7] More precisely, however, the appropriate tax rate should be the asset's effective marginal tax rate. That is, all else being equal, shareholders would prefer the project with the lower effective tax rate if different earning streams are subject to differential tax treatments.

The Denominator

Historically, two approaches have emerged to measure the denominator of the RAROC equation or economic capital at risk.[8] The first approach, following Bankers Trust, develops a market-based measure. The second, following Bank of America among others, develops an experiential or historically based measure.

The original Bankers Trust approach was to measure capital at risk as being equal to the maximum (adverse) change in the market value of a loan over the next year. Starting with the duration equation:

$$\frac{\Delta L}{L} = -D_L \frac{\Delta R}{1 + R_L} \qquad (13.8)$$

$(\Delta L/L)$ is the percentage change in the market value of the loan expected over the next year, D_L is the Macauley duration of the loan, and $\Delta R/(1 + R_L)$ is the expected maximum discounted change in the credit-risk premium on the loan during the next year.[9] We can rewrite the duration equation with the following interpretation:

$$\Delta L \quad = \quad -D_L \quad \times \quad L \quad \times \quad \left(\frac{\Delta R}{1 + R_L}\right) \qquad (13.9)$$

(Dollar capital risk exposure or loss amount)	=	(Duration of the loan)	×	(Risk amount or loan exposure)	×	(Expected discounted change in the credit premium or risk factor on the loan)

The loan's duration (say, 2.7 years) and the loan amount (say, $1 million) are easily estimated. It is more difficult to estimate the maximum change in the credit risk premium on the loan expected over the next year. Publicly available data on loan risk premiums are scarce, so users of this approach turn to publicly available corporate bond market data to estimate credit risk premiums. First, a Standard and Poor's (S&P) or other credit rating is assigned to a borrower. Thereafter, the risk premium changes of all the bonds traded in that particular rating class over the past year are analyzed. The ΔR in the RAROC equation is then:

$$\Delta R = \text{Max} \left[\Delta(R_i - R_G) > 0\right] \qquad (13.10)$$

where $\Delta(R_i - R_G)$ is the change in the yield spread between corporate bonds of credit rating class i (R_i) and matched-duration U.S. Treasury bonds (R_G) over the past year. To consider only the worst-case scenario, the maximum change in yield spread is chosen, as opposed to the average change.

As an example, let us evaluate the credit risk of a loan to an AAA borrower. Assume there are currently 400 publicly traded bonds in that class (the bonds were issued by firms whose rating type is similar to that of the borrower). The first step is to evaluate the actual changes in the credit risk premiums $(R_i - R_G)$ on each bond for the past year. These (hypothetical) changes are plotted in the frequency curve of Figure 13.1. They range from a fall in the risk premium of 1 percent to an increase of 3.5 percent. Because the largest increase may be a very extreme (unrepresentative) number, the 99 percent worst-case scenario is chosen. (Only 4 bonds out of 400 have risk premium increases exceeding the 99 percent worst case.) For the example shown in Figure 13.1, ΔR is equal to 1.1 percent.

The estimate of loan (or capital) risk, assuming that the current average level of rates on AAA bonds is 10 percent, is:

$$\Delta L = -D_L \times L \times \frac{\Delta R}{1 + R_L}$$

$$= -(2.7)(\$1 \text{ million})\left(\frac{.011}{1.10}\right) \qquad (13.11)$$

$$= -\$27,000$$

Thus, although the face value of the loan amount is $1 million, the risk amount, or change in the loan's market value due to a decline in its credit quality, is $27,000.

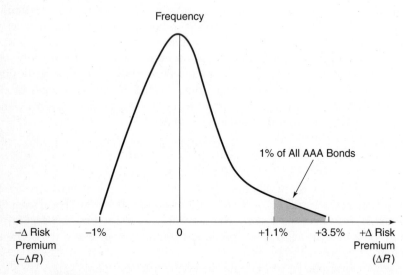

FIGURE 13.1 Estimating the change in the risk premium.

To determine whether the loan is worth making, the estimated loan risk is compared to the loan's adjusted income. For simplicity, we ignore operating costs and marginal corporate tax rates here (although estimates of these could be made). Suppose the annual projected adjusted income is:

$$\text{Spread} = 0.2\% \times \$1 \text{ million} \quad = \$2,000$$
$$\text{Fees} = 0.15\% \times \$1 \text{ million} = \$1,500 \quad\quad (13.12)$$
$$\text{Expected loss} = 0.1\% \times \$0.5 \text{ million} = \underline{\$ \ (500)}$$
$$\$3,000$$

$$\text{RAROC} = \frac{\substack{\text{One-year adjusted}\\\text{income on loan}}}{\text{Capital at risk}(\Delta L)} = \frac{\$3,000}{\$27,000} = 11.1\%$$

If this RAROC (11.1 percent) exceeds the bank's hurdle rate, the loan should be made.[10]

Most banks, however, have adopted a different way to calculate the denominator of the RAROC equation or capital at risk (unexpected loss). The calculation usually involves experiential modeling based on a historic database of loan (or bond) defaults. Essentially, for each type of borrower, the adjusted one-year income is divided by an unexpected default rate, and the result is multiplied by the loss given default (LGD), where the unexpected default rate is some multiple of the historic standard deviation of default rates (σ) for such borrowers. The multiple of σ used will reflect both the desired credit rating of the bank and the actual distribution of losses. For example, suppose the bank wants to achieve an AA rating, thereby requiring that only 0.03 percent of AA firms default in a year. Consequently, the amount of capital needed has to cover up to 99.97 percent of loan (asset) losses. Based on the standardized normal distribution, the standard deviation of losses (σ) would have to be multiplied by 3.4; that is:[11]

$$\text{Unexpected loss}_i = 3.4 \times \sigma_i \times LGD_i \times \text{Exposure}_i \quad\quad (13.13)$$

However, as discussed in Chapters 4 through 8, loan loss distributions tend to be skewed and to have fat tails, and, depending on the fatness of the tail, the multiplier of σ is increased. For example, Zaik, Walter, and Kelling (1996) report that Bank of America uses a multiplier of 6:

$$\text{Unexpected loss}_i = 6 \times \sigma_i \times LGD_i \times \text{Exposure}_i \quad\quad (13.14)$$

Others have argued for a multiplier as high as 10 if a bank wants to achieve AAA status.[12]

THE RAROC DENOMINATOR AND CORRELATIONS

Neither the market-based version [equation (13.8)] nor the experientially based version [equation (13.13)] of the RAROC denominator allows for correlations (and thus diversification) among business line risks, including lending.[13] That the RAROC equation should take such correlations into account can be seen by calculating the RAROC from a one-factor capital asset pricing model (CAPM) that describes the equilibrium risk-return trade-offs among assets and implicitly assumes that loans are tradeable assets like equities. This theoretical RAROC includes an adjustment for correlation in its denominator. Specifically, applying the CAPM following James (1996), Crouhy, Turnbull, and Wakeman (1998), and Ho (1999) as follows:

$$R_i - r_f = \beta_i \, (R_m - r_f) \qquad (13.15)$$

where R_i = the return on a risky asset,
r_f = the risk-free rate,
R_m = the return on the market portfolio,
β_i = the risk of the risky asset,
and

$$\beta_i = \frac{\sigma_{im}}{\sigma^2_m} = \frac{\rho_{im}\sigma_i\sigma_m}{\sigma^2_m} = \frac{\rho_{im}\sigma_i}{\sigma_m} \qquad (13.16)$$

where σ_{im} = covariance between the returns on risky asset i and the market portfolio m,
σ_m = standard deviation of the return on the market portfolio,
ρ_{im} = correlation between the returns on the risky asset i and the market portfolio,
$\rho_{im}\sigma_i\sigma_m = \sigma_{im}$, by definition.

Substituting equation (13.16) into equation (13.15), we have:

$$R_i - r_f = \rho_{im}\sigma_{im}\frac{\left(R_m - r_f\right)}{\sigma_m} \qquad (13.17)$$

and, rearranging:

$$\frac{R_i - r_f}{\rho_{im}\sigma_i} = \frac{R_m - r_f}{\sigma_m} \tag{13.18}$$

$$\text{RAROC} = \text{Hurdle rate}$$

The left side of equation (13.18) is the theoretical RAROC; the right side is the hurdle rate, the excess return on the market per unit of market risk (or the market price of risk). As can be seen by setting $\rho_{im} = 1$, the theoretical RAROC takes the stand-alone form employed by most banks, which is also the traditional Sharpe ratio, $(R_i - r_f)/\sigma_i$, for a risky asset. This will clearly bias against projects for which (excess) returns $(R_i - r_f)$ may be low but which have low correlations with other projects within the bank. Reportedly, some banks are building correlations into their RAROC denominators; that is, they are measuring unexpected loss as:

$$\text{Unexpected loss}_i = \rho_{im} \times \text{Multiplier} \times \sigma_i \times LGD_i \times \text{Exposure}_i \tag{13.19}$$

In doing so, two issues arise. First, looking at the correlation of the loan's return with the market (even if estimable) may be erroneous unless the bank is holding a very well diversified portfolio of tradeable assets (i.e., liquid and marketable assets). Some multifactor specification of equation (13.15) may be more appropriate in many cases. Second, the RAROC formula in equation (13.19) becomes non-implementable if ρ_{im} lies in the range $-1 \le \rho_{im} \le 0$.

Flaws in this analysis emanate from the implied CAPM assumption that once the loan's unsystematic risk is diversified away, all that remains is the loan's systematic risk exposure to market risk. However, if that were true, then the loan's market risk might be more efficiently (and less expensively) managed and hedged using derivatives and there would be no need to allocate capital using RAROC since risk by implication would largely be diversified away (at least for traded derivatives or organized exchanges where the basis risk is small). That is, the RAROC approach was developed to deal with the risk of *untraded* and *unhedgeable* assets, such as loans, for which the CAPM does not generally apply.

Banks specialize in information-intensive relationship lending activities that cannot be efficiently offered by capital markets.[14] Only a fraction of the risk of these loans can be hedged using fairly priced currency and interest rate derivatives; the remainder is often an illiquid credit risk component, although the recent growth in the market for credit derivatives has reduced this illiquid portion somewhat. The bank prices these two components of risk differently. The market portion of the loan's risk is priced in the capital market and is based only on the loan's correlation with systematic market risk factors as previously shown. However, the nontraded or illiquid credit risk component of the loan must be evaluated by each bank individually, with the risk pricing based on the loan's correlation with the credit risk of the bank's own portfolio. Since each bank's portfolio will have a different credit risk exposure, each bank will price a loan differently. That is, a bank with a loan portfolio uncorrelated with the credit risk of the proposed loan will offer the borrower more attractive terms than a bank with a portfolio of loans that is highly correlated with the credit risk of the new loan. Froot and Stein (1998) decompose loan risk into tradeable and nontradeable risk components using a two-factor model.

Suppose that a bank has an opportunity to either accept or reject a loan of a small amount relative to the total portfolio size.[15] Froot and Stein (1998) and James (1996) decompose the loan's total risk ε into a tradeable, market risk component, denoted ε_T, and a nontradeable, illiquid credit risk component, denoted ε_N, as follows:

$$\varepsilon = \varepsilon_T + \varepsilon_N$$

By construction, the nontradeable risk component ε_N is uncorrelated with the market portfolio. In contrast, the tradeable risk component ε_T is fully priced using the CAPM. Froot and Stein (1998) show that the hurdle rate, the required return on the loan, denoted μ^*, can be expressed as:[16]

$$\mu^* = g\,cov\left(\varepsilon_T, m\right) + G\,cov\left(\varepsilon_N, \varepsilon_p\right) \tag{13.20}$$

where μ^* = the loan's hurdle rate,
  ε_T = the tradeable, market risk portion of the loan's total risk,
  ε_N = the nontradeable, illiquid credit risk portion of the loan's total risk,
  ε_p = the nontradeable, illiquid credit risk portion of the entire loan portfolio,
  m = the systematic market risk factor,
  g = the market unit price of systematic risk,
  G = the bank's level of risk aversion.

It can be shown that g is simply the CAPM hurdle rate from equation (13.18); that is:

$$g = \frac{R_m - r_f}{\sigma_m}$$

Thus, the first term in equation (13.20), $g\ cov(\varepsilon_T, m)$, is the market price of the loan's tradeable risk component where the $cov(\varepsilon_T, m)$ term incorporates the covariance (implicitly the correlation) of the tradeable risk on the loan with the market. Moreover, in the second "additional" term, G measures the impact on shareholder wealth of marginal changes in the value of the bank's portfolio. If it is costly for the bank to raise external funds on short notice, then the bank's shareholders will be risk averse with respect to fluctuations in the portfolio's value.[17] Thus, the second term in equation (13.20) is the cost to bank shareholders in terms of capital at risk due to volatility stemming from the loan's untradeable risk component.[18] Equation (13.20) can then be restated as:

$$\text{Hurdle rate} = \begin{array}{c} \text{Market price} \\ \text{of the loan's} \\ \text{traded risk} \end{array} + \begin{array}{c} \text{Bank shareholders'cost} \\ \text{of capital to cover} \\ \text{nontradeable risk} \end{array} \quad (13.20')$$

The bank will make the loan only if the expected return on the loan (the adjusted income) exceeds the risk-adjusted hurdle rate in equation (13.20').

RAROC AND EVA

Equation (13.20') illustrates the link between RAROC and economic value added (EVA), which is a risk-adjusted performance measure increasingly used by banks and other corporations. In the context of lending, EVA requires a loan to be made only if it adds to the economic value of the bank from the shareholders' perspective. In fact, an EVA formula can be directly developed from the RAROC formula.

Assume ROE is the hurdle rate for RAROC. A loan should be made if:

$$RAROC > ROE \quad (13.21)$$

or:

$$\frac{\left(\text{Spread} + \text{Fees} - \text{Expected loss} - \text{Operating costs}\right)}{\text{Capital at risk or economic capital }(K)} > \text{ROE}$$

Rearranging, the EVA per dollar of the loan is positive if the net dollar profit of loan returns exceeds the total dollar capital cost of funding; that is:

$$(\text{Spread} + \text{Fees} - \text{Expected loss} - \text{Operating costs}) - \text{ROE} \times K \geq 0$$

SUMMARY

This chapter has discussed the RAROC model of lending (and other business-unit performance). RAROC is similar to a Sharpe ratio commonly analyzed in assessing the performance of risky assets and portfolios of risky assets (such as mutual funds). There are two different approaches to calculating RAROC: (1) the market-based approach and (2) the experiential approach. A major weakness of the RAROC model is its explicit failure to account for correlations. To correct this, we examine a two-factor model that incorporates the loan's correlation with the bank portfolio's illiquid credit risk exposure. This implies that bank capital is costly and therefore that shareholders are averse to unhedgeable, illiquid credit risks. This is supported by the prevalence of RAROC-type models introduced in response to shareholder initiatives.

CHAPTER 14

Off-Balance-Sheet Credit Risk

The tremendous growth in off-balance-sheet (OBS) over-the-counter (OTC) contracts, such as swaps, forwards, and customized options, has raised questions as to where credit risk exposure really lies: Is it on- or off-the balance sheet? For example, as of December 2000, the total (on-balance-sheet) assets of all U.S. banks was $5 trillion and for Euro area banks it was over $13 trillion. The value of nongovernment debt and bond markets worldwide was almost $12 trillion. In contrast, global derivatives markets exceeded $84 trillion in notional value; see Rule 2001.

Given the growth and importance of OBS exposures, a question arises as to the applicability of the models discussed in Chapters 4 through 13 to OBS activities. To the extent that a model (such as KMV) is seeking to predict the probability of default, it is as applicable to the measurement of counterparty default risk on a swap contract as it is to a borrower's defaulting on a loan contract.[1] Where differences arise, however, is in measuring the *VAR* of an OBS position and assessing the credit exposure of a portfolio of OBS positions.

In this chapter, we will evaluate the credit *VAR* of OBS contracts. Because of the importance of interest rate swaps in most banks' OBS portfolios, much of the discussion will focus on these instruments.

MEASURING THE CREDIT RISK AND *VAR* OF INTEREST RATE SWAPS

As is well known, the credit risk on an interest rate swap is less than the credit risk on an equivalent size loan [see, for example, Smith, Smithson, and Wilford (1990)]. Specifically, apart from the fact that interest rate swap exposure reflects only the difference between two interest-rate-linked cash flows, rather than the full principal amount as in the case of a loan, at least two conditions have to pertain for a counterparty to default on a swap: (1) the swap contract has to be out-of-the-money to a counterparty (i.e., it has to have an $NPV < 0$) and (2) the counterparty has to be in financial distress. In addition to these preconditions, banks and other FIs that engage in swaps have put in place a number of other mechanisms that further reduce the probability of default on a swap contract or the loss given default. These mechanisms are:

1. Rationing or capping the notional value of swap exposure to any given counterparty.
2. Establishing bilateral and multilateral netting across contracts.
3. Establishing collateral guarantee requirements.
4. Marking-to-market long-term swap contracts at relatively frequent intervals.
5. Restricting maturities of contracts.
6. Establishing special-purpose vehicles (with high capitalization) through which to engage in swap contracts.
7. Adjusting the fixed rate of the swap contract for a risk premium that reflects the credit risk of the counterparty.[2]

Building all of these features into a credit VAR model is difficult but not infeasible. Here, we look first at the framework under BIS I for calculating the capital requirement for swaps and other OTC derivative instruments. BIS II proposes to accept the BIS I framework with exceptions for credit risk mitigation. That is, BIS II proposals (described in this chapter) recognize that credit risk can be reduced by collateral, credit derivatives and guarantees, and offsetting positions subject to netting agreements. Finally, we discuss how CreditMetrics and others estimate the credit VAR for a plain-vanilla interest-rate swap contract.

CREDIT RISK FOR SWAPS: THE BIS I MODEL

Under the current BIS I risk-based capital regulations, a major distinction is made between exchange-traded derivative security contracts (e.g., Chicago Board of Trade exchange-traded options) and over-the-counter (OTC) traded instruments (e.g., forwards, swaps, caps, and floors).[3] The credit or default risk of exchange-traded derivatives is approximately zero because when a counterparty defaults on its obligations, the exchange itself adopts the counterparty's obligations in full. However, no such guarantee exists for bilaterally negotiated OTC contracts originated and traded outside organized exchanges. Hence, most OBS futures and options positions have no capital requirements for a bank, although most forwards, swaps, caps, and floors do.

For the purposes of capital regulation under the BIS I codes, the calculation of the risk-adjusted asset values of OBS market contracts requires a two-step approach: (1) credit equivalent amounts are calculated for each contract and (2) the credit equivalent amounts are multiplied by an appropriate risk weight.

Specifically, the notional or face values of all non-exchange-traded swap, forward, and other derivative contracts are first converted into credit equivalent amounts (i.e., "as if" they are on balance sheet credit instruments). The credit equivalent amount itself is divided into a *potential exposure* element and a *current exposure* element:

$$\begin{matrix} \text{Credit equivalent amount} \\ \text{of OBS derivative} \\ \text{security items (\$)} \end{matrix} = \begin{matrix} \text{Potential} \\ \text{exposure (\$)} \end{matrix} + \begin{matrix} \text{Current} \\ \text{exposure (\$)} \end{matrix} \quad (14.1)$$

The potential exposure component reflects the credit risk if the counterparty to the contract defaults in the future. The probability of such an occurrence is modeled as depending on the future volatility of interest rates/exchange rates. Based on a Federal Reserve Bank of England Monte Carlo simulation exercise (see Appendix 14.1), the BIS I came up with a set of conversion factors that varied by type of contract (e.g., interest rate or FX) and by maturity bucket (see Table 14.1). The potential exposure conversion factors in Table 14.1 are larger for foreign exchange contracts than

TABLE 14.1   Credit Conversion Factors for Interest Rate and Foreign Exchange Contracts in Calculating Potential Exposure (as a percent of Nominal Contract Value)

	Conversion Factors For:	
Remaining Maturity	Interest Rate Contracts (%)	Exchange Rate Contracts (%)
1. One year or less	0.0	1.0
2. One to five years	0.5	5.0
3. Over five years	1.5	7.5

Source: Federal Reserve Board of Governors press release, August 1995, Section II.

for interest rate contracts. Also, note the larger potential exposure credit risk for longer term contracts of both types.

In addition to calculating the potential exposure of an OBS market instrument, a bank must calculate its current exposure to the instrument: the cost of replacing a contract if a counterparty defaults today. The bank calculates this replacement cost or current exposure by replacing the rate or price that was initially in the contract with the current rate or price for a similar contract and then recalculates all the current and future cash flows to give a current present value measure of the replacement cost of the contract.

If $NPV > 0$, then the replacement value equals current exposure. However, if $NPV < 0$, then current exposure is set to zero because a bank cannot be allowed to gain by defaulting on an out-of-the money contract.

After the current and potential exposure amounts are summed to produce the credit equivalent amount of each contract, this dollar number is multiplied by a risk weight to produce the final risk-adjusted asset amount for OBS market contracts. In general, the appropriate risk weight under BIS I is .5, or 50 percent, that is:

$$\frac{\text{Risk-adjusted asset value}}{\text{of OBS market contracts}} = \frac{\text{Total credit equivalent}}{\text{amount} \times .5 \text{ (risk weight)}} \qquad (14.2)$$

BIS II proposals remove the 50 percent ceiling on risk weights for over-the-counter derivative transactions. If the derivative is unconditionally cancelable or automatically cancels upon deterioration in the borrower's creditworthiness, then the risk weight is set at 0 percent. In contrast, a risk weight of 100 percent is applied to transactions secured by bank collateral or to transactions in which the bank provides third-party performance guarantees. A 50 (20) percent risk weight is retained for commitments with an original maturity over (less than) one year (see discussion in next section).

An Example

Suppose that the bank had taken one interest-rate hedging position in the fixed-floating interest rate swap market for four years with a notional dollar amount of $100 million, and one two-year forward $/£ foreign exchange contract for $40 million. The credit equivalent amount for each item or contract is shown in Table 14.2.

For the four-year fixed-floating interest rate swap, the notional value (contract face value) of the swap is $100 million. Because this is a long-term, over-one-year, less-than-five-year interest rate contract, its face value is multiplied by .005 to get a potential exposure or credit risk equivalent

TABLE 14.2 Potential Exposure + Current Exposure ($ Millions)

Type of Contract (Remaining Maturity)	Notional Principal ×	Potential Exposure Conversion Factor =	Potential Exposure ($)	Replacement Cost	Current Exposure =	Credit Equivalent Amount
4-Year fixed–floating interest rate swap	$100 ×	.005 =	.5	3	3 =	$3.5
2-Year forward foreign exchange contract	$ 40 ×	.05 =	2	−1	0 =	$2
$A_{gross} = \$2.5$		Net current exposure = $2			Current exposure = $3	

value of $0.5 million (see Table 14.2). We add this potential exposure to the replacement cost (current exposure) of this contract to the bank. The replacement cost reflects the cost of having to enter into a new fixed-floating swap agreement, at today's interest rates, for the remaining life of the swap. Assuming that interest rates today are less favorable, on a present value basis, the cost of replacing the existing contract for its remaining life would be $3 million. Thus, the total credit equivalent amount (current plus potential exposure for the interest rate swap) is $3.5 million.

Next, we look at the foreign exchange two-year forward contract of $40 million face value. Because this is an over-one-year, less-than-five-year foreign exchange contract, the potential (future) credit risk is $40 million × .05 or $2 million (see Table 14.2). However, its replacement cost is – $1 million and, as discussed earlier, when the replacement cost of a contract is negative, the current exposure has to be set equal to zero (as shown). Thus, the sum of potential exposure ($2 million) and current exposure ($0) produces a total credit equivalent amount of $2 million for this contract.

Because the bank in this example has just two OBS derivative contracts, summing the two credit equivalent amounts produces a total credit equivalent amount of $3.5 million + $2 million = $5.5 million for the bank's OBS market contracts. The next step is to multiply this credit equivalent amount by the appropriate risk weight. Specifically, to calculate the risk-adjusted asset value for the bank's OBS derivative or market contracts, we multiply the credit equivalent amount by the appropriate risk weight, which, for virtually all over-the-counter derivative security products, is .5, or 50 percent:[4]

$$\text{Risk-adjusted asset value of OBS derivatives} = \underset{\text{equivalent amount)}}{\$5.5 \text{ million (credit}} \times \underset{\text{weight)}}{0.5 \text{ (risk}} = \$2.75 \text{ million} \quad (14.3)$$

As with the risk-based capital requirement for loans, the BIS I regulations do not directly take into account potential reductions in credit risk from holding a diversified portfolio of OBS contracts. As Hendricks (1994) and others have shown, a portfolio of 50 pay-floating and 50 pay-fixed swap contracts will be less risky than a portfolio of 100 pay-fixed (or floating) contracts (see Appendix 14.2). Nevertheless, although portfolio diversification is not recognized directly, it has been recognized indirectly since October 1995, when banks were allowed to net contracts with the same counterparty under standard master agreements.

The post-1995 BIS netting rules define net current exposure as the net sum of all positive and negative replacement costs (or mark-to-market values of the individual derivative contracts). The net potential exposure is defined by a formula that adjusts the gross potential exposure estimated earlier:

$$A_{net} = (0.4 \times A_{gross}) + (0.6 \times NGR \times A_{gross}) \quad (14.4)$$

where A_{net} is the net potential exposure (or adjusted sum of potential future credit exposures), A_{gross} is the sum of the potential exposures of each contract, and NGR is the ratio of net current exposure to gross current exposure. The 0.6 is the amount of potential exposure that is reduced as a result of netting.[5]

The same example (with netting) will be used to show the effects of netting on the total credit equivalent amount. Here, we assume both contracts are with the same counterparty (see Table 14.2).

The net current exposure is the sum of the positive and negative replacement costs; that is, $3 million + (−$1 million) = $2 million. The total current exposure is $3 million and the gross potential exposure (A_{gross}) is $2.5 million. To determine the net potential exposure, the following formula is used and then substituted into equation (14.4):

$$NGR = \frac{\text{Net current exposure}}{\text{Current exposure}} = \frac{\$2 \text{ million}}{\$3 \text{ million}} = \tfrac{2}{3} \quad (14.5)$$

$$A_{net} = (0.4 \times 2.5) + (0.6 \times \tfrac{2}{3} \times 2.5)$$

$$= \$2 \text{ million}$$

$$\begin{array}{ccccc} \text{Total credit} & = & \text{Net potential} & + & \text{Net current} \\ \text{equivalent amount} & & \text{exposure} & & \text{exposure} \\ \$4 \text{ million} & = & \$2 \text{ million} & + & \$2 \text{ million} \end{array} \quad (14.6)$$

$$\begin{array}{ccccc} \text{Risk-adjusted asset} & & & & 0.5 \text{ (risk} \\ \text{value of OBS} & = & \text{Total credit} & \times & \text{weight)} \\ \text{market contracts} & & \text{equivalent amount} & & \\ \$2 \text{ million} & = & \$4 \text{ million} & \times & 0.5 \end{array} \quad (14.7)$$

As can be seen, using netting reduces the risk-adjusted asset value from $2.75 million to $2 million. And, given the BIS 8 percent capital requirement, the capital required against the OBS contracts is reduced from $220,000 to $160,000.[6] This capital requirement may be reduced even further by BIS II proposals that take credit mitigation into account by adjusting the exposure to reflect the value of collateral, credit guarantees, or netting. We discuss these proposals in the next section.

BIS II CREDIT MITIGATION PROPOSALS

BIS II proposals seek to eliminate incentive incompatability in BIS I regulations that may require more capital against a protected or collateralized obligation than against an obligation fully exposed to credit risk. In this section, we focus on collateral as the form of credit risk mitigation, although the proposals also consider netting and the use of credit derivatives (discussed in Chapter 15).[7]

The methodology of the BIS II credit risk mitigation proposal reduces the exposure level to reflect the protection afforded by credit risk mitigation. That is, credit risk is measured on a portfolio basis; for example, the credit protection offered under master netting agreements permits the transfer of additional (nonpledged) collateral in the event of the failure of the counterparty. Indeed, November 2001 potential modifications incorporate credit risk mitigation that spans the banking and trading books.

Under BIS II proposals, the BIS I risk weights are retained[8] and then applied to an adjusted exposure level that reflects the collateral value. To use the example shown in equation (14.7), if the OBS position was 25 percent collateralized, then the risk-adjusted asset value would be reduced to $1.5 million [= $4m × .5 × (1 − .25)], rather than $2 million. To determine the collateral weight, haircuts are applied to the value of collateral in order to protect against volatility in collateral prices. Table 14.3 shows the standard supervisory haircuts proposed under BIS II.[9]

TABLE 14.3 Standard Supervisory Haircuts for Credit Risk Mitigation Proposals under BIS II

Issue Rating for Debt Securities	Remaining Maturity	Debt Issued by Sovereigns (%)	Debt Issued by Banks/ Corporates (%)
AAA, AA	≤ 1 year	0.5	1
	> 1 year, ≤ 5 years	2	4
	> 5 years	4	8
A, BBB	≤ 1 year	1	2
	> 1 year, ≤ 5 years	3	6
	> 5 years	6	12
BB	≤ 1 year	20	Not eligible
	> 1 year, ≤ 5 years	20	Not eligible
	> 5 years	20	Not eligible
Equities main index		20	20
Other equities		30	30
Cash		0	0
Gold		15	15
Surcharge—foreign exchange risk		8	8

Note: Supervisors may permit banks to calculate haircuts using their own internal estimates of market price volatility and foreign exchange rate volatility. *Source:* BIS (January 2001), p. 20.

The haircuts shown in Table 14.3 are used to calculate the adjusted value of collateral as follows:

$$C_A = \frac{C}{\left[1 + H_E + H_C + H_{FX}\right]} \tag{14.8}$$

where C_A = the adjusted value of collateral,
C = the current value of the collateral,
H_E = the haircut appropriate to the exposure,
H_C = the haircut appropriate to the collateral,
H_{FX} = the haircut for any currency mismatch (set at 8 percent).

The adjusted value of the exposure, denoted E^*, is then calculated as:

$$\begin{aligned} E^* &= E - (1-w)C_A \quad \text{if } C_A < E \text{ and} \\ &= wE \qquad\qquad\quad \text{if } C \geq E \end{aligned} \tag{14.9}$$

where E = the value of the uncollateralized exposure,
   w = the weighting factor to cover remaining risks, set equal to
   0.15 for collateralized transactions,
   C_A = the value of the collateral adjusted by the haircuts.

Thus, if the exposure is fully collateralized, there is a floor (equal to $wE = 0.15E$) capital requirement. For example, a fully collateralized $4 million exposure would have an adjusted exposure value E^* equal to $600,000 (= 0.15 × $4m) for a floor capital level (assuming a 50 percent risk weight and an 8 percent capital requirement) of $24,000 (= $600,000 × 0.5 × 0.08). If, however, the exposure was not fully collateralized, then the adjusted exposure E^* would be calculated using $E - (1 - w)C_A$. For example, if the adjusted collateral value was $1 million on the $4 million exposure, then the adjusted exposure value E^* would be $3.15 million (= $4m - (1 - .15)$1m) for a $126,000 capital charge (= $3.15m × .5 × .08 assuming a 50 percent risk weight and an 8 percent capital requirement).

CREDITMETRICS AND SWAP CREDIT RISK: *VAR*

The BIS is concerned with calculating default risk on an OBS instrument, such as a swap, if default were to occur today (current exposure) or at any future time during the contract's remaining life (potential exposure). CreditMetrics concentrates its *VAR* calculation on the one-year horizon. Assuming some credit event occurs during the next year, how will the value of the swap be affected during its remaining life?

Conceptually, the value of a swap is the difference between two components. The first component is the *NPV* of a swap between two default risk-free counterparties. This involves valuing the swap at the year 1 horizon, based on fixed and expected (forward) government rates, and discounting by the one year forward zero curve (see Chapter 6, Appendix 6.1).

For example, in a three-year plain-vanilla swap (see Figure 14.1), the expected net present value at the one-year horizon [hereafter, swap future value (*FV*)] would be:

$$FV = \frac{\left(\overline{F} - \tilde{f_2}\right)}{\left(1 + {}_1 z_1\right)} + \frac{\left(\overline{F} - \tilde{f_3}\right)}{\left(1 + {}_1 z_2\right)^2} \tag{14.10}$$

where $\overline{F}$ = fixed rate on swap,
   $\tilde{f_t}$ = one year forward rates (expected floating rates) for t year maturity,
   ${}_1 z_t$ = one year forward zero-coupon rates with t year maturity.

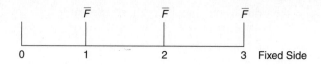

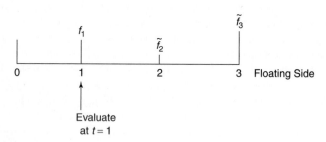

FIGURE 14.1   Calculating the forward value of a default risk-free swap.

Any positive (or negative) FV reflects movements in government yield curves and thus interest-rate (or market) risk on the swap rather than the default risk on the swap—although, as noted earlier and in what follows, it is difficult to separate the two because the more out-of-the-money a contract becomes to any given party, the greater is the incentive to default.[10]

The second component of a swap's value is an adjustment for credit risk. CreditMetrics deducts from the FV of any swap an expected loss amount reflecting credit risk. This expected loss amount will vary by the end of the year-1 horizon rating category of the counterparty (e.g., AAA versus C) and by default (D). Thus, as with loans, eight different expected losses will be associated with the eight different transition states over the one-year horizon (including the counterparty's credit rating remaining unchanged). Hence:

$$
\begin{array}{ccc}
\text{Value of} & FV & \text{Expected loss} \\
\text{swap at} & \text{(risk-free} & \text{rating class } R \\
\text{year 1 for} = & \text{future value} - & \text{(year 1 through} \\
\text{rating class } R & \text{in year 1)} & \text{to maturity)}
\end{array}
\qquad (14.11)
$$

In turn, for each of the seven nondefault ratings, the expected loss is calculated as the product of three variables:

$$
\begin{array}{ccccc}
\text{Expected} & \text{Average} & & \text{Cumulative} & \text{Loss} \\
\text{loss} & \text{exposure} & & \text{probability of} & \text{given} \\
\text{(rating} & = & \text{(year 1} & \times & \text{default (year 1} & \times & \text{default} \\
\text{class } R) & \text{through year } N) & & \text{through year } N) &
\end{array}
\qquad (14.12)
$$

We discuss each variable in the next section.

Average Exposure

As is well known, two general forces drive the default risk exposure on a fixed-floating swap. The first is what may be called the interest-rate diffusion effect—the tendency of floating rates to drift apart from fixed rates with the passage of time. The degree of drift depends on the type of interest rate model employed (e.g., mean reversion or no mean reversion), but, in general, the diffusion effect on exposure may be as shown in Figure 14.2a: increasing with the term of the swap. Offsetting the diffusion effect, in terms of replacement cost, is the maturity effect. As time passes and the swap gets closer to maturity, the number of payment periods a replacement contract must cover declines. Thus, the maturity effect tends to reduce exposure as the time remaining to swap maturity shrinks (see Figure 14.2b). The overall effect of the two forces on future replacement cost (exposure) is shown in Figure 14.2c, which suggests that future exposure levels rise, reach a maximum, and then decline. To measure exposure amounts each year into the future, two approaches are normally followed: (1) a Monte Carlo simulation method or (2) an option pricing method.[11]

Figure 14.2c shows the average annual exposure amount. For a three-year swap, with two years to run beyond the one-year credit-event horizon, the average exposure is the average of the swap's exposure as measured at the beginning of year 2 and year 3.

Cumulative Probability of Default

As discussed in Chapter 8, the cumulative mortality rate (*CMR*) over N years is linked to marginal (annual) mortality rates (*MMRs*) by

$$
CMR = 1 - \prod_{i=1}^{N} \left(1 - MMR_i\right)
\qquad (14.13)
$$

Assuming that transition probabilities follow a stationary Markov process, then the *CMRs* for any given rating can be found by either: (1) using a

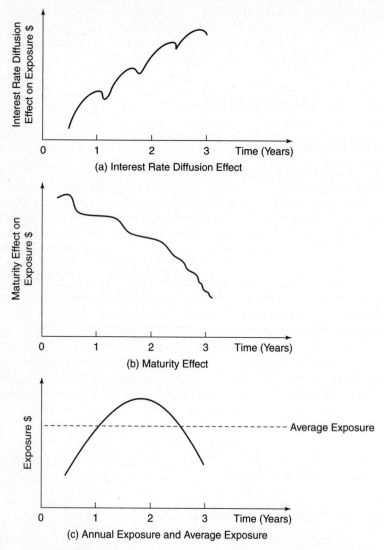

FIGURE 14.2 Measuring swap average exposure.

methodology similar to Altman (1989), that is, calculating the annual *MMR*s and then the appropriate *CMR* for the remaining life of the swap or (2) multiplying the annual transition matrix by itself *N* times (where *N* is the remaining years of the swap contract at the one-year horizon).[12] In the three-year swap, the cumulative mortality rates would be the last column calculated from the matrix:

$$(\text{One-year transition matrix})^2 \qquad (14.14)$$

Loss Given Default, *LGD*

The loss given default or (1 – the recovery rate) should not only reflect the loss per contract, but, where relevant (as under the BIS II proposals), take netting into account.

The product of average exposure (*AE*), the cumulative probability of default (*CMR*), and the loss given default (*LGD*) gives the expected loss for each of the seven nondefault rating transitions. However, in the event of default on or before the credit horizon (1 year), the expected loss is given as:

Expected loss on default = Expected exposure in year 1 × *LGD*   (14.15)

Specifically, in the three-year swap, where default is assumed to occur at the end of year 1, exposure will be measured by the total replacement cost over the remaining two years of the swap.[13]

An Example

Following CreditMetrics, consider the example of a three-year fixed floating rate swap with a notional value of $10 million, an *LGD* of 50 percent, and an average exposure, measured at the end of year 1, of $61,627. Based on historical (bond) transition matrices (and *CMR*s calculated therefrom) for a counterparty rated AA at the end of the one-year credit-event horizon, the value of the swap is:

$$\text{Value of swap at credit horizon} = FV - \text{Expected loss}$$
$$= FV - [AE \times CMR_{AA} \times LGD]$$
$$= FV - [\$61,627 \times 0.0002 \times 0.5]$$
$$= FV - \$6$$

where the FV is the expected future value of the default-free swap at the end of the year. For a three-year swap where the counterparty is rated CCC at the end of the one-year credit horizon:

$$\text{Value of swap at credit horizon} = FV - [\$61{,}627 \times 0.3344 \times 0.5]$$

$$= FV - \$10{,}304$$

The lower value of the CCC counterparty swap reflects the higher CMR of that type of counterparty over the remaining two years of the swap. Note also that the lower rated counterparty may also have a higher LGD, although in this example it is assumed to be the same as the LGD for the AA rated counterparty. If the CCC rated counterparty had a lower LGD than 50 percent, then the swap value would be even lower.

For a swap, where the counterparty defaults during the one-year horizon, expected exposure (EE or replacement cost) over the remaining two years is assumed to be $101,721. Thus:

$$\text{Value of swap at the one-year horizon} = FV - [EE \times LGD]$$

$$= FV - [\$101{,}721 \times 0.5]$$

$$= FV - \$50{,}860$$

Table 14.4 summarizes the expected swap values at the end of year 1 under the seven possible rating transitions and the one default state.

TABLE 14.4 Value of Three-Year Swap at the End of Year 1

Rating of Counterparty	Value ($)
AAA	FV – 1
AA	FV – 6
A	FV – 46
BBB	FV – 148
BB	FV – 797
B	FV – 3,209
CCC	FV – 10,304
D	FV – 50,860

Source: Gupton et al., *Technical Document,* April 2, 1997, p. 51.

The size of the expected and unexpected loss of value on a swap will depend on the initial rating of the counterparty at time 0 (today), the one-year transition probabilities during the first year, and the one-year forward or expected future values (*FV*) calculated in Table 14.5, where the counterparty is rated as AA today (time 0).

Table 14.5 shows that the credit-related expected loss of value on the swap is $21.8, and the 99 percent unexpected loss of value (*VAR*) is approximately $126.2. If the original rating of the swap counterparty is lower, the expected and unexpected losses of value are likely to be higher.

A similar methodology could be used to calculate the credit *VAR* of forwards (swaps can be viewed as a succession of forward contracts) as well as interest rate options and caps. For example, the average exposure on a three-year interest rate cap, as measured at the end of the one-year horizon, would be the average of the replacement cost of the cap (the fair value of the cap premium[14] under an appropriate interest rate model) measured at the beginning of year 2 and the beginning of year 3. As with swaps, replacement costs tend to reflect a similar inverted U-shape, as shown in Figure 14.2c, because of the offsetting effects of the interest rate diffusion effect and the maturity effect.[15]

TABLE 14.5 Expected and Unexpected Loss on a Three-Year $10 Million Swap to an AA Counterparty

Rating at Year 1	One-Year Transition Probability (%)	Value of Swap at One-Year Horizon ($)
AAA	0.7	FV - 1
AA	90.65	FV - 6
A	7.65	FV - 46
BBB	0.77	FV - 148
BB	0.06	FV - 797
B	0.14	FV - 3,209
CCC	0.02	FV - 10,304
D	0.01	FV - 50,860
	100.00	Expected FV − 21.8
		99% Value FV − 148

$$\frac{99\% \text{ unexpected}}{\text{loss of value}} = \left[\text{Expected value } - \text{ 99 percent value}\right] = \$126.2.$$

Source: Gupton et al., *Technical Document*, April 2, 1997.

SUMMARY

In this chapter, we analyzed the way in which a *VAR*-type methodology can be extended to the credit risk of derivative instruments. The BIS model uses a bucketing approach based on the type of contract and its maturity, but newer private-sector models such as CreditMetrics have sought to extend to the calculation of the credit *VAR* on derivative instruments a methodology similar to that used in loan valuation and *VAR* calculation. The BIS II proposals continue the rigid regulatory specification of risk weights and conversion factors for off-balance sheet items, with only a limited reduction in capital requirements available to those banks that meet regulatory requirements on disclosure and internal risk management systems. However, the BIS II proposals reduce bank disincentives to mitigate their credit risk exposure by allowing banks to reduce capital requirements for obligations protected from credit risk exposure by collateral, credit guarantees, and offsetting positions subject to netting agreements.

APPENDIX 14.1
THE BIS MODEL FOR SWAPS

This appendix discusses the underlying Monte Carlo simulation approach used in establishing capital requirements for swaps' potential exposure under BIS I.[16] The proposed New Capital Accord, BIS II, essentially retains this approach with the exception that when the bank provides a guarantee that a third party will perform on its obligations (as when the bank intermediates a swap transaction), then the bank must calculate capital requirements as if it were a party to the transaction (see Chapter 15).

SIMULATION STEPS

1. Choose a random number between 0 and 1. Set this equal to $\Phi(z)$, the area under the standard normal cumulative density function (c.d.f.) to the left of the level z.
2. Look up z for this value of $\Phi(z)$ from the standard normal c.d.f. table.
3. $\Delta(\log r) = \dfrac{zs}{\sqrt{2}}$, for example, assumed log-normal interest rate process.
4. $\log R_{i+1} = \log R_i + \Delta(\log r)$
5. $R_{i+1} = \exp(\log R_{i+1})$
6. Semiannual cash flows (see Figure 14.3).

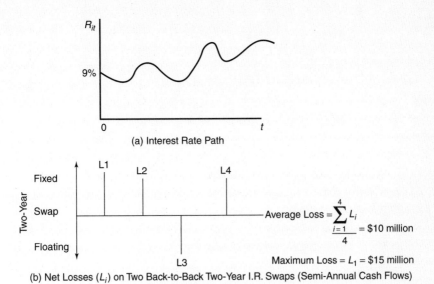

(a) Interest Rate Path

(b) Net Losses (L_i) on Two Back-to-Back Two-Year I.R. Swaps (Semi-Annual Cash Flows)

$$\text{Average Loss} = \frac{\sum_{i=1}^{4} L_i}{4} = \$10 \text{ million}$$

$$\text{Maximum Loss} = L_1 = \$15 \text{ million}$$

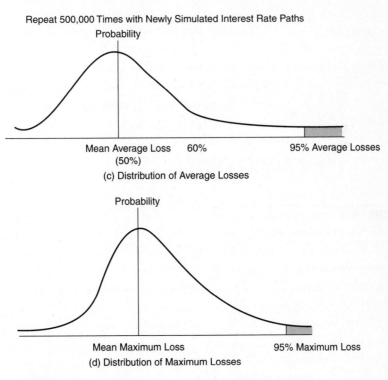

Repeat 500,000 Times with Newly Simulated Interest Rate Paths

(c) Distribution of Average Losses

(d) Distribution of Maximum Losses

FIGURE 14.3   Simulating loss distributions: Simulation 1.

$$\Delta \log r \sim N\left(\frac{0, s^2}{2}\right)$$

$$\frac{\sqrt{2}}{s} \Delta(\log r) \sim N(0,1)$$

$$\Phi(z) = P_r\left(\frac{\sqrt{2}}{s} \Delta(\log r) \le z\right) = P_r\left(\Delta(\log r) \le \frac{zs}{\sqrt{2}}\right)$$

As an example, consider the following initial conditions: $R_0 = 0.09$, $s = 0.182$, where $s = $ the annual standard deviation of interest rate changes.
   Step 1, Simulation 1:

$$\log R_{i+1} = \log R_i + \Delta(\log r)$$

$$= \log(.09) + \frac{zs}{\sqrt{2}}$$

$$= -2.407 + \left[1.127\left(\frac{.182}{1.414}\right)\right]$$

$$= -2.407 + .1449$$

$$= -2.26$$

$$R_{i+1} = \exp[\log R_{i+1}] = e^{-2.26}$$

$$= .1043 \text{ or } 10.43\%$$

See line 1, Simulation 1, in Table 14.6.

TABLE 14.6   Monte Carlo Simulation of Future Interest Rates on Fixed–Floating U.S. Interest Rate Swap

	Simulation 1			
R_i	$\phi(z)$ (Random No.)	z	$\Delta \log r_i$	R_{i+1}
$R_0 = 0.09$	0.87	1.127	0.1449	0.1043
$R_1 = 0.1043$	0.33	−0.44	−0.0566	0.0983
$R_2 = 0.0983$	0.18	−0.915	−0.1178	0.0874
$R_3 = 0.0874$	0.24	−0.706	−0.0909	0.0798
$R_4 = 0.0798$	0.42	−0.202	−0.0260	0.0778
$R_5 = 0.0778$	—	—	—	—

TABLE 14.6 (*Continued*)

	Simulation 2			
R_i	$\phi(z)$ (**Random No.**)	z	$\Delta logr_i$	R_{i+1}
$R_0 = 0.09$	0.28	−0.583	−0.075	0.0835
$R_1 = 0.835$	0.91	1.341	0.1726	0.0992
$R_2 = 0.0992$	0.66	0.412	0.0530	0.1046
$R_3 = 0.1046$	0.15	−1.036	−0.1333	0.0916
$R_4 = 0.0916$	0.98	2.054	0.2643	0.1193
$R_5 = 0.1193$	—	—	—	—

APPENDIX 14.2
THE EFFECTS OF DIVERSIFICATION
ON SWAP PORTFOLIO RISK

A simple example, following Hendricks (1994), can demonstrate the risk of a portfolio of swaps and the effects of diversification.

Suppose there are N contracts in the portfolio and the risk (σ_i) of each is the same. Following MPT, the risk of a portfolio (σ_p) is:

$$\sigma_p = \sigma_i \sqrt{N + 2\sum_{\substack{i=1 \\ }}^{N}\sum_{\substack{j=1 \\ i \neq j}}^{N}\rho_{ij}} \qquad (14.16)$$

Define an average correlation coefficient ($\bar{\rho}$):

$$\bar{\rho} = \frac{\displaystyle\sum_{i=1}^{N}\sum_{j=1}^{N}\rho_{ij}}{\dfrac{\left(N^2 - N\right)}{2}} \qquad (14.17)$$

Then

$$\sigma_p = \sigma_i \sqrt{N + \left(N^2 - N\right)\bar{\rho}} \qquad (14.18)$$

From equation (14.18), the higher the risk (σ_i) of each swap contract, the higher the risk of the swap portfolio; the larger the number of contracts (N) in the portfolio, the higher the risk of the portfolio; and the lower the average correlation coefficient ($\bar{\rho}$), the lower the portfolio risk. Because a more diverse swap portfolio will have a lower $\bar{\rho}$ (e.g., an equal mix of pay fixed/receive floating, and pay floating/receive fixed), the composition of the swap portfolio may be as important as its size in determining the credit risk of an OBS derivatives portfolio.

CHAPTER 15

Credit Derivatives

There has been an explosive growth in the use of credit derivatives. Estimates in June 2001 put the market at approximately US$1 trillion in notional value worldwide.[1] It is clear that the market for credit derivatives is still young, with quite a bit of growth potential. Market participants estimate that currently the worldwide market in credit derivatives is doubling in size each year. Compared to other international derivatives markets, the market for credit derivatives is still in its infancy. For example, BIS data show that the market for interest rate derivatives totaled $65 trillion (in terms of notional principal), foreign exchange rate derivatives exceeded $16 trillion, and equities almost $2 trillion.[2] Given the dominance of credit risk in the portfolios of banks and other FIs, the worldwide market in credit derivatives clearly has considerable room for growth.

The growth in trading of credit derivatives that are designed to transfer the credit risk on portfolios of bank loans or debt securities has facilitated a net overall transfer of credit risk from banks to non-banks, principally insurance companies. This development may have both positive and negative consequences for global financial market stability. By allowing banks to hold more diversified credit portfolios, the use of credit derivatives reduces bank vulnerability to systemic shocks. Moreover, credit is more available and the likelihood of credit crunches reduced when lenders can use credit derivatives to transfer the credit risk of loans that they originate. However, this may create a wedge between borrower and lender, thereby hampering monitoring and restructuring activities.[3] Moreover, by dispersing credit risk throughout the financial system, the impact of those shocks is more broadly felt, thereby increasing systemic risk exposure to economic downturns; see Rule 2001.

In this chapter, we first document the treatment of credit derivatives under the BIS capital standards, and the use of these instruments in solving the "paradox of credit" (see Chapter 10). We then look at the individual instruments: (1) credit options, (2) credit swaps, (3) credit forwards, and (4) credit securitizations.

CREDIT DERIVATIVES AND THE BIS
CAPITAL REQUIREMENTS

The role of credit derivatives in credit risk management can best be seen in the context of the paradox of credit, discussed in Chapter 10 (see Figure 10.1). Given a concentrated loan portfolio, there are at least two ways for a bank to reach the efficient frontier and/or improve its risk-return performance. The first, as discussed in Chapters 10 and 11, is to more actively manage its loan portfolio by trading loans. However, as noted in Chapter 10, this tends to adversely impact customer relationships, especially if a long-term borrower from a bank discovers that his or her loan has been sold.

An alternative way to improve the risk-return trade-off on a loan portfolio is to take an off-balance-sheet position in credit derivatives. As will be discussed next, credit derivatives allow a bank to alter the risk-return trade-off of a loan portfolio without having to sell or remove loans from the balance sheet.[4] Apart from avoiding an adverse customer relationship effect, the use of credit derivatives (rather than loan sales) may allow a bank to avoid adverse timing of tax payments, as well as liquidity problems related to buying back a similar loan at a later date if risk-return considerations so dictate. Thus, for customer relationship, tax, transaction cost, and liquidity reasons, a bank may prefer the credit derivative solution to loan portfolio optimization rather than the more direct (loan trading) portfolio management solution. Figure 15.1 shows the breakdown of market participants buying and selling protection against credit risk. Banks, securities firms, and corporates are net buyers of credit protection, whereas insurance companies, hedge funds, mutual funds, and pension funds are net sellers.[5]

Despite their apparent value as credit risk management tools, credit derivatives have not been well treated under the BIS I capital requirements.[6] According to Wall and Shrikhande (1998), the present U.S. approach is to treat credit derivatives as a loan guarantee, provided the payoff from the credit derivative is sufficiently highly correlated with the loan. If the counterparty is neither a bank nor a government entity, the risk weight is 100 percent (i.e., no risk reduction is recognized). If the counterparty is a bank, the risk weight on the loan for the buyer of the guarantee is 20 percent; however, for the bank that issues the guarantee to the counterparty, the risk weight of the guarantee is 100 percent (i.e., it is as if the counterparty has been extended a loan). Thus, in the aggregate, the combined risk-based capital requirements of the two banks could increase as a result of using the derivative. (Under certain conditions, however, this capital burden may be reduced.)[7,8]

BIS II proposes a harmonization of treatment of credit derivatives under the two approaches—standardized and internal ratings based (IRB) methods (see Chapter 3). For buyers of credit protection that use the standardized

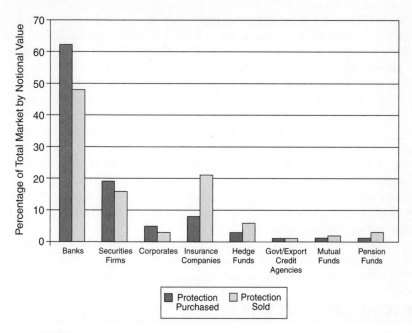

FIGURE 15.1 Breakdown of credit swap market participants.

approach, the risk weight for banking book (and some trading book) exposures protected using credit derivatives is calculated as follows:

$$r^* = [w \times r] + [(1-w)g] \qquad (15.1)$$

where r^* = the effective risk weight of the protected position,
r = the risk weight of the underlying obligor (the borrower),
w = the residual risk factor, set at 0.15 for credit derivatives,[9]
g = the risk weight of the protection provider.

For example, if the credit protection was obtained from a AAA rated insurance company (with a 20 percent risk weight under the standardized approach) for the bank's underlying credit exposure to a B rated corporate borrower (150 percent risk weight), the effective risk weight on the credit derivative would be:

$$39.5\% = (0.15 \times 150\%) + (0.85 \times 20\%)$$

If instead of using the standardized approach, the bank buying credit protection used the IRB approach, the risk weights r and g in equation (15.1) would be replaced by the probabilities of default obtained using the bank's credit risk measurement model.

These risk-adjusted capital requirements are for credit derivatives protecting loans on the banking book. BIS II also proposes specific risk capital charges against trading book positions hedged by credit derivatives. If the reference asset, maturity and currency of the credit derivative exactly matches those of the underlying hedged position, then BIS II allows an 80 percent specific risk offset to avoid risk double counting. If maturities or currencies are mismatched, but the reference assets are identical, only the higher of the specific risk capital charges will be levied against the entire hedged position. November 2001 proposed modifications would further integrate the banking and trading books.

Next, we look at how various types of derivatives can be used to hedge the credit risk of loans or portfolios of loans.

HEDGING CREDIT RISK WITH OPTIONS

The rationale for using option contracts was detailed in Chapter 4, where it was argued that a banker, in making a loan, receives a payoff similar to that of a writer of a put option on the assets of a firm. The upside return on the loan is relatively fixed (as is the premium to a put option writer) and has a long-tailed downside risk (like the potential payout exposure of a put option writer; see Figure 15.2). If a banker making a loan faces a risk equivalent to writing a put option on the assets of the firm, he or she may seek to hedge that risk by buying a put option on the assets of the firm, so as to truncate or limit a part, or all, of the downside risk on the loan (or portfolio of loans).

One early use of options in this context was for farming loans in the Midwest. In return for a loan, a wheat farmer was required to post collateral in the form of put options on wheat purchased from a major Chicago options exchange. If the price of wheat fell, the market value of the loan fell because the probability of the farmer's repaying the loan in full declined (and the *LGD* increased). Offsetting this decline in the implied market value of the loan was the rise in value of the put options on wheat posted as collateral by the borrower. The offsetting effect of the rising value of the wheat put options is shown in Figure 15.2.

There are two problems with this type of hedging vehicle:

1. The farmer may default for idiosyncratic reasons (e.g., divorce, injury, and so on) rather than because the price of the crop falls. As a result, a large "basis risk" is present in the credit risk hedge.

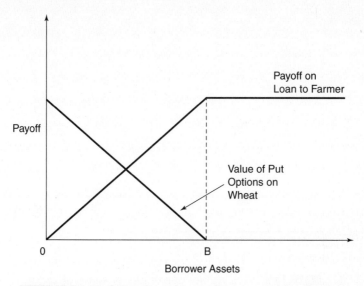

FIGURE 15.2 Hedging the risk on a loan to a wheat farmer.

2. The requirement that the farmer must post collateral (and thus pay an options premium to the exchange) may make the loan contract very expensive—especially if the farmer is required to buy close-to-the-money options—and may harm the bank's relationship with the farmer.

More direct methods of hedging credit risk through options have been developed. A *credit spread call option* is a call option in which the payoff increases as the credit spread on a borrower's specified benchmark bond increases above some exercise spread, S_T. If a bank is concerned that the risk of a loan will increase, it can purchase a credit spread call option to hedge its increased credit risk (see Figure 15.3). As the credit quality of a borrower declines, his or her credit spread rises, and the potential payoffs from the option increase. To the extent that the values of the borrower's (nontraded) loans and publicly traded bonds are highly correlated, the decline in the value of the loan (as credit quality declines) is offset by the increase in the value of the option.[10] Specifically, the payoff from the spread option will be:

$$\text{Payoff on option} = MD \times \text{Face value of option} \times \left[\text{Current credit spread} - S_T\right] \quad (15.2)$$

where MD = the modified duration of the underlying bond in the credit spread option contract;
S_T = the strike spread.[11]

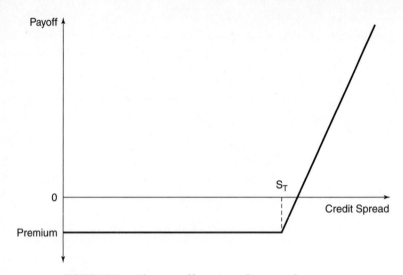

FIGURE 15.3   The payoff on a credit spread option.

A second innovation is the *default option,* an option that pays a stated amount in the event of a loan default (the extreme case of increased credit risk). As shown in Figure 15.4, the bank can purchase a default option covering the par value of a loan (or loans) in its portfolio. In the event of a loan default, the option writer pays the bank the par value of the defaulted loans.

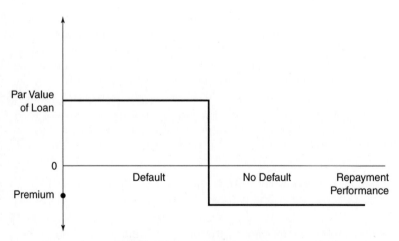

FIGURE 15.4   A default option.

If the loans are paid off in accordance with the loan agreement, however, the default option expires unexercised. As a result, the bank will suffer a maximum loss on the option equal to the premium (cost) of buying the default option from the writer (seller). There are other variants on these simple options; for example, a barrier feature might be written into the credit spread option. If the credit quality of a borrower improves, and spreads fall below some "barrier" spread, the option will cease to exist. In return, the buyer of the credit spread option will pay a lower premium than would be required for the plain-vanilla credit spread option considered earlier.

HEDGING CREDIT RISK WITH SWAPS

Credit options are being used increasingly, but the dominant credit derivative to date has been the credit swap. Rule (2001) cites a British Bankers Association survey that found that 50 percent of the notional value of all credit derivatives are credit swaps, as compared to 23 percent collateralized loan obligations, 13 percent credit-linked notes, 8 percent baskets,[12] and only 6 percent credit spread options. There are two main types of credit swaps: (1) total return swap and (2) pure credit or default swap (CDS).

The Total Return Swap

A total return swap involves swapping an obligation to pay interest at a specified fixed or floating rate for payments representing the total return on a loan or a bond. For example, suppose that a bank lends $100 million to a manufacturing firm at a fixed rate of 10 percent. If the firm's credit risk increases unexpectedly over the life of the loan, the market value of the loan will fall. The bank can seek to hedge an unexpected increase in the borrower's credit risk by entering into a total return swap in which it agrees to to pay a counterparty the total return based on an annual rate, $\bar{F}$, equal to the promised interest (and fees) on the loan, plus the change in the market value of the loan. In return, the bank receives a variable market rate payment of interest annually (e.g., one-year LIBOR that reflects its cost of funds). Figure 15.5 and Table 15.1 illustrate the cash flows associated with the typical total return swap.

Using the total return swap, the bank agrees to pay a fixed rate of interest annually, plus the capital gains or losses on the market value of the loan over the period of the swap. In Figure 15.5, P_0 denotes the market value of the loan at the beginning of the swap payment period, and P_T represents the market value of the loan at the end of a swap payment period (here, one year). If the loan decreases in value over the payment period, the bank pays

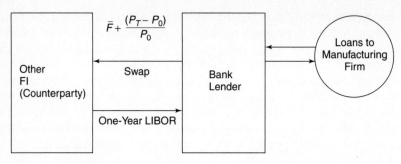

FIGURE 15.5 Cash flows on a total return swap.

the counterparty a relatively small (possibly negative) amount equal to the fixed payment on the swap minus the capital loss on the loan.[13] For example, suppose the loan was priced at par $(P_0 = 100)$ at the beginning of the swap period. At the end of the swap period (or the first payment date), the loan has an estimated market value of 90 $(P_T = 90)$ because of an increase in the borrower's credit risk. Suppose that the fixed rate payment $(\bar{F})$ as part of the total return swap is 12 percent. The bank would send to the swap counterparty the fixed rate of 12 percent minus 10 percent (the capital loss on

TABLE 15.1 Cash Flows on Total Return Swap

	Annual Cash Flow for Year 1 through Final Year	Additional Payment by FI	Total Return (First Payment Period)
Cash inflow (on swap to bank)	1 year LIBOR (11 percent)	—	1 year LIBOR (11 percent)
Cash outflow (on swap to FI)	Fixed rate $(\bar{F})$ (12 percent)	$\dfrac{P_T - P_0}{P_0}$	$\bar{F} + \left[\dfrac{P_T - P_0}{P_0}\right]$
			$12 \text{ percent} + \dfrac{90-100}{100} =$
			$12 \text{ percent} - 10 \text{ percent} = 2 \text{ percent}$
			Net profit $= 11 \text{ percent} - 2 \text{ percent}$
			$= 9 \text{ percent}$

the loan), or a total of 2 percent, and would receive in return a floating payment (e.g., LIBOR = 11 percent) from the counterparty to the swap. Thus, the net profit on the swap to the bank/lender is 9 percent (11 percent minus 2 percent) times the notional amount of the swap contract. This gain can be used to offset the loss of market value of the loan over that period. This example is summarized in Table 15.1 [see Finnerty (1996)].

Pure Credit or Default Swaps

Total return swaps can be used to hedge credit risk exposure, but they contain an element of interest (or market) risk as well as credit risk. For example, in Table 15.1, if the LIBOR rate changes, then the *net* cash flows on the total return swap will also change, even though the credit risk of the underlying loans has not necessarily changed.

To strip out the interest-rate-sensitive element of total return swaps, an alternate swap, called a "pure" credit or default swap, has been developed.[14] The credit default swap (CDS) is characterized by the following terms:

1. The identity of the reference loan [i.e., the notional value, maturity, and the credit spread (over LIBOR) on a risky loan issued by the reference obligor].[15]
2. The definition of a credit event—usually any one of the following: bankruptcy, prepayment, default, failure to pay, repudiation/moratorium, or restructuring.
3. The compensation that the protection seller will pay the protection buyer if a credit event occurs.
4. Specification of either physical settlement (delivery of agreed debt instruments) or cash settlement.[16]

In July 1999, ISDA published a credit swap master agreement to standardize the terms and conditions of CDS transactions.[17] This standardization has facilitated trading and pricing transparency in the market. The premium on the CDS is similar to the credit spread on the reference debt trading at par. Thus, the CDS market promotes price discovery in illiquid debt markets (see discussion of noisy debt prices in Chapter 5), as well as harmonizes pricing across segmented markets, thereby increasing debt market efficiency.

As shown in Figure 15.6, the protection buyer on a CDS (say, the bank lender) will send (in each swap period) a fixed fee or payment (similar to an option premium) to the protection seller (swap counterparty). The fixed fee is known as the swap premium or swap quote. If the CDS reference loan (or loans) does not default, the protection buyer will receive nothing back from

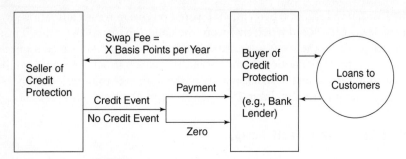

FIGURE 15.6   A credit default swap (CDS).

the swap counterparty. However, if the loan (or loans) defaults, the counterparty will cover the default loss by making a default payment equal to the par value of the original loan (e.g., $P_0 = \$100$) minus the secondary market value of the defaulted loan (e.g., $P_T = \$40$); that is, the counterparty will pay the bank $P_0 - P_T$ ($\$60$, in this example).[18] Thus, the CDS pays out par minus the recovery value of the loan in the event of default. A pure credit swap is similar to buying credit insurance and/or a multiperiod credit option.

Pricing the Credit Default Swap

The CDS fixed fee or premium depends on the probability of default,[19] *PD*, on the reference loan. We have seen that *PD* can be determined using the observed credit spread on the reference loan and the decomposition methodology discussed in Chapter 5 [see equation (5.2)]. That is, consider a one year pure discount loan with $100 face value and a *LGD* of 100 percent; the loan price can be expressed as follows:[20]

$$P = \frac{100}{\left(1+r_f+CS\right)} \tag{15.3}$$

where P = the risky loan price,
       r_f = the risk-free rate,
       CS = the loan's credit spread (specified in the CDS terms and conditions).

If the risky loan price is observable, then equation (15.3) can be rearranged to solve for the *CS* as follows:

$$1 + CS = \left(\frac{100}{P}\right) - r_f \qquad (15.3')$$

However, loan prices are often unavailable and therefore equation (15.3′) cannot be solved directly. In such cases, the *CS* of other similar risk debt obligations is used to price the swap. Recall from Chapter 5 that the loan can be valued as the present value of all cash flows as follows:

$$P = \frac{100(1 - PD)}{(1 + r_f)} \qquad (15.4)$$

Setting equation (15.3) equal to equation (15.4) and solving for the probability of default yields:

$$PD = 1 - \frac{(1 + r_f)}{(1 + r_f + CS)} \qquad (15.5)$$

Incorporating an *LGD* of less than 100 percent alters equation (15.4) as follows:

$$P = \frac{100(1 - PD) + PD(100 - LGD)}{(1 + r_f)} \qquad (15.4')$$

and therefore, solving for default probability:

$$PD = \frac{\left[1 - \frac{(1 + r_f)}{(1 + r_f + CS)}\right]}{\left(\frac{LGD}{100}\right)} \qquad (15.5')$$

Since the CDS pays out *LGD* in the event of default and zero otherwise, the *PD* obtained from either equation (15.5) or (15.5′) can be used to calculate the expected payout on the CDS as $PD \times LGD$. Thus, the credit default swap is always priced off of the loan's credit spread. That is, the CDS premium should equal CS, the premium on the risky loan rate over the benchmark rate, usually LIBOR.[21] Indeed, this equivalence works both ways. As swap markets become more liquid, swap premiums can be used to price risky loans by providing estimates for the CS. However, there are several practical problems that may cause observed credit swap curves to diverge from credit spreads. That is, we observe a basis in CDS markets, defined as the difference between CS and the CDS premium.[22]

One reason for the persistence of a basis in the CDS market is that credit spreads are difficult to calculate because of noise in debt market prices.[23] Many reference loans are not traded and therefore cannot be priced. Moreover, option-like features embedded in some risky debt issues make it impossible to use the simple formulations in equations (15.5) and (15.5'), which do not even consider coupon payments.[24] In practice, spread curves are interpolated from bond prices using bootstrapping methods. Thus, the results are sensitive to the methodologies used, as well as to assumptions about LGD and other parameter values.

Another factor breaking the linkage between CDS premiums and CS is the presence of risk premiums. Although theoretically the CDS premium is a risk neutral probability of default, observable spreads contain risk premiums. One of these risk premiums is the counterparty credit charge (see discussion in next section). Since debt markets tend to be more liquid than CDS markets, there is also a liquidity premium that tends to raise the CDS premium above CS.[25] Moreover, market segmentation also contributes to higher observed premiums in the CDS market since some institutions cannot participate in the default swap market, but can participate in the bond market. However, this market segmentation effect is mitigated somewhat by the existence of participants who prefer the CDS market to equivalent risk bond transactions. There are even CDS markets that have become more liquid than the cash markets for the reference debt instruments, resulting in a negative basis.

Given the equivalence of the CDS premium to the credit spread, any divergence should present market participants with an arbitrage opportunity that quickly dissipates in equilibrium. However, this arbitrage opportunity is particularly costly to exploit. Arbitraging a high CDS premium (positive basis) requires selling credit protection via the CDS and simultaneously shorting the reference security in the debt market. The latter position may be costly or even impossible if repo rates are high or if there are short sale restrictions. (For example, see Appendix 15.1.) Moreover, even if the arbitrage were possible, the position is still subject to basis risk.

TABLE 15.2   CDS Spreads for Different Counterparties

Correlation between the Counterparty and Reference Entity	Counterparty Credit Ratings			
	AAA	AA	A	BBB
0.0	194.4	194.4	194.4	194.4
0.2	191.6	190.7	189.3	186.6
0.4	188.1	186.2	182.7	176.7
0.6	184.2	180.8	174.5	163.5
0.8	181.3	176.0	164.7	145.2

Notes: CDS spreads are in basis points. The reference loan is BBB rated, has a maturity of 5 years, and requires semiannual payments of 10 percent p.a. with an expected recovery rate of 30 percent. Results are based on 500,000 Monte Carlo trials for each set of parameter values. *Source:* Hull and White (2001).

Pricing the Credit Default Swap with Counterparty Credit Risk

Observed CDS premiums typically exceed credit spreads. However, a countervailing factor that reduces this differential by reducing swap premiums is counterparty credit risk. That is, the protection buyer is exposed to possible default by the protection seller, particularly if the protection seller defaults at the same time as a credit event occurs. Since this possibility makes the CDS's credit protection less valuable, the swap premium will generally carry a counterparty credit charge that is deducted from the credit spread (CS). This credit charge will depend on the counterparty's credit risk exposure as well as the correlation between the counterparty's PD and the reference entity's PD. The greater the counterparty credit charge the lower the CDS premium is relative to the reference loan's credit spread. Hull and White (2001) use a reduced form model to price CDS premiums with counterparty credit risk. Table 15.2 shows that the CDS premium varies from 194.4 basis points for a AAA rated counterparty uncorrelated to the reference entity's PD down to 145.2 basis points for a BBB rated counterparty with a PD that has a correlation with the reference entity's PD of 0.8.

Hull and White (2001) use an approximation of the reduced form model to estimate the CDS premium with counterparty default risk. If CS_0 is the CDS premium without counterparty default risk, then:

$$CS = \frac{CS_0(1-g)}{(1-h)} \tag{15.6}$$

where CS = the CDS premium with counterparty credit risk,
g = the proportional reduction in the present value of the expected payoff on the CDS to the buyer of credit protection arising from counterparty defaults,
h = the proportional reduction in the present value of expected payments on the CDS to the seller of credit protection arising from counterparty defaults.

Arbitrarily assuming that there is a 50 percent chance that the counterparty default occurs both before and after the reference entity defaults, then:

$$g = \frac{0.5\,P_{rc}}{Q_r} \tag{15.7}$$

where P_{rc} = the joint probability of default by the counterparty and the reference entity between time 0 and the maturity date of the CDS,
Q_r = the probability of default by the reference entity between time 0 and the maturity date of the CDS.

Moreover, under the assumption of an equal 50 percent chance that either the counterparty or the reference entity defaults first, then the CDS premium payments to the credit protection seller are one-third less than in the no-counterparty default case, then:

$$h = \left(\frac{Q_c}{2}\right) - \left(\frac{P_{rc}}{3}\right) \tag{15.8}$$

where Q_c = the probability of default by the counterparty between time 0 and the maturity date of the CDS.

Substituting equation (15.7) and (15.8) into (15.6) yields:

$$CS = \frac{CS_0\left(1 - \dfrac{1}{2}P_{rc}\right)}{Q_r} \Bigg/ \left(1 - \frac{1}{2}Q_c + \frac{1}{3}P_{rc}\right) \tag{15.9}$$

Although equation (15.9) incorporates many simplifying assumptions, the estimates of the CDS premiums obtained are quite similar to the simulated values shown in Table 15.2. For example, when the correlation between the counterparty and the reference entity is 0.4 or less, then the analytic approximation in equation (15.9) yields estimates within 1.5 basis points of those obtained in Table 15.2 using 500,000 Monte Carlo simulations.

HEDGING CREDIT RISK WITH CREDIT FORWARDS

A *credit forward* is a forward agreement that hedges against an increase in default risk on a loan (decline in credit quality of a borrower) after the loan rate is determined and the loan has been issued. The credit forward agreement specifies a credit spread (a risk premium above the risk-free rate to compensate for default risk) on a benchmark bond issued by the (loan) borrower. For example, suppose the benchmark bond of the borrower was rated BBB at the time a loan was originated from a bank, and it had an interest spread over a U.S. Treasury bond of the same maturity of 2 percent. Then $CS_F = 2$ percent defines the credit spread on which the credit forward contract is written. Figure 15.7 illustrates the payment pattern on a credit forward. CS_T is the actual credit spread on the bond when the credit forward matures (e.g., one year after the loan was originated and the credit forward contract was entered into); MD is the modified duration on the benchmark BBB bond; and A is the principal amount of the forward agreement.

The payment pattern established in a credit forward agreement is detailed in Figure 15.7. The credit forward buyer bears the risk of an increase in default risk on the benchmark bond of the borrowing firm, and the credit forward seller (the bank lender) hedges itself against an increase in the borrower's default risk. Suppose the borrower's default risk increases so that when the forward agreement matures the market requires a higher credit spread on the borrower's benchmark bond (CS_T) than was originally agreed

Credit Spread at End of Forward Agreement	Credit Spread Seller (Bank)	Credit Spread Buyer (Counterparty)
$CS_T > CS_F$	Receives $(CS_T - CS_F) \times MD \times A$	Pays $(CS_T - CS_F) \times MD \times A$
$CS_F > CS_T$	Pays $(CS_F - CS_T) \times MD \times A$	Receives $(CS_F - CS_T) \times MD \times A$

FIGURE 15.7 Payment pattern on a credit forward agreement.

to in the forward contract (CS_F) (i.e., $CS_T > CS_F$). The credit forward buyer then pays the credit forward seller (the bank): $(CS_T - CS_F) \times MD \times A$. For example, suppose the credit spread between BBB bonds and U.S. Treasury bonds widened to 3 percent from 2 percent over the year, the modified duration (MD) of the benchmark BBB bond was 5 years, and the size of the forward contract (A) was $10,000,000. The gain on the credit forward contract to the seller (the bank) would then be $(3\% - 2\%) \times 5 \times \$10,000,000 = \$500,000$. This amount could be used to offset the loss in market value of the loan due to the rise in the borrower's default risk. If the borrower's default risk and credit spread decrease over the year, the credit forward seller pays the credit forward buyer: $(CS_F - CS_T) \times MD \times A$. [However, the maximum loss on the forward contract (to the bank seller) is limited, as will be explained next.]

Figure 15.8 illustrates the impact on the bank from hedging the loan [see Finnerty (1996)]. If the default risk on the loan increases, the value of the loan falls below its value at the beginning of the hedge period. However, the bank hedged the change in default risk by selling a credit forward contract. Assuming the credit spread on the borrower's benchmark bond also increases (so that $CS_T > CS_F$) the bank receives $(CS_T - CS_F) \times MD \times A$ on the forward contract. If the characteristics of the benchmark bond (i.e., credit spread, modified duration, and principal value) are the same as those of the loan to the borrower, the market value loss on the bank's balance sheet is offset completely by the gain from the credit forward. (In our

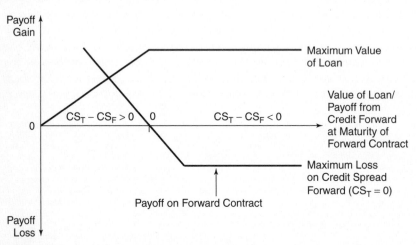

FIGURE 15.8 Hedging loan default risk by selling a credit forward contract.

example, a \$500,000 market value loss in the loan would be offset by a \$500,000 gain from selling the credit forward contract.)

If the default risk does not increase but actually decreases (so that $CS_T < CS_F$), the bank selling the forward contract will pay $(CS_F - CS_T) \times MD \times A$ to the credit forward buyer. However, *this payout by the bank is limited to a maximum*. When CS_T falls to zero (i.e., the default spread on BBB bonds falls to zero), or the original BBB bonds of the borrower are viewed as having the same default risk as government bonds (the rate on the benchmark bond is equal to the risk-free rate), the maximum loss on the credit forward, $[CS_F - (0)] \times MD \times A$, offsets the maximum and limited upside gain (return) on the loan. Anyone familiar with options will recognize that, in selling a credit forward, the payoff is similar to buying a put option.

CREDIT SECURITIZATIONS

Until recently, the growth of commercial credit or loan securitization (as in the case of loan sales and trading) had been hampered by concerns about negative customer relationship effects if loans were removed from the balance sheet and packaged and sold as CLOs (collateralized lending obligations) or CDOs (collateralized debt obligations) to outside investors.[26] Instead, such mechanisms have proved to be popular for more commoditized credits such as mortgages, credit card loans, and auto loans. Thus, until recently, many loan securitizations were conducted in which loans remained on the balance sheet, and asset-backed securities (credit-linked notes, or CLNs) were issued against the loan portfolio.[27] A huge variety of these products has emerged, but the differences among them relate to the way in which credit risk is transferred from the loan-originating bank to the note investor. In general, a subportfolio of commercial loans is segmented on the asset side of the balance sheet, and an issue of CLNs is made. The return and risk of investors vary by type of issue. Some investors are promised a high yield on the underlying loans in return for bearing all the default risk; other investors are offered lower yields in return for partial default protection (i.e., a shared credit risk with the bank). In general, the bank issuer takes the first tranche of default risk but is protected against catastrophic risk (which is borne by the CLN investor).

Although the issuance of CLOs and CLNs may reduce the bank's credit risk exposure, the impact on the bank's economic capital requirements is not reflected in current regulations. Indeed, for a single OBS activity, current rules are inconsistent and vary widely across different regulatory agencies and across different security structures. On January 1, 2002, a new regulation took effect that would standardize the treatment of the credit risk of financial instruments with recourse, direct credit substitutes, and residual interests as supervised by U.S. bank regulators. The rule ties the instrument's risk weight to an external credit rating (as in BIS II's standardized approach; see Chapter 3) with risk weights ranging from 20 percent (for AAA and AA rated obligations) to 200 percent (for BB rated obligations). However, banks are not permitted to use internal models to risk weight unrated obligations and thus, many credit risk enhancements will still be incorrectly evaluated for the purposes of bank capital requirements.

There are several disadvantages to managing a portfolio's credit risk using CLOs or CLNs. First, we have seen that these structures will not offer the bank relief from excessive capital regulations (see also Appendix 15.2). Second, the relatively high spreads in the asset backed securities market causes the cost of financing to be rather high for a low risk bank. Third, transferring ownership of a loan to a special-purpose vehicle (SPV) may require borrower notification and consent, with adverse consequences for the loan relationship. Finally, reputational effects may damage CLO issuers if economic conditions cause unanticipated increases in the underlying portfolio's default rate. For example, in July 2001, American Express was forced to take a pretax charge exceeding $1 billion because default rates on its CDOs were 8 percent (compared to an expected 2 percent default rate) and it was holding many of the high risk tranches.

Synthetic securitization is one response to the disadvantages of loan securitization.[28] In 1997, J.P. Morgan introduced a structure known as BISTRO (Broad Index Secured Trust Offering), illustrated in Figure 15.9. In this structure, the originating bank purchases credit protection from the intermediary bank (e.g., J.P. Morgan Chase) via a CDS subject to a "threshold." That is, the CDS will not pay off unless credit losses on the reference loan portfolio exceed a certain level, 1.50 percent in this example.[29] The intermediary buys credit protection on the same portfolio from an SPV. The BISTRO SPV is collateralized with government securities which it funds by issuing credit-tranched notes to capital market investors. However, the BISTRO collateral is substantially smaller than the notional value of the portfolio. In the example shown in Figure 15.9, only $700 million of collateral backs a $10 billion loan portfolio (7 percent collateralization).[30] This is possible because the portfolio is structured to have enough investment grade loans and diversification that make it unlikely that losses on the loan portfolio would exceed $850 million ($700 million in BISTRO collateral plus the bank's absorption of the first $150 million in possible losses, that is, 1.5 percent of the portfolio's notional value.) This structure significantly reduces the legal, systems, personnel, and client relationship

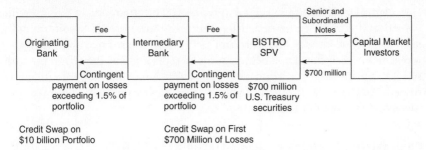

FIGURE 15.9 BISTRO structure. *Note:* Under BIS I market risk capital rules, the intermediary bank can use *VAR* to determine the capital requirement of its residual risk position.

costs associated with a traditional asset backed security (ABS). It permits much greater diversity in the portfolio underlying the BISTRO than is possible for a CLO or CLN. For example, unfunded credit exposures, such as loan commitments, letters of credit, and trade receivables, can be included in the BISTRO portfolio, whereas CLOs are limited to portfolios of funded loans. Moreover, since the BISTRO is unrelated in any way to the originating bank, there should be no reputational risk effects, thereby further reducing capital charges.

PRICING ISSUES

A key question is: What role do the new models play in the credit derivatives market? Apart from identifying counterparty risk, they play a role in pricing. Consider the case of the pure credit swap, discussed earlier. On origination, the *NPV* of the swap should be zero; that is, the present value of the annual (semiannual) premiums paid by the buyer of credit insurance should equal the present value of expected default losses (probability of default × *LGD*) over the swap period. A number of different approaches appear to be used in practice. One approach is to use a KMV-type model to generate *EDF*s for each future swap date and (combined with *LGD*s) project a series of expected losses on the swap. Given a set of appropriate discount rates, the theoretically fair annual premium (annuity) to be paid by the credit risk seller can thus be established. Unfortunately, this would likely misprice the swap since *EDF*s are based on historic data, whereas for pricing purposes, we need expectations of future default rates using risk neutral probabilities (see Chapter 4).[31] The premium is like a credit spread and can be estimated using the term structure of credit spreads, such as Jarrow, Lando, and Turnbull (1997). An alternative approach is to replicate the cash flows of a default swap by replicating its payoffs in the cash market. This assumes instruments in the cash (bond) market are efficiently priced. An example of Merrill Lynch's cash-market replication approach is discussed in Appendix 15.1.[32]

An Example of Pricing a Credit-Linked Note (CLN)[33]

Consider a five-year fixed coupon CLN structured to guarantee payment of principal at maturity. However, all coupon payments will terminate if a default event occurs. We can price the CLN using the CDS swap curve shown in Table 15.3 for a fixed credit spread CS equal to 7 percent and a fixed risk-free rate of 5 percent p.a. Equation (15.5') can be used to determine the cumulative PD for similar risk debt instruments shown in column (2) of Table 15.3. Since the principal is risk free, the present value (at a par value of $100) is: $100/(1.05)^5 = \$78.35$. That leaves $100 - 78.35 = \$21.65$ as the present value of the coupon payments. To calculate the fixed coupon payment, C, that corresponds to this present value, taking into account the PD, note that the expected coupon payment in each year is simply $C(1 - PD)$, as shown in column (3) of Table 15.3. Discounting the expected coupon payments by the risk-free rate of 5 percent p.a. yields the present value of each coupon payment, shown in column (4) of Table 15.3, which sums to $21.65. Solving for C, we obtain a fixed coupon rate of 6.18 percent p.a. for the CLN.

TABLE 15.3 Pricing a Credit-Linked Note Off the Spread Curve

Year (1)	Cumulative Probability of Default (2)	Expected Coupon Payment (3)	Present Value of Coupons (4)
1	7.22%	$(1 - .0722)C$	.8837 C
2	13.91	$(1 - .1391)C$	.7808 C
3	20.13	$(1 - .2013)C$	.6900 C
4	25.89	$(1 - .2589)C$	.6097 C
5	31.24	$(1 - .3124)C$	.5388 C

Notes: C is the fixed coupon payment on the CLN. The risk-free rate is assumed constant at 5 percent p.a. and the credit spread is fixed at 7 percent p.a. *Source: Risk* (2000).

SUMMARY

This chapter has looked at the role that credit derivatives are playing in allowing banks to hedge the credit risk of their loan portfolios. The BIS capital requirements do not actively encourage the use of credit derivatives (especially loan or debt securitizations), but banks are attracted to them because of their potential in improving loan risk-return trade-offs without harming customer relationships. Some simple examples of credit options, credit default swaps, credit forwards, and credit securitizations were discussed, as was the issue of credit derivative pricing.

APPENDIX 15.1
CASH MARKET REPLICATION TO PRICE/VALUE
A PURE CREDIT OR DEFAULT SWAP

The expected value of credit risk (in a credit swap) is already captured by credit spreads in the cash market for bonds and the market for fixed-floating rate swaps. Figure 15.10 (from Merrill Lynch) shows how the risk on a pure credit swap can be replicated through cash market transactions and plain-vanilla swap transactions where the "investor" sells protection under a pure credit swap.

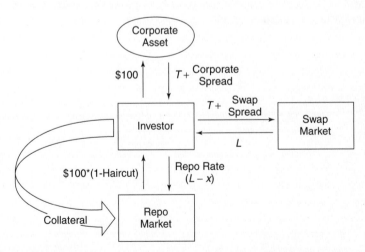

FIGURE 15.10   Replicating default swap exposure, protection for the swap seller. *Source:* "Credit Default Swaps," Merrill Lynch, Pierce, Fenner, and Smith, Inc. (October 1998), p. 12.

In this replication, the investor (swap risk seller):

1. Purchases a cash bond with a spread of $T + S_c$ for par,
2. Pays fixed on a swap $(T + S_s)$ with the maturity of the cash bond and receives LIBOR (L),
3. Finances the position in the repo (repurchase agreement) market [the repo rate is quoted at a spread to LIBOR $(L - x)$].
4. Pledges the corporate bond as collateral and is charged a haircut by the repo counterparty.

Transactions 1 and 2 hedge the underlying interest rate risk involved in purchasing the corporate bond (since we are concerned with only credit risk exposure). Transactions 3 and 4 reflect the cost of financing the purchase of the risky corporate bond through the repo market, where a lender charges a collateral haircut on the amount borrowed and $L - x$ reflects the cost of repo finance. Table 15.4 shows the net cash flows of the four transactions (with the collateral haircut set equal to zero for simplicity).

The credit risk exposure of the swap seller (via replication) equals $(S_c - S_s) + x$; for example, the spread between the corporate bond risk premium and the swap spread in the fixed-floating swap market, plus an amount x that reflects the degree to which the investor can borrow below LIBOR in the repo market. If $x = 0$, then the credit exposure is $S_c - S_s$, which is analytically equivalent to the (fair) premium or fee that has to be paid to the seller of credit risk insurance in a pure credit (or default) swap transaction, in return for providing default risk insurance.

TABLE 15.4   Cash Flows of Default Swap Replication

	Receive	Pay
Cash bond	$T + S_c$	$100
Swap hedge	L	$T + S_s$
Repo transaction	$100	$(L - x)$
	$S_c - S_s + x$	

S_c = corporate spreads; S_s = swap spread. Assume no "haircut."

Source: Credit Default Swaps, Merrill Lynch, Pierce, Fenner, and Smith, Inc., October 1998, p. 13.

APPENDIX 15.2
BIS II CAPITAL REGULATIONS FOR ASSET
BACKED SECURITIES (ABS)

Arbitrage of capital regulations has contributed to rapid growth in the issuance of asset backed securities, in which a portfolio of relatively homogenous loans is repackaged into a collateralized debt obligation (CDO) and resold as a marketable ABS. By removing the securitized assets from the bank's balance sheet, the originating bank can reduce its capital requirements. BIS II proposes fairly strict tests to ascertain whether a "clean break" has been made before the assets can be removed from the originating bank's balance sheet for the purposes of capital regulations. A "clean break" has occurred if:

1. The transferred assets have been legally separated from the originating bank so that they are beyond the reach of the bank's creditors in the event of the bank's bankruptcy; and
2. The assets underlying the ABS are placed into a special-purpose vehicle (SPV); and
3. The originating bank has neither direct nor indirect control over the assets transferred into the SPV.

Even when the conditions for a "clean break" are met, the originating bank may still be required to hold capital against the assets in the ABS pool if regulators believe that the bank is subject to reputational risk. That is, to prevent damage to the originating bank's reputation, the bank might offer "implicit recourse," which may take the form of the following possible responses to credit deterioration in the asset pool underlying the ABS: the bank may repurchase or substitute for credit-impaired assets in the pool, loans may be made to the SPV, or fee income associated with the ABS structure may be deferred. Under such circumstances, regulators may force the bank to hold capital against *all* assets in *all* ABSs issued, even those for which implicit recourse was not granted, as if all assets in all ABS pools remained on the bank's balance sheet. Thus, the finding of the provision of implicit recourse engenders punitive regulatory action that is made public by bank regulators.

Originating banks not satisfying conditions for a "clean break" (e.g., by providing credit enhancements for an ABS or servicing the loan cash flows in the underlying pool of assets) may still be allowed to limit the risk of the assets for capital regulatory purposes if all credit enhancements are provided up front at the issuance of the ABS. In general, however, the value of any credit enhancements must be deducted from the bank's capital using the full risk-based capital charge. Moreover, if the ABS has any provisions that may force an early wind down of the securitization program if the credit quality of the underlying loans in the asset pool deteriorates beyond a certain point, then the originating bank must apply a minimum 10 percent conversion factor to the notional value of all off-balance-sheet assets in the pool underlying the ABS in order to calculate the capital charge.

Banks that invest in ABS, as opposed to originating banks, must hold capital charges according to the risk weights shown in Table 15.5. This schedule conforms with the risk weights under the standardized approach of BIS II (see Chapter 3), except for the lowest quality ABS (B+ and below or unrated) where there is "in effect" a one-to-one capital charge if a bank invests in these bonds. Indeed, the stringency of this capital charge is to off-set the type of regulatory arbitrage apparent under BIS I.

Consider the following example of regulatory arbitrage under BIS I. A bank with $100 million of BBB loans on the balance sheet would pay a capital charge of $8 million under BIS I. Suppose these loans were placed in an SPV and two tranches of bonds were issued as shown in Figure 15.11. The first tranche of $80 million was rated AA because it was structured to absorb default losses only after the first 0.3 percent of losses on the entire $100 million loan portfolio (corresponding to the historical default rate of bonds with a BBB rating) were borne by the second tranche of $20 million. Because of the low quality of the second tranche they were rated B. Suppose that the high quality tranche was sold to outside investors, but the bank or its subsidiaries (as commonly happens) ended up owning (buying) the residual B rated tranche. Because BIS I treated all commercial credit risks with equal weight, the capital requirement on the $20 million of purchased bonds (that have virtually the same credit risk as the original $100 million BBB portfolio) would be subject to a capital charge of only $20 million × 8 percent = $1.6 million. That is, the bank has "arbitraged" a capital savings of $8 million minus $1.6 million = $6.4 million through the securitization. Under the January 2002 rule and proposed BIS II, the capital charge on the

TABLE 15.5 Risk Weights

External Credit Assessment	AAA to AA–	A+ to A–	BBB+ to BBB–	BB+ to BB–	B+ and Below or Unrated
	20%	50%	100%	150%	Deduction from capital RW = 1250%

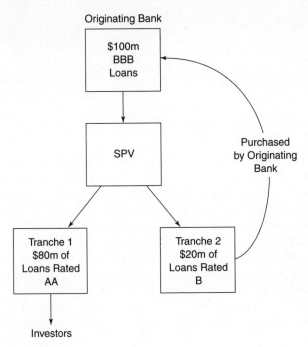

Originating Bank

$100m
BBB
Loans

SPV

Purchased
by Originating
Bank

Tranche 1
$80m of
Loans Rated
AA

Tranche 2
$20m of
Loans Rated
B

Investors

FIGURE 15.11 Regulatory arbitrage under BIS I.

$20 million tranche would be $20 million, thereby eliminating arbitrage incentives. For those investing banks that use the internal ratings-based approaches instead, the probability of default can be measured for each tranche of each ABS. However, the BIS II proposals assume an LGD of 100 percent for ABS, in contrast to the 50 percent assumed under the IRB foundations approach for senior unsecuritized loans.

Banks can also sponsor SPVs that purchase assets from non-banks which then issue ABS. Although sponsoring banks are neither the loan originators nor servicers, they may provide credit enhancements, which must be deducted from capital.[34] However, if sponsoring banks sell any of their own assets to the sponsored SPV they are treated as if they were originating banks and subject to the onerous regulations for ABS originators.

bibliography

Acharya, V. V. "A Theory of Systemic Risk and Design of Prudential Bank Regulation." Dissertation Thesis, New York University, January 2001.

Acharya, V. V., and J. N. Carpenter. "Callable Defaultable Bonds: Valuation, Hedging and Optimal Exercise Boundaries." Working paper 27, New York University Salomon Center, June 1999.

Acharya, V. V., and J. N. Carpenter. "Corporate Bonds: Valuation, Hedging, and Optimal Call and Default Policies." Working paper 24, New York University Salomon Center, March 2000.

Acharya, V. V., J. Huang, M. G. Subrahmanyam, and R. K. Sundaram. "Costly Financing, Optimal Payout Policies, and the Valuation of Corporate Debt." Working paper 8, New York University Salomon Center, February 2000.

Aguais, S. D., L. Forest, S. Krishnamoorthy, and T. Mueller. "Creating Value from Both Loan Structure and Price." *Commercial Lending Review* (Spring 1998): 13–24.

Allen, L. "Discussion." In *Ratings, Rating Agencies, and the Global Financial System,* edited by R. Levich. New York: Kluwer Academic Press, 2002 (forthcoming).

Allen, L., J. Boudoukh, and A. Saunders. *Value at Risk in Theory and Practice.* London: Blackwell, 2002 (forthcoming).

Altman, E. I. "Financial Ratios, Discriminant Analysis and the Prediction of Corporate Bankruptcy." *Journal of Finance* (September 1968): 589–609.

Altman, E. I. "Measuring Corporate Bond Mortality and Performance." *Journal of Finance* (September 1989): 909–922.

Altman, E. I. *Corporate Financial Distress,* 2nd ed. New York: Wiley, 1993.

Altman, E. I. "Predicting Financial Distress of Companies: Revisiting the Z-Score and Zeta Models." Working paper, Department of Finance, New York University, July 2000.

Altman, E. I., T. K. N. Baidya, and L. M. R. Dias. "Assessing Potential Financial Problems for Firms in Brazil." *Journal of International Business Studies* 10, no. 2 (1979): 9–24.

Altman, E. I., and B. Brady. "Explaining Aggregate Recovery Rates on Corporate Bond Defaults." Working Paper, New York University Salomon Center, November 2001.

Altman, E. I., and D. L. Kao. "The Implications of Corporate Bond Ratings Drift." *Financial Analysts Journal* (May–June 1992): 64–75.

Altman, E. I., and B. Karlin. "Defaults and Returns on High Yield Bonds: Analysis Through 2000 and Default Outlook." Working Paper 10, New York University Salomon Center, February 2001a.

Altman, E. I., and B. Karlin. "Defaults and Returns on High Yield Bonds: Analysis Through the First Half of 2001 and Default Outlook." Working Paper 11, New York University Salomon Center, June 2001b.

Altman, E. I., and V. M. Kishore. "Defaults and Returns on High-Yield Bonds: Analysis Through 1997." Working paper 1, New York University Salomon Center, January 1998.

Altman, E. I., G. Marco, and F. Varetto. "Corporate Distress Diagnosis: Comparisons Using Linear Discriminant Analysis and Neural Networks (the Italian Experience)." *Journal of Banking and Finance* (May 1994): 505–529.

Altman, E. I., and P. Narayanan. "An International Survey of Business Failure Classification Models." *Financial Markets, Instruments and Institutions* 6, no. 2 (1997).

Altman, E. I., and A. Saunders. "Credit Risk Measurement: Developments over the Last Twenty Years." *Journal of Banking and Finance* (December 1997): 1721–1742.

Altman, E. I., and A. Saunders. "An Analysis and Critique of the BIS Proposal on Capital Adequacy and Ratings." *Journal of Banking and Finance* (January 2001a): 25–46.

Altman, E. I., and A. Saunders. "Credit Ratings and the BIS Reform Agenda." Paper presented at the Bank of England Conference on Banks and Systemic Risk, London, May 23–25, 2001b.

Altman, E. I., and H. J. Suggitt. "Default Rates in the Syndicated Loan Market: A Mortality Analysis." Working paper 39, New York University Salomon Center, December 1997.

Anderson, R., S. Sundaresan, and P. Tychon. "Strategic Analysis of Contingent Claims." *European Economic Review* (April 1996): 871–881.

Anderson, R., and S. Sundaresan. "A Comparative Study of Structural Models of Corporate Bond Yields: An Exploratory Investigation." *Journal of Banking and Finance* (January 2000): 255–269.

Angbazo, L., J. P. Mei, and A. Saunders. "Credit Spreads in the Market for Highly Leveraged Transaction Loans." *Journal of Banking and Finance* (October 1998): 1249–1282.

Arrow, K. K. "Le Role des Valeurs Boursieres pour la Repartition de la Meilleure des Risques." *Econometrie* 40 (1953): 91–96.

Asarnow, E. "Managing Bank Loan Portfolios for Total Return." Paper presented at a Conference on "A New Market Equilibrium for the Credit Business," Frankfurt, Germany, March 11, 1999.

Asarnow, E., and J. Marker. "Historical Performance of the U.S. Corporate Loan Market, 1988–1993." *Journal of Commercial Lending* (Spring 1995): 13–22.

Asarnow, E., and D. Edwards. "Measuring Loss on Defaulted Bank Loans: A 24-Year Study." *The Journal of Commercial Lending* (March 1995): 11–23.

Asquith, P., D. W. Mullins, and E. D. Wolff. "Original Issue High Yield Bonds: Aging Analysis of Defaults, Exchanges and Calls." *Journal of Finance* (September 1989): 923–952.

Astebro, T., and F. Rucker. "Foresight Beats Hindsight: Maximizing Portfolio Returns by Optimizing the Cut-Off Credit Score." *The RMA Journal* (February 2000): 65–69.

Babbel, D. F. "Insuring Banks Against Systematic Credit Risk." *Journal of Futures Markets* (November 6, 1989): 487–506.

Bahar, R., and K. Nagpal. "Modeling the Dynamics." *Credit* (March 2000).

Bali, T. "The Generalized Extreme Value Distribution: Implications for the Value at Risk." Working Paper, Baruch College Zicklin School of Business, February 2001.

Bangia, A., F. X. Diebold, and T. Schuermann. "Ratings Migration and the Business Cycle, with Applications to Credit Portfolio Stress Testing." Working Paper 26, Wharton Financial Institutions Center, April 2000.

Bank for International Settlements. *Standardized Model for Market Risk.* Basel, Switzerland: Bank for International Settlements, 1996.

Bank for International Settlements. "Credit Risk Modeling: Current Practices and Applications." Basel Committee on Banking Supervision, Document No 49, April 1999a.

Bank for International Settlements. "Sound Practices for Loan Accounting and Disclosure." Basel Committee on Banking Supervision, Document No 55, July 1999b.

Bank for International Settlements. "Range of Practice in Banks' Internal Ratings Systems." Basel Committee on Banking Supervision, Document No 66, January 2000.

Bank for International Settlements. "The New Basel Capital Accord," January 2001.

Bank for International Settlements. "Long-term Rating Scales Comparison," April 30, 2001.

Bank for International Settlements. "Working paper on the Regulatory Treatment of Operational Risk," September 2001.

Bank for International Settlements. "Results of the Second Quantitative Impact Study," November 5, 2001a.

Bank for International Settlements. "Potential Modifications to the Committee's Proposals," November 5, 2001b.

Barnhill, T. M., Jr., and W. F. Maxwell. "Modeling Correlated Interest Rate, Spread Risk, and Credit Risk for Fixed Income Portfolios." *Journal of Banking and Finance* 26/2–3 (February 2002).

Barniv, R., and A. Raveh. "Identifying Financial Distress: A New Nonparametric Approach." *Journal of Business, Finance and Accounting* 16, no. 3 (Summer 1989): 361–383.

Basak, S., and A. Shapiro. "A Model of Credit Risk, Optimal Policies, and Asset Prices." Working Paper, New York University, June 2001.

Belkin, B., L. R. Forest, S. D. Aguais, and S. J. Suchower. "Credit Risk Premiums in Commercial Lending (I)." KPMG, New York, August 1998a (mimeo).

Belkin, B., L. R. Forest, S. D. Aguais, and S. J. Suchower. "Credit Risk Premiums in Commercial Lending (II)." KPMG, New York, August 1998b (mimeo).

Belkin, B., S. J. Suchower, and L. R. Forest. "The Effect of Systematic Credit Risk on Loan Portfolio Value at Risk and Loan Pricing." *CreditMetrics Monitor* (winter 1998): 17–28.

Belkin, B., S. J. Suchower, D. H. Wagner, and L. R. Forest. "Measures of Credit Risk and Loan Value in LAS." KPMG Risk Strategy Practice, 1998 (mimeo).

Black, F., and M. Scholes. "The Pricing of Options and Corporate Liabilities." *Journal of Political Economy* (May–June 1973): 637–654.

Bohn, J. R. "Characterizing Credit Spreads." KMV Corporation, June 1999.

Bohn, J. R. "An Empirical Assessment of a Simple Contingent-Claims Model for the Valuation of Risky Debt." *Journal of Risk Finance* 1, no. 4 (2000a): 55–77.

Bohn, J. R. "A Survey of Contingent Claims Approaches to Risky Debt Valuation." *Journal of Risk Finance* 1, no. 3 (2000b): 53–71.

Bongini, P., L. Laeven, and G. Majnoni. "How Good is the Market at Assessing Bank Fragility: A Horse Race between Different Indicators." Working Paper, World Bank, January 2001.

Boot, A. W. A., and T. T. Milbourn. "Credit Ratings as Coordination Mechanisms." Working Paper, University of Amsterdam, April 10, 2001.

Boudoukh, J., M. Richardson, and R. Whitelaw. "Expect the Worst." *Risk Magazine* (September 1995): 101–105.

Brenner, M., and Y. H. Eom. "No Arbitrage Option Pricing: New Evidence on the Validity of the Martingale Property." Working Paper 10, New York University Salomon Center, June 1997.

Cantor, R. "Moody's Investors Service Response to the Consultative Paper Issued by the Basel Committee on Bank Supervision 'A New Capital Adequacy Approach.'" *Journal of Banking and Finance* (January 2001): 171–186.

Cantor, R., and F. Packer. "Determinants and Impacts of Sovereign Credit Ratings." *Economic Policy Review,* Federal Reserve Bank of New York, (October 1996): 37–53.

Caouette, J. B., E. J. Altman, and P. Narayanan. *Managing Credit Risk: The Next Great Financial Challenge.* New York: Wiley, 1998.

Carty, L. V., and D. Lieberman. "Corporate Bond Defaults and Default Rates 1938–1995." Moody's Investors Service, Global Credit Research, January 1996.

Carey, M. "Credit Risk in Private Debt Portfolios." *Journal of Finance* (August 1998): 1363–1387.

Carey, M. "Dimensions of Credit Risk and Their Relationship to Economic Capital Requirements." Working Paper 7629, NBER, March 2000.

Carey, M. "Consistency of Internal versus External Credit Ratings and Insurance and Bank Regulatory Capital Requirements." Working Paper, Federal Reserve Board, February 2001a.

Carey, M. "A Policymaker's Guide to Choosing Absolute Bank Capital Requirements." Working Paper, Federal Reserve Board, June 3, 2001b, Presented at the Bank of England Conference on Banks and Systemic Risk, May 23–25, 2001b.

Carey, M., and M. Hrycay. "Parameterizing Credit Risk Models with Rating Data." *Journal of Banking and Finance* 25, no. 1 (2001): 197–270.

Carey, M., M. Post, and S. A. Sharpe. "Does Corporate Lending by Banks and Finance Companies Differ? Evidence on Specialization in Private Debt Contracting." *Journal of Finance* (June 1998): 845–878.

Carty, L. V. "Bankrupt Bank Loan Recoveries." Moody's Investors Service, *Rating Methodology,* June 1998.

Carty, L. V., and D. Lieberman. "Defaulted Bank Loan Recoveries." Moody's Investors Service, *Special Report,* November 1996.

Cathcart, L., and L. El-Jahel. "Valuation of Defaultable Bonds." *Journal of Fixed Income* (June 1998): 65–78.

Cavallo, M., and G. Majnoni. "Do Banks Provision for Bad Loans in Good Times? Empirical Evidence and Policy Implications." Working Paper 2691, World Bank, June 2001.

Chang, G., and S. M. Sundaresan. "Asset Prices and Default-Free Term Structure in an Equilibrium Model of Default." Working Paper, Columbia University, October 1999.

Chen, R. R., and J. Z. Huang. "Term Structure of Credit Spreads, Implied Forward Default Probability Curve, and the Valuation of Defaultable Claims." Working Paper, Department of Management, Rutgers University, July 2000.

Choudhury, S. P. "Choosing the Right Box of Credit Tricks." *Risk Magazine* (November 1997): 17–22.

Clow, R. "Bond Yield." *Institutional Investor* (February 2000): 41–44.

Coates, P. K., and L. F. Fant. "Recognizing Financial Distress Patterns Using a Neural Network Tool." *Financial Management* (Summer 1993): 142–155.

Collin-Dufresne, P., and R. Goldstein. "Do Credit Spreads Reflect Stationary Leverage Ratios?" *Journal of Finance,* LVI, no. 5 (October 2001): 1929–1957.

Collin-Dufresne, P., and B. Solnik. "On the Term Structure of Default Premia in the Swap and LIBOR Markets." *Journal of Finance* (June 2001): 1095–1115.

Credit Suisse Financial Products (CSFP). "CreditRisk+: A Credit Risk Management Framework," Technical Document, 1997.

Crouhy, M., and R. Mark. "A Comparative Analysis of Current Credit Risk Models." Paper presented at the Bank of England Conference on Credit Risk Modeling and Regulatory Implications, London, September 21–22, 1998.

Crouhy, M., D. Galai, and R. Mark. "A Comparative Analysis of Current Credit Risk Models." *Journal of Banking and Finance* (January 2000): 57–117.

Crouhy, M., and R. Mark. "Prototype Risk Rating System." *Journal of Banking and Finance* (January 2001): 47–95.

Crouhy, M., S. M. Turnbull, and L. M. Wakeman. "Measuring Risk-Adjusted Performance." Paper presented at Center for Economic Policy Research (CEPR) Conference, London, September 20, 1998.

Cruz, M., R. Coleman, and G. Salkin. "Modeling and Measuring Operational Risk." *The Journal of Risk* 1, no. 1 (Fall 1998): 63–72.

Cunningham, A. "Bank Credit Risk In Emerging Markets." Moody's Investors Service, *Rating Methodology,* July 1999.

Dahiya, S., M. Puri, and A. Saunders. "Bank Borrowers and Loan Sales: New Evidence of the Uniqueness of Bank Loans." Working Paper, Department of Finance, New York University, 2001.

Das, S., and P. Tufano. "Pricing Credit-Sensitive Debt When Interest Rates, Credit Ratings, and Credit Spreads are Stochastic." *Journal of Financial Engineering* (June 1996): 161–198.

Delianedis, G., and R. Geske. "Credit Risk and Risk-Neutral Default Probabilities: Information About Rating Migrations and Defaults." Paper presented at the Bank of England Conference on Credit Risk Modeling and Regulatory Implications, London, September 21–22, 1998.

Dembo, R. S., A. R. Aziz, D. Rosen, and M. Zerbs. "Mark-to-Future: A Framework for Measuring Risk and Reward." Toronto: Algorithmics Publications, May 2000.

Dermine, J. "Pitfalls in the Application of RAROC in Loan Management." *The Arbitrageur* (Spring 1998): 21–27.

DeSantes, R. "An Appetite for Risk." *CreditRisk* (October 1999): 18–19.

De Stefano, M. T. "Basel Committee's New Capital Standards Could Strengthen Banking." Standard & Poor's Credit Week, August 18, 1999, pp. 19–22.

Diamond, D. "Financial Intermediation and Delegated Monitoring," *Review of Economic Studies* 51 (1984): 393–414.

Diebold, F., and R. Mariano. "Comparing Predictive Accuracy." *Journal of Business and Economic Statistics* (May 1995): 253–264.

Duffee, G. R. "The Relation Between Treasury Yields and Corporate Bond Yield Spreads." *Journal of Finance* 53 (1998): 2225–2242.

Duffee, G. R. "Estimating the Price of Default Risk." *The Review of Financial Studies* (Spring 1999): 197–226.

Duffie, D., and M. Huang. "Swap Rates and Credit Quality." *Journal of Finance* (July 1996): 921–950.

Duffie, D., and D. Lando. "Term Structures of Credit Spreads with Incomplete Accounting Information." *Econometrica* 69 (2001): 633–664.

Duffie, D., L. H. Pedersen, and K. J. Singleton. "Modeling Sovereign Yield Spreads: A Case Study of Russian Debt." Working Paper, Graduate School of Business, Stanford University, April 2000.

Duffie, D., and K. J. Singleton. "Simulating Correlated Defaults." Paper presented at the Bank of England Conference on Credit Risk Modeling and Regulatory Implications, London, September 21–22, 1998.

Duffie, D., and K. J. Singleton. "Modeling Term Structures of Defaultable Bonds." *Review of Financial Studies* 12 (1999): 687–720.

The Economist. "Banking Supervision: The Basel Perplex" (November 10, 2001): 65–66.

Elmer, P. J., and D. M. Borowski. "An Expert System Approach to Financial Analysis: The Case of S&L Bankruptcy." *Financial Management* (Autumn 1988): 66–76.

Elton, E. J., and M. J. Gruber. *Modern Portfolio Theory and Investment Analysis,* 5th ed. New York: Wiley, 1995.

Eom, Y. H., J. Helwege, and J. Z. Huang. "Structural Models of Corporate Bond Pricing: An Empirical Analysis." Working Paper, January 2001.

Erlenmaier, H. and H. Gersbach. "Default Probabilities and Default Correlation." Working Paper, University of Heidelberg, February 2001.

Estrella, A. "Formulas or Supervision? Remarks on the Future of Regulatory Capital." Federal Reserve Bank of New York, *Economic Policy Review,* October 1998.

Fadil, M. W. "Problems with Weighted-Average Risk Ratings: A Portfolio Management View." *Commercial Lending Review* (Spring 1997): 23–27.

Falkenheim, M., and A. Powell. "The Use of Credit Bureau Information in the Estimation of Appropriate Capital and Provisioning Requirements." Working Paper, Central Bank of Argentina, 2001.

Federal Reserve System Task Force Report. "Credit Risk Models at Major U.S. Banking Institutions: Current State of the Art and Implications for Assessments of Capital Adequacy." Washington, DC, May 1998.

Fehle, F. "Market Structure and Swap Spreads: International Evidence." Working Paper, University of South Carolina, September 1998.

Fender, I., M. S. Gibson, and P. C. Mosser. "An International Survey of Stress Tests," *Current Issues in Economics and Finance,* Federal Reserve Bank of New York, November 2001.

Ferri, G., L. G. Liu, and G. Majnoni. "The Role of Rating Agency Assessments in Less Developed Countries: Impact of the Proposed Basel Guidelines." *Journal of Banking and Finance* (January 2001): 115–148.

Financial Times. "Fears over Banks Prompt Surge in Credit Derivatives." (October 7, 1998): 1.

Finger, C. C. "Conditional Approaches for CreditMetrics Portfolio Distributions." *RiskMetrics Monitor* (April 1999).

Finger, C. C. "Toward a Better Estimation of Wrong-Way Credit Exposure." *RiskMetrics Journal* (Spring 2000a): 25–40.

Finger, C. C. "A Comparison of Stochastic Default Rate Models." *RiskMetrics Journal* (November 2000b): 49–75.

Finnerty, J. D. "Credit Derivatives, Infrastructure Finance and Emerging Market Risk." *The Financier* (February 1996): 64–78.

Flannery, M. J., and S. Sorescu. "Evidence of Bank Market Discipline in Subordinated Debenture Yields: 1983–1991." *Journal of Finance* (September 1996): 1347–1377.

Flood, M. "Basel Buckets and Loan Losses: Absolute and Relative Loan Underperformance at Banks and Thrifts." Working Paper, Office of Thrift Supervision, March 9, 2001.

Fons, J. "Using Default Rates to Model the Term Structure of Credit Risk." *Financial Analysts Journal* (September–October 1994): 25–32.

Fraser, R. "Stress Testing Credit Risk Using Credit Manager 2.5." *RiskMetrics Journal* 1 (May 2000): 13–23.

Freixas, X., B. Parigi, and J. C. Rochet. "Systemic Risk, Interbank Relations, and Liquidity Provision by the Central Bank." *Journal of Money, Credit and Banking* 32, no. 3, part II (August 2000).

Froot, K. A., and J. C. Stein. "Risk Management, Capital Budgeting, and Capital Structure Policy for Financial Institutions: An Integrated Approach." *Journal of Financial Economics* (January 1998): 55–82.

General Accounting Office. "Risk-Based Capital: Regulatory and Industry Approaches to Capital and Risk." Report No. 98-153, General Accounting Office, July 1998.

Geske, R. "The Valuation of Corporation Liabilities as Compound Options." *Journal of Financial and Quantitative Analysis* (November 1977): 541–552.

Ginzberg, A., K. Maloney, and R. Wilner. "Risk Rating Migration and Valuation of Floating Rate Debt." Working Paper, Citicorp, March 1994.

Gordy, M. B. "A Comparative Anatomy of Credit Risk Models." *Journal of Banking and Finance* (January 2000): 119–149.

Gordy, M. B. "A Risk-Factor Model Foundation for Ratings-Based Bank Capital Rules." Working Paper, Board of Governors of the Federal Reserve System, February 5, 2001.

Gorton, G., and A. Santomero. "Market Discipline and Bank Subordinated Debt." *Journal of Money, Credit and Banking* (February 1990): 117–128.

Granger, C. W. J., and L. L. Huang. "Evaluation of Panel Data Models: Some Suggestions from Time-Series." Discussion Paper 97-10, Department of Economics, University of California, San Diego, 1997.

Griep, C., and M. De Stefano. "Standard & Poor's Official Response to the Basel Committee's Proposal." *Journal of Banking and Finance* (January 2001): 149–170.

Gully, B., W. Perraudin, and V. Saporta. "Risk and Economic Capital for Combined Banking and Insurance Activities." Paper presented at the Bank of England Conference on Banks and Systemic Risk, London, May 23–25, 2001.

Gupton, G. M. "Bank Loan Loss Given Default." Moody's Investors Service, *Special Comment,* November 2000.

Gupton, G. M., D. Gates, and L. V. Carty. "Bank-Loan Loss Given Default." Moody's Investors Service, *Global Credit Research,* November 2000.

Gupton, G. M., C. C. Finger, and M. Bhatia. *CreditMetrics.* RiskMetrics Technical Document, April 1997.

Hammes, W., and M. Shapiro. "The Implications of the New Capital Adequacy Rules for Portfolio Management of Credit Assets." *Journal of Banking and Finance* (January 2001): 97–114.

Hancock, D., and M. L. Kwast. "Using Subordinated Debt to Monitor Bank Holding Companies: Is it Feasible?" *Journal of Financial Services Research* 20, no. 2/3 (October/December 2001): 147–187.

Harrison, J. M. *Brownian Motion and Stochastic Flow Systems*. Melbourne, FL: Krieger, January 1990.

Harrison, J. M., and D. Kreps. "Martingales and Arbitrage in Multi-Period Security Markets." *Journal of Economic Theory* (1979): 381–408.

Harrison, J. M., and S. R. Pliska. "Martingales and Stochastic Integrals in the Theory of Continuous Trading." *Stochastic Processes and Their Applications* (August 1981): 215–260.

Hawley, D. D., J. D. Johnson, and D. Raina. "Artificial Neural Systems: A New Tool for Financial Decision-Making." *Financial Analysts Journal* (November/December 1990): 63–72.

Hendricks, D. "Netting Agreements and the Credit Exposures of OTC Derivatives Portfolios." Federal Reserve Bank of New York, *Quarterly Review* (Spring 1994): 36–69.

Hirtle, B. J., M. Levonian, M. Saidenberg, S. Walter, and D. Wright. "Using Credit Risk Models for Regulatory Capital: Issues and Options." *Economic Policy Review,* Federal Reserve Bank of New York (March 2001): 19–36.

Ho, T. S. "Allocate Capital and Measure Performance in a Financial Institution," *Financial Markets, Institutions, and Instruments* 8, no. 5 (1999): 1–23.

Hoggarth, G., R. Reis, and V. Saporta. "Costs of Banking System Instability: Some Empirical Evidence." Paper presented at the Bank of England Conference on Banks and Systemic Risk, London, May 23–25, 2001.

Hu, Y. T., R. Kiesel, and W. Perraudin. "The Estimation of Transition Matrices for Sovereign Credit Ratings." Working Paper, May 2001.

Huang, J. Z., and M. Huang. "How Much of the Corporate-Treasury Yield Spread is Due to Credit Risk? Results from a New Calibration Approach." Working Paper, Penn State University and Stanford University, August 2000.

Hull, J., and A. White. "Valuing Credit Default Swaps II: Modeling Default Correlations," *Journal of Derivatives* (Spring 2001): 12–21.

IIF/ISDA. Institute of International Finance and International Swaps and Derivatives Association, "Modeling Credit Risk: Joint IIF/ISDA Testing Program," February 2000.

Institute of International Finance. "Response to the Basel Committee on Banking Supervision Regulatory Capital Reform Proposals," September 2000.

Inter-American Development Bank Research Network Project. "Determinants and Consequences of Financial Constraints Facing Firms in Latin America and the Caribbean." Project: Credit Constraints in Argentina, June 2001.

International Swaps and Derivatives Association (ISDA). *Credit Risk and Regulatory Capital,* New York/London, March 1998.

Jackson, P., W. Perraudin, and V. Saporta. "Setting Minimum Capital for Internationally Active Banks." Paper presented at the Bank of England Conference on Banks and Systemic Risk, London, May 23–25, 2001.

James, C. "RAROC-Based Capital Budgeting and Performance Evaluation: A Case Study of Bank Capital Allocation." Working Paper, University of Florida, September 1996.

James, J. "Credit Derivatives: How Much Should They Cost?" *CreditRisk, Risk* Special Report (October 1999): 8–10.

Jarrow, R. A. "Default Parameter Estimation Using Market Prices." *Financial Analysts Journal* (September/October 2001): 75–92.

Jarrow, R. A., and S. M. Turnbull. "Pricing Derivatives on Financial Securities Subject to Credit Risk." *Journal of Finance* 50, no. 1 (March 1995): 53–85.

Jarrow, R., D. Lando, and S. M. Turnbull. "A Markov Model for the Term Structure of Credit Spreads." *Review of Financial Studies* (Summer 1997): 481–523.

Jarrow, R. A., and S. M. Turnbull. "The Intersection of Market and Credit Risk." *Journal of Banking and Finance* 24, no. 1 (2000).

Jarrow, R. A., and D. R. van Deventer. "Practical Usage of Credit Risk Models in Loan Portfolio and Counterparty Exposure Management." Credit Risk Models and Management, *Risk Publications,* March 1999.

Jewell, J., and M. Livingston. "A Comparison of Bond Ratings from Moody's, S&P, and Fitch." *Financial Markets, Institutions, and Instruments* 8, no. 4 (1999).

Jones, D. "Emerging Problems with the Basel Capital Accord: Regulatory Capital Arbitrage and Related Issues." *Journal of Banking and Finance* 24 (2000): 35–58.

Jones, E. P., S. P. Mason, and E. Rosenfeld. "Contingent Claims Analysis of Corporate Capital Structures: An Empirical Investigation." *Journal of Finance* (July 1984): 611–625.

J. P. Morgan & Co., and RiskMetrics Group. "The JP Morgan Guide to Credit Derivatives with Contributions from the RiskMetrics Group." London: Risk Publications, 1999.

Kaminsky, G., and S. Schmukler. "Emerging Markets Instability: Do Sovereign Ratings Affect Country Risk and Stock Returns?" Working Paper, World Bank, February 28, 2001.

Kao, D. L. "Estimating and Pricing Credit Risk: An Overview." *Financial Analysts Journal* (July/August 2000): 50–60.

Karels, G. V., and A. J. Prakash. "Multivariate Normality and Forecasting of Business Bankruptcy." *Journal of Business, Finance and Accounting* (Winter 1987): 573–593.

Kealhofer, S. "Portfolio Management of Default Risk." San Francisco: KMV Corporation, November 15, 1993.

Kealhofer, S. "Managing Default Risk in Derivative Portfolios." In *Derivative Credit Risk: Further Advances in Measurement and Management,* 2nd ed. London: Risk Books, January 1999.

Kealhofer, S. "The Quantification of Credit Risk." San Francisco: KMV Corporation, January 2000 (unpublished).

Kealhofer, S., and M. Kurbat. "The Default Prediction Power of the Merton Approach Relative to Debt Ratings and Accounting Variables." KMV, May 2001.

Kealhofer, S., S. Kwok, and W. Weng. "Uses and Abuses of Bond Default Rates." KMV, March 1998.

Keenan, S. C. "Historical Default Rates of Corporate Bond Issuers, 1920–1999." *Special Comment,* Moody's Investors Service, January 2000.

Keswani, A. "Estimating a Risky Term Structure of Brady Bonds." Working Paper, London School of Economics, November 23, 1999.

Kiesel, R., W. Perraudin, and A. Taylor. "The Structure of Credit Risk: Spread Volatility and Rating Transitions." Working Paper, Bank of England, June 2001.

Kim, J. "Conditioning the Transition Matrix." *Credit Risk* (October 1999): 37–40.

Kim, J. "Hypothesis Test of Default Correlation and Application to Specific Risk." *RiskMetrics Journal* 1 (November 2000): 35–48.

Kim, K. S., and J. R. Scott. "Prediction of Corporate Failure: An Artificial Neural Network Approach." Working Paper, Southwest Missouri State University, September 1991.

KMV. "Credit Monitor Overview." San Francisco: KMV Corporation, 1993 (mimeo).

KMV. "Global Correlation Factor Structure." San Francisco: KMV Corporation, August 1996 (mimeo).

KMV. "KMV and CreditMetrics." San Francisco: KMV Corporation, 1997 (mimeo).

KMV. "The KMV EDF Credit Measure and Probabilities of Default." San Francisco, KMV Corporation, 2000.

KMV. "Portfolio Manager Model." San Francisco: KMV Corporation, undated.

Koyluoglu, H. U., A. Bangia, and T. Garside. "Devil in the Parameters." New York: Oliver, Wyman & Company, July 26, 1999.

Koyluoglu, H. U., and A. Hickman. "A Generalized Framework for Credit Risk Portfolio Models." Working Paper, New York: Oliver, Wyman and Co., July 1998.

KPMG. *VAR: Understanding and Applying Value-At-Risk.* New York: Risk Publications, 1997.

KPMG. "Loan Analysis System." New York: KPMG Financial Consulting Services, 1998.

Krahnen, J. P., and M. Weber. "Generally Accepted Rating Principles: A Primer." *Journal of Banking and Finance* 25, no. 1 (2001): 3–23.

Kreps, D. "Multiperiod Securities and the Efficient Allocation of Risk: A Comment on the Black-Scholes Option Pricing Model." In *The Economics of Information and Uncertainty*, edited by J. J. McCall. Chicago: University of Chicago Press, 1982.

Kupiec, P. H. "Techniques for Verifying the Accuracy of Risk Measurement Models." *The Journal of Derivatives* (Winter 1995): 73–84.

Kupiec, P. H., D. Nickerson, and E. Golding. "Assessing Systemic Risk Exposure Under Alternative Approaches for Capital Adequacy." Paper presented at the Bank of England Conference on Banks and Systemic Risk, London, May 23–25, 2001.

Kuritzkes, A. "Transforming Portfolio Management." *Banking Strategies* (July/August 1998).

Layish, D. N. "A Monitoring Role for Deviations From Absolute Priority in Bankruptcy Resolution." Dissertation Thesis, Baruch College, 2001.

Leland, H. "Agency Costs, Risk Management and Capital Structure." *Journal of Finance* (August 1998): 1213–1243.

Leland, H. "Corporate Debt Value, Bond Covenants and Optimal Capital Structure." *Journal of Finance* (September 1994): 1213–1252.

Leland, H., and K. Toft. "Optimal Capital Structure, Endogenous Bankruptcy, and the Term Structure of Credit Spreads." *Journal of Finance* (July 1996): 987–1019.

Leonhardt, D. "More Falling Behind on Mortgage Payments." *New York Times* (June 12, 2001): A1, C5.

Libby, R. "Ratios and the Prediction of Failure: Some Behavioral Evidence." *Journal of Accounting Research* (Spring 1975): 150–161.

Libby, R., K. T. Trotman, and I. Zimmer. "Member Variation, Recognition of Expertise, and Group Performance." *Journal of Applied Psychology* (February 1987): 81–87.

Lim, F. "Comparative Default Predictive Power of EDFs and Agency Debt Ratings." San Francisco: KMV, December 1999 (mimeo).

Linnell, I. "A Critical Review of the New Capital Adequacy Framework Paper Issued by the Basel Committee on Banking Supervision and its Implications for the Rating Agency Industry." *Journal of Banking and Finance* (January 2001): 187–196.

Litterman, R., and T. Iben. "Corporate Bond Valuation and the Term Structure of Credit Spreads." *Journal of Portfolio Management* (Spring 1991): 52–64.

Longstaff, F. A., and E. F. Schwartz. "A Simple Approach to Valuing Risky Fixed and Floating Rate Debt." *Journal of Finance* (July 1995): 789–819.

Longin, F., and B. Solnik. "Extreme Correlation of International Equity Markets." *Journal of Finance* 56, no. 2 (April 2001): 649–676.

Lopez, J. A., and M. R. Saidenberg. "Evaluating Credit Risk Models." *Journal of Banking and Finance* 24, no. 1/2 (January 2000): 151–165.

Lown, C., and D. P. Morgan. "The Credit Cycle and the Business Cycle: New Findings Using the Survey of Senior Loan Officers." Working Paper, Federal Reserve Bank of New York, June 25, 2001.

Maclachlan, I. "Recent Advances in Credit Risk Management." Ninth Melbourne Money and Finance Conference, June 19, 1999.

Madan, D. B., and H. Unal. "Pricing the Risks of Default." *Review of Derivative Research* 2 (1998): 121–160.

Madan, D. B., and H. Unal. "A Two-Factor Hazard-Rate Model for Pricing Risky Debt and the Term Structure of Credit Spreads." *Journal of Financial and Quantitative Analysis* (March 2000): 43–65.

McAllister, P. M., and J. J. Mingo. "Commercial Loan Risk Management, Credit Scoring, and Pricing: The Need for a New Shared Database." *Journal of Commercial Lending* (May 1994): 6–22.

McKinsey and Co. *Credit Portfolio View.* New York: McKinsey and Co., 1997.

McNeil, A. J. "Extreme Value Theory for Risk Managers." Working Paper, Department of Mathematics, Swiss Federal Technical University, Zurich, May 1999.

McQuown, J. A. "A Comment on Market vs. Accounting-Based Measures of Default Risk." San Francisco: KMV Corporation, September 1993.

McQuown, J. A. "The Illuminated Guide to Portfolio Management." *Journal of Lending and Credit Risk Management* (August 1997): 29–41.

McQuown, J. A., and S. Kealhofer. "A Comment on the Formation of Bank Stock Prices." San Francisco: KMV Corporation, April 1997.

Meissier, W. F., and J. V. Hansen. "Inducing Rules for Expert System Development: An Example Using Default and Bankruptcy Data." *Management Science* 34, no. 12 (December 1988): 1403–1415.

Mella-Barral, P., and W. Perraudin. "Strategic Debt Service." *Journal of Finance* (June 1997): 531–556.

Merrill Lynch. "Credit Default Swaps." New York: Global Fixed Income Research, October 1998.

Merton, R. C. "On the Pricing of Corporate Debt: The Risk Structure of Interest Rates." *Journal of Finance* (June 1974): 449–470.

Mester, L. "What's the Point of Credit Scoring?" Federal Reserve Bank of Philadelphia, *Business Review* (September/October 1997): 3–16.

Miller, R. "Refining Ratings." *Risk Magazine* (August 1998).

Mingo, J. J. "Policy Implications of the Federal Reserve Study of Credit Risk Models at Major U.S. Banking Institutions." *Journal of Banking and Finance* (January 2000): 15–33.

Monfort, B., and C. Mulder. "Using Credit Ratings for Capital Requirements on Lending to Emerging Market Economies—Possible Impact of a New Basel Accord." Working Paper WP/00/69, International Monetary Fund, 2000.

Moody, J., and J. Utans. "Architecture Selection Strategies for Neural Networks: Application to Corporate Bond Rating Prediction." In *Neural Networks in Capital Markets,* edited by A. P. Refenes, 277–300, New York: Wiley, 1994.

Mueller, C. "A Simple Multi-Factor Model of Corporate Bond Prices." Doctoral Dissertation, University of Wisconsin-Madison, October 29, 2000.

Nagpal, K. M., and Bahar, R. "An Analytical Approach for Credit Risk Analysis Under Correlated Defaults." *CreditMetrics Monitor* (April 1999): 51–74.

Nakada, P., H. Shah, H. U. Koyluoglu, and O. Collignon. "P&C RAROC: A Catalyst for Improved Capital Management in the Property and Casualty Insurance Industry." *The Journal of Risk Finance* (Fall 1999): 52–69.

Nandi, S. "Valuation Models for Default-Risky Securities: An Overview." Federal Reserve Bank of Atlanta, *Economic Review,* Fourth Quarter 1998, 22–35.

Neftci, S. N. "Value at Risk Calculations, Extreme Events, and Tail Estimation." *Journal of Derivatives* 7, no. 3, (Spring 2000): 23–38.

Nickell, P., W. Perraudin, and S. Varotto. "Stability of Rating Transitions." *Journal of Banking and Finance* 24, no. 1/2 (2001a): 203–228.

Nickell, P., W. Perraudin, and S. Varotto. "Ratings versus Equity-Based Credit Risk Modeling: An Empirical Analysis." Working Paper 132, Bank of England, May 2001b.

Oda, N., and J. Muranaga. "A New Framework for Measuring the Credit Risk of a Portfolio: The 'ExVAR' Model." Monetary and Economic Studies, Bank of Japan, December 1997.

Paul-Choudhury, S. "Taming the Wild Frontier." *CreditRisk,* Risk Special Report (October 1999): 14–15.

Phelan, K., and C. Alexander. "Different Strokes." *CreditRisk,* Risk Special Report (October 1999): 32–35.

Poddig, T. "Bankruptcy Prediction: A Comparison with Discriminant Analysis." In *Neural Networks in Capital Markets,* edited by A. P. Refenes, 311–323, New York: Wiley, 1994.

Powell, A. "A Capital Accord for Emerging Economies?" Working Paper, World Bank, July 11, 2001.

Rajan, R. "Insiders and Outsiders: The Choice between Informed and Arm's Length Debt." *Journal of Finance* (September 1992): 1367–1400.

Reinhart, C. "Sovereign Credit Ratings Before and After Financial Crises." Department of Economics, University of Maryland. February 21, 2001, presented at the Conference on Rating Agencies in the Global Financial System, Stern School of Business New York University, June 1, 2001.

Reisen, H. "Revisions to the Basel Accord and Sovereign Ratings." In *Global Finance From a Latin American Viewpoint, IDB/OECD*, edited by R. Hausmann and U. Hiemenz. Development Centre, 2000.

Reisen, H., and J. von Maltzan. "Boom and Bust and Sovereign Ratings." *International Finance* 2, no. 2 (July 1999): 273–293.

Ronn, E., and A. Verma. "Pricing Risk-Adjusted Deposit Insurance: An Option-Based Model." *Journal of Finance* (September 1986): 871–895.

Rule, D. "The Credit Derivatives Market: Its Development and Possible Implications for Financial Stability." *Financial Stability Review* (June 2001): 117–140.

Sanvicente, A. S., and F. L.C. Bader. "Filing for Financial Reorganization in Brazil: Event Prediction with Accounting and Financial Variables and the Information Content of the Filing Announcement." Working Paper, Sao Paulo University, October 1998.

Saunders, A. *Financial Institutions Management: A Modern Perspective*. 4th ed. BurrRidge, IL: Irwin/McGraw-Hill, August 2002 (forthcoming).

Saunders, A., A. Srinivasan, and I. Walter. "Price Formation in the OTC Corporate Bond Markets: A Field Study of the Inter-Dealer Market." *Journal of Economics and Business* (2002, forthcoming).

Schultz, P. "Corporate Bond Trading Costs: A Peek Behind the Curtain." *Journal of Finance* (April 2001): 677–698.

Schwartz, T. "Estimating the Term Structures of Corporate Debt." *The Review of Derivatives Research* 2, no. 2/3 (1998): 193–230.

Shearer, A. "Pricing for Risk Is the Key in Commercial Lending." *American Banker* (March 21, 1997): 1.

Shepheard-Walwyn, T., and R. Litterman. "Building a Coherent Risk Measurement and Capital Optimization Model for Financial Firms." *Economic Policy Review*, Federal Reserve Bank of New York, October 1998.

Shimko, D., N. Tejima, and D. R. van Deventer. "The Pricing of Risky Debt when Interest Rates Are Stochastic." *Journal of Fixed Income* (September 1993): 58–65.

Singleton, J. C., and A. J. Surkan. "Bond Rating with Neural Networks." In *Neural Networks in Capital Markets*, edited by A. P. Refenes, 301–307, New York: Wiley, 1994.

Smith, C. W., W. Smithson, and D. S. Wilford. *Managing Financial Risk*. Cambridge, MA: Ballinger, 1990.

Sobehart, J. R., R. M. Stein, V. Mikityanskaya, and L. Li. "Moody's Public Firm Risk Model: A Hybrid Approach to Modeling Short Term Default Risk." Moody's Investors Service, *Rating Methodology* (April 2000).

Sobehart, J. R., S. Keenan, and R. M. Stein. "Benchmarking Quantitative Default Risk Models: A Validation Methodology." Moody's Investors Service, *Rating Methodology* (March 2000).

Society of Actuaries. "1986–1992 Credit Loss Experience Study: Private Placement Bonds." Schaumburg, IL: Society of Actuaries, 1996.

Stahl, G. "Confidence Intervals for Different Capital Definitions in a Credit Risk Model." Paper presented at Center for Economic Policy Research (CEPR) Conference, London, September 20, 1998.

Standard and Poor's. "Rating Performance 1997-Stability and Transition." New York: Standard and Poor's Research Report, 1998 (mimeo).

Stein, R. M. "Evidence on the Incompleteness of Merton-type Structural Models for Default Prediction." Moody's Technical Paper, December 6, 2000.

Stiglitz, J., and A. Weiss. "Credit Rationing in Markets with Imperfect Information." *American Economic Review* (June 1981): 393–410.

Sundaram, R. K. "Equivalent Martingale Measures and Risk-Neutral Pricing: An Expository Note." *Journal of Derivatives* (Fall 1997): 85–98.

Sundaram, R. K. "The Merton/KMV Approach to Pricing Credit Risk." *Extra Credit,* Merrill Lynch (January/February 2001): 59–67.

Swidler, S., and J. A. Wilcox. "Information about Bank Risk from Options Prices." Paper presented at the Bank of England Conference on Banks and Systemic Risk, London, May 23–25, 2001.

Taylor, J. D. "Cross-Industry Differences in Business Failure Rates: Implications for Portfolio Management." *Commercial Lending Review* (Winter 1998): 36–46.

Theodore, S. S. "Rating Methodology: Bank Credit Risk (An Analytical Framework for Banks in Developed Markets)." Moody's Investors Service, *Rating Methodology,* April 1999.

Treacy, W., and M. Carey. "Internal Credit Risk Rating Systems at Large U.S. Banks." *Federal Reserve Bulletin* (November 1998).

Treacy, W. F., and M. Carey. "Credit Risk Rating Systems at Large U.S. Banks." *Journal of Banking and Finance* (January 2000): 167–201.

Turnbull, S. M. "Capital Allocation and Risk Performance Measurement in a Financial Institution." *Financial Markets, Institutions & Instruments* 9, no. 5 (2000): 325–357.

Unal, H., D. Madan, and L. Guntay. "A Simple Approach to Estimate Recovery Rates with APR Violation from Debt Spreads." Working Paper 7, Wharton Financial Institutions Center, February 2001.

Vasicek, O. "Probability of Loss on a Loan Portfolio." San Francisco: KMV Corporation, February 1987.

Wall, L. D., and T. W. Koch. "Bank Loan-Loss Accounting: A Review of the Theoretical and Empirical Evidence." Federal Reserve Bank of Atlanta, *Economic Review* (Second Quarter 2000): 1–19.

Wall, L., and M. M. Shrikhande. "Credit Derivatives." Paper presented at the FMA Conference, Chicago, October 1998.

Warga, A. Fixed Income Securities Database. University of Houston, College of Business Administration (www.uh.edu/~awarga/lb.html), 1999.

White, L. "The Credit Rating Industry: An Industrial Organization Analysis." Presented at the Conference on Rating Agencies in the Global Financial System, Stern School of Business New York University, June 1, 2001.

Wilson, T. "Credit Risk Modeling: A New Approach." New York: McKinsey & Co., 1997a (mimeo).

Wilson, T. "Portfolio Credit Risk (Parts I and II)." *Risk Magazine* (September and October 1997b).

Wilson, T. "Portfolio Credit Risk." Federal Reserve Bank of New York, *Economic Policy Review* (October 1998): 71–82.

Yang, Z. R., M. B. Platt, and H. D. Platt. "Probabilistic Neural Networks in Bankruptcy Prediction." *Journal of Business Research* (February 1999): 67–74.

Zaik, E., J. Walter, and J. G. Kelling. "RAROC at Bank of America: From Theory to Practice." *Journal of Applied Corporate Finance* (Summer 1996): 83–93.

Zhou, C. "A Jump Diffusion Approach to Modeling Credit Risk and Valuing Defaultable Securities." Working Paper, Federal Reserve Board of Governors, March 1997.

Zhou, C. "An Analysis of Default Correlations and Multiple Defaults." *The Review of Financial Studies* (Summer 2001): 555–576.

notes

Chapter 1   Why New Approaches to Credit Risk Measurement and Management?

1. A consensus among the IIF/ISDA survey participants asserted that data on emerging market debt were insufficient to model migration risk, correlations of default probabilities, and portfolio volatilities of default and migration risk. The existing data on emerging market debt were sufficient to measure only default risk.
2. Arguably, technology and the increased liquidity in the secondary market for loans (along with the development of credit derivatives) have helped move the "lending paradigm" away from a buy-and-hold strategy to one in which loans and credit risk are actively managed in a portfolio framework. [See, for example, Kuritzkes (1998) and Hammes and Shapiro (2001).]
3. The difference in the time horizons for market risk's *VAR* (defined over 10 days) as compared to credit risk's *VAR* (defined over 1 year) highlights one of the primary difficulties in obtaining sufficient data to implement credit risk measurement models.
4. The market value is the present value of all future cash flows discounted at a risk-adjusted rate of return reflecting the security's risk exposure.

Chapter 2   Traditional Approaches to Credit Risk

1. Libby (1975) conducts a controlled experiment in which 43 commercial loan officers, drawn from both small banks (in Urbana-Champaign, Illinois) and large banks (in Philadelphia, Pennsylvania) were asked to independently evaluate the creditworthiness of an identical pool of 60 business loan applicants. He finds a considerable dispersion in the accuracy rate which ranged from 27 to 50 correct, out of the 60 cases. Three of the loan officers were unable even to outperform chance in accurately predicting firms failure. In another test, Libby, Trotman, and Zimmer (1987) find that, 75.9 percent of the time, the average expert correctly classified those Australian land development firms that ultimately entered bankruptcy. The best member of the group had an 86.6 percent correct classification rate.
2. Treacy and Carey (1998) argue that loan review departments are further mechanisms through which common standards can be applied across lending officers.

3. A type 1 error misclassifies a bad loan as good. A type 2 error misclassifies a good loan as bad.

4. The maximal, fully connected two-layer network, with 10 input variables and 12 hidden units, has a maximum of $1 + 12(10 + 2) = 145$ number of weights. All possible combinations of these weights within the two layers (treating the ordering of the connections as unique) is: $2^{145} = 4.46 \times 10^{43}$.

5. We focus on internal ratings in contrast to the external ratings publicly released by any independent rating agency designated by the SEC as a "nationally recognized statistical rating organization" (NRSRO). See White (2001) and Boot and Milbourn (2001) for a discussion of the role of external ratings.

6. The Central Bank of Argentina requires banks to classify all loans on a scale of 1 to 5 and makes the database, which contains over 6 million entries available on its Web site: www.bcra.gov.ar [see Falkenheim and Powell (2001)].

7. Carey (2001a) compares the capital requirements imposed on insurance companies by the NAIC to those proposed for banks, and finds that the banks' capital requirements under the BIS Internal Ratings-Based Approach are two to four times greater, thereby raising the prospect of regulatory arbitrage in diversified FIs.

8. Treacy and Carey (2000) find that the median number of grades on the internal rating scales of large banks is five pass grades and three or four problem asset grades. The BIS (2000) find an average of 10 grades for performing loans and three for impaired loans. Smaller banking organizations tend to have fewer grades on their scales, or no rating systems at all. To qualify for the internal ratings-based approach to the new Basel Capital Accord (see Chapter 3), an internal ratings system must have at least six to nine performing classifications and two nonperforming risk classifications.

9. In recognition that consumer or retail assets are less amenable to independent credit risk analysis, the new Basel Capital Accord proposal of 2001 (see Chapter 3) permits the grouping of retail assets into similar risk segments. See Appendix 3.2.

10. A short time horizon may be appropriate in a mark-to-market model in which downgrades of credit quality are considered, whereas a longer time horizon may be necessary for a default mode model that considers only the default event. See Hirtle et al. (2001).

11. To adopt the internal ratings-based approach in the new Basel Capital Accord, banks must adopt a risk rating system that assesses the borrower's credit risk exposure separately from that of the transaction.

12. Krahnen and Weber (2001) describe the necessary prerequisites for design of an internal rating system. Crouhy and Mark (2001) present a prototype based on the CIBC internal ratings model.

13. However, Mester (1997) reports that only 8 percent of banks with up to $5 billion in assets used scoring for small business loans. In March 1995, in order to make credit scoring of small business loans available to small banks, Fair, Isaac introduced its Small Business Scoring Service, based on five years of data on small business loans, collected from 17 banks.

14. More recently, the discriminant model fit has been improved by considering a nonparametric approach [Barniv and Raveh (1989)], selecting explanatory variables with a multivariate normal distribution [Karels and Prakash (1987)], and incorporating a neural network [Coates and Fant (1993)].
15. Astebro and Rucker (2000) demonstrate the economic implications of the choice of cut-off point in a credit scoring model of European cell phone customers. If economic conditions are ignored, the cut-off point is the Z value midway between the average Z of the failed (bankrupt) group and the average Z of the matched sample of nonfailing firms.
16. In comparing the accuracy of internal ratings and credit scoring models, Carey and Hrycay (2001) find that long time periods of data across several points of the business cycle must be utilized in order to reduce the models' distortions.

Chapter 3   The BIS International Bank Capital Accord: January 2002

1. The Basel Committee consists of senior supervisory representatives from Belgium, Canada, France, Germany, Italy, Japan, Luxembourg, the Netherlands, Sweden, Switzerland, the United Kingdom, and the United States. It usually meets at the Bank for International Settlements in Basel where its permanent Secretariat is located.
2. More than 100 countries have adopted BIS I.
3. Tier 1 consists of the last, residual claims on the bank's assets, such as common stock and perpetual preferred stock. Tier 2 capital is slightly more senior than Tier 1 (e.g., preferred stock and subordinated debt).
4. An indication of BIS I's mispricing of credit risk for commercial loans is obtained from Flood (2001) who examines the actual loan loss experience for U.S. banks and thrifts from 1984 to 1999. He finds that in 1984 (1996) 10 percent (almost 3 percent) of the institutions had loan losses that exceeded the 8 percent Basel capital requirement. Moreover, Falkenheim and Powell (2001) find that the BIS I capital requirements for Argentine banks were set too low to protect against the banks' credit risk exposures. See the International Swaps and Derivatives Association (ISDA, 1998) for an early discussion of the need to reform BIS I.
5. However, Jones (2000) and Mingo (2000) argue that regulatory arbitrage may not be all bad because it sets into motion the forces of innovation that will ultimately correct the mispricing errors inherent in the regulations.
6. The original time line was pushed back a year. The final draft of the proposals is scheduled for January 2002. The comment period will end in June 2002, leading to a final accord in December 2002 and implementation in 2005.
7. The Federal Housing Authority (FHA) reported at the end of the first quarter of 2001 that the percentage of homeowners whose mortgage payments were more than 30 days late exceeded 10 percent for the first time ever (Leonhardt, 2001).
8. McKinsey estimates that operational risk represents 20 percent, market risk comprises 20 percent, and credit risk is 60 percent of the overall risk of a typical

commercial bank or investment bank. [See Hammes and Shapiro (2001), p. 106. Reprinted from *Journal of Banking and Finance,* January 2001 issue by W. Hammes and M. Shapiro, "The Implications of the New Capital Adequacy Rules for Portfolio Management of Credit Assets," copyright 2001, with permission from Elsevier Science.] However, the November 2001 modifications to BIS II reduce the share of operational risk to 12 percent.

9. The basic indicator approach levies a single operational risk capital charge for the entire bank, the standardized approach divides the bank into eight lines of business, each with its own operational risk charge, and the advanced measurement approach (AMA) uses the bank's own internal models of operational risk measurement to assess a capital requirement. [See BIS (September 2001).]

10. For more details on the market and operational risk components of regulatory capital requirements, see the BIS Web site at http://www.bis.org/.

11. Moreover, accounting rules differ from country to country so that often the loan loss reserve is a measure of current or incurred losses, rather than expected future losses. [See Wall and Koch (2000) and Flood (2001).] Indeed, Cavallo and Majnoni (2001) show that distorted loan loss provisions may have a procyclical effect that exacerbates systemic risk. In particular, many Latin American countries require large provisions for loan losses (averaging 8 percent of gross financing), which raises the possibility of excessive capital requirements in these countries due to double counting of credit risk [see Powell (2001)].

12. BIS II makes no changes to the Tier 1, Tier 2, and Tier 3 definitions of capital. Carey (2001b) suggests that because subordinated debt is not useful in preserving soundness (i.e., impaired subordinated debt triggers bank insolvency), there should be a distinction between equity and loan loss reserves (the buffer against credit risk, denoted Tier A) and subordinated debt (the buffer against market risk, denoted Tier B). Jackson et al. (2001) also show that the proportion of Tier 1 capital should be considered in setting minimum capital requirements.

13. The one exception to this regards insurance subsidiaries. Banks' investments in insurance subsidiaries are deducted for the purposes of measuring regulatory capital. However, this distinction ignores the diversification benefits from combining banking and insurance activities; see Gully et al. (2001).

14. Capital requirements are just the first of three pillars comprising the BIS II proposals. The second pillar consists of a supervisory review process that requires bank regulators to assess the adequacy of bank risk management policies. Several issues, such as interest rate risk included in the banking book, have been relegated to the second pillar (i.e., supervisory oversight) rather than to explicit capital requirements. The third pillar of BIS II is market discipline. The Accord sets out disclosure requirements to increase the transparency of reporting of risk exposures so as to enlist the aid of market participants in supervising bank behavior. Indeed, the adequacy of disclosure requirements is a prerequisite for supervisory approval of bank internal models of credit risk measurement.

15. The EAD for on-balance-sheet items is the nominal outstanding amount. EAD for off-balance-sheet items is determined using most of the same credit conversion factors from BIS I, with the exception of loan commitments maturing in

less than one year that now have a 20 percent conversion factor rather than the 0 percent under BIS I.

16. Korea and Mexico (both OECD members) will move, under the proposals, from a zero risk weight to a positive risk weight corresponding to their credit ratings. Powell (2001) uses the standardized approach to estimate that capital requirements for banks lending to Korea (Mexico) will increase by $3.4 billion ($5 billion), resulting in an estimated increase in bond spreads of 74.8 basis points for Korea and 104.5 basis points for Mexico. If the internal ratings-based approach is used, the impact is even greater.

17. That is, an AAA rating would normally warrant a 0 percent risk weight; instead, the risk weight is set one category higher, at 20 percent.

18. However, if the contract is expected to roll over upon maturity (e.g., an open repo), then its effective maturity exceeds three months and the bank supervisor may consider it ineligible for the preferential risk weights shown in Table 3.3.

19. Similarly, Powell (2001) finds insufficient convexity in the standardized risk weights for sovereign debt.

20. Because actual loss data are used and the samples are finite, there are standard errors around these estimates. Moreover, BIS II is calibrated to a 99.9 percent level, not the higher 99.97 percent used in the Altman and Saunders study.

21. One year has become the common time horizon for credit risk models. One year is perceived as being of sufficient length for a bank to raise additional capital (if able to do so). However, Carey (2001b) contends that this time horizon is too short.

22. For less developed countries (LDCs), the proportion of companies with external credit ratings is much lower than for developed countries. Powell (2001) reports that only 150 corporates in Argentina are rated, although the central bank's credit bureau lists 25,000 corporate borrowers. Thus, Ferri et al. (2001) surmise that borrowers in less developed countries are likely to suffer a substantial increase in borrowing costs relative to those in developed countries upon adoption of BIS II.

23. Linnell (2001) and Altman and Saunders (2001b) suggest that, at the very least, the unrated classification risk weight should be 150 percent. There is evidence that the failure ratio on nonrated loans is similar to the failure ratio in the lowest (150 percent) rated bucket; see Altman and Saunders (2001b).

24. To mitigate this problem, Griep and De Stefano (2001) suggest that more unsolicited ratings be used. German bank associations plan to pool credit data so as to address the problem of unrated small and medium sized businesses. Because of the importance of this market sector to the German economy, Chancellor Schroder has threatened to veto the BIS II proposal. See *The Economist,* November 10, 2001.

25. Moody's, in its ratings of about 1,000 banks worldwide, uses a complex interaction of seven fundamental factors: (1) operating environment (competitive, regulatory, institutional support); (2) ownership and governance; (3) franchise value; (4) recurring earning power; (5) risk profile (credit, market, liquidity risks, and asset-liability management, agency, reputation, operational, etc.) and

risk management; (6) economic capital analysis; (7) management priorities and strategies. See Cunningham (1999) and Theodore (1999).

26. Moreover, the usefulness of external ratings for regulatory purposes is questionable because the rating incorporates the likelihood that the firm will be bailed out by the government in the event of financial distress. Only Fitch, IBCA, and Moody's provide stand-alone creditworthiness ratings, but these cannot be used to calculate the probability of default; see Jackson et al. (2001).

27. Jewell and Livingston (1999) find that Fitch ratings were slightly higher on average than ratings from S&P and Moody's. Fitch is the only rating agency that explicitly charges for a rating.

28. Moreover, contagious regional financial crises in confidence may lead to excessive downgradings of sovereign ratings, see Cantor and Packer (1996), Ferri et al. (2001), and Kaminsky and Schmukler (2001).

29. In this chapter, we focus on the BIS II regulations as applied to on-balance sheet activities. In Chapter 15, we describe the BIS II proposals for off-balance-sheet activities.

30. As noted earlier, the use of a one-year time horizon assumes that banks can fully recapitalize any credit losses within a year. Carey (2001b) argues that a two- to three-year time horizon is more realistic.

31. Maturity is the weighted average life of the loan (i.e., the percentage of principal repayments in each year times the year(s) in which these payments are received). For example, a two-year loan of $200 million repaying $100 million principal in year 1 and $100 million principal in year 2 has a weighted average life (WAL) = $[1 \times (100/200)] + [2 \times (100/200)] = 1.5$ years.

32. According to Carey (2001b), the January 2001 IRB proposal was calibrated to a 4.75 percent Tier 1 capital ratio with a Tier 2 subordinated debt multiplier of 1.3 and a *PD* error multiplier of 1.2. This resulted in a target capital ratio minimum of $4.75 \times 1.3 \times 1.2 = 7.4$ percent. Since the BIS I 8 percent ratio incorporates a safety factor for operational risk, it makes sense that the pure credit risk IRB minimum capital requirement would be calibrated to a number less than 8 percent.

33. The format of the IRB approach is to use *PD, LGD,* and *M* to determine the loan's risk weight and then to multiply that risk weight times the *EAD* times 8 percent in order to determine the loan's capital requirement.

34. However, there is now a 20 percent conversion factor for loan commitments maturing in less than one year. Under BIS I this conversion factor was 0 percent.

35. The foundation approach assumes a constant *LGD.* Altman and Brady (2001) find that *LGD* is directly related to *PD.*

36. *PD* is expressed in decimal format in all formulas.

37. Historical insolvency for AA (A) rated bonds corresponds to a 99.97 percent (99.95 percent) target loss percentile. Jackson et al. (2001) use CreditMetrics to show that BIS I provides a 99.9 percent solvency rate (equivalent to a BBB rating) for a high-quality bank portfolio, and 99 percent (BB rating) for a lower quality bank portfolio.

38. Treacy and Carey (2000) document that bank internal ratings systems generally have more than 10 rating classifications.

39. In contrast to the advanced IRB approach, the foundation IRB approach does not input the loan's actual maturity into the risk weight calculation.

40. Gordy (2001) estimates that on average the largest 10 percent of the exposures account for about 40 percent of the portfolio value. Moreover, McQuown and Kealhofer (1997), using KMV data on *PD* and *LGD*, find that 40 percent of bank equity is required to back up the credit risk of just 20 concentrated corporate obligations.

41. As of December 2001, there were still unresolved questions about the structure of the granularity adjustment.

42. The portfolio *TEAD* is calculated by simply summing the *EAD*s for all non-retail exposures. There is no granularity adjustment for retail (consumer) loans unless the bank has a very high proportion of its portfolio in retail loans.

43. A loan Herfindahl index is used to adjust for the fact that granularity will depend on the distribution of loan sizes within the portfolio. For example, the granularity of a portfolio containing 1,000 loans, where 100 loans accounted for 40 percent of the total portfolio exposure, is much higher than the granularity of a portfolio of 1,000 equal-size loans.

44. Carty (1998) finds that the mean *LGD* for senior unsecured (secured) bank loans is 21 percent (13 percent). Carey (1998) finds a mean *LGD* of 36 percent for a portfolio of private placements. Asarnow and Edwards (1995) find a 35 percent *LGD* for commercial loans. Gupton (2000) finds a 30.5 percent (47.9 percent) *LGD* for senior secured (unsecured) syndicated bank loans. Gupton et al. (2000) obtain similar estimates for expected *LGD*, but find substantial variance around the mean.

45. This may incorporate a mark-to-market adjustment. However, the mark-to-market adjustment in BIS II does not incorporate the transition risk (deterioration in credit quality) and spread risk (change in the market price of credit risk) components of a comprehensive mark-to-market model. There is also an alternative specification of the *b(PD)* adjustment based on the default mode assumption.

46. That is, for loans with maturities longer than 3 years, the increase in the capital requirement relative to the *BRW* decreases as the loan quality deteriorates. This could increase the relative cost of long term bank credit for low risk borrowers. See Allen (2002).

47. Hoggarth et al. (2001) show that cumulative output losses during systemic crises average 15 percent to 20 percent of annual GDP.

48. That is, the IRB frameworks are calibrated to an asset correlation of 0.20, which is higher than actual correlations that averaged 9 percent to 10 percent for Eurobonds; see Jackson et al. (2001). The November 2001 potential modifications to BIS II proposals incorporate a correlation coefficient that is inversely related to the *PD*. However, Freixas et al. (2000) show that systemic crises may occur even if all banks are solvent.

49. Jackson et al. (2001) show that BIS II is calibrated to achieve a confidence level of 99.9 percent (i.e., an insolvency rate of .1 percent), whereas banks choose a solvency standard of 99.96 percent (an insolvency rate of .04 percent) in response to market pressures. This conforms to observations that banks tend to hold capital in excess of regulatory requirements.

50. Jackson et al. (2001) find that a decrease in the bank's credit rating from A+ to A reduces swap liabilities by approximately £2.3 billion.

51. If *EAD* cannot be determined, the bank can use an estimate of expected losses, or $PD \times LGD$.

52. The lower retail capital charges reflect BIS concern that certain retail portfolios may generate expected margin income sufficient to cover expected losses (*EL*). Thus, the proposed risk weights which cover both *EL* and *UL* may overstate capital requirements.

Chapter 4 Loans as Options: The KMU and Moody's Models

1. In many cases, the models can also be applied to private firms by proprietary "mapping" models (e.g., KMV's Private Firm model). See Appendix 11.1.

2. In fact, if there are direct and indirect costs of bankruptcy (e.g., legal costs), the lender's loss on a loan may exceed principal and interest. This makes the payoff in Figure 4.1 even more similar to the one shown in Figure 4.2 (i.e., the loan may have a negative dollar payoff).

3. Specifically, most corporate bonds are traded over-the-counter. Price information is extremely difficult to get because most trades are interdealer. In September 1998, the Securities and Exchange Commission (SEC) announced a special joint initiative with the National Association of Securities Dealers (NASD) to improve the quality of corporate bond price information over the next two years. The introduction of on-line trading and underwriting systems should also improve bond market efficiency and transparency; see Clow (2000). However, Hancock and Kwast (2001) find significant discrepancies among commercial bond pricing services, Bloomberg, and Interactive Data Corporation in all but the most liquid bond issues.

4. Jarrow and van Deventer (1999) test a Merton-type model using bond quotes (spreads) for one bank (Interstate Bankcorp) over the January 3, 1986, to August 20, 1993, period, and found considerable instability in implied default probabilities. This may, in part, be due to the use of bond quotes rather than transaction prices.

5. See the Bibliography for references to KMV publications and the KMV Web site at www.kmv.com.

6. For example, if the assets are liquidated at current market values and the resulting funds are used to meet borrowing obligations.

7. In the event of liquidation of the firm's assets, the model assumes that the shareholders receive nothing. However, in practice, more than 75 percent of all bankrupt firms' debt structures are renegotiated so as to allow some deviation from absolute priority, in which the equity holders receive some payment even if the bondholders are not fully paid; see Layish (2001). Acharya et al. (2000) extend the Merton model to include renegotiation in the event of default.

8. The volatility of a firm's equity value, σ, may be calculated using historical equity prices or backed-out-of-option prices; Swidler and Wilcox (2001) solve for the implied volatility of large bank equity prices using option prices.

9. KMV has found that most firms do not default immediately upon reaching the technical insolvency point when the market value of assets has declined to equal the firm's total liabilities. The firm may have lines of credit or other cash-generating mechanisms that permit the servicing of debt even after the technical point of insolvency is reached. KMV sets the default point equal to total short-term liabilities plus one half of long-term liabilities as a somewhat arbitrary way of modeling this lag between technical insolvency and default. However, Mella-Barral and Perraudin (1997) suggest that default may begin before technical insolvency is reached, because shareholders can extract concessions on coupon payments.

10. KMV also doesn't make distinctions in the liability structure as to seniority, collateral, or covenants. Convertible debt and preferred stock are treated as long-term liabilities. It might be noted, however, that the user can input whatever value of B he or she feels is economically appropriate. Geske (1977) has extended the Merton model to include coupon payments, covenants, and so on.

11. Bongini et al. (2001) show that external credit ratings lagged behind default-risk-adjusted Ronn and Verma deposit insurance premiums in forecasting the 1998 Asian banking crisis.

12. Where σ_A is the annual standard deviation of asset values expressed in dollar terms, or percentage standard deviation times the market value of assets.

13. Distance to default $= [A(1 + g) - B]/ \sigma_A = (\$110 - \$80)/\$10 = 3$ standard deviations. KMV Credit Monitor uses a constant asset growth assumption for all firms in the same market, which is the expected growth rate of the market as a whole. The rationale for this assumption is that, in an efficient market, differences in growth rates between the market and individual firms are fully discounted (i.e., arbitraged away) and incorporated in the stock prices (and hence into asset value) of the firm. Thus, in equilibrium, there is no difference between asset growth of individual firms and the market. The only other adjustment to this constant (across-the-board) asset growth rate is for firm-specific payouts such as dividends or interest payments. The adjusted number is then applied to the implied current asset value in the distance-to-default formula.

14. Under the assumption of normality, half of the 9,500 firms in KMV's North American database have a distance to default of 4.0 or more, implying that more than half of the firms are better than BBB rated—a conclusion at odds with actual ratings; see KMV (2000). In reality, asset values have considerably fatter tails than those that characterize the normal or lognormal distributions.

15. Of course, there is something unappealing about using the normality assumption to back out estimates of A and σ_A in order to get to this point in the model, and then dropping the assumption when it comes to the final step. See Sundaram (2001).

16. However, this methodology raises a question: Does KMV's empirical *EDF* measure firm-specific default or is it a composite measure particular to the database used? This criticism does not apply to Moody's empirical *EDF* scores because the influence of each key variable is determined for each firm individually, at each point in time.

17. For simplicity, interest rates, r, are assumed constant in the Merton model, although Acharya and Carpenter (2000) show that declines in interest rates may trigger default. Longstaff and Schwartz (1995) model stochastic interest rates.

18. As of June 2001, the database included 10,000 nonfinancial firms in North America, 6,500 firms in Europe, 6,500 firms in the Asia–Pacific Region, 5,500 multinational financial institutions, and 500 firms in Latin America.

19. As shown in Figure 4.8, even Altman's credit scoring model (for non-manufacturing firms) outperformed agency ratings in forecasting Enron's financial distress.

20. Both financial and nonfinancial firms were included in the sample. All firms had ratings 12 months prior to the event of default, which was defined as a failure to pay any scheduled liability on time due to financial condition; most defaults (but not all) were reflected in a "D" rating. See Lim (1999).

21. Another reason for the better predictability of KMV scores over the short horizon is that Standard & Poor's and Moody's calibrate their ratings to default experience over the past 30 years. Their probabilities therefore reflect a "cycle average" view. By comparison, KMV's *EDF*s reflect strong cyclicality over the business cycle. Some studies have shown that *EDF*s do not offer any advantage for time horizons over two years; see Miller (1998).

22. If the assets have no systematic risk, then the two probabilities (KMV *EDF* and risk-neutral *EDF*) are identical. Anderson and Sundaresan (2000) show that the risk-adjusted *EDF* performs better than the risk-neutral *EDF* in replicating historical bond defaults and that fluctuations in leverage and asset volatility explain most of the variations in bond spreads over time. Bohn (2000a) finds that KMV empirical *EDF*s explain 60 percent of credit spread volatility.

23. Bond spreads for low-credit-risk issues are higher than would be implied by KMV empirical *EDF*s alone because the market Sharpe ratio scaling parameter tends to increase with the bond's term, thereby increasing observed bond spreads; see Kealhofer (2000). Bohn (1999) finds that low-credit-quality bond issues have humped-shape or downward sloping credit spread term structures, whereas high-credit-quality bond issues have upward sloping credit spread term structures. Maclachlan (1999) asserts that credit spread levels fluctuate over the business cycle and display a tendency for short maturity credit spreads to increase the most during recessions. KMV's Portfolio Manager estimates this macroeconomic effect using a multifactor model; see Chapter 11.

24. See, for example, Jones, Mason, and Rosenfeld (1984).

25. For example, the boundary will become stochastic if there are liquidation costs. This gives firms power to renegotiate. See Longstaff and Schwartz (1995).

26. For example, an insider might sell a large block if he or she has private information about the adverse nature of future prospects for the firm, although the time between the sale and actual default will likely be short, thereby mitigating the benefits of a KMV-type model as an "early warning system."

27. Both KMV and Moody's have models that estimate empirical *EDF* scores for private companies.

28. Kealhofer (2000) claims that the KMV model could incorporate multiple debt and nondebt fixed liabilities, debt with embedded options, maturity differences,

dividend payouts, and coupon payments. The way this is accomplished is by converting a complex debt structure into a zero-coupon-equivalent single-default point value B. Bohn (2000a) surveys different specifications of structural models that vary with respect to their assumptions about asset value, the default-free rate, the default point, and recovery rates (LGD).

29. Because asset values have a positive drift term, whereas leverage is assumed constant, Merton models imply a negative slope of the term structure of credit spreads, for example, default risk approaches zero as the debt's maturity increases because asset values drift higher than the fixed default point. In general, this is not observed in actual risky bond spreads.

30. See the Bibliography for references to Moody's publications and the Web site www.moodysrms.com. Although Moody's uses the notation EDP (estimated default probability) as a way of distinguishing its model outputs from KMV's EDF scores, we use EDF throughout the book for all models.

31. Each variable's influence level is calculated relative to the industry/sectoral average. An influence level of zero implies that the variable is no more nor less influential for this firm than average; positive (negative) influence levels increase (decrease) the firm's EDF.

32. The Moody's definition of default includes bankruptcy, Chapter 11, distressed exchange, modification of an indenture, dividend omission, and missed principal or interest payments.

33. To prevent this, the model is re-optimized many times using different subsets of the in-sample data in order to ensure that the total residual forecast error is acceptable and that the model performance is stable across all subsets of the in-sample data set.

34. Kealhofer and Kurbat (2001) find that Moody's bond ratings did not add any predictive power to KMV empirical EDFs.

35. Stein (2000) conducts a "walk-forward test" of the predictive ability of the Merton model (adjusted for excess volatility) and the ROA conditioned on the Merton model and finds that the addition of the additional variable significantly improved predictive ability. See Sobehart, Keenan, and Stein (2000) for a discussion of validation tests.

36. This is based on Babbel (1989). Source: "Insuring Banks Against Systematic Credit Risk," by D. F. Babbel, *Journal of Futures Markets,* November 6, 1989, 487–506. Copyright ©1989. Reprinted by permission of John Wiley & Sons, Inc.

Chapter 5   Reduced Form Models: KPMG's Loan Analysis System and Kamakura's Risk Manager

1. For pricing of derivative assets, when the underlying asset is traded, the risk-neutral price is the correct one, irrespective of investor preferences. This is because, with an underlying asset, the derivative can be perfectly hedged to create a riskless portfolio. When a portfolio is riskless, it has an expected return equal to the risk-free rate.

2. This assumes that the default probability is independent of the security's price, something that does not hold for swaps with asymmetric counterparty credit

risk, for example. Duffie and Singleton (1999) specify that one should use a "pure" default-free rate r that reflects repo specials and other effects. The U.S. Treasury short rate, typically used as the empirical proxy for r, may be above or below the pure default-free rate.

3. To illustrate the double subscript notation, the yield on a B-rated two-year maturity zero-coupon bond to be received one year from now would be denoted $_1y_2$. This bond would mature three years from today—one year until it is delivered on the forward contract and then two years until maturity from then. Spot rates are for transactions with immediate delivery; the first subscript of a spot rate is always zero.

4. Although many intensity-based models assume that LGD is fixed, Unal et al. (2001) find that LGD varies intertemporally and cross-sectionally.

5. Duffie and Singleton (1999) show that PD and LGD could not be separately identified in defaultable bond prices because risky debt is priced on the credit spread, $PD \times LGD$.

6. Structural models can be viewed as a special case of reduced form models in which the default process is endogenously determined by the relationship between stochastic asset values and the default point if asset values are assumed to follow a jump process that makes it possible for assets to jump past the default point. See Duffie and Lando (2001), which specified the hazard rate in terms of asset value volatility that is known only imperfectly through past and present accounting data. Imperfect information about asset values allows the default stopping time to be modeled as a jump process. Cathcart and El-Jahel (1998) achieve this by assuming that default occurs when a stochastic signaling process hits the default barrier.

7. A Poisson distribution describes the random arrival through time such that the exponentially distributed intensity of the Poisson process jumps by a certain amount at each arrival time (corresponding to default or credit migration); the interarrival times are assumed to be statistically independent.

8. There would not have been enough observations for the Unal et al. (2001) study if the sample were limited to zero coupon, noncallable debt; therefore, junior and senior debt issues were matched by choosing the closest possible duration and coupon rates. There were only 11 companies with enough data to fully estimate the model.

9. In this chapter, we focus on credit spreads for corporate borrowers. Duffie et al. (2000) use a reduced form model to estimate the credit risk of Russian dollar-denominated sovereign country debt.

10. Huang and Huang (2000) use the Longstaff-Schwartz structural model to find average yield spreads (credit risk spreads) for 10-year corporate bonds as follows: Aaa: 63 bp (10.2 bp), Aa: 91 bp (13.5 bp), A: 123 bp (20 bp), Baa: 194 bp (46 bp), Ba: 299 bp (174 bp), B: 408 bp (373.6 bp). Moreover, they find that the credit spread is even lower for investment grade bonds with shorter maturities.

11. In 2000, there was a total of $17.7 trillion in domestic (traded and untraded) debt outstanding; see Basak and Shapiro (2001).

12. As of 1998, about $350 billion of bonds traded each day in the United States as compared to $50 billion of stocks that are exchanged; see Bohn (1999).

13. Chang and Sundaresan (1999) endogenize the relationship between the *PD* and economic conditions by noting that when default risk increases during economic downturns, investors become more risk averse ("flight to quality"), thereby causing risk-free rates to decline and building in an inverse relationship between default risk and the default-free term structure.

14. The tree diagram shows only five possible transition ratings: A, B +, B, C, or D (default) and thus is considerably simpler than reality in which there are 22 possible ratings transitions alone. Moreover, default need not be an absorbing state in reality if restructuring is possible.

15. As Belkin, Suchower, and Forest (1998c) have shown, the LAS model can also be used to calculate *VAR* figures. For example, a simple *VAR* figure could be calculated by using LAS to value the loan at the one year (credit-event) horizon. Alternatively, model spread volatility can be introduced by allowing the transitions themselves to be variable (KPMG calls this Z-risk). Kiesel et al. (2001) show that stochastically varying spreads contribute significantly to credit risk, with spread risk increasing for higher credit quality exposures.

16. Using the credit rating agencies' transition matrices to estimate the default probability inserts error into the model since the empirically observed ("natural") default rates are lower than risk neutral default rates. See the discussion in Chapter 4 converting KMV empirical *EDF*s to risk neutral *EDF*s by adjusting for expected asset returns. KPMG obtains risk neutral default rates by solving for the empirical credit spreads for one year option-free term loans and using iterative arbitrage pricing methods to price two state (default or nondefault) reference loans as contingent claims on the one-year loans.

17. In practice, the other possibilities could include exercise of embedded options, prepayments, restructuring, as well as finer gradations of ratings migrations.

18. Thus, the *PD* in the first period is the probability that the B-rated loan will default, 5 percent, and in the second period, it is the sum of the probabilities that the A-rated loan defaults, 0.34 percent, plus the *PD* for the B-rated loan, 5 percent, for the 5.34 percent *PD* we found in the solution to equation (5.6).

19. Recall that the one year risk-free forward rate is obtained using the 8 percent one-year spot risk-free yield and the two year spot risk-free yield shown in Figure 5.1 so that: $(1 + .10)^2 = (1 + .08)(1 + {}_1r_1)$ to obtain ${}_1r_1 = 12.04$ percent p.a.

20. To solve for *CS*, we choose the positive solution of the quadratic equation. Alternatively, we could follow Belkin et al. (1998b) and assume that the risk premium has a flat term structure. In practice, however, this assumption does not hold; see Chen and Huang (2000).

21. Note that the credit spread, *CS*, is assumed to be constant over time (i.e., in years 1 and 2 in this example).

22. Not only is the risk neutral *PD* higher than the empirical *PD*, but Duffee (1999) finds that the risk neutral *PD* is nonstationary, whereas the empirical *PD* is mean reverting.

23. Nickell et al. (2001a) find that rating transitions are volatile and depend on the industry (banks versus industrials), the domicile of the obligor (United States versus non-United States), and the stage of the business cycle.

24. Duffee (1999) finds misspecification in these models, particularly for below investment-grade bonds.

25. Jarrow (2001) makes the interesting point that, prior to this work, structural models used only equity prices, eschewing debt prices as too noisy, whereas reduced form models used only debt prices. This is claimed to be the first model to use both debt and equity prices to assess credit risk exposure.

26. Repurchase agreements (also known as repos) are short-term loans collateralized by marketable debt securities. Although Treasury and Agency securities are most often used as collateral on repurchase agreements, corporate bonds can be used as well.

27. Equity prices consist of a stream of dividend payments plus a "liquidating dividend" which is the payment to the equity holder in the event of default on the firm's debt. Since equity represents the residual claim on the firm's assets, the implied value of this liquidating dividend can be used to solve for the bondholders' *LGD*.

28. This example was adapted from Duffie and Singleton (1998). © 2001 by Darell Duffie and Kenneth Singleton. All rights reserved. You may read and browse this material at this Web site. However, no further copying, downloading, or linking is permitted. No part of this material may be further reproduced in any form by any electronic or mechanical means (including photocopying, recording, or information storage and retrieval) without permission in writing from the publishers. Users are not permitted to mount this file on any network servers.

29. Using equation (5.7) to calculate the *PD* over a five-year time horizon, we obtain a *PD* of .005 for the A-rated firm and .2212 for the B-rated firm.

30. The intensity of the sum of independent Poisson processes is just the sum of the individual processes' intensities; therefore, the portfolio's total intensity is: $1,000*.001 + 100*.05 = 6$ defaults per year.

31. Indeed, with constant intensity, the two terms are synonymous.

32. For risk-neutral investors, this expression for survival probabilities, particularly in its continuous-time form, is mathematically equivalent to the current price of a zero coupon bond with maturity t discounted at interest rate h.

33. The parameters would have to be adjusted to remove the risk premium in order to obtain the risk-neutral credit spread.

34. Moody's computes that the average default rate of B (Baa) rated corporate issues over the period 1920–1997 was 442 (32) basis points.

Chapter 6 The *VAR* Approach: CreditMetrics and Other Models

1. The capital requirements for market risk contain a general market risk component and a specific risk component. For example, with respect to corporate bonds that are held in the trading book, an internal model calculation of specific risk would include features such as spread risk, downgrade risk, and concentration risk. Each of these is related to credit risk. Thus, the 1996 BIS market risk capital requirement contains a credit risk component.

2. See Gupton et al., *CreditMetrics, Technical Document,* J.P. Morgan, New York, April 2, 1997. In 1998, the group developing the RiskMetrics and CreditMetrics products formed a separate company called RiskMetrics Group. Technical information may be obtained from the Web site at www.riskmetrics.com.

3. The one-year horizon is controversial [see Carey (2001)]. For example, if there is some autocorrelation or trend over time toward default, a longer window (say, two years or more) might be appropriate.

4. As will be discussed in Chapter 11, to calculate the *VAR* of a loan portfolio we also need to calculate default correlations among counterparties.

5. This example is based on the one used in Gupton et al., *CreditMetrics-Technical Document* (1997).

6. As will be discussed later, the choice of transition matrix has a material effect on the *VAR* calculations. Moreover, the choice of bond transitions to value loans raises again the question of how closely related bonds and loans are.

7. If the + / – modifiers ("notches") are utilized, there are 22 different rating categories, see Bahar and Nagpal (2000).

8. The rating transitions are based on U.S. corporate bond data. For non-U.S. companies a "mapping" is required for the non-U.S. company into a U.S. company or else the development of a non-U.S. or country-specific rating transition matrix is required.

9. Technically, from a valuation perspective the credit-event occurs (by assumption) at the very end of the first year. Currently, CreditMetrics is expanding to allow the credit event "window" to be as short as three months or as long as five years.

10. In CreditMetrics documentation, the first subscript is suppressed for simplicity; because all valuations take place one year into the future, the first subscript is always one for all terms, e.g., $_1r_1$ $(_1r_2)$ denotes the zero-coupon riskfree rate on a one-year (two-year) maturity U.S. Treasury to be delivered in one year. See discussion of the double subscript notation in Chapter 5 and in Appendix 6.1.

11. The assumption that interest rates are deterministic is particularly unsatisfying for credit derivatives because fluctuations in risk-free rates may cause the counterparty to default as the derivative moves in or out of the money. Thus, the portfolio *VAR*, as well as *VAR* for credit derivatives, (see for example CIBC's CreditVaR II) assume a stochastic interest rate process that allows the entire risk-free term structure to shift over time. See Crouhy et al. (2000).

12. In this case, the discount rates reflect the appropriate zero-coupon rates plus credit spreads (s_i) on A-rated loans (bonds). If the borrower's rating were unchanged at BBB, the discount rates would be higher because the credit spreads would reflect the default risk of a BBB borrower. The credit spreads used in CreditMetrics are generated by Bridge Information Systems, a consulting firm, which updates these rates every week.

13. Net of the first year's coupon payment, the loan's price would be $108.66 million – $6 million = $102.66 million.

14. Recent studies have suggested that this *LGD* may be too high for bank loans. A Citibank study of 831 defaulted corporate loans and 89 asset-based loans for 1970–1993 finds recovery rates of 79 percent (or equivalently *LGD* equal to 21 percent). Similarly, high recovery rates are found in a Fitch Investor Service report in October 1997 (82 percent) and a Moody's Investor Service Report of June 1998 (87 percent). See Asarnow (1999).

15. In the calculation in Table 6.4, we look at the risk of the loan from the perspective of its mean or expected forward value ($107.09). Using an alternative

perspective, we would look at the distribution of changes in value around the value of the loan if it continued to be rated BBB over the whole loan period. In Table 6.3, the forward value of the loan, if its rating remains unchanged over the next year, is \$107.55. Using this BBB benchmark value, the mean and the variance of the value changes are, respectively, mean $= -\$0.46$ and $\sigma = \$2.96$. We obtain expected losses using the probability-weighted distribution of bond value changes as shown in Table 6.3: $.0002(109.37 - 107.55) + .0033(109.19 - 107.55) + .0595(108.66 - 107.55) + .053(102.02 - 107.55) + .0117(98.10 - 107.55) + .0012(83.64 - 107.55) + .0018(51.13 - 107.55) = -0.46$. Similarly, the loss variance is: $.0002(1.82 + 0.46)^2 + .0033(1.64 + .46)^2 + .0595(1.11 + .46)^2 + .053(- 5.53 + .46)^2 + .0117(- 9.45 + .46)^2 + .0012(- 23.91 + .46)^2 + .0018(- 56.42 + .46)^2 = 8.77$. The 1 percent *VAR* under the normal distribution assumption is then $(2.33 \times - \$2.96) + (- \$0.46) = - \$7.36$.

16. In 99 years out of 100, the 1 percent *VAR* capital requirement would allow the bank to survive unexpected credit losses on loans. Note that under the specific risk component for market risk, which measures spread risk, downgrade risk, and concentration risk for tradable instruments like corporate bonds, the 1 percent one day *VAR* has to be multiplied by a factor of 3 or 4 (the stress-test multiplier), and the holding period is 10 days rather than one year; this leads to a $\sqrt{10}$ multiplier of one-day *VAR* for a liquidity risk adjustment.

17. However, they also find that the 3-to-4 multiplication factor badly underestimates extreme losses if there are "runs" of bad periods (e.g., as might be expected in a major long-term economic contraction). Neftci (2000) uses Extreme Value Theory to solve for market *VAR* and finds that the BIS multiplication factor of 3 is excessive; instead, his estimates range from 1.02 to 1.33.

18. We discuss EVT from the perspective of assessing additional capital to cover catastrophic risk events. However, Neftci (2000) describes how the *VAR* itself could be more accurately measured using EVT. An advantage of the EVT approach is that it estimates the positive and negative tails of the underlying parent distribution separately, thereby allowing for distributional asymmetries in long and short positions. Longin and Solnik (2001) use EVT and find correlation increases across assets in bear markets (negative tails), but not in bull markets (positive tails).

19. Because of this property, EVT can also be used to measure operational risk. See Allen et al. (2002).

20. For large samples of identically distributed observations, Block Maxima Models (Generalized Extreme Value, or GEV distributions) are most appropriate for extreme values estimation. However, the Peaks-over-Threshold (POT) models make more efficient use of limited data on extreme values. Within the POT class of models is the Generalized Pareto Distribution (GPD). See Appendix 6.2, McNeil (1999) and Neftci (2000). Bali (2001) uses a more general functional form that encompassed both the *GPD* and the GEV called the Box-Cox-GEV.

21. Using the simple approach to calculating a transition matrix, suppose we have data for 1997 and 1998. In 1997, 5.0 percent of bonds rated BBB were downgraded to B. In 1998, 5.6 percent of bonds rated BBB were downgraded to B. The average transition probability of being downgraded from BBB to B is therefore

5.3 percent. In practice, however, historical average default rates are not accurate measures of default probability; that is, average historical default probability typically overstates the default rate, see Crouhy et al. (2000).

22. Finger (2000a) uses both an extended CreditMetrics model and an intensity-based model to examine correlated default probabilities over varying time horizons and finds considerable impact on economic capital requirements.

23. Credit Portfolio View (see Chapter 7) utilizes a macroeconomic model of systematic risk factors in contrast to the CreditMetrics approach that simply conditions the default probability function on a forecast of the credit cycle index, Z. Koyluoglu et al. (1999) show that results were robust to differences in modeling the conditional default distributions as a function of economic conditions.

24. The credit cycle index, Z, is constructed from the default probabilities on speculative grade bonds (equal to and lower than Moody's Ba rating) regressed (using a probit model) on four factors: (1) the credit spread between Aaa and Baa; (2) the yield on 10-year Treasury bonds; (3) the quarterly consumer price index; and (4) the quarterly growth of GDP. To obtain Z, the model parameters are estimated using historical quarterly data, then projected forward to the next quarter and transformed into a standard normal distribution. Kim (1999) backtests this specification and finds that it decreases forecasting errors by more than 30 percent when compared to the historical average. Bangia et al. (2000) use NBER designations of contractions and expansions to obtain conditional probabilities of default. Using 1 percent *VAR,* they find that economic capital is nearly 30 percent higher for a contraction year than for an expansion year. [See also Nickell et al. (2001a).]

25. That is, the transition matrix can be built around KMV's *EDF* scores rather than bond ratings. The correlation between KMV's transitions and rating agencies' transitions is low. In the new December 2001 version of CreditMetrics, risk neutral probabilities are used instead of historical migration probabilities. Alternatively, Algorithmics Mark to Future™ *VAR* uses scenario analysis as an alternative to valuations based on ratings transition matrices (see discussion in Chapter 12).

26. The assumption of nonstochastic interest rates is also consistent with Merton (1974). Nevertheless, Shimko, Tejima, and van Deventer (1993) extend the Merton model to include stochastic interest rates.

27. Gupton et al., *CreditMetrics-Technical Document,* p. 30 (1997). Whether or not recovery rates are constant, an additional capital requirement of $0.46 million, in our example, must be held as reserves against expected losses.

28. Unal et al. (2001) show that *LGD*s on bonds are extremely volatile across time and cross-sectionally. See the discussion in Chapter 5.

29. Or, using the "99th percentile" comparison: $2.33 \times \$2.99 = \$6.97$ million versus $2.33 \times \$2.07 = \$4.82$ million.

30. As we discussed, the assumption of fixed credit spreads is quite contentious.

31. We abstract here from variations in the length of each semiannual coupon payment period that may range from 180 to 184 days. Daycount differentials and the precision of the calculations may cause rounding errors. All risk-free rates are denoted r, all risky corporate bond rates are denoted y, and all zero coupon risk-free rates are denoted z.

32. All one-year forward rates deliver in two half years; hence the first subscript 2 for all one-year forward yields. The forward rates obtained in this section must be multiplied by 2 in order to transform them from semi-annual rates to annual rates.

33. If $\xi = 0$, then the distribution is exponential and if $\xi < 0$ it is the Pareto type II distribution.

34. These estimates are obtained from McNeil (1999) who estimates the parameters of the GPD using a database of Danish fire insurance claims. The scale and shape parameters may be calculated using maximum likelihood estimation in fitting the (distribution) function to the observations in the extreme tail of the distribution.

Chapter 7   The Macro Simulation Approach: The Credit Portfolio View Model and Other Models

1. The exceptions are the models that condition the transition matrix on a realization or a forecast of economic conditions. See Bangia et al. (2000), Finger (1999), Kim (1999), and Nickell et al. (2001a) and discussion in Chapter 6.

2. Treacy and Carey (2000) find that 65 percent of the loans outstanding are rated either BBB or BB according to the banks' internal ratings.

3. The relationship between macroeconomic conditions and loan quality may reflect a credit cycle. Lown and Morgan (2001) show that fluctuations in commercial credit standards at banks lead to fluctuations in both the Fed funds rate and in the level of commercial lending activity, which in turn lead to fluctuations in credit quality. Using Federal Reserve surveys, they find that all recessions since 1967 have been preceded by an increase in the percentage of loan officers reporting tightening credit standards for commercial loans or credit lines. Moreover, changes in the business failure rate account for about 10 percent of the change in credit standards.

4. Originated by McKinsey, CreditPortfolio View is now independent.

5. For example, Nickell et al. (2001a) fit transition matrices to observed credit standings for subsamples of issuer years broken down according to: (1) five domiciles (United States, the United Kingdom, Japan, Europe excluding the United Kingdom, and other), (2) 10 industry categories (banking, finance, industrial, insurance, other nonbank, public utility, securities, sovereign, thrifts, and financial institutes); and (3) three business cycle states (normal, trough, and peak). See discussion in Chapter 6.

6. Nickell et al. (2001a) show that business cycle effects impact ratings volatility more than ratings levels; that is, the volatility of rating transitions decreases during expansions and increases in recessions, although there is no systematic increase (decrease) in upgrade probabilities during business expansions (recessions).

7. In fact, all the probabilities in the final column of the transition matrix (p_{AAAD}, p_{AAD}, and so on) will move cyclically and can be modeled in a fashion similar to p_{CD}. See Appendix 7.1.

8. In Wilson (1997a and 1997b), equation (7.1) is modeled as a logistic function of the form $p = 1/(1 + e^{-y})$. This constrains p to lie between 0 and 1. See discussion of equation (7.9) in Appendix 7.1.

9. The specific form of equation (7.2) is presented in Appendix 7.1 as equation (7.10).

10. In Wilson (1997a), the macroeconomic variables are modeled as levels of variables (rather than changes in levels), and the X_{it} variables are related to their lagged values by a second-order autoregressive process. See discussion of equation (7.8) in Appendix 7.1.

11. Technically, the variances and covariances of V_t and ε_{it} are calculated from the fitted model (the Σ matrix). The Σ matrix is then decomposed using the Cholesky decomposition $\Sigma = AA'$, where A and A' are symmetric matrices and A' is the transpose of A. Shocks can be simulated by multiplying the matrix A' by a random number generator: $Z_t \sim N(0,1)$.

12. The specific format of equation (7.5) is shown as equation (7.12) in Appendix 7.1.

13. The precise procedure for doing this is described in the *Approach Document* to CreditPortfolio View, Chapter 10. Basically, it involves the use of a shift operator (called the systematic risk sensitivity parameter) along with the imposition of the constraint that the shifted values in each row of the migration matrix sum to one. See Appendix 7.1 for a detailed description of the methodology.

14. Alternatively, using a default mode (DM) set-up with default (p)/no default $(1 - p)$, unexpected loss rates can be calculated for different stages of the business cycle.

15. As of April 1999, McKinsey reported that the R^2 of this nonlinear regression for Germany was 94 percent, and over 80 percent for other countries, thereby demonstrating the high explanatory power of macroeconomic conditions on default rates.

16. Wilson (1997b) shows the need for a multifactor model of macroeconomic conditions; the first factor alone explains only 23.9 percent of the U.S. systematic risk index, 56.2 percent of the United Kingdom's and 66.8 percent of Germany's.

17. Risk segments are obtained by classifying each obligation in the portfolio by industry, by credit rating, and by level of diversification. CPV-Macro obtains correlations across industry and risk segments by considering common macroeconomic variables affecting all default distributions, as well as correlated systemic risk factors. CPV-Direct directly examines distributional correlations. Wilson (1998) uses a simple example to show how loans can have a positive conditional correlation even though their unconditional correlation coefficient is zero, because each loan is correlated to common macroeconomic factors. We examine portfolio correlations in Chapter 11.

18. This is adapted from CreditPortfolio View, *Approach Document,* version 1.1, 1998.

19. Wilson (1997b) shows very high R-squared values for the estimation of equation (7.8). However, Jarrow and Turnbull (2000) point out that *changes* in macroeconomic variables should have an impact on default rates, not levels. When Altman (1993) uses changes in macroeconomic variables, the explanatory

power decreases and there is a *negative* relation between changes in the number of business failures and changes in the following macroeconomic variables: real GDP, the money supply, the S&P 500 index, and new business formation.

20. Equation (7.8) represents the precise specification of the general form presented as equation (7.3) in the text.

21. Explanatory processes for each macroeconomic variable are assumed to be independent of each other. This unrealistic assumption can be corrected by estimating equation (7.8) using a vector auto regressive moving average; see Lown and Morgan (2001).

22. The model allows the use of insolvency rate data or empirical *EDF*s, in place of default rates in the estimation of equation (7.9).

23. For simplicity, we consider only four rating classes: A, B, C, and the absorbing state D.

24. The example uses discrete approximations to the continuous time values of λ and r used in CPV-Macro.

25. The values of the shift operator sum to zero across the entire row; that is $\Delta p_{CD} + \Delta p_{CC} + \Delta p_{CB} + \Delta p_{CA} = 0$.

26. Utilizing bond data, the ratio of unexpected default rate changes to the expected default rate for highly rated obligors tends to be quite a bit higher than the ratio for non-investment grade obligors and this variation is not well explained by macroeconomic events; see CreditPortfolio View, *Approach Document*, 1998, pp. 92–93.

Chapter 8 The Insurance Approach: Mortality Models and the CSFP Credit Risk Plus Model

1. Combining the volatility of annual *MMR*s with *LGD*s can produce unexpected loss calculations as well [see Altman and Saunders (1997)].

2. That is, a mortality rate is binomially distributed; see McAllister and Mingo (1994) for further discussion.

3. In most published studies, mortality tables have been built on total samples of around 4,000 bonds and loans [see Altman (1989) and Altman and Suggitt (1997)]. However, the Central Bank of Argentina has recently built transition matrices and mortality tables based on over 5 million loan observations, although less than 20,000 of these observations are usable [see Inter-American Development Bank study (2001)]. These Argentinean credit registry data are available on the Central Bank's Web site: www.bcra.gov.ar.

4. That is, there is a constant probability that any given house will burn down (or equivalently, a loan will default) within a predetermined time period. Credit Risk Plus has the flexibility to calculate default probabilities over a constant time horizon (say, one year) or over a hold-to-maturity horizon.

5. Moreover, the probability of default is assumed to be constant over time. This is strictly true for only the simplest of the models in Credit Risk Plus. A more sophisticated version ties loan default probabilities to the systematically varying mean default rate of the "economy" or "sector" of interest.

6. The continuous time extension of Credit Risk Plus is the intensity-based model of Duffie and Singleton (1998) which stipulates that over a given short time interval, the probability of default is independent across loans and proportional to a fixed default intensity function. The evolution of this intensity process follows a Poisson distribution as assumed in the discrete version Credit Risk Plus [see Finger (2000b)].

7. The most speculative risk classifications' default probabilities are most sensitive to these shifts in macroeconomic conditions [see Crouhy et al. (2000)].

8. The assumption of independence may be violated if the volatility in mean default rates reflects the correlation of default events through interrelated macroeconomic factors.

9. The nominal dollar size of these loans can be very different. One loan may have a nominal size of $100,000; another, a nominal size of $25,000. What is similar is the dollar severity of loss on default.

10. The term 3! equals $1 \times 2 \times 3 = 6$. 0! is defined to be one, so that the probability of 0 defaults is $(e^{-3}3^0/0!) = 5$ percent.

11. The cumulative probability of 7 (8) or fewer defaults is 98.8 (99.6) percent.

12. Loan loss reserves, if set equal to expected losses, would be $60,000, and would be included in capital requirements as per the January 2001 BIS II proposals.

13. In "adding" the two loss distributions, one has to calculate the probabilities by taking into account the possible combination of losses on the two portfolios that might produce some aggregate dollar loss. Thus, assuming a mean number of defaults $m = 3$ in both bands $v = 1,2$:

Aggregate Portfolio Loss ($)	(Loss on $v = 1$, Loss on $v = 2$) in $20,000 units	Probability
0	(0, 0)	$(.0497 \times .0497)$
20,000	(1, 0)	$(.1493 \times .0497)$
40,000	[(2, 0) (0, 1)]	$[(.224 \times .0497) + (.0497 \times .1493)]$
60,000	[(3, 0) (1, 1)]	$[(.224 \times .0497) + (.1493)^2]$
80,000	[(4, 0) (2, 1) (0, 2)]	$[(.168 \times .0497) + (.224 \times .1493) + (.0497 \times .224)]$
⋮	⋮	⋮

14. Default correlations can be derived from the specified default rate volatilities and assumed sectoral sensitivity factors.

Chapter 9 A Summary and Comparison of New Internal Model Approaches

1. However, Jarrow and Turnbull (2000) contend that market risk and credit risk are inseparable.

2. Essentially the difference between the DM and the MTM models is whether the loan matures at the credit horizon (DM) or matures beyond the credit horizon (MTM).

3. For a good discussion of multifactor models, see Elton and Gruber (1995).

4. For example, Froot and Stein (1998) examine a two-factor model in a RAROC framework.

5. Because mortgages are more sensitive to specific local economic conditions than are other debt instruments, the study's participants could not agree on a meaningful common base case portfolio to be used to compare publicly available credit risk models for the mortgage portfolio. Differences of opinion among the bank participants in the survey dealt with issues such as: the interaction between interest rate and credit risk, the role of collateral and mortgage insurance, portfolio "seasoning" or diversification of tenor, and cross-country differences in securitization.

6. This is adapted from IIF/ISDA (2000), pp. 2–3. Reprinted with permission from the Institute of International Finance. The complete study is available for purchase from http://www.iif.org.

7. Table 9.3 understates the degree of variability in credit risk estimates, particularly for internal models. When banks undertook their own practice runs using their own parameter settings, the range of outputs increased dramatically. For example, estimates of 1 percent *VAR* ranged from 3.1 percent to 13.0 percent for the middle market portfolio using the banks' parameterization of their proprietary internal models.

8. Estimates using KMV Portfolio Manager were obtained using hypothesized parameter values (regarding *EDF*, systematic R^2 risk factors, etc.) because most retail portfolios are not publicly traded.

9. However, the large portfolio had fewer separate obligors (166,467) in contrast to 346,940 distinct borrowers for the small retail portfolio.

10. Expanding Gordy's (2000) framework, CreditPortfolio View clearly uses the same model structure as both Credit Risk Plus and CreditMetrics, with the macroeconomic factors explicitly modeled rather than simply drawn from either a normal or a gamma distribution.

11. Gordy's (2000) simulations were calibrated using data from Carey (1998) and the Society of Actuaries (1996) study of insurance companies' privately placed bond portfolios and portfolio losses from 1986 to 1992.

12. Koyluoglu et al. (1999) use three alternative assumptions for default rate volatility in Credit Risk Plus: (1) Default rate volatility is calibrated to the Carty and Lieberman (1996) results of an unconditional default rate of 116 basis points and a standard deviation of default rate of 90 basis points to obtain a coefficient of variation of 78 percent on average across all obligations; (2) Default rate distributions are differentiated by Moody's credit grades, with coefficients of variation ranging from 300 percent for the highest quality to 55 percent for the lowest quality; (3) The coefficient of variation is set to be a constant such that the unexpected losses (*UL*) calculated by Credit Risk Plus matches the average *UL* calculated by CreditMetrics and KMV. Estimates of *UL* show a considerable amount of variation across these three alternative assumptions in the Credit Risk Plus model.

13. Moody's empirical *EDF*s are averaged over historical experience and therefore are likely to reflect past business cycles, whereas KMV empirical *EDF*s rely more on forward-looking market prices (see Chapter 4).

Chapter 10   Overview of Modern Portfolio Theory and Its Application to Loan Portfolios

1. Moreover, the BIS I and the standardized model in BIS II are both linearly additive across individual loans. See Rajan (1992) for an example of the "customer relationship" model.
2. See Elton and Gruber (1995) for proofs.
3. In practice, KMV finds that portfolio risk can often be reduced by 20 percent to 50 percent simply by choosing asset allocations that move the portfolio to the efficient frontier. In many portfolios, as few as 5 percent of the assets account for up to 40 percent of the total risk.
4. It might be noted that in identifying point D, it is assumed that investors (FIs) can borrow and lend at the same (risk-free) rate. This unrealistic assumption can be relaxed without changing the fundamentals of the model.
5. Although, arguably, as the number of loans in a portfolio gets bigger, the distribution of returns tends to become more "normal." Alternatively, all a manager may care about maximizing is a quadratic utility function, that depends by definition, only on the mean and variance of returns.
6. However, the Loan Pricing Corporation now tracks secondary market prices on syndicated loans. Currently, over 50,000 loans are contained in their database, which contains detailed information about spreads, loan covenants, and maturities. However, the database is not constructed as a time series. Therefore, the loans are not tracked over time; they are only priced as of the loan origination date and at intermittent points in time, thereby making it difficult to update the optimal MPT portfolio over time.

Chapter 11   Loan Portfolio Selection and Risk Measurement

1. One implication of using excess returns instead of gross returns is that the line drawn from the return axis to find the most efficient portfolio (shown in Figure 10.2, Chapter 10) would now originate from the origin rather than the r_f point on the return axis (as shown).
2. In the DM model, there are only two possible outcomes—default and no default; hence the binomial probability distribution. Equation (11.3) holds precisely only if the initial loan is valued at par and matures at the credit valuation horizon (say, in one year).
3. KMV's Portfolio Manager assumes that LGD follows a Beta distribution with a variance equal to $LGD(1 - LGD)/k$ where k is determined by the distribution's shape parameters.
4. KMV's Portfolio Manager MTM calculation of σ_i can be interpreted in a CreditMetrics framework as a mapping of $EDFs$ into score ranges corresponding to different rating classifications. The valuation volatility, $VVOL$, is then obtained from the migration matrix across all classes except default. Thus, KMV Portfolio Manager and CreditMetrics yield similar estimates for UL. However, the IIF/ISDA comparison study discussed in Chapter 9 found that the models'

results diverged if the risk-neutral pricing method (as opposed to risk-adjusted matrix pricing) was used to obtain the KMV valuations.

5. KMV's Portfolio Manager uses a multifactor model to estimate asset correlations; see discussion in the next section of this chapter.

6. Conditional on the realization of systematic risk, the distribution of portfolio value converges to normal when the portfolio consists of many loans of roughly the same size with relatively low levels of asset correlation. In contrast, Wilson (1998) shows that the loss distribution of undiversified portfolios tends to be bimodal—corresponding to the two events: default and nondefault.

7. If the two assets (Ford and General Electric) were uncorrelated then the isocircles would be perfectly circular in shape. Figure 11.2 represents them as ellipses, suggesting that asset values are positively correlated; that is, there is greater probability of either a good outcome for both F and G (a move in the northeast direction of Figure 11.2) or a bad outcome for both (a move in the southwest direction) than if the two assets were uncorrelated.

8. If G and F were uncorrelated, then the $JDF_{GF} = EDF_G EDF_F$ and $\rho_{GF} = 0$.

9. Another way that correlations can increase is for the isocircles to become more elliptical (say, because of greater correlations in migration probabilities), thereby increasing the probability weight in the shaded area, even holding leverage ratios constant.

10. KMV, CreditMetrics, CreditPortfolio View, Credit Risk Plus and reduced form models (such as Kamakura) all use multifactor models in order to estimate correlations because (1) using historical correlations could introduce sampling error and (2) linking correlations to fundamental factors reduces the number of pairwise correlation coefficients that must be estimated.

11. CreditMetrics estimates the sensitivity of equity prices to systematic risk factors, whereas Portfolio Manager delevers equity prices and uses asset returns to estimate multifactor systematic risk coefficients. [See Barnhill and Maxwell (1999).]

12. Phelan and Alexander (1999) note the opportunities for risk reduction through diversification as a result of the low correlations across bank loans (between 0.5 percent to 2.5 percent) compared to equity correlations of 40 percent and asset correlations which range between 10 to 60 percent. Moreover, debt portfolios tend to be more diverse than equity portfolios with ranges of 300 to 1 in risk differentials across individual assets as compared to 10 to 1 for equity portfolios.

13. McQuown (1997) asserts that KMV's Portfolio Manager's optimized portfolio weights double the portfolio's Sharpe ratio. However, a substantial portion of this gain may be obtained from the exploitation of mispricing of debt securities, rather than from risk diversification.

14. However, gains to diversification are somewhat mitigated in bad economic states because default correlations typically increase as credit quality decreases, thereby exacerbating the portfolio's credit risk as the credit quality of individual assets declines.

15. Barnhill and Maxwell (1999) examine the historical correlation structure from 1987 to 1996 and find that changes in the short-term U.S. Treasury rate are negatively correlated with returns on the S&P 500 (correlation coefficient

of –0.33) and negatively correlated with 14 out of 15 different industry indices (automotive, banking, chemicals, building, energy, health, insurance, manufacturing, oil and gas, paper, technology, telecommunications, textiles, and utilities), with a slightly positive correlation (0.02) with the entertainment industry index.

16. About 100 factors worldwide are used to account for virtually all empirically discernible correlations; see McQuown (1997).

17. It is used for U.S. loans only because "customer relationships" are weaker for its U.S. borrowers than for its Canadian borrowers (i.e., U.S. loans can be viewed as being more commoditized for this bank).

18. Another way of defining the marginal risk contribution in equation (11.10) is $MRC_i = \sigma_{ip}/\sigma_p$ where σ_{ip} is the covariance between i and the portfolio p. KMV estimates that the MRC for an individual asset typically ranges from 4 percent to 68 percent of the UL of the portfolio.

19. Note that equation (11.11) can be viewed simply as a restatement of the portfolio risk equation (10.2) in Chapter 10, where σ_i = the UL of firm i.

20. In recent presentations, KMV has been using a multiple of 10. That is, Capital = $UL_p \times 10$. However, if the loss distribution was normal and the critical cut-off point was the 99th percentile, then capital would equal $UL_p \times 2.33$. Clearly, the difference between the multiplicative factors, 2.33 and 10, reflects: (1) the degree of skewness in a bank's portfolio loss distribution, and (2) its desired level of capital protection against insolvency (or percentile cut-off point) and thus its desired credit rating. For example, Bank of America uses a multiple of 6 to achieve a 99.97 percent cut-off. Since a 99.97 percent cut-off implies a 0.03 percent probability of default, this has been historically consistent with the one year default probabilities of AA rated firms [see James (1996)].

21. Returns are calculated as the loan value on the horizon date (net of the bank's cost of funds) divided by the current loan value. However, returns may be undefined, particularly if the maturity of the loan exceeds the horizon date or if the horizon period is more than one year.

22. In all models, exposures are assumed to be independent of default risk. Finger (2000a) extends CreditMetrics to consider marketwide credit events (such as the 1997 Asian crisis) which could impact exposure values, as for credit derivatives; see Chapter 15.

23. Table 11.1 shows the transition matrix using historical migration probabilities. In the new December 2001 version of CreditMetrics, KMV-type risk-neutral probabilities are used instead.

24. A standardized return is an actual return that is divided by its estimated standard deviation after subtracting the mean return. Thus, a standardized normal distribution has a mean of zero and a standard deviation of unity. In Figure 11.3, we illustrate the link between asset volatility and rating transitions using a BB rated borrower; similar figures would be drawn for the BBB rated and A rated loans in the sample portfolio.

25. There is a 2.06 percent probability (1.06 percent + 1.00 percent) that the BB-rated borrower will be downgraded to CCC or below.

26. J.P. Morgan and other vendors offer software (e.g., Portfolio Manager) to perform this function.

27. Arguably, we should be measuring correlations between loans and not borrowers. For example, a low-quality borrower with a highly secured loan would find the loan rated more highly than the borrower as a whole.

28. CreditMetrics requires the user to input the factor sensitivity coefficients.

29. By construction of the factor sensitivities, the bank and insurance indices are independent of each other. Note the correlation between the unsystematic return components U_A and U_Z is zero by assumption.

30. To find this, the probabilities have to be counted backwards: the worst loan outcome, then the next worst, and so on until one reaches the loan value where the cumulative probability (starting from the worst case) is 1 percent (i.e., the 99th percentile *VAR*).

31. In this case, the bank's capital requirement falls from 14.8 percent to $9.23/$200 million or 4.62 percent.

32. This approach can be computationally intensive, particularly for large portfolios. Nagpal and Bahar (1999) suggest an analytic solution that transforms correlated defaults into mutually exclusive scenarios with independent default probabilities. The number of scenarios is independent of the number of assets in the portfolio, thereby making their method computationally efficient for large portfolios. However, the methodology is not always feasible because it may generate negative probabilities.

33. Technically, decompose the correlation matrix (Σ) among the loans using the Cholesky factorization process, which finds two matrices A and A' (its transpose) such that $I = AA'$. Asset return scenarios (y) are generated by multiplying the matrix A' (which contains memory relating to historical correlation relationships) by a random number vector z (i.e., $y = A'z$.)

34. This can be quite computationally intensive. In the new December 2001 version of CreditMetrics, variance-reduction techniques are used to cut down the number of required simulations by a factor of between 10 and 100. Rather than sampling the distribution around the origin, the new version of CreditMetrics extrapolates the entire distribution from concentrated sampling in the tails.

35. Since this version of CreditMetrics does not incorporate returns, we cannot fully perform this risk-reward tradeoff. The most recent version of CreditMetrics permits incorporation of returns to obtain the efficient frontier for the portfolio.

36. Duffie and Singleton (1998) also consider another specification of multivariate correlated intensities; that is, all default intensities are modeled as log-normally distributed. In contrast to the example presented in the text, portfolio default losses are relatively insensitive to default intensity correlations under the lognormal specification.

37. The parameter value $h(0) = .001$ reflects an initial mean default arrival rate of one default per thousand years. This is roughly equivalent to the historical average rate of default arrival for bonds rated by Moody's at A or Aa over the period 1920 to 1997.

38. As v approaches zero, the model converges to the independent default intensity model with zero correlations. As v approaches one, the jump intensities become

perfectly correlated (identical), thereby eliminating any potential gains to portfolio diversification.

39. In contrast to CPV-Macro, CPV-Direct moves away from the macroeconomic modeling of default correlations and simply assumes joint probability distributions of default.

40. The firm specific and systematic risk factors are independent and identically distributed standard normal random variables.

41. KMV's Portfolio Manager also offers an analytical solution as an alternative to the simulated loss distribution presented in this section. As long as enough iterations are performed, however, the simulated distribution provides a very good approximation without the need to make restrictive assumptions. However, the simulation may take between one hour and several days to run, depending on the computing facilities and the size of the portfolio.

42. Alternatively, the marginal annual *EDF* can be assumed to be constant over time and the cumulative *EDF*s can be calculated using the exponential function. In the following numerical example (see Tables 11.8 and 11.9), the marginal *EDF* is found to be 1 percent p.a. and so the *t*-year cumulative *EDF* is calculated as: $1 - (1 - .01)^t$.

43. KMV uses the *EDF* rather than the QDF to evaluate the loan in equation (11.25).

44. KMV Portfolio Manager actually offers several additional algorithms (linear and exponential) to calculate portfolio returns. We present the risk comparable valuation methodology.

45. Note that, as discussed in Chapter 4, the *QDF* is always greater than the *EDF*. The difference between the *QDF* and the *EDF* increases as the market risk premium increases, the R-squared (i.e., the systematic risk component in equation 11.21) of the assets increases, and as the *EDF* increases (up to an *EDF* of 50 percent).

Chapter 12   Stress Testing Credit Risk Models: Algorithmics Mark-to-Future

1. Under the internal model rules of the BIS for market risk, the bank's internal *VAR* has to be multiplied by a minimum value of 3. Intuitively, this 3 can be viewed as a stress-test multiplier accommodating outliers in the 99 percent tail of the distribution. If, in back-testing a model, regulators/auditors find that the model underestimated *VAR* on fewer than 4 days out of the past 250 days, it is placed in a green zone and the *VAR* multiplier remains at its minimum value of 3. If between 4 days and 9 days of underestimated risk are found (out of 250 days), the model is placed in the yellow zone and the multiplier is increased to a range from 3.4 to 3.85. If more than 10 daily errors are found, the multiplication factor for the internal *VAR* is set at 4 (the model is placed in the red zone). Some observers have labeled this regulatory punishment system "the traffic-light" system.

2. Kupiec (1995) describes how a minimum of 1,000 observations is necessary to stress test a market *VAR* model if the underlying loss function is assumed to be

symmetric. If, as is the case, the distribution is not symmetric, even more data are required. For example, McNeil's (1999) model using extreme value theory back-tests for market risk with more than 5,000 daily observations. (See Appendix 6.2 for a discussion of extreme value theory.)

3. Even this is somewhat optimistic; not even the rating agencies have default histories going back that far. Currently, most banks have perhaps two or three years' usable data; see Carey and Hrycay (2001).

4. For example, Nickell et al. (2001b) conclude that their results suggesting that both KMV and CreditMetrics underestimate the credit risk of Eurobonds should be treated with caution since they only have 10 years of data.

5. Only active monitoring can reduce classification gaming designed either to minimize bank capital requirements or to maximize loan officer bonuses.

6. Some models may perform better at different points in the credit cycle. Keswani (1999) uses Brady bond prices and finds that structural models outperform (underperform) reduced form models in the period before (after) the 1994 Mexican peso crisis.

7. The analogy with back-testing market risk models using time-series data measures how representative the past period is (i.e., the last 250 days under the BIS rules).

8. Altman and Karlin (2001b) average bond defaults over 1978 to 2001 and find that *LGD* is inversely related to bond seniority; that is, median *LGD* is lowest (42.58 percent) for senior secured debt, next for senior unsecured (57.73 percent) and highest (68.04 percent) for subordinated debt. However, that effect has been somewhat unstable in recent years; see Table 12.3.

9. Finger (2000a) proposes an extension of CreditMetrics that would incorporate the correlation between market risk factors and credit exposure size. This is particularly relevant for the measurement of counterparty credit risk on derivatives instruments because the derivative can move in or out of the money as market factors fluctuate. In June 1999, the Counterparty Risk Management Policy Group called for the development of stress tests to estimate "wrong-way credit exposure" such as experienced by U.S. banks during the Asian currency crises; that is credit exposure to Asian counterparties increased just as the foreign currency declines caused FX losses on derivatives positions.

10. Fraser (2000) finds that a doubling of the spread between Baa rated bonds over U.S. Treasury securities from 150 basis points to 300 basis points increases the 99 percent *VAR* measure from 1.77 percent to 3.25 percent for a Eurobond portfolio.

11. Since other models assume credit risk to be independent of market risk (e.g., see Chapter 6 for a discussion of CreditMetrics' assumption of fixed credit spreads), then MtF estimates must be compared to the sum of market risk and credit risk exposures obtained in other models.

12. Although the default boundary is not observable, it can be computed from the (unconditional) default probability term structure observed for BB rated firms.

13. Default is assumed to be an absorbing state, so Figure 12.1 shows that the curve representing the firm's asset value in scenario 1 coincides with the default boundary for all periods after year 3.

Chapter 13   Risk-Adjusted Return on Capital

1. According to Zaik, Walter, and Kelling (1996), Bank of America applied its RAROC model to 46 different business units within the bank.
2. In general, WACC will be less than ROE, especially if debt costs are tax deductible.
3. The RAROC approach essentially assumes that all assets are either perpetuities or pure discount instruments with the same maturity date. To adjust for differences across assets in the timing of cash flows, capital budgeting's net present value approach should be used with the discount rate adjusted for the risk of each individual asset. Analyzing RAROC for property and insurance companies, Nakada et al. (1999) use the present value of all cash flows (discounted at the insurer's marginal borrowing rate) in both the numerator and denominator of equation (13.1).
4. Turnbull (2000) defines the term structure of economic capital as the schedule of required capital over the long term planning horizon, which is determined by the timing and risk of project cash flows.
5. However, Machlachlan (1998) notes a circularity in valuing projects and investment allocations using economic capital (EC) when the project's market value itself must be used to obtain the measure of EC.
6. Nevertheless, some banks take a "customer relationship" approach and calculate the RAROC for the whole relationship.
7. In applying RAROC to the investment decisions of insurance companies, Nakada et al. (1999) solve for a combined RAROC that balances the diversification effects against the tax penalty. Similarly, the tax penalty in Turnbull (2000) is the tax that bank shareholders pay on the risk-free interest received from the interim investment of economic capital until it is needed either in the event of default or at the maturity of the loan to repurchase equity. Alternatively, the tax penalty may be viewed as the debt tax shield foregone because of the use of economic capital (equity) rather than debt to finance part of the loan.
8. The economic capital required in the initial period of the loan is used in the denominator even if economic capital requirements vary over the life of the loan. Some [e.g., Nakada et al. (1999)] have argued that the present value of economic capital over the life of the project should be used in the denominator, but Turnbull (2000) shows that any adjustment for the stream of economic capital should instead be included in the numerator.
9. Credit risk is distinguished from market risk in that the interest rate on the loan can be decomposed into: $R_L = r_f + R$ where R_L is the loan rate, r_f is the credit-risk free (Treasury rate) on a similar duration bond, and R is the credit spread. Here, we are not concerned with changes in r_f (Δr_f) that affect the loan's market value, but rather with the effects of shifts in R (ΔR), the credit spread.
10. Suppose the bank's hurdle was its ROE of 10 percent. Then the loan would be profitable and should be made under the RAROC criterion.
11. As discussed earlier, one simple way to calculate σ is to use the binomial model. Based on N years of data, where p_i is the default rate in year i for this borrower type: $\sigma = \sqrt{\dfrac{\sum_{i=1}^{N} p_i(1-p_i)}{N}}$

12. As of August 2001, no bank and only eight corporations had AAA status in the United States.

13. Maclachlan (1998) shows that maximizing RAROC may not produce efficient portfolio allocations, particularly in the event of increases in the tail density of return distributions (i.e., since RAROC is a point estimate of the reward to risk, it may result in overinvestment in correlated risky outlier assets).

14. Indeed, without a comparative advantage in providing monitoring and information services, there would be no reason for banks to exist in private economies.

15. If this assumption is relaxed, then the required return (hurdle rate) cannot be expressed as a constant, as in the standard RAROC formulation, but rather as an increasing function of the amount invested in the loan. The form of the Froot and Stein result differs from the standard RAROC formulation shown in equation (13.1); instead, Froot and Stein solve for the optimal level of investment in the new project (the loan) as a function of the bank's risk aversion, the loan's unhedgeable risk, and the loan's expected return.

16. In Froot and Stein (1998), the result in equation (13.20) is driven by the assumption of convex costs of issuing equity to meet the bank's economic capital requirements. Turnbull (2000) achieves the same result assuming that the role of economic capital is to lower any particular loan's default probability to a desired level (say, commensurate with the bank's chosen credit rating). Therefore, for any marginal loan, the economic capital is calculated on a marginal, not a stand-alone basis. Thus, diversification of the loan portfolio may reduce the amount of economic capital required for any particular loan; that is, capital can be considered sub-additive and the result in equation (13.20) obtains.

17. James (1996) offers empirical evidence documenting the sensitivity of loan growth to bank financing constraints and capital costs. Ho (1999) uses insurance company data to simulate the cost of capital adjustments and finds an S&P convexity charge of 34.7 basis points, where the S&P convexity charge is defined to be the price shock (capital charge) in the event of a 300 basis point parallel shift in the yield curve for a bond with negative convexity compared to an option-free bond of the same duration.

18. This term can be viewed as the cost per unit of bank capital times the amount of capital that may be lost due to unhedgeable fluctuations in the loan's value.

Chapter 14   Off-Balance-Sheet Credit Risk

1. Arguably, net short-term obligations (payments) on swap and other OBS contracts have to be added to short-term liabilities on the balance sheet when defining the default exercise point (see Chapter 4).

2. Evidence by Fehle (1998) and Duffie and Huang (1996) suggest that a default risk premium of between $\frac{1}{2}$ bp and 1 bp exists in the spread between the fixed swap rate and a similar maturity Treasury bond in the United States.

3. The 1996 amendment to BIS I incorporated the capital requirements for counterparty credit risk on OBS derivatives discussed in this chapter. BIS II proposes changes to the capital treatment of credit derivatives (see Chapter 15), as well as to the capital requirements for asset backed securities (see Appendix 15.1).

4. The capital requirement under BIS I would then be 8 percent of $2.75 million, or $220,000. BIS II proposes to change the 50 percent conversion factor to 20 percent for business commitments with an original maturity up to 1 year; beyond 1 year, the conversion factor would stay at 50 percent. There are two exceptions: (1) a 0 percent conversion factor for commitments that are unconditionally cancelable or automatically cancelled in the event of a deterioration in the borrower's creditworthiness, and (2) a 100 percent conversion factor for the lending of securities, including repo transactions.

5. See Federal Reserve Board of Governors press release, August 29, 1995, p. 17.

6. Note that the net to gross current exposure ratio (NGR) will vary across different contracts, whereas the 0.4 and 0.6 weights remain unchanged.

7. Eligible collateral consists of cash on deposit with the lending bank, securities rated BB- and above issued by sovereigns and selected public-sector entities, securities issued by FIs rated BBB- and above, equities included in a main index, and gold.

8. The one exception is in the case of a maturity mismatch in which the maturity of the hedge is less than that of the underlying exposure. If the maturity mismatch exceeds one year, then BIS II proposes an adjusted risk weight that is a function of the ratio of the maturities.

9. In November 2001, the Basel Committee on Banking Supervision released potential modifications of the BIS II proposals that would eliminate the "weighting" factor in equation (14.9) from minimum capital requirements and replace the treatment of residual risks with Pillar II supervisory oversight. See BIS (November 5, 2001b).

10. Finger (2000a) proposes an extension of CreditMetrics that would incorporate the correlation between credit exposure size and counterparty credit risk on derivatives instruments. In June 1999, the Counterparty Risk Management Policy Group called for the development of stress tests to estimate "wrong-way credit exposure" such as experienced by U.S. banks during the Asian currency crises (i.e., credit exposure to Asian counterparties increased just as foreign currency declines caused FX losses on derivatives positions).

11. See Appendix 14.2 and Smith, Smithson, and Wilford (1990). The intuition behind using a Black-Scholes-type options pricing model to measure potential exposure can be seen by looking at the five variables that would determine the option value to default on a swap [i.e., the original interest rate on the swap (the strike price s), the current interest rate (the current underlying price p), the volatility of interest rates (σ), the short-term interest rate (r), and the time to maturity of the swap (τ)]. That is, potential exposure = $f(s, p, \sigma, r, \tau)$.

12. The question is which transition matrix to use. Arguably, because the cash flows on swaps are similar to the coupon flows on bonds, a bond transition matrix may prove to be adequate.

13. This is an approximation. Default can occur at any time between time 0 and the end of the 1-year credit-event horizon.

14. A cap can be valued as a call option on interest rates or a put on the price of a bond.

15. CreditMetrics currently allows for the estimation of the VAR for OBS activities, such as loan commitments, asset backed securities, and credit guarantees (such as letters of credit).

16. For additional information, see Bank of England and Board of Governors of the Federal Reserve System, *Potential Credit Exposure on Interest Rate and Foreign Exchange Rate Related Instruments,* March 1997.

Chapter 15   Credit Derivatives

1. Comprehensive global data on the size of OTC derivatives markets do not exist, so Rule (2001) estimates the size of the market using Office of the Comptroller of the Currency data showing that U.S. commercial banks held $352 billion notional credit derivatives outstanding on March 31, 2001 pro-rated for U.S. banks' share using a British Bankers Association Survey showing that the global market totalled $514 billion in 1999.
2. However, since all derivatives are subject to counterparty credit risk, their pricing requires evaluation of each counterparty's credit quality. See Nandi (1998) for a discussion of how asymmetric credit quality affects the pricing of interest rate swaps.
3. It is also unclear whether insurance companies collectively have sufficient capital to withstand systemic credit shocks inherited from the sale of credit derivatives.
4. Although, the borrower's consent may still be needed to transfer the loan if the credit derivative specifies physical delivery upon occurrence of a credit event.
5. DeSantes (1999) describes how insurance companies leverage their high credit ratings and increase earnings by selling credit protection in the credit derivatives market.
6. This may account for the observation that only the largest U.S. banks use credit derivatives at all. Moreover, total credit derivatives exposure at U.S. banks as of March 31, 2001, comprised less than 1 percent of all U.S. banks' notional derivative exposures; 64 percent of the total credit derivatives exposure was held by J.P. Morgan Chase alone. See Rule 2001.
7. Wall and Shrikhande (1998) note that "the combined regulatory capital requirements may be reduced if three conditions are met: (1) the bank selling the credit risk is bound by the risk-based guidelines, (2) the counterparty's (the buyer of the credit risk) required capital under the leverage standard exceeds its required capital under the risk-based standard, and (3) the counterparty does not already have such a high level of off-balance-sheet commitments that the regulators impose a judgmental increase in its leverage requirement. In this case, the bank holding the loan and selling its risk would reduce its capital requirement for the loan to one-fifth the original level (moving from a 100 percent weighting to a 20 percent weighting). Further, the counterparty may not experience any increase in its capital requirements since the credit derivative would not be included in the calculation of its leverage ratio" (p. 10).
8. Since July 1998, banks in the United Kingdom have been permitted to include credit derivatives in their trading book, provided that they can be hedged and that market makers exist. Under this treatment, the bank holds capital against the underlying asset only, thereby avoiding a capital charge on both the underlying and the derivative.

9. The residual risk factor w reflects the possibility of default on the credit derivative itself. ISDA has criticized the proposal to set $w = 0.15$ as both unnecessary and excessive. In November 2001, the Basel Committee on Banking Supervision released potential modifications to the BIS II proposals that would eliminate the w factor from minimum capital requirements; residual risk would instead be subject to regulatory oversight under Pillar II of the BIS II proposals.

10. We have shown payoffs on the loan as piecewise linear; in reality the loan payoff will have some convexity.

11. For additional discussion, see Finnerty (1996).

12. Baskets are credit derivatives based on a small portfolio of loans or bonds, such that all assets included in the underlying pool are individually listed. In contrast, the contents of larger portfolios are described by their characteristics. A basket credit default swap (CDS), also known as a first-to-default swap, is structured like a regular CDS, but the reference security consists of several securities. The first reference entity to default triggers a default payment of the par value minus the recovery value and then all payments end.

13. Total return swaps are typically structured so that the capital gain or loss is paid at the end of the swap. However, in the alternate structure used in this example, the capital gain or loss is paid at the end of each interest period during the swap. If a specified credit event causes the principal to become due for immediate repayment, then the structure used in this example applies.

14. A pure credit swap is like a default option (e.g., see the earlier discussion), but a key difference is that the fee (or premium) payments on the swap are paid over the life of the swap, whereas for a default option the whole fee (premium) is paid upfront. Premiums are paid quarterly on an actual/360 day calendar. Another difference is that for a credit swap the protection buyer has an obligation to settle the transaction if a credit event occurs, whereas the option holder has the right, but not the obligation.

15. Both the obligor and the specific reference debt instrument must be specified. The reference instrument is usually a senior unsecured debt obligation, although a CDS can be written on subordinated debt as well.

16. Early credit swaps were cash settled, but now physical delivery is the most common settlement method.

17. Paul-Choudhury (1999) describes the advantages of the standardized ISDA master agreements as greater certainty (i.e., less "documentation arbitrage"), enhanced flexibility, and broader coverage.

18. Default payments are usually computed in one of three ways: (1) par minus a final loan price as determined by a poll of dealers (such as Creditex and Credit-Trade); (2) payment of par by the counterparty in exchange for physical delivery of the defaulted loan; and (3) a fixed dollar amount contractually agreed to at the swap origination. Increasingly, method (2) is the favored method of settlement because of the difficulty in getting accurate secondary market prices on loans around credit event dates.

19. Actually, the probability that a credit event will occur.

20. Alternatively, a multiplicative credit spread can be used as in *JP Morgan Guide* (1999).

21. An arbitrage position that is equivalent to selling credit protection using a CDS consists of two simultaneous transactions: (1) holding a risky loan with a floating rate equal to LIBOR plus a credit spread and (2) selling a risk-free security paying LIBOR. The net cash flow on the arbitrage position is always equal to the credit spread alone.

22. Typically, the observed basis is positive; that is, the CDS premium exceeds the credit spread *CS*. Theoretically, however, the CDS premium should be a risk-neutral credit spread. In practice, both the CDS premium and the *CS* are distorted by risk premiums.

23. James (1999) describes the difficulty in pricing credit derivatives if bond price data are noisy or unavailable. See also discussion in Chapter 5.

24. Aside from the impact on the valuation expressions in equations (15.3) to (15.5), the size of the coupon payment may affect the *LGD* since accrued interest up until the default is considered a valid claim, but interest due after default is not.

25. Collin-Dufresne and Solnik (2001) find that the spread between LIBOR and the fixed-floating rate swap curve can be explained by default risk differentials that may also include a liquidity premium.

26. See Dahiya et al. (2001).

27. However, one motive for issuing asset backed securities (ABS) is to reduce capital requirements by removing assets from the balance sheet. See Appendix 15.2 for a discussion of how the BIS II proposals assess the credit risk of ABS for capital requirements.

28. Fitch reported in February 2001 that more than 50 percent of all CDOs were synthetic CDOs.

29. This threshold can be viewed as equivalent to the credit enhancement offered by the originating bank in a CLO or CLN.

30. Typically, BISTRO collateralization ranges from 5–15 percent of the notional value of the loan portfolio.

31. In a KMV context, *QDFs* rather than *EDFs* should be used; see Chapter 4.

32. Currently, the cash replication approach appears to be the most used. Credit spread models appear to be used more to "benchmark" the premium calculated via cash replication models.

33. This example is taken from *Risk* (2000).

34. First-loss credit enhancements are deducted from capital, whereas a capital charge is levied against subordinated second-loss credit enhancement using risk weights determined by the assets in the ABS.